TALKING AND TESTING

STUDIES IN BILINGUALISM (SiBil)

EDITORS

Kees de Bot
University of Nijmegen

Thom Huebner
San José State University

EDITORIAL BOARD

Michael Clyne (Monash University)
Kathryn Davis (University of Hawaii at Manoa)
Charles Ferguson (Stanford University)
Joshua Fishman (Yeshiva University)
François Grosjean (Université de Neuchâtel)
Wolfgang Klein (Max Planck Institut für Psycholinguistik)
Georges Lüdi (University of Basel)
Christina Bratt Paulston (University of Pittsburgh)
Suzanne Romaine (Merton College, Oxford)
Merrill Swain (Ontario Institute for Studies in Education)
Richard Tucker (Carnegie Mellon University)

Volume 14

Richard Young and Agnes Weiyun He (eds)

Talking and Testing
Discourse approaches to the assessment of oral proficiency

TALKING AND TESTING

DISCOURSE APPROACHES TO THE ASSESSMENT OF ORAL PROFICIENCY

RICHARD YOUNG
University of Wisconsin-Madison

AGNES WEIYUN HE
SUNY Stony Brook

JOHN BENJAMINS PUBLISHING COMPANY
AMSTERDAM/PHILADELPHIA

The paper used in this publication meets the minimum requirements of American National Standard for Information Sciences — Permanence of Paper for Printed Library Materials, ANSI Z39.48-1984.

Library of Congress Cataloging-in-Publication Data

Talking and testing : discourse approaches to the assessment of oral proficiency / [edited by] Richard Young, Agnes Weiyun He.
    p.   cm. -- (Studies in Bilingualism, ISSN 0928-1533 ; v. 14)
   Includes bibliographical references and index.
   1. Language and languages--Ability testing. 2. Conversation--Ability testing. 3. Oral communication--Ability testing.
P53.4.T35   1998
418'.0076--dc21   98-24277
ISBN 90 272 4120 1 (Eur.) / 1-55619-548-6 (US) (Hb; alk. paper)   CIP

© Copyright 1998 - John Benjamins B.V.
No part of this book may be reproduced in any form, by print, photoprint, microfilm, or any other means, without written permission from the publisher.

John Benjamins Publishing Co. • P.O.Box 75577 • 1070 AN Amsterdam • The Netherlands
John Benjamins North America • P.O.Box 27519 • Philadelphia PA 19118-0519 • USA

Contents

Preface ix
    Marianne Celce-Murcia

Chapter 1
Language Proficiency Interviews: A Discourse Approach 1
    Agnes Weiyun He and Richard Young

Part 1   Language Proficiency Interviews and Conversation

Chapter 2
Re-analyzing the OPI:
How Much Does It Look like Natural Conversation? 27
    Marysia Johnson and Andrea Tyler

Chapter 3
Evaluating Learner Interactional Skills: Conversation at the Micro Level 53
    Heidi Riggenbach

Chapter 4
What Happens When There's No One to Talk to? Spanish Foreign
Language Discourse in Simulated Oral Proficiency Interviews 69
    Dale April Koike

Part 2   Turns and Sequences in Language Proficiency Interviews

Chapter 5
Answering Questions in LPIs: A Case Study 101
    Agnes Weiyun He

Chapter 6
Framing the Language Proficiency Interview as a Speech Event:
Native and Non-Native Speakers' Questions   117
  Carol Lynn Moder and Gene B. Halleck

Chapter 7
Miscommunication in Language Proficiency Interviews of
First-Year German Students: A Comparison with Natural Conversation   147
  Maria M. Egbert

Part 3   Knowledge and Communication in Language Proficiency Interviews

Chapter 8
Knowledge Structures in Oral Proficiency Interviews
for International Teaching Assistants   173
  Bernard Mohan

Chapter 9
The Use of Communication Strategies in Language Proficiency
Interviews   205
  Yumiko Yoshida-Morise

Chapter 10
Meaning Negotiation in the Hungarian Oral Proficiency
Examination of English   239
  Lucy Katona

Part 4   Language Proficiency Interviews as Cross-Cultural Encounters

Chapter 11
Maintaining American Face in the Korean Oral Exam:
Reflections on the Power of Cross-Cultural Context   271
  Catherine E. Davies

Chapter 12
Confirmation Sequences as Interactional Resources
in Korean Language Proficiency Interviews   297
  Kyu-hyun Kim and Kyung-hee Suh

Chapter 13
Divergent Frame Interpretations in Oral Proficiency
Interview Interaction   333
   Steven Ross

Chapter 14
"Let Them Eat Cake!" or How to Avoid Losing Your Head in
Cross-Cultural Conversations   355
   Richard Young and Gene B. Halleck

Index of Names   383

Index of Topics   391

Preface

Marianne Celce-Murcia
University of California, Los Angeles

This volume is a unique contribution to applied linguistics in that it brings together assessment and discourse analysis. The editors have compiled a remarkable collection of current research that documents various dimensions of the ways in which the language learner and the language proficiency interviewer use language to accomplish oral language assessment tasks.

Rather than speculate as to what will happen or what might have happened in language proficiency interviews (henceforth LPIs), all contributions to this volume are based on audio- and/or videotaped data from actual LPI sessions. All data have been carefully transcribed prior to analysis. This is particularly significant in view of the fact that, although there exists a literature on using interviews for the assessment of second language oral proficiency, until very recently studies of LPIs ignored the central validity issue of oral proficiency assessment—namely, the ways in which the LPI is accomplished through discourse.

The introduction and thirteen chapters in this book address various questions, including:

- How do participants locally manage the activity of the LPI?
- How do participants construct their linguistic identities and linguistic competence through language use?
- How do participants draw on their social, cultural, and interactional resources?
- How do interviewers form their knowledge of and judgments about the learner's interactional abilities?
- What does an LPI mean to the participants?
- Does the meaning of an LPI change from one speech community to another? If so, how?

To answer such questions, the authors contributing to this volume draw on a variety of analytical perspectives, including the ethnography of speaking, ethnomethodology, conversation analysis, second language acquisition, language socialization, sociolinguistic variation theory, sociological human interaction research, systemic functional linguistics, and discourse domain theory. The book also examines LPIs conducted in several languages other than English, including French, German, Korean, and Spanish.

At least two guidelines emerge from this collection that can serve others working in similar areas: (1) record, transcribe, and analyze the actual talk that takes place between the interviewer(s) and the learner; and (2) adopt a multidisciplinary approach to research in language assessment.

This book will be of considerable interest to language testers, discourse analysts, second language acquisition researchers, foreign language teaching specialists, and anyone who is concerned with oral proficiency issues in language teaching. I commend the authors and editors and hope that this collection will be a stimulus to others doing cross-disciplinary research. We need further related research if we are to arrive at a richer and more complete understanding of what oral proficiency means in a second/foreign language in particular and what constitutes communicative competence in general.

Language Proficiency Interviews:
A Discourse Approach

Agnes Weiyun He
State University of New York at Stony Brook

Richard Young
University of Wisconsin-Madison

1 Introduction: Assessing Second Language Speaking Ability

This book begins with a practical question: How can we best assess how well someone speaks a second language? The contributors to the book all examine one particular answer to that question: The best way of assessing how well a learner speaks a language is to get him or her to speak; in particular, to get the learner to have an interview with a proficient speaker of the language. Although there are certain practical problems associated with setting up an interview with a learner—there has to be a native or very proficient speaker available, and there has to be enough time available for a reasonable conversation to develop between the interviewer and each learner—if these problems can be overcome, then interviews have proved to be a very popular way of assessing speaking ability in a second language.

Do interviews deserve their popularity? One way of answering that question is to consider interviews in terms of the qualities that contemporary language testing theory suggests are desirable in language tests. For example, Bachman and Palmer (1996), in their book *Language Testing in Practice*, lay out four qualities of a useful language test: *reliability, construct validity, authenticity,* and *interactiveness*. The first two of Bachman and Palmer's criteria—reliability and construct validity—are familiar to test designers because they are essential qualities if tests are to be used as ways of measuring learners' abilities. Reliability is the consistency with which a test measures ability and one way in which interviews may be *un*reliable is if two different examiners judge the speaking ability of the same learner differently. Such a threat to reliability, however, is well known, and modern testing agencies take considerable pains to train interviewers and to develop rating scales that minimize the amount of disagreement between interviewers.

Construct validity is the quality of a test that allows us to make interpretations of the scores on the test. By saying that an interview is a good test of speaking ability in a second language, we make a statement about the construct validity of the test, namely, that an interview measures speaking ability rather than, say, second language reading ability or speaking ability in the learner's mother tongue. This clearly requires that we have an understanding of what speaking ability in a second language is, independently of the interview that we use to measure it. If not, we run the risk of circularity by saying that the definition of speaking ability in a second language is simply whatever is measured by the interview. Defining the construct of speaking ability on the basis of test scores is not a good idea because it does not help us think about what is the best way to design the test.

Defining the construct of speaking ability in a second language is in fact a theoretically challenging undertaking. Before we can say what speaking ability is, we have to have an understanding of the properties of naturally occurring spoken language and of what it means for someone to speak a language better or worse than someone else. Many of the contributors to this book have struggled with these questions and have put forward in their respective chapters a broad-based theory of second language spoken ability that we call *interactional competence* discussed in considerable detail below.

In addition to reliability and construct validity, Bachman and Palmer (1996) recognize two other qualities of a useful language test: authenticity and interactiveness. By authenticity they refer to the degree of correspondence between the characteristics of a task that learners are required to perform on a test and the characteristics of a non-test task in the second language. Authenticity is an important quality of language tests because an authentic test allows us to make generalizations from learners' performances on a test to their performances on real-life tasks in the target language community. On the surface, at least, interviews appear to be an authentic task: learners are involved in spoken interaction with a proficient speaker of the language, a task that appears to be very similar to many kinds of face-to-face conversations in the target language community outside the testing room. Until very recently, however, this correspondence between interviews and native/non-native conversations was something that was taken on trust because few researchers had made any systematic comparisons between interviews and conversations. The unique contribution of this book is to make such comparisons available, not only between interviews in English and English conversations but also—and for the first time—comparisons in Spanish, German, and Korean as well. The general consensus among contributors to this book is that, for reasons that we will discuss below, the characteristics of an interview are quite different from the characteristics of ordinary conversation. Interviews, that is, are *not* authentic tests of conversation.

The fourth and final quality of useful language tests recognized by Bachman and Palmer is interactiveness. This refers not to interaction between the test taker and the administrator of the test but to the degree to which the learner simultaneously draws on different kinds of knowledge—both cognitive and affective—in doing a test. There are several kinds of knowledge that according to Bachman and Palmer can interact in the learner's performance of a test task: knowledge of the second language, knowledge of how to overcome communication difficulties in performance (strategic competence), knowledge of how to organize and plan a task (metacognitive strategies), topical knowledge, and learners' emotional reactions to particular topics and tasks (affective schemata). Examples of highly interactive tests according to Bachman and Palmer include a role-play and an extended conversation because both tests require language, require learners to plan ahead, and involve learners in topics that interest them.

Bachman and Palmer's emphasis on interaction between and/or integration of various knowledges internal to the speaking individual is largely a psychological model that neglects the social, dialogic dimension of cognition and emotion—that is to say, cognition and emotion are not located in the mind of a single individual, but are instead embedded in distributed systems and are shaped and accomplished interactionally (Hutchins 1995, Lave 1988, Rogoff 1990). As McNamara (1997) points out, an exclusive focus on the learner's internal abilities suggests that the learner be held solely accountable for the results of proficiency interviews; while in fact even the display of what is in an individual's head is mediated by moment-by-moment interactional contingencies.

The two questions that we now wish to address arise from our previous discussion of Bachman and Palmer's qualities of a language test. How can speaking ability be defined independently of a language proficiency interview that is designed to assess it? And to what extent is a language proficiency interview an authentic representation of normal conversation in the target language?

2 Interactional Competence

The ability to speak a second language is a subset of a learner's overall ability—or proficiency—in the language. Thus the question of what speaking ability is, is closely related to the question of what it means to know a second language. Historically, two theories of second language knowledge have been influential in the design of language tests: Robert Lado's structuralist theory (Lado 1957) and Canale and Swain's theory of communicative competence (Canale and Swain 1980). Lado maintained that knowledge of a second language could be divided into five parts: the ability to comprehend the spoken language, the ability to speak the language, the ability to read it, the ability to write it, and an understanding of the culture of the target-language community. Lado's four skills (the fifth skill, knowing about the culture, was often ignored) were the basis for much curriculum development and language assessment in the two decades following the publication of *Linguistics Across Cultures*, and to some extent are still in use today. Within each skill, knowledge was further broken down into knowledge of the traditional linguistic levels of phonology, morphology, lexis, and syntax. According to this view, second language knowledge consisted in knowing the four skills and their components. How well a learner knew a language could be assessed by testing each of the four skills and their components separately in what came to be known as discrete-point testing (Davies 1990).

The theory of communicative competence was based on the greater understanding of the interrelationship between linguistic form and social context developed through the work of linguists such as Firth (1957), anthropologists such as Malinowski (1923), and philosophers such as Austin (1962), but mainly through the broad and integrating perspective on language use put forward by Hymes as *communicative competence* (1972, 1974). Canale and Swain's framework, which is by now well known, adds to the purely linguistic perspective of Lado and characterizes a learner's competence in a language in terms of linguistic, pragmatic, discourse, and strategic competence. Without doubt, by broadening our concept of linguistic knowledge from a narrow focus on the four skills and on knowledge of linguistic structure, the Canale and Swain framework has given rise to much useful research and provided a rich view of the knowledge and skills that an individual speaker needs to command in order to communicate accurately, appropriately, and effectively in a second language. In language testing, communicative competence has been influential through Bachman's application of the theory to the design of language tests (Bachman 1990). And in the assessment of speaking ability, as Young (1995a) has indicated, several modern language proficiency interviews are designed specifically to assess components of communicative competence such as pragmatic competence (e.g., the functional descriptions of proficiency in the ACTFL OPI) and strategic competence (e.g., the rating scales of the Cambridge Assessment of Spoken

English interview developed by the University of Cambridge Local Examinations Syndicate).

The focus of the Canale and Swain framework is on an individual learner in a social context; that is, the framework helps us understand what an individual needs to know and do in order to communicate. Such exclusive focus on a single individual's contribution to communication should, we believe, be problematized in view of current research that has advanced the position that abilities, actions, and activities do not belong to the individual but are *jointly* constructed by *all* participants. This position has been put forward by—among others—cognitive anthropologists who focus on participants' actions in a social context, by ethnomethodologists whose objective is to understand how participants' actions organize and sustain the context, by cultural-historical psychologists who demonstrate the contributions of social interaction to the development of the mind, and by phenomenologists who have qualitatively described and interpreted experiences in historical and social context (Chaiklin and Lave, 1993).

This constructivist, practice-oriented view of interaction and competence has also been articulated by various applied linguists under different names. In an early paper, Kramsch (1986) referred to it as *interactional competence*.[1] A more recent term was introduced by Jacoby and Ochs (1995:171), who refer to it as *co-construction,* which they define as "the joint creation of a form, interpretation, stance, action, activity, identity, institution, skill, ideology, emotion, or other culturally meaningful reality." Although the term *co-construction* may suggest that joint creations are made by means of cooperative or supportive interaction, Jacoby and Ochs make clear that co-construction is not necessarily affiliative or supportive interaction: an argument, for example, is just as much co-constructed as a conversation.

A second applied linguistic perspective that advances the interactive nature of communicative activity is Hall's idea of *interactive practices* (1993, 1995). In talking of interactive practices, Hall indicates that participation in talk does not involve the individual in spontaneous creation of individual utterances free from social constraints; rather "talk is comprised of interactive practices, structured moments of face-to-face interaction—differently enacted and differently valued— whereby individuals come together to create, articulate, and manage their collective histories via the use of sociohistorically defined and valued resources" (Hall 1995:207–208). Interactive practices, according to Hall, are recurring episodes of talk that are of sociocultural significance to a community of speakers.

Interactive practices are co-constructed by participants, each of whom contributes linguistic and pragmatic resources to the practice. Participants bring the following resources, among others, to a given practice: a knowledge of rhetorical scripts, a knowledge of certain lexis and syntactic patterns specific to the practice, a knowledge of how turns are managed, a knowledge of topical organization, and a knowledge of the means for signaling boundaries between practices and transitions within the practice itself.

A few examples will show the kinds of resources participants bring to different practices. Participants bring knowledge of *rhetorical scripts* (Ranney 1992), or sequences of speech acts that help define a particular interactive practice. For example, He (1993) has shown that students distinguish between acceptable and unacceptable peer reviews of their written work by whether certain obligatory acts are present in a certain sequence in the reviews.

Second, participants bring to a practice *specific lexis and syntactic structures*. For example, in discussing complimenting behavior in American English, Wolfson (1984) found that a very limited range of syntactic patterns and adjectives were used in compliments and that the choice of adjective depends to some degree on the gender of the person who is being complimented.

Third, different interactive practices involve different *strategies for managing turns*. Research done by Young and others on the discourse of language proficiency interviews (LPIs) has shown that turns are allocated in a very similar way in LPIs to how turn-taking is managed in classrooms (Young 1995b, Young and Milanovic 1992). That is, the interviewer (like the teacher) can claim a turn at any time and has the right to allocate a turn to the interviewee by means of questions and other turn-allocation devices. This turn-taking system is very different from turn-taking patterns in ordinary conversations among peers, where no single individual has the exclusive right to allocate turns and where there can be much competition for the floor.

Fourth, the *management of topics* differs in different interactive practices. Topic management includes preferences for certain topics over others and decisions as to who has the right to introduce a given topic, how long a topic persists in discourse, and who has the right to change the topic. A simple example of differences in topic management in different interactive practices comes from a comparison of conversations between couples in intimate relationships (Crow 1983) and conversations in language proficiency interviews. Crow found that the couples in his study shifted the conversational topic on average every 48 seconds. In contrast, in certain kinds of language proficiency interviews, Young (1995a) found that topic shifts were far less frequent: in intermediate-level interviews participants shifted topics on average every 67 seconds, and in advanced-level interviews they shifted every 84 seconds.

Finally, the means for *signaling the boundaries* of an interactive practice differ from one practice to another. Hartford and Bardovi-Harlig (1992) have shown that the ways closings are managed in academic advising sessions between a professor and a student differ quite markedly from the ways closings have been described in ordinary conversations (Schegloff and Sacks 1973). In closing academic advising sessions, it is not legitimate to reinvoke topics that have already been dealt with during the session, whereas in closing ordinary conversations, reinvocations are used to indicate that none of the participants has any new topics to introduce.

Interactional competence, as we have described it, differs from communicative competence in several respects. In one respect, interactional competence is a further elaboration of second language knowledge; in other words, to discourse, pragmatic, and strategic competence, we must now add competence in (at least) the five interactional features described above. In another respect, however, interactional competence is fundamentally different from communicative competence. Whereas communicative competence has been interpreted in the testing literature as a trait or bundle of traits that can be assessed in a given individual, interactional competence—we wish to stress—is co-constructed by all participants in an interactive practice and is specific to that practice. Participants' knowledge and interactive skills are *local*: they apply to a given interactive practice and either do not apply or apply in a different configuration to different practices.

Because knowledge and interactional skills are local and practice-specific, the joint construction of an interactive practice involves participants making use of the resources they have acquired in previous instances of the *same* practice. According to this view, individuals do not acquire a general, practice-independent communicative competence; rather they acquire a practice-specific interactional competence by participating with more experienced others in specific interactive practices. Interactional competence in a specific practice, that is, involves participants making skillful use of resources, such as those five that we have detailed, in the "joint creation of a form, interpretation, stance, action, activity, identity, institution, skill, ideology, emotion, or other culturally meaningful reality" (Jacoby and Ochs 1995:171). Interactional competence is not an attribute of an individual participant, and thus we cannot say that an individual is interactionally competent; rather we talk of interactional competence as something that is jointly constructed by all participants (including an analyst if the interaction is subjected to analysis). Equally, interactional competence is not a trait that is independent of the interactive practice in which it is (or is not) constituted.

The theoretical framework of interactional competence suggests that we should interpret language proficiency interviews rather differently from the way they have been interpreted up until now. Positivistic language assessment suggests that an individual's language proficiency can be discovered via scientific (i.e., often quantitative) methods. It removes from consideration the situationally and sequentially grounded and culturally shared understandings of LPIs as particular types of speech situations. It encourages us to focus on what each utterance means in isolation from other utterances and neglects the fact that interaction itself creates meaning and constructs proficiency.

In language proficiency interviews, interaction is a medium for comprehension and knowing and judging. Each LPI is an instantiation of interaction between the examiner and the language learner that is socially and institutionally organized and exhibits describable features. LPIs are nothing other than the interactional achievements from which interview results can be extracted. From their interactions with learners, examiners must extract an object that can be heard as an answer upon which an assessment of language proficiency can be made. Like other forms of interview, the LPI is an interaction between two persons who influence each other and react in relation to each other.

LPIs do not simply sample an ability that exists in the learner prior to the interview; rather they actually produce or fabricate the abilities they supposedly measure. (For example, feedback from the examiner affects the amount of information provided by the learners and the manner in which they provide it.) Shared understandings are developed and negotiated between participants in the course of an ongoing interaction. It is through interaction that each participant connects his or her own identities, emotions, tasks, and activities with those of others. These connections, accomplished by ongoing interaction, provide the basis for what Rommetveit (1985) has called *intersubjectivity*. It is from within this dynamically sustained context that what is talked about gets its meaning.

3 Authenticity

Is an LPI an instance of natural conversation? This is a question posed by several researchers in language assessment (Lazaraton 1992, Riggenbach 1991, van Lier 1989) and for educational tests in general (e.g., Schaeffer 1991). Van Lier (1989) questions the supposedly conversational nature of OPIs and proposes an alternative modular approach to the existing OPI format so as to transform an OPI into a conversation. Lazaraton (1992, 1996) examines the overall structural organization of the LPI as well as examiners' question design and the interactively co-constructed nature of the assessment of the learners' language ability. She shows that, although

LPIs import their fundamental structural and interactional features from conversation, they are identifiably instances of interviews for the participants.

Contributors to this book continue the discussion by making explicit comparisons between the characteristics of LPIs and the characteristics of naturally occurring conversations. In so doing they delineate the interactional and structural features specific to LPIs. In particular, contributors highlight three salient differences between LPIs and ordinary conversation: (1) as interviews, the topical and turn-taking systems of LPIs differ from ordinary conversation, (2) as instances of institutional discourse, the speech exchange system and the goal-orientedness of LPIs differ from ordinary conversation, and (3) as cross-cultural encounters, participants in LPIs often have very different understandings of what is going on in the LPI, a situation that may not occur in ordinary NS-NNS conversations. These three challenges to the authenticity of LPIs will be discussed below.

3.1 *LPIs as Interviews*

As a research methodology, interviews range from informal and open-ended to formal instruments used in survey research. Interviews have been used in a wide variety of social science disciplines, including sociology, history, anthropology, the ethnography of communication, quantitative studies of linguistic variation, and the sociology of language. Interviews, including LPIs, tell us something that we did not know before. As representational devices, they are means of gathering information.

But what is an interview? A few definitions are presented below. In examining therapeutic interviews, Labov and Fanshel (1977) define the interview as a speech event in which one person, A, extracts information from another person, B, that was contained in B's biography. In the context of interviews of college students by academic counselors, Erickson and Shultz (1982) take interviews to be a brief encounter, usually between strangers, in which one person has the authority to make decisions that affect the other's future. Mishler (1986) proposes that interviews are a form of discourse having structures that reflect and shape several types of normative rules, including rules of syntax, semantics, and pragmatics. As is true of other culturally grounded norms, these rules guide the ways interviewers and interviewees enter into situations, define and frame their sense of what they can appropriately say, and provide the basis for their understandings of questions and responses.

When an interview is conducted for the purpose of assessing second language speaking ability, it is often referred to as an "oral proficiency interview." But that term is also used to refer to the particular kind of interview designed and developed by the American Council on the Teaching of Foreign Languages. For this reason, we prefer in this book to use the term *language proficiency interview*—abbreviated as LPI—to refer to any interview used for the assessment of second language speaking ability, including the ACTFL OPI. In particular, we define a language proficiency interview as a face-to-face spoken interaction usually between two participants (although other combinations do occur), one of whom is an expert (usually a native or near-native speaker of the language in which the interview is conducted) and the other a non-native speaker (NNS) or learner of the language as a second or foreign language. The purpose of the LPI is for the expert speaker—the interviewer—to assess the NNS's ability to speak the language in which the interview is conducted. The participants meet at a scheduled time, at a prearranged location such as a classroom or school office, and for a limited period. In the case of scripted interviews, an agenda specifying the topics for conversation and the activities to take place during the LPI is prepared in advance. The agenda is always known to the interviewer but not necessarily to the NNS. In addition to the agenda, the interviewer (but usually not the NNS) has access to one or more scales for rating the NNS's ability in the language of the interview.

Talk in LPIs is subject to global rules of interviewing, resulting from the formal relationship between the interviewer and the learner, who use language to reconstruct their prescribed role identities. The ultimate purpose of the LPI, as one type of interview, is to discover target information—the learner's second language speaking ability—of which the interview result is a sign or representation. It can be characterized as a speech event in which: (1) the interviewer extracts linguistic data from the language learner, data that are supposedly representative of the learner's language use in ordinary settings; (2) the interviewer has the authority to pass judgments about the learner's level of linguistic competence; and (3) specific rules of syntax, semantics, pragmatics, and conversational exchange are exhibited that may or may not be equally familiar to both parties.

3.2 *LPIs as Institutional Discourse*

Conversation and interviews are two kinds of talk-in-interaction. Interviews reflect the institutional context in which they are embedded through their speech exchange system and its goal-orientedness. In ordinary conversation, topics and turns are not prescribed by specific speech activity; none of the participants has a predefined role in managing the interaction. In LPIs, however, there are specific constraints on participants' contributions in terms of turn-taking and reduction or re-specification of conversational options. As it is often the interviewer who controls the topic and who exercises a consistently predominant role in managing turn-taking, the authenticity of LPIs presents itself as a particularly important issue. We suggest that the speech exchange system of the LPI does not necessarily invalidate the learner's responses. After all, linguistic competence that is revealed in the LPI setting is a social, interactional construction and constitutes at least one type of exhibited competence, as long as it is interpreted within the right frame.

Another way in which the LPI, as a genre of institutional discourse, differs from ordinary conversation is in its goal-orientation. While ordinary conversation suggests symmetrical social relations, unconstrained topic flow, and informality of style, institutional discourse involves one speaking party who represents to some extent an institution encountering another person seeking its services. Institutional discourse is characterized by formal task-, role-, or goal-based activities (Agar 1985, Drew and Heritage 1992). As we remarked earlier, interviewers have as their goal to extract language samples from the interviewee and often have a predefined agenda for the encounter. Learners and examiners both contribute to constructing an LPI context, and yet they know different things, have varying linguistic abilities, speak with different interests and different global perceptions of the interview, and bring with them different social and cultural experiences. The learner's global definition of the LPI's purpose may differ from that of the interviewer's, and this may influence his or her contribution to the interaction and hence the interview results, because both interviewer and candidate select what to say and how to say it in ways that are congruent with their own perceptions of the "activity type" (Levinson 1979) of the LPI. The learner's definition of the LPI in general and, in particular, of the purpose of specific questions the examiner asks has important interactional consequences.

LPIs are situated interviews in an institutional setting. The assessment of language proficiency is accomplished through interactional practices involving the language learner and the examiner, who are related to each other in multiple and heterogeneous ways, who may have different interests and goals, and for whom a failure in the LPI is as much a collaborative activity as a success. Despite the unspoken assumption of much previous discussion on LPIs that the interview is seen in a similar light by both participants, many contributors to this book challenge the harmony of interests, goals, and perceptions that is so often assumed in existing research. And they propose alternative views that emphasize the heterogeneous, multifocal character of the LPI.

3.3 LPIs as Cross-Cultural Encounters

It might appear superfluous to say that LPIs are most often instances of communication between participants from different cultures; the mere fact that the language learner is a non-native speaker makes this self-evident. What is perhaps easily overlooked, however, is that LPIs constitute instances of cross-cultural communication because the parties bring to the LPI different views of the learning process and of communication, which, as Ochs (1982, 1988) argues, are closely related to their views regarding language acquisition, language teaching, and the evaluation of communicative competence.

Briggs (1986), an ethnographer examining the interview, reports that this interactive practice is not found in all cultures. He points out that, some speech communities have methods other than interviews for gathering information and so Western researchers may be imposing their folk theories of reality and communication on speech communities organized along different lines. That is, there may exist an incompatibility between interview techniques used in social science research and native systems of communication. Briggs cites both the nature of the interview itself as a communicative event and the nature of the data it produces. He highlights the fact that the interviewee may apply rules learned in other speech events (e.g., those in ordinary conversation or those in another cultural context) and may reject attempts to impose interview rules. He argues that the validity of interviews could be improved if interviewees could use culturally natural forms of talk. Similarly, Gumperz (1992) describes how NNSs map L_1 rhetorical strategies onto L_2 situations in cross-cultural interviewing.

Clearly, the relationship between learners' language use in the LPI setting and in ordinary conversational settings requires further investigation. Several contributors to this book address issues of divergent cultural norms, frames, views of face, knowledge structures, and communication strategies in LPI discourse.

4 Interdisciplinary Orientation

Contributors to this book have approached the description and interpretation of LPIs from a number of different methodological orientations. In fact, research into the discourse of LPIs owes a lot to the increasingly rich body of theoretical and empirical work on situated language use by linguists, sociolinguists, anthropologists, sociologists, philosophers, and psychologists.

In philosophy, speech act theorists (Austin 1962; Searle 1969, 1979) have heightened awareness of the formulaic and performative character of speech.

Phenomenological and hermeneutic traditions (Gadamer 1975, Schutz 1962) have brought increased sophistication in the interpretation of meaning. Literary criticism and sociohistorical psychology have provided insights into the process of analyzing texts, genres, and performance (Bakhtin 1981, Derrida 1976, Voloshinov 1973). Conversation analysis and ethnomethodology have shown how sociality resides in and is reshaped by details of talk-in-interaction (Sacks 1992; Sacks, Schegloff, and Jefferson 1974). Work in interactional sociolinguistics (Goffman 1981, Hymes 1974), cross-cultural communication (Brown and Levinson 1987, Gumperz 1992), classroom discourse (McHoul 1978, 1990; Sinclair and Coulthard 1975), and psycholinguistics (Douglas and Selinker 1985) has much to offer in terms of methodology for analyzing LPI discourse.

This section focuses on three analytic traditions that we believe will give new impetus to research on LPIs, and that the authors of this volume draw on as theoretical frames: conversation analysis/ethnomethodology, the ethnography of speaking, and speech acts and Gricean pragmatics.

4.1 *Conversation Analysis/Ethnomethodology*

As we argued in Section 3, LPIs are first and foremost talk-in-interaction. Thus the work of ethnomethodologists and conversation analysts (Garfinkel 1984, Sacks, Schegloff, and Jefferson 1974) has particularly important relevance to research in LPI discourse as well as to the study of communication and social behavior in general. Questioning such traditional sociological methods as questionnaires and interviews, these researchers focused on the actual lived stuff of social reality by closely scrutinizing the methods used by participants themselves to manage their lives interactively. Accordingly, in the analysis of talk-in-interaction, the rules used to account for the orderly and collaborative nature of interaction are seen as those that participants themselves use to make sense of their moment-by-moment interaction. This approach to interaction allows for great flexibility and pays special attention to the fluidity of interaction. Some of the major insights offered by CA/ethnomethodology are summarized below.

CA focuses on the structural conversational mechanisms through which talk is accomplished and by means of which practical knowledge is realized and created. One such structure is the *adjacency pair* (Schegloff and Sacks 1973): a sequence of two utterances adjacent to each other, produced by different speakers—ordered as a first part and second part—and typed, so that a first part requires a particular second part or range of second parts. Questions-answers are one type of paired utterances that play an important part in LPI interactions as well as in other institutional encounters such as courtroom discourse (Atkinson and Drew 1979), medical consultations (Heath 1989), psychotherapy (Labov and Fanshel 1977), academic counseling encounters (Erickson and Shultz 1982, He 1994, 1996), news interviews (Clayman 1992, Greatbatch 1988), job interviews (Button 1987), and standardized oral testing discourse (Marlaire and Maynard 1990).

Central to CA is the concept of *turn-taking* (Sacks, Schegloff, and Jefferson 1974), which can be described as a set of rules with ordered options that operate on a turn-by-turn basis as a locally, sequentially managed system. This system explains how speakers "earn" their right to speak, how speaking rights are negotiated and interactionally managed, how the next speaker is selected, how overlaps occur and how they are resolved, and how speakers fix problems in comprehension and miscommunication. A turn is constructed with turn-constructional units (TCUs) that are mapped onto syntactic, lexical, intonational, or pragmatic units (Ford and Thompson 1996). The rules of turn-taking apply at the end of each TCU, which is called a transition relevance place.[2]

Part of displaying conversational competence in everyday talk is appropriately projecting and using possible transition relevance places. Questions project a transition relevance place; learners need to display comprehension and competence by projecting the beginning of their turn and by recognizing the upcoming completion of the question. Several chapters in this volume (He, Moder and Halleck, Kim and Suh) directly address issues of turn-taking and adjacency pairs.

Closely associated with turn-taking is *topic organization* (Button and Casey 1984). Like other institutional representatives (e.g., a counselor, a doctor, a 911 operator), the LPI examiner uses the first pair part in the adjacency pair (question of question-answer) to elicit not just any information but information that will fit the learner's specific linguistic abilities to the institution's definition of language proficiency levels. When the learner does ask questions, it is often at the examiner's invitation. Questions are used by the examiner to control the flow of information, to introduce and/or terminate topics, and to provide an interactional space for the learner to demonstrate his/her linguistic competence.

CA is particularly relevant to the LPI interaction because it provides a powerful tool for understanding and analyzing problems in communication with its description of *repair organization* (Schegloff, Jefferson, and Sacks 1977). When trouble in conversation occurs, it is noticed and then corrected, either by the party whose turn contains the source of trouble or by another party. This sequence of trouble + initiation-of-correction + correction is known as a *repair trajectory*. Repair occurs when one party corrects his or her own talk or that of another party, and it can be accomplished in a number of ways.

In LPIs, a common repair sequence is examiner-initiated probing (see Egbert, this volume). Probing may occur when an answer that would be adequate in ordinary conversation is considered less than adequate for the purpose of language assessment. In LPIs, there seems to be a preponderance of these probing question-answer sequences. Oftentimes, elaboration of an answer is required and encouraged in LPIs, whereas a simple, straightforward answer might have sufficed in ordinary conversation (see He this volume, Ross this volume).

These and other structural conversational mechanisms are resources that participants may draw on in order to carry out the activity of the LPI. An understanding of the ways these mechanisms are used reveals not only the characteristics of the interaction in any particular LPI but also the basis for judgments regarding the learner's level of language proficiency.

4.2 *Ethnography of Speaking*

We stated earlier that LPIs are situated, occasioned activities in the sense that they occur among specific participants, for specific purposes, and in specific settings. The range of parameters that need to be taken into consideration when characterizing the LPI as a "speech event" can be summarized by Hymes's (1972) SPEAKING acronym, which stands for Situation (setting or scene), Participants (addressor and addressee), Ends (goals and outcomes), Act sequence (message form and message content), Key (the affective tone of the event), Instrumentalities (channel, forms of speech), Norms (norms of interaction and norms of interpretation), and Genre (the type of speech event).

Hymes uses the term *speech event* to refer to activities or aspects of activities that are directly governed by rules for language use. A community that shares rules for the conduct and interpretation of speech is called a *speech community*. As a speech event, an LPI is "directly governed by rules or norms for the use of speech" (Hymes 1972:56). Viewing the LPI as a speech event stresses the role of communicative norms in guiding talk and interaction.

In a similar vein, Gumperz (1982) emphasizes the emergence of meaning through interaction in his definition of a *speech activity* as a set of social relationships enacted around a set of schemata in relation to some communicative goal. According to this view, participants in speech activities (e.g., as a lecture or a job interview), have specific expectations about thematic progression, turn-taking rules, form and outcome of the interaction, and constraints on context.

Defining interviews as speech events (Hymes 1972) or speech activities (Gumperz 1982) alerts us to discourse features of LPIs that have been largely neglected until now. Speech events or speech activities occur within a context of situation and context of culture (Malinowski 1923). Situations and cultures with the associated knowledges and norms that native members are assumed to have and observe can affect language use considerably. As knowledges and norms differ from one speech community to another, problems may arise in cases where interactants use the same linguistic code but have different cultural frames and codes. Different ways of speaking can convey different cognitive and affective values, some of which are more appropriate or pleasing than others. Even quantitative features such as amount of talk, length of turns, and rate of speaking can be assessed qualitatively. Fluency, verbosity, taciturnity, and so forth are viewed as more or less desirable in different situations and different cultures.

The chapters in this volume address the nature of the LPI speech event from a variety of perspectives. The chapter by Johnson and Tyler examines whether an LPI is distinctly different from natural conversation as a speech event. The chapter by Koike focuses on the issue of participants. The chapters by He, by Moder and Halleck, by Egbert, by Kim and Suh, and by Yoshida-Morise describe specific act sequences. The chapters by Davies, by Ross, and by Young and Halleck highlight situations where there is a lack of fit between the examiner's ways of speaking and those of the learner, and point out that sometimes it is the examiner's that are promoted at the expense of the learner's.

4.3 *Speech Acts and Gricean Pragmatics*

Contributors to this volume address not only the mechanics of talk-in-interaction and the contexts of language use but also speaker intentions and the associated processes and procedures for interpreting meaning. In this regard, speech act theory and Gricean pragmatics are of particular relevance.

As speech act theory (Austin 1962, Searle 1969) can be applied to the area of second language learning and teaching (Blum-Kulka, House, and Kasper 1989), so can it be useful to the understanding of language assessment, including LPIs. The concept of a speech act highlights the fact that speakers use language not only to describe things but to do things. Austin (1962) points out that some utterances cannot be assessed with regard to truth and falsity, but they may be assessed in relation to felicity conditions for the successful performance of the acts. He focuses on the sorts of things that utterances accomplish and the conditions required for their accomplishment.

Searle (1969, 1979), in an effort to systematize Austin, proposes five major classes of acts that utterances perform: representatives (e.g., asserting, stating), directives (e.g., requests), commissives (e.g., promises), expressives (e.g., apologies, compliments), and declarations (e.g., naming). Related to these major classes is Searle's general theory of illocutionary acts, which classifies various rules and conditions according to which aspect of text and context is focused upon in the speech act. According to Searle, the uttering of words is an utterance act; referring and predicating are propositional acts; and stating, questioning, and promising are illocutionary acts. Illocutionary acts are rule-governed and intentional. The consequences of illocutionary acts are perlocutionary acts.

Equally useful to the understanding of the cognitive, psychological aspect of discourse in LPIs is the work of Paul Grice. Grice (1989) distinguishes between natural meaning (as in "Those spots mean measles") and speaker meaning, which is intended by the speaker to achieve a desired effect in the hearer and to be recognized by the hearer as such. The notion of speaker meaning makes clear that speakers can use utterances for various purposes and that the same utterance can be used to elicit different responses. Further, Grice (1989) sets out the conditions for communication, which he contends is rational and to which he assigns a general principle—the cooperative principle. He then specifies more detailed maxims that are related to this general principle—maxims of quality, quantity, relevance, and manner (Levinson 1983).

Speech act theory and Grice's work have developed along different logical, semantic, and pragmatic lines and have been subject to debate and revision. We will pursue here their roles in the analysis of interaction. It is possible to analyze language use by combining the analysis of the propositional content of utterances with their illocutionary force, permitting us to draw inferences about the inner worlds of each participants in a conversation— their beliefs, assumptions, desires, attitudes, stances, and so forth. It is also possible for us to examine participants' intentions and their effects on interaction.

In this volume, several contributors (Yoshida-Morise, Mohan, Katona, Moder and Halleck, and Young and Halleck) discuss directly or indirectly the impact of the illocutionary force of speakers' utterances on the framing of meaning interpretation and meaning negotiation. They compel us to (re)evaluate the specific rules and conditions of making meaning and making sense of meaning in the LPI context. The contributors to this volume also note that Gricean maxims take on special characteristics in the context of LPIs. For instance, Johnson and Tyler, He, and Ross find that the maxim of quality appears to count for more than that of quantity; the maxim of relevance hardly applies; and the maxim of manner often requires speakers to be verbose rather than clear.

5 Overview of the Book

The following thirteen chapters were all written specifically for this book. Each of the chapters is an in-depth analysis of LPIs recorded on audio- or videotape. It is remarkable to us that this book should be the first such collection of empirical studies, given that the means of assessing second language speaking proficiency through interviews have been around for some time.[3,4]

We deliberately invited contributions from scholars with a wide range of disciplinary orientations. In order to help the reader identify similar research questions and approaches, we have grouped the thirteen chapters into four sections.

In the first section, *Language Proficiency Interviews and Conversation*, we collect those contributions that make explicit comparisons between the discourse of LPIs and other kinds of discourse. In "Re-Analyzing the OPI: How Much Does It Look like Natural Conversation?" Marysia Johnson and Andrea Tyler compare an oral proficiency interview used in the training of interviewers with previous research about the structure of ordinary conversation. Heidi Riggenbach, in "Evaluating Learner Interactional Skills: Conversation at the Micro Level," conducts a microanalysis of an informal conversation between a learner of English and her roommate, and makes specific comparisons between that conversation and the discourse of LPIs. This section concludes with Dale April Koike's "What Happens When There's No One to Talk to? Spanish Foreign Language Discourse in Simulated Oral Proficiency Interviews." Koike makes a quantitative and qualitative comparison of the discourse of direct oral tests and semidirect tests in which the learner has to respond to prompts recorded on tape.

The three contributions to the second section, *Turns and Sequences in Language Proficiency Interviews*, examine LPI discourse from a conversational-analytic framework. Agnes Weiyun He, in "Answering Questions in LPIs: A Case Study," describes the interactional features of an LPI that contributed to an individual's failing the test and thus not being granted a teaching assistantship. Carol Lynn Moder and Gene B. Halleck, in "Framing the Language Proficiency Interview as a Speech Event: Native and Non-Native Speakers' Questions," compare interviews with native and non-native speakers and conclude that the interview frame, rather than the fact that the interviewee is a non-native speaker, determines the types of questions asked in an LPI. The concluding contribution to this section is Maria M. Egbert's comparison of repair in LPIs with repair in informal conversations between native speakers, "Miscommunication in Language Proficiency Interviews of First-Year German Students: A Comparison with Natural Conversation."

The third section, *Knowledge and Communication in Language Proficiency Interviews*, consists of three descriptions of how knowledge is constructed in LPIs through speech acts and practical reasoning. In "Knowledge Structures in Oral Proficiency Interviews for International Teaching Assistants," Bernard Mohan shows clearly how the interviewer and interviewee co-construct knowledge in the interview. Yumiko Yoshida-Morise, in "The Use of Communication Strategies in Language Proficiency Interviews," shows how Japanese interviewees at different levels of proficiency in English use their strategic resources to match their speaking ability with the communicative demands of the interview. The final contribution to this section is "Meaning Negotiation in the Hungarian Oral Proficiency Examination of English" by Lucy Katona. In this chapter, Katona investigates the effect of an important variable in face-to-face interaction—familiarity between the candidate and examiner—on the discourse of LPIs conducted in Hungary.

In the fourth and final section, *Language Proficiency Interviews as Cross-Cultural Encounters*, four chapters examine the differing interpretations placed on the LPI by examiners and candidates coming from different cultural backgrounds. In "Maintaining American Face in the Korean Oral Exam: Reflections on the Power of Cross-Cultural Context," Catherine E. Davies gives an interactional/sociolinguistic perspective on Americans taking an LPI in Korean with a Korean interviewer. In "Confirmation Sequences as Interactional Resources in Korean Language Proficiency Interviews," Kyu-hyun Kim and Kyung-hee Suh analyze a specific interactional routine in Korean that is a marker of how well candidates understand and accept the hierarchical structure of social interaction among Koreans. In "Divergent Frame Interpretations in Oral Proficiency Interview Interaction," Steven Ross explains Japanese candidates' reluctance to elaborate on their answers to interviewers' questions in terms of the differing cultural expectations regarding the role of the interviewee in Japanese and American society. Finally, in "'Let Them Eat Cake!' or How to Avoid Losing Your Head in Cross-Cultural Conversations," Richard Young and Gene B. Halleck compare Mexican and Japanese interviewees in English-language LPIs in terms of talkativeness, and suggest that the comparative taciturnity of the Japanese leads to a lower assessment of proficiency.

We began this introduction with a practical question—How can we best assess how well someone speaks a second language? We have argued that this question needs to be asked within the context of interactional competence of all participants in an LPI. None of the contributions to this book provides a practical answer to that question. What our contributors *do* provide are thorough, empirically based, and theoretically motivated analyses of the discourse of language proficiency interviews.

Collectively, we show how LPIs are constructed via specific moment-by-moment, sequential, lexicogrammatical organizations that embody situational, institutional, and cultural contexts. Through these analyses, a rich and detailed picture of interactional competence emerges. In the tradition of applied linguistics, good practice develops only after a foundation of empirical research and theory-building. We hope to provide that indispensable foundation in this book.

Notes

1. As far as we are aware, the term *interactional competence* was first used by Kramsch (1986). We have, however, greatly extended the meaning of the term in applying it to a theory of second language knowledge that embraces co-construction as well as the specific resources that participants deploy in interactive practices.

2. For further readings on the theoretical assumptions of CA and ethnomethodology, see Heritage (1984); for further readings on the specific rules of turn-taking, see Levinson (1983).

3. Spolsky (1995) mentions the Spanish oral interviews conducted at Yale beginning in 1932 as perhaps the first instance of a face-to-face spoken interaction for the purpose of assessing students' oral ability. But he specifies (p. 99) that "pride of place for a direct measurement of oral language proficiency is generally now granted to the oral interview created by the Foreign Service Institute (FSI) of the U.S. State Department, developed originally between 1952 and 1956."

4. One could argue that Valdman (1987) was such a volume, although with a different emphasis.

References

Agar, Michael. 1985. "Institutional Discourse." *Text* 5.147–168.
American Council on the Teaching of Foreign Languages. 1989. *ACTFL Proficiency Guidelines*. Yonkers, NY: Author.
Atkinson, J. Maxwell, and Paul Drew. 1979. *Order in Court: The Organization of Verbal Interaction in Judicial Settings*. London: Macmillan.
Austin, John L. 1962. *How to Do Things with Words*. Oxford: Oxford University Press.
Bachman, Lyle F. 1990. *Fundamental Considerations in Language Testing*. Oxford: Oxford University Press.
Bachman, Lyle F., and Adrian S. Palmer. 1996. *Language Testing in Practice: Designing and Developing Useful Language Tests*. Oxford: Oxford University Press.
Bakhtin, Mikhail M. 1981. *The Dialogic Imagination*. Austin: University of Texas Press.
Blum-Kulka, Shoshana, Juliane House, and Gabriele Kasper. 1989. "Investigating Cross-Cultural Pragmatics: An Introductory Overview." In *Cross-Cultural Pragmatics*, ed. by Shoshana Blum-Kulka, Juliane House, and Gabriele Kasper, 1–34. Norwood, NJ: Ablex.

Briggs, Charles L. 1986. *Learning How to Ask: A Sociolinguistic Appraisal of the Role of the Interview in Social Science Research*. Cambridge: Cambridge University Press.
Brown, Penelope, and Stephen Levinson. 1987. *Politeness: Some Universals in Language Usage*. Cambridge: Cambridge University Press.
Button, Graham. 1987. "Answers as Interactional Products: Two Sequential Practices in Interviews." *Social Psychology Quarterly* 50.160–171.
Button, Graham, and Neil Casey. 1984. "Generating Topic: The Use of Topic Initial Elicitors." In *Structures of Social Action: Studies in Conversation Analysis*, ed. by J. Maxwell Atkinson and John Heritage, 167–190. Cambridge: Cambridge University Press.
Canale, Michael, and Merrill Swain. 1980. "Theoretical Bases of Communicative Approaches to Second Language Teaching and Testing." *Applied Linguistics* 1.1–47.
Chaiklin, Seth, and Jean Lave, eds. 1993. *Understanding Practice*. Cambridge: Cambridge University Press.
Clayman, Steve E. 1992. "Footing and the Achievement of Neutrality: The Case of News Interview Discourse." In *Talk at Work*, ed. by Paul Drew and John Heritage, 163–198. Cambridge: Cambridge University Press.
Crow, Bryan K. 1983. "Topic Shifts in Couples' Conversations." In *Conversational Coherence: Form, Structure, and Strategy*, ed. by Robert T. Craig and Karen Tracy, 136–156. Beverly Hills, CA: Sage.
Davies, Alan. 1990. *Principles of Language Testing*. Oxford: Basil Blackwell.
Derrida, Jacques. 1976. *Of Grammatology*. Baltimore, MD: Johns Hopkins University Press.
Douglas, Dan, and Larry Selinker. 1985. "Principles for Language Tests Within the 'Discourse Domains' Theory of Interlanguage." *Language Testing* 2.205–226.
Drew, Paul, and John Heritage, eds. 1992. *Talk at Work*. Cambridge: Cambridge University Press.
Erickson, Frederick, and Jeffrey Shultz. 1982. *The Counselor as Gatekeeper*. New York: Academic Press.
Firth, J. R. 1957. *Papers in Linguistics: 1934–1951*. London: Oxford University Press.
Ford, Cecilia, and Sandra Thompson. 1996. "Interactional Units in Conversation: Syntactic, Intonational, and Pragmatic Resources for the Management of Turns." In *Interaction and Grammar*, ed. by Elinor Ochs, Emanuel A. Schegloff, and Sandra Thompson, 134–184. Cambridge: Cambridge University Press.
Gadamer, Hans-Georg. 1975. *Truth and Method*. New York: Seabury Press.
Garfinkel, Harold. 1984. *Studies in Ethnomethodology*. Cambridge: Polity Press.
Goffman, Erving. 1981. *Forms of Talk*. Philadelphia: University of Pennsylvania Press.
Greatbatch, David. 1988. "A Turn-taking System for British News Interviews." *Language in Society* 17.401–430.
Grice, H. Paul. 1989. *Studies in the Ways of Words*. Cambridge, MA: Harvard University Press.
Gumperz, John J. 1982. *Discourse Strategies*. Cambridge: Cambridge University Press.

Gumperz, John J. 1992. "Interviewing in Cross-Cultural Situations." In *Talk at Work*, ed. by Paul Drew and John Heritage, 302–327. Cambridge: Cambridge University Press.

Hall, Joan K. 1993. "The Role of Oral Practices in the Accomplishment of Our Everyday Lives: The Sociocultural Dimension of Interaction with Implications for the Learning of Another Language." *Applied Linguistics* 14.145–166.

Hall, Joan K. 1995. "(Re)creating Our Worlds with Words: A Sociohistorical Perspective of Face-to-face Interaction." *Applied Linguistics* 16.206–232.

Hartford, Beverly S., and Kathleen Bardovi-Harlig. 1992. "Closing the Conversation: Evidence from the Academic Advising Session." *Discourse Processes* 15.93–116.

He, Agnes W. 1993. "Language Use in Peer Review Texts." *Language in Society* 22.403–420.

He, Agnes W. 1994. "Withholding Academic Advice: Institutional Context and Discourse Practice." *Discourse Processes* 18.297–316.

He, Agnes W. 1996. "Narrative Processes and Institutional Activities: Recipient Guided Storytelling in Academic Counseling Encounters." *Pragmatics* 6.205–216.

Heath, Christian. 1989. "Pain Talk: The Expression of Suffering in the Medical Consultation." *Social Psychology Quarterly* 52.113–125.

Hutchins, Edwin. 1995. *Cognition in the Wild*. Cambridge, MA: MIT Press.

Hymes, Dell. 1972. "On Communicative Competence." In *Sociolinguistics: Selected Readings*, ed. by John B. Pride and Janet Holmes, 269–293. Harmondsworth, Middlesex: Penguin.

Hymes, Dell. 1974. *Foundations in Sociolinguistics: An Ethnographic Approach*. Philadelphia: University of Pennsylvania Press.

Jacoby, Sally, and Elinor Ochs. 1995. "Co-construction: An Introduction." *Research on Language and Social Interaction* 28.171–183.

Kramsch, Claire. 1986. "From Language Proficiency to Interactional Competence." *Modern Language Journal* 70.366–372.

Labov, William, and David Fanshel. 1977. *Therapeutic Discourse: Psychotherapy as Conversation*. New York: Academic Press.

Lado, Robert. 1957. *Linguistics Across Cultures*. Ann Arbor, MI: University of Michigan Press.

Lave, Jean. 1988. *Cognition in Practice*. New York: Cambridge University Press.

Lazaraton, Anne. 1992. "The Structural Organization of a Language Interview: A Conversation Analytic Perspective." *System* 20.373–386.

Lazaraton, Anne. 1996. "Interlocutor Support in Oral Proficiency Interviews: The Case of CASE." *Language Testing* 13.151–172.

Levinson, Stephen. 1979. "Activity Types and Language." *Linguistics* 17.365–399.

Levinson, Stephen. 1983. *Pragmatics*. Cambridge: Cambridge University Press.

Malinowski, Bronislaw. 1923. "The Problem of Meaning in Primitive Languages." In *The Meaning of Meaning*, ed. by Charles K. Ogden and Ivor A. Richards, 296–336. London: Harcourt, Brace and World.

Marlaire, Courtney L., and Douglas W. Maynard. 1990. "Standardized Testing as an Interactional Phenomenon." *Sociology of Education* 63.83–101.
McHoul, Alexander. 1978. "The Organization of Turns at Formal Talk in the Classroom." *Language in Society* 7.183–213.
McHoul, Alexander. 1990. "The Organization of Repair in Classroom Talk." *Language in Society* 19.349–377.
McNamara, Tim F. 1996. "'Interaction' in second language performance assessment: Whose performance?" *Applied Linguistics* 18.446–466.
Mishler, Elliot G. 1986. *Research Interviewing: Context and Narrative*. Cambridge, MA: Harvard University Press.
Ochs, Elinor. 1982. "Talking to Children in Western Samoa." *Language in Society* 11.77–104.
Ochs, Elinor. 1988. *Culture and Language Development*. Cambridge: Cambridge University Press.
Ranney, Susan. 1992. "Learning a New Script: An Exploration of Sociolinguistic Competence." *Applied Linguistics* 13.25–50.
Riggenbach, Heidi R. 1991. "Towards an Understanding of Fluency: A Microanalysis of Nonnative Speaker Conversations." *Discourse Processes* 14.423–441.
Rogoff, Barbara. 1990. *Apprenticeship in Thinking: Cognitive Development in Social Context*. New York: Oxford University Press.
Rommetveit, Ragnar. 1985. "Language Acquisition as Increasing Linguistic Structuring of Experience and Symbolic Behavior Control." In *Culture, Communication and Cognition: Vygotskyan Perspectives*, ed. by James V. Wertsch, 183–204. Cambridge: Cambridge University Press.
Sacks, Harvey. 1992. *Lectures on Conversation*. Vols. I and II, ed. by Gail Jefferson, with an introduction by Emanuel A. Schegloff. Cambridge, MA: Blackwell.
Sacks, Harvey, Emanuel A. Schegloff, and Gail Jefferson. 1974. "A Simplest Systematics for the Organization of Turn-taking for Conversation." *Language* 50.696–735.
Schaeffer, Nora C. 1991. "Conversation with a Purpose—or Conversation? Interaction in the Standardized Interview." In *Measurement Errors in Surveys*, ed. by Paul P. Biemer, Robert M. Groves, Lars E. Lyberg, Nancy A. Mathiowetz, and Seymour Sudman, 367–391. New York: Wiley.
Schegloff, Emanuel A., Gail Jefferson, and Harvey Sacks. 1977. "The Preference for Self-Correction in the Organization of Repair in Conversation." *Language* 53.361–382.
Schegloff, Emanuel A., and Harvey Sacks. 1973. "Opening Up Closings." *Semiotica* 8.289–327.
Schutz, Alfred. 1962. "Some Leading Concepts of Phenomenology." In *Alfred Schutz, Collected Papers*, vol. 2, 99–117. The Hague: Martinus Nijhoff.
Searle, John R. 1969. *Speech Acts: An Essay in the Philosophy of Language*. Cambridge: Cambridge University Press.
Searle, John R. 1979. *Expression and Meaning: Studies in the Theory of Speech Acts*. Cambridge: Cambridge University Press.

Sinclair, John M., and Malcolm Coulthard. 1975. *Towards an Analysis of Discourse: The English Used by Teachers and Pupils.* Oxford: Oxford University Press.

Spolsky, Bernard. 1995. *Measured Words: The Development of Objective Language Testing.* New York: Oxford University Press.

Valdman, Albert, ed. 1987. *Proceedings from the Symposium on the Evaluation of Foreign Language Proficiency.* Bloomington, IN: Indiana University Press.

van Lier, Leo. 1989. "Reeling, Writhing, Drawling, Stretching, and Fainting in Coils: Oral Proficiency Interviews as Conversation." *TESOL Quarterly* 23.489–508.

Voloshinov, Valentin N. 1973. *Marxism and the Philosophy of Language.* New York: Seminar Press.

Wolfson, Nessa. 1984. "Pretty Is as Pretty Does: A Speech Act View of Sex Roles." *Applied Linguistics* 5.236–244.

Young, Richard. 1995a. "Discontinuous Interlanguage Development and Its Implications for Oral Proficiency Rating Scales." *Applied Language Learning* 6.13–26.

Young, Richard. 1995b. "Conversational Styles in Language Proficiency Interviews." *Language Learning* 45.3–42.

Young, Richard, and Michael Milanovic. 1992. "Discourse Variation in Oral Proficiency Interviews." *Studies in Second Language Acquisition* 14.403–424.

Part 1

Language Proficiency Interviews and Conversation

Re-analyzing the OPI:
How Much Does It Look like Natural Conversation?

Marysia Johnson
Arizona State University

Andrea Tyler
Georgetown University

1 Introduction

Advocates of the Oral Proficiency Interview (OPI) claim that "a well-structured oral proficiency interview tests speaking ability in a real-life context—a conversation.[1] It is almost by definition a valid measure of speaking ability" (Educational Testing Service 1982). But one of the central characteristics of naturally occurring conversation—as Gumperz (1982) and Wolfson (1976), among others, have pointed out—is that language users are largely unaware of how conversation is typically structured and managed. When asked to articulate conversational practices, native-speaker pronouncements are often at odds with what speakers actually do (Wolfson 1989). Much of how everyday conversation works is so deceptively familiar that people studying and testing language often overlook fundamental characteristics of conversation. It is precisely on these grounds that van Lier (1989) has challenged the ETS's claim that the OPI measures speaking ability in the context of a conversation. Van Lier (1989:494) simply asks, "Is it really a conversation?"

We will contribute to this investigation by analyzing a representative OPI used widely in official language proficiency tester training workshops in government and nongovernment institutions in the United States to illustrate appropriate elicitation techniques and language characteristics of a Level Two speaker. Since we have analyzed only one interview, our results must be viewed with caution. The fact that this interview has been put forward as a model for tester performance and has been used widely to train OPI testers, however, suggests that the patterns found in this exchange are likely to be widespread. Of course, further investigation involving a larger sample is necessary to confirm the present findings.

Our analysis reveals that in terms of such prototypical aspects of everyday conversation (Sacks, Schegloff, and Jefferson 1974) as turn-taking phenomena and topic nomination, this model OPI does not conform to normal conversation. In addition, the analysis of the interviewers' contributions reveals a distinct lack of the features of conversational involvement (Gumperz 1982, Tannen, 1989) and shows of responsiveness (McCarthy 1991) that are prevalent in natural, friendly, everyday conversation (Goodwin and Goodwin 1992, Hatch 1992, Meritt 1982, Tannen 1985). We conclude that the face-to-face exchange that occurs in this OPI interview cannot be considered a valid example of a typical, real-life conversation.

2 The Oral Proficiency Interview

2.1 Overview

The Oral Proficiency Interview is a widely used instrument for assessing second and foreign language speaking ability within U.S. government institutions such as the Foreign Service Institute (FSI) and the Defense Language Institute (DLI). It is also used by nongovernment institutions such as the Educational Testing Service (ETS), and the American Council on the Teaching of Foreign Languages (ACTFL).

In the OPI, the candidate converses face-to-face with one or two trained testers on a variety of topics for 10 to 30 minutes.[2] The elicited sample is then rated on a scale ranging from 0 (no functional ability) to 5 (proficiency equivalent to that of a well-educated native speaker). It is estimated that several thousand OPI tests are administered each year. Professional careers, future job assignments, pay increases, and entrance to or exit from college language programs frequently depend on the rating obtained in an OPI.

2.2 Structure of the Oral Proficiency Interview

The OPI has both a general and a level-specific structure as described in the *ILR Handbook on Oral Interview Testing* (Lowe 1988) and in Clark and Clifford (1988). It consists of four phases: Warm-Up, Level Check, Probes, and Wind-Down. The Warm-Up phase consists of social courtesies at a level that is very easy for the candidate. The Warm-Up serves three purposes: (1) putting the candidate at ease, (2) reacquainting the candidate with the language (if necessary), and (3) giving the testers a preliminary indication of the candidate's level. This preliminary indication must be confirmed in the next phase of the interview, the Level Check. The purpose of the Level Check is to find out the candidate's highest sustainable level of speaking proficiency. In the Level Check phase, testers have the candidate perform the tasks assigned to a given level. When the candidate successfully passes the Level Check, his/her performance provides a floor for the rating. The next phase—Probes—aims to find the ceiling. The purpose of the Probes phase is to show the tester(s) whether the candidate has reached his/her highest level of speaking proficiency. If the candidate passes a given Probe level, this level becomes a new Level Check and the process repeats itself. In order to probe, testers have the candidate attempt to perform a task or tasks one level above the level of proficiency established by the Level Check. The Level Check and Probes are interwoven, so that the candidate is alternately stressed and relaxed, and not constantly pushed ever higher. The last phase is called the Wind-Down, and its purpose is to leave the candidate with a feeling of accomplishment. It also gives testers a last chance to check any aspect of the candidate's speaking ability that may have been assessed incompletely.

2.3 *Elicitation Techniques*

To obtain a ratable sample (i.e., a sample of the candidate's spoken language to which a rating can be assigned), testers must make sure that not only general but level-specific requirements have been fulfilled. Level-specific requirements include a series of tasks and functions that are assigned to a given level. To elicit level-specific tasks and functions, testers use questions and role-play situations.

A variety of question types constitutes the core of the OPI elicitation procedures, and a given set of question types is recommended for a particular level or levels of speaking proficiency. For instance, for Level 0+, Yes/No and Choice Questions are recommended; for Levels 1 and 2, Information Questions; and for Levels 3, 4 and 5, Hypothetical and Supported Opinion Questions are required. Examples of these question types from Lowe (1988) are presented below.

Yes/No Question:	Do you live in Washington?
Choice Question:	Would you like tea or coffee?
Information Question:	What did you do last summer?
Hypothetical Question:	If you were the Prime Minister, what would you do to improve the economic situation in your country?
Supported Opinion Question:	Why are you against this type of policy?

2.4 Principles of the OPI Rating Procedures[3]

In the OPI, ratings are expressed in global terms. The totality of the candidate's speaking performance is compared with the ILR descriptors at each level. Six factors that contribute to the candidate's overall speaking proficiency: pronunciation, fluency, grammar, vocabulary, tasks, and sociolinguistic/cultural factors. The candidate's speaking level of proficiency is evaluated to reflect his/her ability to integrate all these factors/subskills in performing a variety of language functions and tasks (Lowe 1983, 1986, 1988).

3 Literature Review

3.1 Critical Analysis of the OPI

A group of researchers (Bachman 1988, 1990; Bachman and Savignon 1986; Lantolf and Frawley 1985, 1988; Savignon 1985) working in the field of language testing and teaching have voiced strong criticism of the OPI. Their criticisms center primarily on the OPI's validity and the theory of proficiency the OPI claims to represent.

A recent critic of the OPI, van Lier (1989), also calls for a thorough investigation of the OPI's construct validity. But unlike the authors mentioned above, he does not insist on developing an external criterion (i.e., a theoretical framework) against which the construct of the OPI should be evaluated. He calls instead for a thorough examination of the OPI from within. He advocates an ethnographic approach to determine what kind of speech event the OPI is, to find the answer to the question, "Is it really a conversation?"

Van Lier finds it difficult to accept that the OPI represents an instance of natural conversation because the goal of the OPI is to elicit a ratable sample, not to conduct a conversation. Using Jones and Gerard's (1967) model of dyadic interaction, van Lier points to different distributions of rights and duties in interviews and in conversations. An interview is characterized by asymmetrical contingency (i.e., the interviewer has a predefined plan and conducts the interview to execute the plan). Friendly, everyday conversation, in contrast, is based on mutual contingency with equal distributions of rights and duties. It is unclear how the OPI might accommodate these mutually exclusive types of contingency. Van Lier's claims about the asymmetrical contingency of the OPIs have been supported by Young and Milanovic (1992), but his claims about conversation have yet to be substantiated. Van Lier (1989:500) also rightfully points out that "every manifestation of speaking is speaking in context; every contextual manifestation of speaking ability requires, in addition to speaking ability, context-specific skills and experience." If the OPI does not measure speaking ability in the form of conversation, as it claims to measure, then the users of the system may be misled about candidates' abilities to actually carry on real-life conversations.

Furthermore, the OPI may very well be a unique speech event with its own unique norms and rules. These norms and rules may not adhere to those of any naturally occurring speech events. In that case, the ability to generalize OPI scores beyond the OPI context could be severely undermined. Precisely for these reasons, the investigation of the question "Is it really a conversation?" is of the utmost importance.

3.2 Typical Features of Everyday Conversation

As noted above, supporters of the OPI have argued that it is a valid measure of speaking ability because it represents a real-life context—a face-to-face conversation. But this assertion can be maintained only if careful analyses of OPIs show that they contain the established features of natural conversation. We turn now to a consideration of the research examining features of conversation.

The work of Schegloff and Sacks (1973), Sacks, Schegloff, and Jefferson (1974), and Schegloff, Jefferson, and Sacks (1977) has established the highly organized and locally managed system operating within conversation. Key features of the locally managed system are systematic turn-taking mechanisms and adjacency pairs. The local management system accounts for the patterns of stable and recurrent actions responsible for creating order in conversation. Examination of everyday conversation reveals that it is produced on a turn-by-turn basis. Although the turn-taking is normally accomplished smoothly, virtually no aspect of it is specified in advance. Turn size, turn order, and turn distribution are not fixed. In other words, at the beginning of a conversation the participants do not know and cannot accurately predict how much any one participant will contribute, in which order participants will talk, or how frequently any one participant will talk. Neither is the content of a participant's remarks specified in advance. According to Sacks et al. (1974:710), the turn-taking organization for natural conversation, by contrast with interviews and other speech exchange systems, "makes no provision for the content of any turn, nor does it constrain what is (to be) done in any turn." Indeed, the unplanned nature and unpredictable outcomes constitute primary characteristics of natural conversation.

One systematic feature of conversational structure that does provide a kind of predictability is the regular occurrence of ordered sequences produced by different speakers, which Schegloff and Sacks (1973) call adjacency pairs. Adjacency pairs are ordered as a first part and a second part, and are typed in such a way that the occurrence of the first part requires a particular second part. For instance, greetings require greetings, and offers require acceptance or rejection (Levinson 1983, Schiffrin 1994). The basic rule that governs the operation of adjacency-pair use is "given the recognizable production of a first part, on its first possible completion its speaker should stop and a next speaker should start and produce a second pair part from the pair type in which the first is recognizably a member" (Schegloff and Sacks 1973:296). Perhaps the most prototypical adjacency pair is the question-response sequence (Schiffrin 1994).

Another salient feature of everyday conversation is spontaneously created and negotiated topics. Although researchers have failed to agree upon an operational definition of topic, topic can be regarded as a "pre-theoretical notion of what is being talked about" (Brown and Yule 1983:71) through some series of turns at talk.[4] In natural conversation, topic is negotiated and topical coherence is "constructed across turns by collaboration of participants" (Levinson 1983:313). This collaboration involves participants picking up elements from other participants' contributions to the preceding discourse and incorporating these elements into their own contributions (Brown and Yule 1983, Tannen 1989). Brown and Yule (1983) specify that speaking topically involves the process of making contributions that fit closely to the most recent element incorporated in the topic framework. They distinguish speaking topically from speaking on a topic, which they characterize as occurring when participants concentrate their talk on a particular individual or issue.

In natural conversation, topic emerges spontaneously, and as Ochs points out "is relatively unplanned and locally managed" (Ochs 1970:58). Agreeing with Ochs, Brown and Yule (1983) argue that a regular feature of conversation is that "topics are not fixed beforehand but are negotiated in the process of conversing. Throughout a conversation, the next topic of conversation is developing. Each speaker contributes to the conversation in terms of both the existing topic framework and his personal topic" (Brown and Yule 1983:89). According to Jones and Gerard (1967) and their notion of mutual rights and mutual contingencies, one expects roughly balanced distribution among participants in naturally occurring conversation in terms of initiation of topic as well as turns at talk, length of turn, and speaker selection.

Finally, typical everyday conversation involves an affective quality that goes beyond a smoothly orchestrated exchange of speakership. Gumperz (1982) argues that the interlocutors' displays of willingness to be engaged in and value the exchange—an affective stance he terms "conversational involvement"—are an inherent part of normal conversation. Along the same lines, Meritt (1982) argues that everyday conversation is typified by an observable state of interlocutors being engaged in coordinated interaction. Similarly, Tannen (1985) notes that one fundamental aspect of normal face-to-face communication is the display of connectedness with one's interlocutor(s), which is accomplished through shows of solidarity, friendliness, and interestedness in the content of the other participants' utterances. Indeed, the observation that topic is emergent and collaboratively constructed argues that interlocutors must be responsive to and display interest in one another's contributions.

One important way of displaying interestedness involves assessment of the content of the contributions made by other participants (Goodwin and Goodwin 1992). McCarthy (1991:123) notes that in everyday conversation, speakers often "evaluate (or at least react to) the content of their interlocutor's contribution." Moreover, the content of one's assessment would appear to be subject to ritual constraints that involve obligations to help others maintain the image of being competent communicators (Goffman 1967, 1974, 1976). As Hatch (1992:67) points out, "Ritual constraints on communication include not only ways of presenting self, but ways we give face to others. In everyday discourse, we often reassure our partners and we avoid open disagreement." This is not to say that all real-life conversations are friendly and devoid of face-threatening acts. Certainly we must acknowledge that disagreement and conflict are part of natural conversation. In the absence of aggressive or insulting remarks on the part of a participant, however, we do not expect other interlocutors to engage in face-threatening behavior. As Goodwin and Goodwin (1992) point out, a participant's assessment of an interlocutor's contribution is usually positive, but if it is challenging, it tends to be cloaked in indirection and hedges in order to help others maintain face. This would seem to be the case particularly if those interlocutors have the avowed goal of leaving the other participant with a sense of conversational accomplishment, as is the stated case for interviewers in the OPIs. (Recall that a specified goal of the Wind-Down phase of the OPI is to leave the candidate with a sense of accomplishment.)

4 Analysis

4.1 *Data Description*

We turn now to an analysis of a representative sample of the OPI that is widely used in official oral proficiency tester training workshops. In U.S. government agencies, this OPI video is used in conjunction with the Inter-Agency Language Roundtable (ILR) level descriptors to illustrate language characteristics of a Level Two speaker and appropriate elicitation techniques.

In this Level Two OPI, a Korean woman in her early thirties (the NNS) is being interviewed by two experienced American testers, one female in her early thirties (the IRF) and one male in his early forties (the IRM). The candidate volunteered to participate in the OPI. She was not assigned to take the OPI for any external reasons such as job or academic requirements. The two American testers were certified OPI testers for English as a second language. The interview took place in Monterey, California, in the early 1980s.

The analysis that follows seeks to determine how much this OPI looks like natural conversation in terms of such prototypical aspects of everyday conversation as turn-taking, adjacency pairs, and topic nomination as well as features of conversational involvement.

4.2 *Turn-Taking*

4.2.1 *Distribution and Content of Turns*

In normal conversation, we expect turn order, length of turns, and turn distribution to be unspecified prior to the exchange. Once the conversation is under way, we expect to see aspects of collaboration and negotiation in construction of the emerging topic. An analysis of the Level Two OPI video reveals that, in contrast, turn order, length of turns, and turn distribution appear to be largely fixed and controlled by the testers who execute them in a highly systematic way specific to this interaction.

A quantitative analysis of the distribution and content of turns appears in Table 1. In this study, a turn refers to an actual occurrence of holding the floor (i.e., turns were counted when transfer of speakers occurred). Turns were also classified according to the function they performed as information questions, clarification questions, neutral minimal responses, or expressions of experience, opinion, or assessment. Information questions are those utterances whose illocutionary force is to seek information and in which the speaker's stance toward the information appears to be neutral. They include *Where are you from?* and *How did you come here?*. Turns involving expression of personal experience or opinion are those in which a participant reveals some personal experience or opinion. Expression of assessment of the content of another speaker's contributions is also included in this category. Assessment can be either positive or negative. A positive expression of assessment may take the form of an expression of solidarity in which a speaker

Table 1. Distribution and Content of Turns in the Level Two OPI

	Tester			NNS	Total
	IRF	IRM	Both		
Number of turns, of which...	23	41	64	60	124
information questions	19	20	39	5	44
clarification questions	3	0	3	4	7
neutral minimal responses	2	5	7	5	12
expressions of experience, opinion, assessment	0	10	10	42	52

offers support for the previous speaker's position by overtly agreeing or sympathizing (Boxer 1993) or by adding information in harmony with the previous speaker's position, as in Excerpt 1.

```
(1) Candidate's expressions of personal experience and
opinion

IRM:  So when I go to the store and I look at the way the
      prices=
NNS:  Yes
IRM:  =going up it's just incredible
NNS:  Everything
```

The IRM's utterances reveal personal experience (the speaker has gone to stores and observed rising prices) as well as personal opinion (the speaker finds the rising prices surprising). The NNS's responses are analyzed as showing positive assessment in the first instance in explicitly agreeing with the speaker by choosing the full lexical item *yes* rather than a more neutral backchannel. In the second instance they show agreement (or in Boxer's terms commiseration) with the speaker's complaint about rising prices through the response *Everything*. The NNS's responses imply that she has experienced the same phenomenon the IRM is relating and that she sees it from a similar perspective. According to Tannen (1989), such utterances are attempts to build rapport or solidarity.

Questions can also reveal an assessment. For instance, consider the male tester's question, *Is he really all that inflexible?* This utterance, while requesting information, also carries a challenge to the accuracy with which the speaker has characterized her uncle's flexibility. Thus the utterance indicates the speaker's assessment of the content of the candidate's utterance—in this case a somewhat negative assessment. In cases such as this, utterances are not double counted. According to the scheme used in this analysis, this utterance is classified as assessment, not as an information question.

Quantitative analysis reveals that within the conversational sections of the exchange (excluding the role-play sequences and the sequence in which the candidate is explicitly directed to ask questions), 44 out of 124 or one-third of all the turns involve information questions, and these questions are predominately produced by the testers, who contribute 39 out of 44 (89%). In contrast, information questions make up only 5 out of 60 (8%) of the candidate's turns.

4.2.2 *Order of Turns*

A turn-by-turn analysis reveals the turn order in these sections of the interaction: one of the testers asks a question and the candidate has an obligation to respond. This obligation does not necessarily apply to the testers, as is evident from the fact that two out of five of the candidate's information questions go unanswered while two others are answered with another question, as exemplified in Excerpt 2.

```
(2)  The candidate attempts to involve the female
     interviewer in the discussion of the economy

IRM: Yeah . . uh Why are prices going up? Why do you think
     it is so?
NNS: Well, I don't really know about that . . but when the
     price go up . . and you get pay more too . . right? I
     mean everybody when, when they work . . Is
 →   that what is it? (directed to IRF) (Silence)
IRM: What do you mean?
     . .
IRM: Do you think that people are generally keeping up?
NNS: I don't think so.
IRM: Why not? I mean why they are not keeping up?
NNS: Well . . because it is hard to live that way. Don't
 →   you think? (addressed to IRF)
 →   (Silence)
IRM: What do you think . . are the reasons for that?
```

Although there are three interlocutors present at all times, the exchanges tend to be two-way interactions between one of the testers and the candidate; there is virtually no interaction between the testers themselves. The testers tend to alternate in asking questions only if there is a change in task. Table 2 illustrates this point.

Table 2. Number of Turns Taken by Testers on Each Task in the Level Two OPI

Task	IRM	IRF
1. Narration in past	0	6
2. Narration in present	10	1
3. Description	9	9
4. Role-play: *Getting a doctor's appointment*	4	18
5. Candidate asks questions	0	0
6. Role-play: *Giving directions*	36	0
7. Role-play: *Getting a driver's license*	0	18
8. Supported opinion task: *Discussion of the economy*	13	0

It appears that the testers have specified their roles and turns in advance. They appear to be adhering to an agreement of noninterference during the other tester's task time. The one possible exception to this pattern takes place in the task of description, in which the two interviewers take an equal number of turns. This might lead the reader to conclude that the two interviewers were simultaneously contributing to this section of the interview. But the quantitative analysis masks the fact that this task was actually enacted in two discrete segments. First the female interviewer asked a series of questions such as *Tell me about your cousin. What is she like?*. Their purpose, assuming she is following ILR guidelines, was to elicit descriptions. After several turns that fail to produce adjective-laden descriptive language from the candidate, the female interviewer responds to the candidate's utterance with a minimal *I see*, followed by a pause. At this point the male interviewer steps in with the functionally equivalent questions, *What kind of man is your uncle? What kind of person is your uncle?* Once the male tester asks his questions, the female tester remains silent until the male tester announces the next task. There was no simultaneous dual tester involvement during the description section of the interview. In fact, the video reveals that while the male tester is asking his questions, the female tester is looking through a set of note cards rather than overtly attending to the ongoing exchange. Although the candidate continually scans both interviewers' faces, only the male tester meets her gaze.

In sum, in contrast to natural conversation, interactional tasks appear to largely have been set before the interview. The pattern of question-answer-question-answer led exclusively by only one of the testers, one at a time, does not look like natural conversation. As McCarthy (1991:126) notes, "Conversational data do contain stretches where initiate-respond-initiate-respond is the pattern, but rarely for long

Table 3. Average Length of Response in the Level Two OPI

	Testers	Candidate	Combined
Average length of response (in words)	4.3	19.5	10.4

Note. Conventionalized non-lexical verbalizations indicating backchanneling such as *mhm* were analyzed as words.

periods of time; such a pattern extended over a whole conversation would almost certainly lead the person on the receiving end of the questions to assess the event as having been like an interrogation." While such exchanges occur on occasion in real life, they are not the norm and are distinctly uncomfortable.

4.2.3 *Length of Turns*

A second striking feature of the exchange is the extreme imbalance in the amount of talk produced by the individual participants in the OPI. The bulk of the talking is done by only one of the participants—the candidate.

Table 3 gives the length of responses to questions for all three participants. The information in Table 3 reveals that the candidate's responses are, on average, four times as long as the testers' responses. The candidate's responses seem to be monitored by the testers as to appropriate length in terms of the expected linguistic features. If the candidate's response does not satisfy the linguistic requirements of a given level, she is forced to answer more questions. This is illustrated in Excerpt 3, which is the portion of the interaction attempting to elicit a narration in the past. The female tester keeps asking questions about the candidate's arrival in the U.S. because the candidate does not produce discourse consistently using the past tense; she often switches to present and future activities.

```
(3)  The female interviewer attempts to elicit past-tense
     narration from the candidate

15→IRF:  Oh, how did you come here?
16  NNS: Well, my uncle . . he was in the States long time .
17       . and my uncle . . he invited me over in the USA and
18       me and my brother . . but my brother . . he is in
19       Texas now and he's got this business over there . .
20       and he wanted me to come and live with him but
21       weather is so hot down there . . and I always get
22       sick with hot weather so I could not make . . and I
23       have a lots of cousins . . and she went to MPC in
24       Monterey and I came with her here.
25→IRF:  Is that from Korea you came with her?
```

```
26  NNS:   No, no, no, that's my uncle's children.
27→IRF:   Uhuhm so did you come with your brother or did you
28         come by yourself?
29  NNS:   Yes . . yes . . me and my brother and when I first
30         arrived in the USA I liked it even though I had uh
31         you know lots of problems with the English, but I
32         went to school English from long times, almost all
33         my life you know . . but I talked with lots of
34         people . . and uhm always learn every day.
35→IRF:   So you came to LA first.
36  NNS:   I stayed at LA almost three years . . weather was
37         hot.
38→IRF:   Uhm did you study English or did you work in LA?
39  NNS:   Well, I used to work for my uncle. He has a grocery
40         store in LA and . . I . . I was mopping the floors
41         and little things like that you know . . I did not
42         like it and I always wanted to be a nurse so I am
43         going to school for nurse and I work for a nurse a
44         little bit, but I really wanna uh to become RN so .
45         . that's what I'm doing. It's really hard because .
46         . you know . . it's a second language=
47  IRM:   Sure.
48  NNS:   =but at least I'm trying.
```

The same regulation of the candidate's turn length by syntactic and morphological production may be observed during the task of description. The candidate's response to the male tester's question in Excerpt 4—which was apparently intended to elicit a description—does not fulfill the linguistic requirements for Level Two. The candidate does not produce description—a paragraph that includes adjectives—and therefore the male tester keeps returning to the same task.

(4) The male interviewer attempts to elicit description from the candidate

```
→ IRM:   What does he look like . . originally looked?
  NNS:   Well, he just looks like any other Oriental man . .
         Korean man. (Silence) He is big though, like uh he
         weighs about 180 pounds and . . he is about six
         foot.
→ IRM:   What about his eyes? What are they?
  NNS:   Well, uh I think he has . . dark brown. Uhm . . all
         my family are big you know, my father is big except
         my mother she is kinda . . little . . and my brother
         is big and he uh . . well we don't want to change
```

```
                the subject and start talking about my brother
                (laughs). I always do that
→   IRM:        Well, that's okay. So what kind of person is your
                brother?
```

Note that the interviewer's determination to elicit description results in the exchange itself being somewhat incoherent with a locally emerging topic being ignored. In response to the query concerning what her uncle looks like, after noting that he looks like a typical Korean man, the candidate attempts to give information that might distinguish him, i.e., that her brother is big. Rather than following up on this remark, the interviewer asks about eye color. This question strikes one as odd for two reasons. First, it ignores the immediate focus of the previous remark. Second, it seems to violate the maxim of relevance. Typical Koreans have brown eyes. By saying her uncle looks like a typical Korean, the candidate has implied he has brown eyes. We argue that interactions such as these are governed by the requirements of the interview that aims to elicit particular grammatical structures, such as adjective-laden sentences, rather than the normal dynamics of mutual, emergent topic negotiation.

Excerpt 3 illustrates yet another point. As noted above, Brown and Yule (1983) argue that a typical pattern in conversation is for the current speaker to fit his or her comment closely to the immediately preceding discourse. Note that the interviewer's queries at lines 27, 35, and 38 do not display this close fit. Rather than fitting her utterances to the candidate's commentary concerning her brother who has set up a business in Texas, the physical difficulty she has with hot weather, or her decision to move to Monterey with one of her cousins, the female tester makes a series of unusual and disjunctive moves. Note that the tester in fact marks her contributions as unusual or unexpected with *Uhuhm* in line 27, *So* in line 35, and *Uhm* in line 38. After marking the disjunction, she poses a question that draws the candidate back to giving narration pertaining to her arrival. The tester's contributions seem to fit what McCarthy calls the journalistic interview style, in which the interviewer fails to offer follow-up moves found in most natural conversations. As McCarthy (1991:126) notes, "Interview style patterns are fine if interview language is the desired goal; they are a poor substitute for natural conversational patterns."

Finally, the testers appear to have determined ahead of time that their turn size would be kept to an absolute minimum. While this may be consistent with goals of the OPI, it is abnormal in everyday conversation where a fundamental assumption is that holding the floor and contributing to a conversation is positive. As Hatch (1992) argues, there is a sense in which each interlocutor is expected to uphold her/his end of the conversation through the addition of relevant comments. To consistently fail to take a turn when it is offered or to do so only minimally is one aspect of what Goffman (1967) refers to as being a "faulty participant." One of the primary effects of this strategy is to strip the testers' contributions of a sense of responsiveness to the candidate's utterances, or what Goodwin and Goodwin (1992) refer to as assessment. One of the most striking instances of the testers' lack of response occurs in Excerpt 5, when the candidate reveals her brother's expertise in Tae Kwon Do. This revelation is a follow-up to her earlier statement, *I am so proud of my brother.*

(5) Testers fail to respond to candidate's contribution.

```
NNS:  . . and he was very good . . and he went to Germany for
      the team . . and he got a black belt. . he is very good
      and I tell him "Don't you every use that on me"
      (laughs) and he never did.
IRM:  Let's try a situation here.
```

The length of turns, like the turn order, in the OPI is predictable and fixed. The testers' turns consist of a single sentence or question (except for the introduction to the role-play situations), with minimal assessment or responsiveness to the candidate's contributions. The candidate's turns consist of at least a few connected sentences. The candidate's turns are predictably longer than the testers'. Moreover, the length of the candidate's turns seems largely to be tied to her production of the syntactic and morphological constructions that the testers are seeking to elicit.

4.2.4 *Selection of Next Speaker*

According to Sacks et al. (1974), at the point where the current speaker is ready to relinquish the floor—called the turn transition-relevance point—the transfer of speakers occurs according to this rule: the current speaker selects the next speaker, or there is a self-selection, or the current speaker continues if there is no self-selection. According to Sacks et al. (1974), self-selection often involves some competition for the floor. This competition reflects a sense that contributing to the conversation or having an opportunity to hold the floor is valued by the participants.

The analysis of this OPI shows that at nearly all transition-relevance points, the testers select the next speaker. The right to select the next speaker does not apply to the candidate, even though she may be the current speaker. The candidate's few attempts to select the next speaker are either reluctantly accepted or totally ignored by the testers, as we saw in Excerpt 2. Once the candidate completes her turn, the turn goes back automatically to the tester (usually the one who posed the question to the candidate). Rather than taking the turn as an opportunity to add to the content of the candidate's remarks or express the tester's perspective, the tester asks another question or introduces a new activity such as a role-play situation and selects the candidate as the next speaker. Selection of next speaker is entirely controlled by the testers and adheres to the following pattern.

- Tester selects the candidate as the next speaker.
- Candidate responds.
- After the candidate's response, the turn returns to the same tester, or the other tester if a new task is introduced.

The candidate participates in the selection of next speaker only under the testers' specific instruction as is shown in Excerpt 6, the introduction to the Candidate Asks Questions task.

```
(6)  Testers instruct candidate to ask questions.

IRM: We have been asking you a lot of questions about
     yourself . . and we would like you to ask some
     questions about us . . our background, education, our
     job, family, how old we are. You can ask one or both of
     us.
```

4.3 *Adjacency Pairs*

Throughout much of the interview, the participants adhere to the strict adjacency pair format where the first part is immediately followed by the second part. The first part of the adjacency pairs—a question—is provided by one of the testers and the second part—an answer—is provided by the candidate. The candidate's answer is then followed by another question posed by a tester. This pattern is illustrated as follows.

    IR: Question
NNS: Answer
    IR: Question

Sacks et al. (1977) note that perhaps the most prototypical example of an adjacency pair is the question and response. In natural conversation between non-intimates, failure to respond to a question is rare. In a study of preferred responses to questions, Pomerantz (1984) found no instances of non-intimate interlocutors failing to respond to questions. Fishman (1983) found examples of husbands failing to respond to wives' questions, but this was seen as producing negative perturbations in the conversations and negative consequences for the wives. Thus it is particularly striking that the candidate attempts to answer all 39 information questions directed at her while the testers attempt to answer only one of the candidate's five information questions, and that one with a minimal response of *No, what is it?* What also seems striking is that the testers fill the second part of question-answer adjacency pairs structurally but not semantically, as shown in Excerpt 7.

```
(7)   Tester's minimal response to candidate's question

NNS:  Do you know what Tae Kwon Do means? Have you ever heard
      that?
      (Silence)
IRM:  No, what is it?
```

The candidate's four remaining questions are either left unanswered as shown in Excerpt 2 or responded to by other questions. It may be that the female interviewer's lack of response to the candidate's questions is connected with the previously described testers' agreement of non-interference during the other tester's task-time. Since the section of the interview in which the unanswered questions occurs was introduced by the male tester, the female tester may have perceived that this was his time and his responsibility to interact with the candidate. Whatever the reason, the failure to respond to four out of five of the candidate's information questions is atypical of natural conversation.

4.4 *Topic Nomination*

As reported in Table 2, the entire OPI can be divided into eight sections on the basis of topic and activity. The boundaries of these sections are surprisingly unambiguous, as they were marked by explicit bracketing phenomena. For instance, sections 4 and 6 begin with explicit announcements concerning role-playing a situation; sections 5, 6, and 7 end with the interviewer explicitly thanking the candidate for her responses.

In normal conversation we would not expect such explicit bracketing of topics (McCarthy 1991), nor would we expect one party to exclusively control the shift to new topics. In the OPI under consideration, however, explicit bracketing of the beginning and end of seven of the eight major topics is provided by the interviewers (the only potential exception is that the candidate may prompt the end of the roleplay in section 4). We believe that the strict segmentation of the OPI under the explicit direction of the testers comes about because the trained testers follow the OPI protocol to obtain a ratable sample. The prescribed format of the interview, not the emergent discourse, controls both the local and overall structure of the exchange.

Even within these sections, the candidate has a restricted role in negotiating or changing a topic, as Excerpt 8 illustrates. Note that the candidate sometimes sounds as if she feels the need to obtain the testers' permission to change a topic.

```
(8)   Tester grants candidate limited permission to change
      topic.

NNS:  . . well we don't want to change the subject and start
      talking about my brother (laughs). I always do that
IRM:  Well, that's okay. So what kind of person is your
      brother?
```

In Excerpt 8, although the candidate does receive permission to talk about her brother, she is also reminded that she has to return to the prior topic selected by the testers. The testers' power to draw the candidate back to the topic they have nominated is evident in many places; the most revealing is when they are discussing the economy in Excerpt 9. Despite the candidate's repeated objections, she is forced to continue to talk about this topic by the male tester.

```
(9)   Candidate is forced to express her opinion about the
      economy

IRM:  So when I go to store and look at the way the prices
NNS:  Yes
IRM:  =are going up it's just incredible.
NNS:  Everything
IRM:  Yeah . . uh Why are prices going up? Why do you think
      it is so?
NNS:  Well, I don't really know about that . . but when the
      price go up . . and you get pay more too . . right? I
      mean everybody when, when they work . . Is that what is
      it? (directed to IRF) (Silence)
IRM:  What do you mean?
NNS:  You get, get pay for the same thing right? Let's say uh
      . . one loaf of bread was 50 cent okay? Now is one
      dollar you=
IRM:  Uhm
```

NNS: =you was making only five dollar at the time when bread was 50 cent right? Now you make eight dollars an hour . . so is not it almost the same?
IRM: Uhm except that if the bread is going up to eight fifty and I'm making only eight dollars.
(IRM and IRF laugh)
NNS: Well . . but still that was an example . . I mean what I'm trying to say . . it goes . . you know together your income goes up, you know . . things go up too.
IRM: Do you think that people are generally keeping up?
NNS: I don't think so.
IRM: Why not . . I mean why they are not keeping up?
NNS: Well, because it is hard to live that way . . Don't you think? (addressed to IRF)
(Silence)
IRM: What do you think . . are the reasons for that?
NNS: Oh! Everybody says inflation right? But I don't know about that why because . . you know . . that's the government . . you know job . . they, they . . they take care of that . . Don't they? (addressed to IRM)
IRM: They take care of what?
NNS: You know . . things like that
IRM: What? Inflation! Do you think that the government is causing inflation?
NNS: No! No! No!. . I'm not saying that . . I just Oh! I really don't know about that kind of stuff. I don't have any question about it. I don't have any, you know, doubts about it. I just live, you know, with it and it doesn't, doesn't bother me, you know, I don't want things to, you know, everybody is getting harder . . not just here everywhere, everywhere, everywhere . . I guess, you know, lots of people . . I

The discussion of the economy/inflation in Excerpt 9 represents for the testers a crucial moment in the process of decision-making as to the candidate's speaking proficiency level. The format of the question *Why do you think so?* indicates that the tester is probing the candidate by asking her to perform a Level Three task (a Supported Opinion Question). The candidate's responses are taken as evidence that the candidate does not have the linguistic abilities to perform Level Three tasks, and therefore she is given a Level Two rating. One may only wonder if the candidate's performance (and thus the rating) might have been different had the topic been changed from the economy to nursing.

Furthermore, the testers tend to select topics that are determined by the elicitation of certain prescribed speech genres such as narration and description. The testers introduce these topics by picking up on some of the candidate's prior remarks, but these remarks are frequently tangential to the immediate focus of the conversation. This is illustrated in Excerpt 3 in the exchange concerning narration in the past. As we saw earlier, the tester ignores the candidate's immediate information about the weather, her sickness from hot weather, her brother, her coming to Monterey with her cousin, and her problem with learning English, and instead keeps asking questions that focus on eliciting the past tense.

Other than in Excerpt 6, when the candidate is explicitly instructed to ask questions about the testers, the testers rarely reveal information about personal experiences or opinions. For instance, the candidate mentions early in the OPI that although her brother would like her to join him in Texas, she finds the weather too hot; the female interviewer does not reveal that she is from Texas herself until considerably later in the exchange, and then only in response to the direct question *Where are you from?*. McCarthy (1991) notes that in real world conversation, interlocutors tend to express interest in or at least react to the content of their interlocutor's utterances. One of the most typical ways to express reaction is to respond to an interlocutor's revelations with follow-up that involves relevant personal experience or opinion (Boxer 1993).

In contrast to the testers' uninvolved, noncommittal behavior, the candidate spontaneously offers her personal experiences. In Excerpt 10, upon hearing that the male tester had studied in Chicago, she immediately reveals her familiarity with the city.

(10) Candidate reacts to tester's contribution

```
IRM:  I graduated college in Chicago.
NNS:  I see. Oh! I've been there in Chicago for three days .
      . I didn't like it.
```

This type of responsiveness is not observable in the testers' contributions. It seems that the testers' role in an interview is to ask questions and monitor the candidate's responses. This monitoring of the candidate's responses gives the impression that the purpose of the interaction is to test rather than engage in a typical conversation.

4.5 A Final Note on Assessment and Face

We have already noted that the bulk of the testers' contributions are in the form of information questions. As Table 1 shows, of the 64 turns taken by the testers, only ten can be construed as assessments—either explicit affiliative statements (limited to *Sure* and *We wish you luck* and *I think you will*) or utterances that express personal experience or opinion relevant to the content of the preceding speaker's remarks.

Given the paucity of assessments made by the testers, we find it particularly noteworthy that five of the ten are fairly direct challenges of statements the candidate has just made. Such challenges are generally regarded as face-threatening and tend to be avoided or at least softened with hedges in natural conversation among non-intimates (Brown and Levinson 1987, Hatch 1992). The most direct challenges occur during the discussion concerning the economy in which the male tester questions the accuracy or logic of the statement the candidate has just made. As shown in Excerpt 11, the candidate eventually reacts with apparent discomfort, as demonstrated by her denial of the male tester's interpretation of her earlier remark and her denial of any interest in the topic.

```
(11)   Tester challenges candidate's contribution.

IRM:   What? Inflation! Do you think that . . the government
       is causing inflation?
NNS:   No! No! No!. . I'm not saying that . . I just . . Oh! I
       really don't know about that kind of stuff. I don't
       have any question about it . . I don't have any, you
       know, doubts about it . . I just live, you know with it
       and it doesn't, doesn't bother me, you know I don't
       want things to, you know, everything is getting harder
       . . not just here everywhere, everywhere, everywhere .
       . I guess . . you know lots of people . . I
```

As we noted earlier, this section is crucial in determining the candidate's rating. We cannot help but wonder about the effect that the degree of discomfort expressed by the candidate had on the rating given her by the testers.

5 Conclusion

The analysis of this model OPI interview shows that salient features of natural conversation involved in turn-taking and negotiation of topic are not present. In natural conversation turn distribution, order, and size are locally managed and mutually negotiated; in the OPI they seem to be largely set in advance and controlled by the testers. Throughout this investigation we have argued, along with researchers such as Goodwin and Goodwin, Gumperz, Hatch and McCarthy, that naturally occurring conversation is by its very nature interactive, and that a crucial part of this interactiveness is a sense of involvement or reactiveness among interlocutors. As Tannen (1989:12) notes, "What may seem at first like the self-evident claim that it takes more than one person to have a conversation is actually a more subtle and significant one: that conversation is not a matter of two (or more) people alternatively taking the role of speaker and listener, but rather that both speaking and listening include elements and traces of the other." We have noted that the testers' contributions consistently lack this quality of conversational involvement. Thus this case study raises questions about the nature of the OPI speech event.

Since this analysis is based on only one case study, caution should be observed in generalizing its findings. As Lazaraton (1992), van Lier (1988), and Young (1995a, b) suggest, more descriptive studies involving detailed analyses of the participants' speech in the LPI need to be conducted. These descriptive studies are indispensable for examining the construct validity of language proficiency interviews, and for designing better instruments for assessing oral proficiency.

Acknowledgments

We are indebted to John L. D. Clark for permission to use the data. Marysia Johnson would like to thank Jeff Connor-Linton for guidance, support, and comments; Deborah Schiffrin for knowledge acquired from her seminar and books; and Leo van Lier for his inspiration and encouragement. These people planted the seeds of most of the ideas developed here.

Notes

1. The term *Oral Proficiency Interview*, or OPI, refers to any interview of the American Council on the Teaching of Foreign Languages, the Educational Testing Service, and U.S. government agencies such as the Foreign Language Institute, the Federal Bureau of Investigation, and the Defense Language Institute. Another term, *Language Proficiency Interview* or LPI, refers to any interview conducted for the purpose of assessing speaking language proficiency in a second language. The term LPI obviously includes the OPI.

2. Two testers are often used in OPIs carried out by agencies of the U.S. government. Non-government uses of the OPI usually involve only one tester.

3. Currently U.S. government agencies are conducting a validation study of a modified version of the OPI that is still based on the original ILR guidelines but includes the following new factors/subskills: interactive comprehension, lexical control, structural control, delivery, social/cultural

appropriateness, and communication strategies.

4. Topic is difficult to define because it encompasses various aspects of the communicative process such as message, code, speaker, and interactions (Schiffrin 1988). Van Lier (1988:147) explicitly recognizes the difficulty of providing an operational definition of topic. He points out, however, that this is nothing new in science. In psychology, for instance, some psychological constructs, such as personality and motivation "have survived many years of non-definition." He suggests that the focus in regard to topic should be on *when* a topic is rather than *what* a topic is. Young (1995:7) also points out that it is easier to "identify places in the discourse where topics change rather than to specify the topic of a given stretch of discourse."

References

Bachman, Lyle F. 1988. "Problems in Examining the Validity of the ACTFL Oral Proficiency Interview." *Studies in Second Language Acquisition* 10.149–174.
Bachman, Lyle F. 1990. *Fundamental Considerations in Language Testing*. Oxford: Oxford University Press.
Bachman, Lyle F., and Sandra Savignon. 1986. "The Evaluation of Communicative Language Proficiency: A Critique of the ACTFL Oral Interview." *Modern Language Journal* 70.380–390.
Boxer, Diana. 1993. *Complaining and Commiserating*. New York: Peter Lang.
Brown, Gillian, and George Yule. 1983. *Discourse Analysis*. Cambridge: Cambridge University Press.
Brown, Penelope, and Stephen C. Levinson. 1987. *Politeness: Some Universals in Language Usage*. New York: Cambridge University Press.
Clark, John L. D., and Ray T. Clifford. 1988. "The FSI/ILR/ACTFL Proficiency Scales and Testing Techniques: Development, Current Status, and Needed Research." *Studies in Second Language Acquisition* 10.129–147.
Educational Testing Service. 1982. *Oral Proficiency Testing Manual*. Princeton, NJ: Author.
Fishman, Pamela. 1983. "Interaction: The Work Women Do." In *Language, Gender, and Society*, ed. by Barrie Thorne, Cheris Kramarae, and Nancy Henley, 89–101. Rowley, MA: Newbury House.
Goffman, Erving. 1967. *Interaction Ritual: Essays on Face-to-Face Behavior*. New York: Anchor Books.
Goffman, Erving. 1974. *Frame Analysis*. New York: Harper and Row.
Goffman, Erving. 1976. "Replies and Responses." *Language in Society* 5.254–313.
Goodwin, Charles, and Marjorie H. Goodwin. 1992. "Assessments and Construction of Context." In *Rethinking Context: Language as an Interactive Phenomenon*, ed. by Alessandro Duranti and Charles Goodwin, 147–190. Cambridge: Cambridge University Press.
Gumperz, John J. 1982. *Discourse Strategies*. New York: Cambridge University Press.

Hatch, Evelyn. 1992. *Discourse Analysis and Language Education*. Cambridge: Cambridge University Press.

Jones, Edward E., and Harold B. Gerard. 1967. *Foundations of Social Psychology*. New York: Wiley.

Lantolf, James P., and William Frawley. 1985. "Oral Proficiency Testing: A Critical Analysis." *Modern Language Journal* 69.337–345.

Lantolf, James P., and William Frawley. 1988. "Proficiency: Understanding the Construct." *Studies in Second Language Acquisition* 10.181–195.

Lazaraton, Anne. 1992. "The Structural Organization of a Language Interview: A Conversation Analytic Perspective." *System* 20.373–386.

Levinson, Stephen C. 1983. *Pragmatics*. New York: Cambridge University Press.

Lowe, Pardee. 1983. "The ILR Oral Interview: Origins, Applications, Pitfalls, and Implications." *Unterrichtspraxis* 16.230–244.

Lowe, Pardee. 1986. "Proficiency: Panacea, Framework, Process? A Reply to Kramsch, Schulz, and Particularly, to Bachman and Savignon." *Modern Language Journal*. 70.391–397.

Lowe, Pardee. 1988. *ILR Handbook on Oral Interview Testing*. Washington, DC: Defense Language Institute/Foreign Service Institute Oral Interview Project.

McCarthy, Michael. 1991. *Discourse Analysis for Language Teachers*. Cambridge: Cambridge University Press.

Meritt, Marilyn. 1982. "Distributing and Directing Attention in Primary Classrooms." In *Communicating in the Classroom*, ed. by Louise Cherry Wilkinson, 223–244. New York: Academic Press.

Ochs, Elinor. 1979. "Transcription as Theory." In *Developmental Pragmatics*, ed. by Elinor Ochs and Bambi B. Schieffelin, 43–72. New York: Academic Press.

Pomerantz, Anita. 1984. "Agreeing and Disagreeing with Assessments: Some Features of Preferred/Dispreferred Turn Shapes." In *Structures of Social Action: Studies in Conversational Analysis*, ed. by John Atkinson and John Heritage, 57–101. The Hague: Mouton.

Sacks, Harvey, Emanuel A. Schegloff, and Gail Jefferson. 1974. "A Simplest Systematics for the Organization of Turn-taking in Conversation." *Language* 50.696–735.

Savignon, Sandra. 1985. "Evaluation of Communicative Competence: The ACTFL Provisional Proficiency Guidelines." *Modern Language Journal* 69.129–133.

Schegloff, Emanuel A., Gail Jefferson, and Harvey Sacks. 1977. "The Preference for Self-Correction in the Organization of Repair in Conversation." *Language* 53.361–82.

Schegloff, Emanuel A., and Harvey Sacks. 1973. "Opening Up Closings." *Semiotica* 8.287–327.

Schiffrin, Deborah. 1994. *Approaches to Discourse*. Cambridge, MA: Blackwell.

Tannen, Deborah. 1985. "Relative Focus on Involvement in Oral and Written Discourse." In *Literacy, Language, and Learning: The Nature and Consequences of Reading and Writing*, ed. by David R. Olson, Nancy Torrence, and Angela Hildyard, 124–148. Cambridge: Cambridge University Press.

Tannen, Deborah. 1989. *Talking Voices: Repetition, Dialogue and Imagery in Conversational Discourse.* Cambridge: Cambridge University Press.
van Lier, Leo. 1989. "Reeling, Writhing, Drawling, Stretching, and Fainting in Coils: Oral Proficiency Interviews as Conversation." *TESOL Quarterly* 23.489–508.
Wolfson, Nessa. 1976. "Speech Events and Natural Speech: Some Implications for Sociolinguistic Methodology." *Language in Society* 5.189–209.
Wolfson, Nessa. 1989. *Perspectives: Sociolinguistics and TESOL.* New York: Harper and Row.
Young, Richard. 1995a. "Conversational Styles in Language Proficiency Interviews." *Language Learning* 45.3–42.
Young, Richard. 1995b. "Discontinuous Interlanguage Development and Its Implications for Oral Proficiency Rating Scales." *Applied Language Learning* 6.13–26.
Young, Richard, and Michael Milanovic. 1992. "Discourse Variation in Oral Proficiency Interviews." *Studies in Second Language Acquisition* 14.403–424.

Evaluating Learner Interactional Skills: Conversation at the Micro Level

Heidi Riggenbach
University of Washington

1 Introduction

This chapter explores the ways in which audiotaped conversations can provide information about a learner's oral proficiency and informal interactional skills. Besides supplying the usual information about learners' spoken language subskills (grammar, pronunciation, fluency, etc.), such conversation data can also provide valuable information about the micro skills that contribute to learners' discourse and strategic competence: their ability to claim and maintain turns of talk, to backchannel and initiate repair, and to self-repair and ensure comprehension on the part of the interlocutor. With greater flexibility in topic choice and control, unstructured conversations as opposed to more traditional, prearranged interviews may, in fact, more authentically reflect learners' interactional skills. In addition, a case is made in this chapter for the development of an oral language portfolio that includes conversation data as one of several kinds of samples that together provide a comprehensive profile of a learner's oral proficiency.

Language proficiency interviews (LPIs) have long been a primary means of assessing non-native speakers' (NNSs) oral production skills. Attention has been paid to the ways in which an interview might best be conducted to obtain a thorough and representative—i.e., valid—sample of a learner's speech (Cohen and Manion 1985, Nunan 1992, Spradley 1979). Another related area of concern is how to best approach these oral data samples in terms of subskills or components of speech (Bachman 1988, Byrnes 1989, Canale 1981, Cohen 1994, Underhill 1987).

When approaching this latter topic, it is necessary to consider crucial questions such as the following: How is oral proficiency demonstrated? What, about a learner's oral production, is important? What components of learner language are and should be judged by native speaker evaluators? Clearly these questions are of interest to those involved in language teaching, language testing, and any research that makes assumptions about language and language competence. But not until relatively recently have researchers concerned themselves with the *nature* of the LPI and the limitations associated with the interview genre itself (Lazaraton 1992, van Lier 1989, Young and Milanovic 1992).

This chapter proposes an alternative or supplement to the LPI—natural conversation data, gathered by learners themselves. In their ESL courses, learners are assigned to tape-record a conversation outside of class with a native speaker or, in EFL settings where access to a pool of native speakers may be limited, with advanced or proficient speakers (e.g., someone who has lived or studied in an English-speaking country). The interlocutor should preferably someone the learner has known for a period of time so the conversation is as authentic as possible on topics of mutual interest, rather than simply a question-answer introduction to each other.

The discourse structure of an unplanned conversation under these conditions can provide information about learners' language that is quite different from that elicited in the LPI. In a conversation, learners are more likely to exhibit the ability to claim and maintain turns of talk, to backchannel and initiate repair, and to self-repair and ensure comprehension on the part of the interlocutor.

This chapter will emphasize the richness of conversation as a source of data, pointing out the kinds of features displayed. It will then suggest the methods of data collection most likely to ensure authentic samples of conversation data. Next, a sample of conversation data will serve to illustrate the skills specific to the genre of conversation. And finally a case will be made for the development of an oral language portfolio as a means of assessment that could serve as an alternative or supplement to more traditional speaking test formats. An oral language portfolio can include not only audiotaped conversation data but also audio or video recordings of the learner engaged in a variety of orally communicated exchanges, among them the LPI.

2 The LPI as a Data Source

If an interview is regarded as a mutually constructed communication, then both the interviewer and interviewee are responsible for constructing meaning and thus responsible to some degree for the learner's performance. Even with efforts to control for the effect of the interviewer, a truly neutral stance is not possible. In a communicative exchange, interlocutors *are* and *must be* affected to some degree by each other (Atkinson and Heritage 1984, Goffman 1976). Adjustments are made, many of them at the micro level, verbally or nonverbally—more or fewer backchannels, for example, or more or fewer repairs and/or repair initiations (Fiksdal 1990, Saville-Troike 1982). These adjustments may be unconscious and may be made in response to a whole array of possible factors, such as the perceived level of the NNS interlocutor, learner accent, L_1, and even the personal style of both interlocutors and their perceptions of rapport or lack of rapport.

In the interview situation, controlling for the interviewer effect can involve thorough interviewer training sessions and conducting interviews with the same, trained interviewer(s). These methods are designed to encourage in the interviewer neutrality of reactions and standardization of question and response type. Another way to control for reliability, which takes into account the variability of responses an interviewer may make in interaction with different learners, is to set up a highly structured interview with no unplanned questions and no deviation from a prepared script. But then the resulting problems have to do with the *authenticity* of the exchange.

Highly structured interviews solve some problems, but they inherently pose threats to both reliability (Are learners exhibiting language behavior different from what would emerge in a less structured, more genuinely communicative exchange?) and validity (Are learners demonstrating *actual* oral production skills?). One of the overriding issues, then, in choosing a testing context is representativeness of data. With conversation samples as opposed to structured interviews, some standardization of topic may be lost, but much is gained in terms of learner comfort level and the authenticity of the communicative exchange.

It is not unusual in an oral interview to include items that aim to isolate skills for the purpose of obtaining information about a learner's linguistic competence, in particular the traditional subcomponents of speaking: pronunciation, grammar, vocabulary, and fluency. Examples of such discrete point items or interview questions are read-aloud tasks, sentence completion tasks, and even items designed to elicit specific rhetorical modes (e.g., description, process, classification), which are also intended as opportunities for a demonstration of a learner's vocabulary range. Items such as these and their corresponding rating scales target pronunciation, vocabulary, or grammar, and may, in fact, be providing some information that contributes to the whole picture—the learner's ability to speak effectively. But is *actual* speaking ability being tested? As with the testing of writing, a response to this validity issue may call for more holistic methods of evaluation (e.g., portfolio assessment). Such an approach to testing speaking may prove to be more compelling in that multiple and varied data samples can provide a more comprehensive picture of learners' ability.

3 Learner Conversation as a Data Source

With greater flexibility in topic choice and topic control, unstructured conversations may more authentically reflect learners' interactional skills and their moment-by-moment construction of social and linguistic identity than do prearranged interviews. Since the data sample—an audiotaped spontaneous conversation—is an *actual* communicative exchange, sample validity is no longer an issue. As many discourse analysts and language researchers have pointed out, informal spoken language bears little resemblance to formal written language (Kroll 1981, Tannen 1982, Ochs 1979), although interview questions are sometimes designed to elicit formal structures usually associated with writing. Yet in spontaneous conversation, native speaker speech is filled with fragments—phrases, clauses, and repairs—rather than the kind of complex complete sentences and sophisticated vocabulary usage that would be appropriate in writing. Although it is possible for conversation data to provide the usual information about a learner's linguistic skills—pronunciation, grammar, vocabulary, fluency—these oral data may not resemble deliberately elicited formal structures.

Perhaps the richest area of investigation involves the micro-level skills that contribute to learners' discourse and strategic competence. In the widely cited Canale and Swain (1980) model of communicative competence, there are four types of language competence that contribute to overall communicative ability. Besides linguistic and sociolinguistic competence, which look respectively at accuracy and social appropriateness, two other types of language competence are proposed: discourse competence and strategic competence. *Discourse competence* is the ability to connect utterances so that there is cohesiveness. Speakers use devices to connect spoken discourse in a similar way that writers use cohesion devices, although speakers may use nonverbal as well as verbal devices (e.g., a nodding of the head, a puzzled look) that serve to keep the exchange flowing. *Strategic competence* is the ability to avoid breakdown of communication. In conversation this may be displayed in the strategies learners use to keep the conversation going when their language abilities prevent complete automaticity.

These four types of communicative competence are not mutually exclusive. There can be cohesion, for example, not only in terms of topic and syntax but also in terms of social elements. The ability to register lack of understanding may be displayed in a way that does not disrupt the flow of the discourse. This ability in turn requires the ability to know how to do that in a socially appropriate way (e.g., overlapping at a clause or phrase boundary with a brief clarification request rather than interrupting in the middle of an extended explanation).

Some of the skills that display a learner's discourse and strategic competence in conversation are listed below. These skills, micro both in the sense of relative length and functional scale, are necessary elements in coherent, fluid turn-taking (discourse competence) and in successful negotiation of meaning in the case of potential communication breakdown (strategic competence).

Conversation Micro Skills

1. The ability to claim turns of talk
2. The ability to maintain turns of talk, once claimed
3. The ability to yield turns of talk
4. The ability to backchannel
5. The ability to self-repair
6. The ability to ensure comprehension on the part of the listener (e.g., comprehension checks such as *Does that make sense? Are you with me? Get it?*)
7. The ability to initiate repair when there is a potential breakdown (e.g., clarification requests)
8. The ability to employ compensatory strategies (e.g., avoidance of structures or vocabulary beyond the learner's proficiency, word coinage, circumlocution, and even shifting topics or asking questions that stimulate the other interlocutor to share the responsibility for maintaining the conversation flow)

Instructional value, or positive backwash, is one of the most important reasons to analyze learner-collected conversation data. Many learners express frustration at not being able to get a word in edgewise when they are speaking with native speakers. In other words, they have difficulty claiming turns. Or, once the native speaker interlocutor has finally yielded a turn, the learner is not able or does not have time to say what she or he wants to say; the difficulty in this case is maintaining the turn. The problem also may be due to conventions in the English turn-taking system that differ from a learner's native language. For example, many learners feel that they are being interrupted in the case of overlaps. In some languages and cultures, overlaps are considered socially inappropriate: speakers must wait until another speaker is silent before beginning a turn (see, for example, Barnlund 1989 and Ramsey 1984 on turn-taking conventions in Japanese; Tao and Thompson 1991 on Chinese Mandarin conventions and English interference; Phillips 1983 and Crago

1992 on tendencies toward silence in Navajo children and Inuit children, respectively; and Tannen 1984 on New York vs. California English turn-taking conventions). But in most dialects of North American English, friends in conversation tend to avoid gaps, or silences, between turns. Except with family members or very close friends, long gaps between turns are sources of discomfort, and short overlaps are completely normal and appropriate. Using authentic conversation data in the classroom can be helpful in raising learners' and instructors' awareness about the discourse structure of conversation.

4 Data Collection Procedures

In order for a conversation sample to be as natural as possible, it is important that learners be in control of the data collection process: they self-select their interlocutors and audiotape an unplanned conversation. This allows learners a level of comfort not possible in most interview settings, since they can select people they are familiar with and converse about things that interest them rather than answer questions about topics that are predetermined and interviewer-controlled.

Ideally, the interlocutor is a native speaker of English (with little or no proficiency in the learner's native language). This ensures that the natural medium of exchange is the target language. But this kind of task is also possible in a foreign language setting (Riggenbach 1988), whereby the learner selects a speaker considered proficient or fluent in English—someone who has lived or worked in an English-speaking country, for example, or someone who has studied English for a greater period of time than the learner.

Researchers are often mistrustful of conversation data because of reliability issues. Interlocutors' familiarity with each other, the nature of the topics that are raised, the setting, the relationship dynamics, the energy level of the interlocutors, and even self-consciousness about the presence of a tape recorder may all affect the direction and the naturalness of a conversation. Clearly there are fewer controls in conversation data in comparison with a structured interview. I maintain, however, that self-selection of interlocutors provides the level of comfort and flexibility of topic necessary for a communicatively authentic conversational exchange.

5 Conversation Data Sample and Analysis

The following learner-recorded data sample was audiotaped in a dormitory room, where the learner had lived for six months with her native speaker interlocutor. The excerpt is ten minutes into the recording, following a discussion about abortion and

Evaluating Learner Interactional Skills 59

adoption, topics that the learner had been discussing that week in her ESL conversation class. The NNS's native language is Japanese; there were no attempts by the transcriber to phonetically represent accent. Unfamiliar transcription conventions used here may include: (hh) = laughter particles, :: = sound stretch/extended vowel, and [= overlap.

```
1  NS:    Well what do you think about um mothers who um have
2         their baby [and they leave them in garbage
3  NNS:              [Uh-huh
4  NS:    cans
5         (1.5)
6  NNS:   Huh? What do you [
7  NS:                     [They have- they have their baby?
8  NNS:   My mom?
9  NS:    No no (hh) Not your(hh hh) — Mothers.
10 NNS:   Uh huh. Mothers uh huh
11 NS:    They have their baby?
12 NNS:   Uh huh
13 NS:    And then- they leave it in garbage cans.
14        (.8)
15 NNS:   Garbage?
16 NS:    Garbage cans. Like big garbage c(hh)ans. Outside
17        of businesses.
18 NNS:   Uh h[uh
19 NS:        [and apartments
20 NNS:   Ahh:: [
21 NS:          [You know what I mean?
22 NNS:   No I don't know. I d- I understand garbage.
23 NS:    Ye[ah. You know dumpsters? where- You know
24 NNS:     [Garbage.
25 NS:    Our garbage?
26 NNS:   Garbage?
27 NS:    Uh huh
28 NNS:   Ah yeah
29 NS:    Yeah. And they'll have a baby and they'll leave
30        it in there
31        (2.0)
32 NNS:   Uh yu:h? ((tone displays shock))
33 NS:    Yeah. For someone to- to take it or for it to die.
34 NNS:   Die? Ahh:: Like a (just lea[ve it)
35 NS:                              [Mm-hm
36 NNS:   I know. ((clears throat)) What do yo[u
37 NS:                                        [It's mean.
38 NNS:   What's mean?
```

```
39  NS:    No- It's mean. It's mean.
40 NNS:    Mean.
41  NS:    Yeah(hh hh) It's bad.
42 NNS:    It's bad. Uh- I know (( unintelligible [x xx))
43  NS:                                            [Mm-hm
44 NNS:    Because baby is not thing is y'[know
45  NS:                                   [Baby's what?
46 NNS:    Not thing. Baby is a animal- (hh) I(hh)don't know.
47         Humor.
48  NS:    Human ye[ah
49 NNS:            [So I can't do that. I ca:n't do that. I
50         can't sell, I can't- I can't throw garba[ge
51  NS:                                            [Throw
52         it awa[y.
53 NNS:          [Throw away.
54  NS:    Yeah.
55 NNS:    But- I can't kill because it's human.
```

When approaching these data with a focus on the learner's oral skills, it is necessary to consider what factors contributed to the success of the interaction in terms of coherence, information exchange, negotiated meaning, and avoidance of communication breakdown. Another parallel question is aimed at identifying what is unsuccessful about the exchange: what skills are *not* displayed by the learner, and what strategies might have been used at potential or actual communication breakdowns?

In line 3, the NNS's backchannel *Uh-huh* is understood by the NS interlocutor as a continuer, a turn-yielding device, since the NS's turn is maintained rather than challenged by the NNS with further talk. The long pause in line 5 is the first signal of the NNS's lack of comprehension (we would expect this to be accompanied by a puzzled look, perhaps, that a videotaped exchange would most likely reveal), and this pause is followed by a repair initiator, and an informal, native-like one at that: *Huh?*. The next partial fragment seems to be interpreted by the NS as a follow-up to the *Huh* and starts out with a question word, *What*. Although the NNS's question is not completed, the NS overlaps with her answer to the partial question, a strategy that resembles a collaborative completion in that one interlocutor's utterance functionally serves to finish what the first interlocutor's utterance has begun.

At this point we can judge the NNS's repair initiator as effective, since the NS complies—she repairs. How she goes about the repair is itself interesting, since she parses the initial part of the utterance and follows this with rising intonation, *They have — they have their baby?*. The question intonation requires a response from the interlocutor, which the NNS provides. In her response, she demonstrates comprehension of the NS's initial (line 1) utterance, and she displays an understanding of the fact that *they* refers to *mothers. My mom?* is her response in line 8, a question aimed at clarification.

The NS's answer to this, marked with laughter particles, provides the clarification called for. It is interesting that the stress on *Mothers* in line 9, along with the zero article, are enough to depersonalize the noun so that it is understood as generic (i.e., mothers in general). The NNS indicates her understanding in line 10 with two affirming *Uh huh's* and a repetition of *mothers*. The next potentially problematic exchange has to do with the word *garbage*. This is problematic in the sense that the learner displays a lack of comprehension of part of the native speaker's utterance. It is not problematic in the whole sense of the exchange: meaning is negotiated, and the conversation proceeds. In line 15, the NNS successfully locates the problem. *Garbage?* she says, with rising intonation. Her *Ahh* in line 20 seems to display understanding of the NS's attempts to define and/or clarify *garbage cans* (the voice quality adds important interpretive information here: the volume increases and the pitch is high initially, and then drops, as in an I-get-it *Ahh*). The NS checks this out with *You know what I mean?* But line 22 is another example of the NNS's persistence in specifically identifying her problem in comprehension for her interlocutor by process of elimination. Her answer to *You know what I mean?* is a direct *No I don't know*, and then she points out the part she *does* understand. *I understand garbage*. This is effective in that it forces the NS to infer what is *not* understood, and thus more clarification of the dumpsters/garbage can concept ensues.

It is possible that line 25, *Our garbage*, is accompanied by a nonverbal gesture that indicates the location of their (the dormitory's) garbage dumpster, but we can only guess at this. The important information for analysts/evaluators of this exchange is that in line 28, the NNS gets it, and registers comprehension with *Ah yeah*. It is clear from the NNS's reaction in lines 32, 34, and 36 that she now understands the babies-in-dumpsters comment. Her tone in line 32 is one of shock and disgust, evident only by listening to the tape, not by reading the transcript.

The NS's line 37 initiates another potentially problematic exchange, this one short and quickly resolved. Line 38 is another place where the transcript does not fully represent the meaning carried by the intonation contour of *What's mean?*. A paraphrase, based on the NNS's rising intonation, would be *You're asking me "What's it mean?"* rather than *What's "mean" mean?* This is impossible to see from a reading of the transcript alone. But the NS's reaction in line 39 displays that she does understand it in this sense. She repeats *It's mean*, and this is echoed by the NNS in line 40, which serves to elicit from the NS the definition of "mean"—bad.

It is not until line 42 that we get the NNS's answer to the question posed by the NS in lines 1–4 of this excerpt, *Well what do you think about um mothers who um have their baby and they leave them in garbage cans.* The fact that the NNS does eventually address this question is itself evidence of discourse competence, since she is displaying the ability to track back through the talk to this original question, and to respond to it with an answer—the second part of the adjacency pair.

In her answer, she is able to elicit the word *human* from the NS. She does not directly ask for this word but she exhibits strategic competence in her attempts. She defines the word by negation, *Not thing.* She paraphrases, *a animal.* She admits lack of knowledge or lack of access to the word, *I don't know.* And finally, she approximates the word phonetically, *Humor.* In the last few lines of this short (1 minute, 15 seconds) excerpt, the learner uses three words that were either problematic words or problematic concepts earlier in the exchange: *garbage* in line 50, *throw away* in lines 50–52, and *human* in line 55. Certainly this is evidence of success, both in terms of the meaning negotiated in this conversational exchange and in terms of the language learning taking place.

6 Discussion: Assessing Language-in-Conversation

Clearly, the analysis of conversation data can be a complex undertaking. For the purpose of assessing conversation skills, it would be necessary to simplify how data are examined. One way of streamlining this process would be simply to create a checklist of skills—i.e., a criterion-referenced scale—that together are important in maintaining conversation coherence and in demonstrating the ability to participate in a conversation. (Brown, Anderson, Shillcock, and Yule 1984 offer useful suggestions for developing scoring protocol for audiotaped data.) Such a scale for conversation data would target micro skills such as the following (also discussed earlier in this chapter): Did the learner display the ability to (1) claim turns of talk, (2) maintain turns of talk, (3) yield turns of talk, (4) backchannel, (5) self-repair, (6) ensure comprehension on the part of the listener, (7) initiate repair, and (8) employ compensatory strategies?

This list is only a beginning. Researchers and teachers interested in using conversation for assessment purposes would want to put some thought into how to (and whether or not to) weigh these criteria. Another consideration is the *effectiveness* with which skills are displayed. For example, an interlocutor who backchannels frequently may be overusing this strategy. Hawkins (1984) reveals that learners' backchannels are often understood by their interlocutors as signals of comprehension and rapport when they may be intended only as continuers (turn-yielding devices).

Evaluating a speaker's participation in a conversation in terms of micro skills does not automatically imply that the display of these skills is equivalent to exhibiting native-like conversational skill. Rather, one objective of dissecting a conversational exchange is to identify the elements of conversation that allow it to move forward, thereby examining the learner's role in contributing to that forward movement: how smoothly hitches are resolved or not resolved, how topics are pursued or dropped, and thus how meaning is negotiated or surrendered. This stance prevents grand claims about native speaker skills, since conversation must be looked at as mutually constructed, dependent on the joint participation of interlocutors. Conversation is a complex endeavor, and participants share responsibility for how it proceeds, moment by moment.

Besides supplying data on conversation micro skills, a conversation sample can also provide information about elements traditionally thought of as the sub-components of speech: grammar, vocabulary, pronunciation, and fluency. But in examining these, consideration must be given to the genre of conversation itself. For example, native speaker conversational talk is filled with language not considered grammatical in the prescriptive sense. It contains fragments, repairs, repetitions, and nonstandard or grammatically inaccurate structures. In lines 2–4 of the excerpt, for instance, there is a lack of agreement between the pronoun *them* and its referent *baby* in the native speaker's statement: *Mothers who um have their baby, and they leave them in garbage cans.*

In addition to using conversation-specific grammar, native speakers also exhibit differences in their conversation vocabulary when compared with the breadth of lexical items used in other genres such as a university lecture, an academic paper like this one, or a job interview. Conversation with friends calls for common, simple, familiar vocabulary. When students in my third year undergraduate/junior level "Introduction to Language Studies" course at the University of Washington first listen in depth to an excerpt of dinner table conversation involving four native speaker adults, their first impressions often include descriptions of the native speakers as uneducated, based, in part, on their simple, unremarkable vocabulary usage.

This impression also applies to native speaker fluency. For novice conversation analysts, the amount of repair, hesitation, and lack of smoothness in normal native speaker conversation comes as something of a shock. Traditional definitions of fluency—reflected in rating scales designed to assess non-native speaker speech such as the Test of Spoken English—include phrases such as "smoothness of speech," "effortlessness," and "speech exhibiting automaticity" (also see comprehensive discussions of fluency in Schmidt 1992, Riggenbach 1991, and Weir 1993). Typical native speaker speech in conversation is often lacking in these qualities.

Unlike fluency, vocabulary, and grammar, which may exhibit different features in conversation, pronunciation is the one subcomponent likely to remain stable across genres. Certainly some relaxing of phonetic rules occurs, displayed for example in contractions and ellipses, but in North American English, pronunciation may not vary extensively from genre to genre. (News broadcasting is a case where more strict phonetic rules *would* apply: speech is slowed somewhat, and words are enunciated more carefully and clearly.)

7 The Oral Language Portfolio

Like data from the LPI, conversation data can provide some but certainly not all of the information about a learner's actual speaking ability. Speaking tests with highly structured items may elicit formal structures and a greater range of words and phonemes than would occur in conversation. And while certain speech events *may* occur naturally in the course of a conversation (e.g., agreeing or disagreeing, complimenting, describing, and requesting), an unplanned conversation would likely be an inappropriate way of evaluating learners' knowledge of socially and linguistically appropriate formulas associated with specific speech events. Where the objective is to develop more formal speaking skills—as is the case, for example, with international teaching assistants and visiting scholars at American universities—tasks that resemble actual performance may be more appropriate.

In most communicative settings, however, the goal is rarely only to deliver. Even in a monologue-type situation (e.g., a lecture), the speaker is reliant on and responds to cues from listeners. Thus it is possible that the features exhibited in a conversation have greater generalizability than those displayed in other, more highly structured, less relaxed genres. Valuable skills in any but the most formal settings are some of those demonstrated by the learner in the excerpt analyzed earlier: paraphrasing and approximating words, directly asking for clarification, and displaying understanding by using appropriate backchannels.

Another inherent weakness in the use of conversation as the *only* method of assessing speaking skills involves the issue of practicality/efficiency. Testers and instructors may be unfamiliar with the elements that contribute to success or coherence in conversation and would need to be informed and/or trained. The development of rating scales appropriate for conversation data certainly requires further thought. Issues such as the following would need to be considered in developing rating skills: What skills and criteria are essential? Whether and how should the criteria/skills be weighed? How should *effectiveness* be handled (e.g., is a repair initiator actually effective in that the interlocutor repairs an utterance? If so, should it have a higher rating?). Should the skills targeted in achievement tests reflect what is being taught in the classroom?

In addition, since some explanation is required in order to have students function as the data collectors (which I claim is *the* way to obtain authentic samples), there may be some problem in logistics if the intention is for larger-scale, beyond-the-classroom testing (e.g., for placement purposes). It would be necessary to conduct some kind of orientation for students in order to explain the data-gathering procedures. An option is to consider arranging for a pool of native or expert speakers to function as conversation partners. But the loss, as with the LPI, is in the validity and authenticity of the exchange.

Given how genre-specific are some of the features displayed in conversation, one important question that must be addressed is how representative of a more general *proficiency* is the language that is exhibited in conversation. If conversation samples are to be used as the *only* method of assessing speaking skills, then these reliability and validity issues must be seriously considered. Conversation data for assessment purposes might be most appropriate where the focus of the course *is* conversation, and where conversation skills are explicitly targeted.

It is logical, however, to make a case for considering student-collected audiotaped conversations as only *one* of *several* types of data that would be gathered together in an oral language portfolio. An oral language portfolio could include audio or video recordings of the learner engaged in a variety of orally communicated exchanges, some of which are monologues, some dialogues, some structured (e.g., read-aloud tasks), some semi-structured (e.g., tasks), some rehearsed (e.g., short lectures), and some spontaneous (e.g., role- plays). This approach to oral skills testing offers a more holistic and comprehensive assessment that could serve as an alternative to more traditional speaking test formats that rely on a single sample and/or a single genre.

References

Atkinson, John and John Heritage, eds. 1984. *Structures of Social Action: Studies in Conversation Analysis.* Cambridge: Cambridge University Press.

Bachman, Lyle. 1988. "Problems in Examining the Validity of the ACTFL Oral Proficiency Interview." *Studies in Second Language Acquisition* 10.149–64.

Barnlund, Dean C. 1989. *Communicative Styles of Japanese and Americans: Images and Realities*. Belmont, CA: Wadsworth.

Brown, Gillian, Anne Anderson, Richard Shillcock, and George Yule. 1984. *Teaching Talk: Strategies for Production and Assessment*. Cambridge: Cambridge University Press.

Byrnes, Heidi. 1989. "The Rating Scale." In *The ACTFL Oral Proficiency Interview Tester Training Manual*, ed. by Kathryn Buck, Heidi Byrnes, and Irene Thompson, 2.2–2.16. Yonkers, NY: The American Council on the Teaching of Foreign Languages.

Canale, Michael. 1981. "On Some Dimensions of Language Proficiency." In *Current Issues in Language Testing Research*, ed. by John Oller, 333–342. Rowley, MA: Newbury House.

Canale, Michael, and Merrill Swain. 1980. "Theoretical Bases of Communicative Approaches to Second Language Teaching and Testing." *Applied Linguistics* 1.1–47.

Cohen, Andrew D. 1994. *Assessing Language Ability in the Classroom*. Boston: Heinle and Heinle.

Cohen, Louis, and Lawrence Manion. 1985. *Research Methods in Education* (2nd ed.). London: Croom Helm.

Crago, Martha. 1992. "Communicative Interaction and Second Language Acquisition: An Inuit Example." *TESOL Quarterly* 26.487–506.

Fiksdal, Susan. 1990. *The Right Time and Pace: A Microanalysis of Cross-cultural Gatekeeping Interviews*. Norwood, NJ: Ablex.

Goffman, Erving. 1976. "Replies and Responses." *Language in Society* 5.254–313.

Hawkins, Barbara. 1984. "Is an Appropriate Response Always So Appropriate?" In *Input in Second Language Acquisition*, ed. by Susan M. Gass and Carolyn G. Madden, 162–178. Rowley, MA: Newbury House.

Kroll, Barry M. 1981. "Developmental Relations Between Speaking and Writing." In *Exploring Speaking-Writing Relationships: Connections and Contrasts*, ed. by Barry M. Kroll and Roberta J. Vann, 32–54. Urbana, IL: National Council of Teachers of English.

Lazaraton, Anne. 1992. "The Structural Organization of a Language Interview: A Conversation Analytic Perspective." *System* 20.373–386.

Nunan, David. 1992. *Research Methods in Language Learning*. New York: Cambridge University Press.

Ochs, Elinor. 1979. "Planned and Unplanned Discourse." In *Discourse and Syntax*, ed. by Talmy Givón, 51–60. New York: Academic Press.

Phillips, Susan U. 1983. *The Invisible Culture: Communication in Classroom and Community on the Warm Springs Indian Reservation*. New York: Longman.

Ramsey, S. Robert. 1984. "Double Vision: Nonverbal Behavior East and West." In *Nonverbal Behavior: Perspectives, Applications, Intercultural Insight*, ed. by Aaron W. Wolfgang, 139–170. Lewiston, NY: Hogrefe.

Riggenbach, Heidi. 1988. "Tapping a Vital Resource: Student-generated Materials." In *Materials for Language Learning and Teaching*, ed. by Bikram Das. Singapore: SEAMEO Regional Language Centre.

Riggenbach, Heidi. 1991. "Towards an Understanding of Fluency: A Microanalysis of Nonnative Speaker Conversations." *Discourse Processes* 14.423–441.

Saville-Troike, Muriel. 1982. *The Ethnography of Communication*. Baltimore: University Park Press.

Schmidt, Richard. 1992. "Psychological Mechanisms Underlying Second Language Fluency." *Studies in Second Language Acquisition* 14.357–385.

Spradley, James P. 1979. *The Ethnographic Interview*. New York: Holt, Rinehart and Winston.

Tannen, Deborah. 1982. "Oral and Literate Strategies in Spoken and Written Narratives." *Language* 58.1–21.

Tannen, Deborah. 1984. *Conversational Style: Analyzing Talk Among Friends*. Norwood, NJ: Ablex.

Tao, Hongyin, and Sandra Thompson. 1991. "English Backchannels in Mandarin Conversations: A Case Study of Superstratum Pragmatic 'Interference'." *Journal of Pragmatics* 16.209–223.

Underhill, Nic. 1987. *Testing Spoken Language: A Handbook of Oral Testing Techniques*. Cambridge: Cambridge University Press.

van Lier, Leo. 1989. "Reeling, Writhing, Drawling, Stretching, and Fainting in Coils: Oral Proficiency Interviews as Conversation." *TESOL Quarterly* 23.489–508.

Weir, Cyril J. 1993. *Understanding and Developing Language Tests*. New York: Prentice Hall.

Young, Richard, and Michael Milanovic. 1992. "Discourse Variation in Oral Proficiency Interviews." *Studies in Second Language Acquisition* 14.403–424.

What Happens When There's No One to Talk to? Spanish Foreign Language Discourse in Simulated Oral Proficiency Interviews

Dale April Koike
University of Texas at Austin

1 Introduction

In the past two decades, direct tests of foreign language oral proficiency that use the format of a face-to-face interview have enjoyed a wide popularity (Clark 1986). An example of such a test is the American Council on the Teaching of Foreign Languages (ACTFL) oral proficiency interview (OPI), which is a systematic interview conducted by a trained interviewer who asks the interviewee questions on a variety of topics and also engages the interviewee in a role-play situation. The questions and topics are such that the language produced by the interviewees reveals linguistic functions and content presumably reflective of their highest level of proficiency. After the interview, the language samples produced are evaluated in terms of a rating scale that describes different levels of proficiency (ACTFL 1986). The ACTFL OPI and guidelines for rating are currently used widely in academic, government, military, and business contexts in the U.S.

The past ten years have also witnessed the increased use of semidirect tests, or those in which the testees listen to a prerecorded set of questions and role-play tasks under language laboratory conditions and record their answers on an audiocassette. This simulated oral proficiency interview (SOPI) is parallel to the OPI in terms of content, functions, and rating scales, and is considerably more efficient in time and cost of administering and grading the test. Studies have reported on the high degree of concurrent validity of the two tests by comparing the functions and tasks required on both (Shohamy, Gordon, Kenyon, and Stansfield 1989, Stansfield and Kenyon

1992). Moreover, researchers such as Shohamy (1994) have claimed that the SOPI is actually a more uniform test than the OPI because the interviewer variable is eliminated and all testees taking a given test perform the same tasks and answer the same questions. On the other hand, in the OPI, the interviewer asks questions of increased difficulty until the testees appear unable to answer or answer only with great difficulty.

Despite this reported high degree of concurrent validity, the differences in testing procedure raise the question of whether or not the two tests actually elicit the same kind of language and, by extension, whether or not they measure the same trait. The objective of the present study is to compare the discourse produced by Intermediate-High and Advanced learners of Spanish on the two kinds of tests and to account for discourse differences in terms of contextual, strategic, organizational, and discourse factors.

2 Background

Previous studies have examined the discourse produced on the two types of tests. Shohamy, Donitsa-Schmidt, and Waizer (1993) examined the effect of the elicitation mode on language obtained in direct and semidirect tests and analyzed specific features of the oral language produced. The elicitation procedures varied on two dimensions: (a) a higher status or an equal peer human interlocutor; and (b) stimuli presented over the telephone, on a videotape, or by an audiotape recorder. Testees were asked to respond to a series of speech act stimuli by expressing complaints and requests. The researchers found that some differences in fluency and accuracy could be attributed to the mode of elicitation but the results were not consistent. They reported a more frequent use of social and pragmatic markers, such as polite and softening expressions and terms of address in the face-to-face tests, but differences were more closely related to the topic of the stimulus than to the modality of the test.

Another study of the validity of direct versus semidirect tests is that of Shohamy (1994). This study serves as a point of departure for the present one in that it looks at differences in communicative strategies and discourse features resulting from the two testing modalities. In comparing ten randomly chosen OPIs of native Hebrew speakers speaking English as a foreign language with their speech in SOPI conditions, Shohamy (1994) found that the SOPI required a wider range of functions and topics of lower proficiency testees, and so was less restrictive than the OPI for testees at that level. No differences in morphological, syntactic, or lexical features were observed, but more self-correction and paraphrasing occurred in the SOPI, indicating that the testees self-monitored more for linguistic accuracy under tape-mediated conditions. There was a significantly greater use of the first language on the OPI, and the discourse of the OPI contained more oral markers such as elaborations, expansion of ideas, and sharing of information. One of Shohamy's conclusions is that the SOPI may elicit more formal speech, while the OPI sample may represent more colloquial language.

Shohamy also noted differences in discourse features, lexical and grammatical density, rhetorical functions and structures, genre, communicative properties, speech functions, and discourse markers. Her main conclusion about the differences between the performances elicited by the two types of tests is that they are a result of the different contexts of elicitation even more than the elicitation tasks themselves. She concludes that the elicitation method—face-to-face or tape-mediated interviews—affects the language produced by the testees. In discussing this work in another study, however, she cautions that since the tasks and questions of the two tests she examined were not identical, some of the discrepancies reported may be due to differences in the stimuli themselves (Shohamy et al. 1993).

3 Research Questions

Shohamy's findings are valuable and point to the need for a closer look at the differences in discourse produced in direct and semidirect tests. The present study purports to describe differences found in responses in OPI and SOPI contexts for more monologic tasks by Intermediate-High and Advanced Spanish learners.[1] In this investigation, the focus is on four of the tasks that characterize an advanced level of oral proficiency according to the ACTFL guidelines: narrating, instructing, comparing advantages and disadvantages, and stating an opinion. In Shohamy et al. (1993), these types of monologic language samples were largely eliminated from the analysis, since the researchers were more interested in characteristics reflective of dialogic, conversational discourse such as terms of address and polite and softening expressions. But since many of the stimuli found in semidirect tests used to evaluate a professional or advanced level of proficiency involve more monologic answers, in which testees need more time to make several points and to develop an adequate reply to the stimulus, it is important to examine the language produced in these contexts as well. Dialogic tasks such as offering an apology usually involve shorter replies centered on a given speech act, with some adjunct elements such as explanations and polite expressions. It is also easier for an interviewer to ask questions or make comments during the completion of a dialogic task without interrupting the testee's initial reply, since the reply is often much briefer and less complex than a monologic task requires. One must keep in mind that monologic discourse is unavoidable in the SOPI, while the testee in the OPI may in fact perform one or more of the functions of the task over a series of interactive exchanges with the interviewer.

Formally stated, the research questions addressed in this study are:
1. What are the differences in the discourse produced in SOPI as opposed to OPI conditions by the same Intermediate-High and Advanced Spanish learners in four Advanced-level tasks?
2. Can these differences be attributed to factors of context (test modality and type of stimulus), strategies (management strategies such as pauses, fillers, and false starts), and discourse elements (structural components such as propositions, supporting statements, and speech acts)?

4 Methodology

Data were collected in two contexts. This section describes the test instruments, the testees, and the features examined, including management strategies and structural components.

4.1 *The SOPI*

The SOPI used in this study is a series of practice test stimuli based on the Spanish Texas Oral Proficiency Test (TOPT) by Stansfield (1993). This test is required of all prospective elementary and secondary Spanish and bilingual education teachers in the state of Texas, and one must be rated at the Advanced level to pass the test and receive certification to teach. Many of the tasks found on this test require lengthy monologic answers of approximately 60 to 90 seconds in length.[2] This study focuses on some tasks that presumably require more linguistic skill than the others—specifically, the tasks of comparing advantages and disadvantages, narration, giving instructions, and giving and supporting an opinion. The stimuli used for these tasks are shown in the Appendix. Successful performance on these tasks is considered to be indicative of the Advanced level of proficiency according to the ACTFL guidelines.

The data are drawn from practice SOPIs done in a language laboratory at the end of a semester-long course aimed at preparing potential Spanish-language teachers of the elementary and high school levels to take the TOPT. The practice test stimuli, given in the Spanish American variety of Spanish, were created to simulate as closely as possible the content, functions, and format of the TOPT. One difference between the practice and live TOPT that should be noted is that on the practice tests, testees are usually given two minutes to answer each question, approximately thirty seconds more than on the typical Advanced-level TOPT question.

As in the earlier format of the TOPT, testees heard the test stimuli in English over a headset in individual language laboratory booths and recorded their answers in Spanish on individual audiocassette tapes. The tapes were then graded by the instructor for such features as fluency, organization, grammar, vocabulary, and appropriateness of language. Particular responses on the tapes that corresponded to the targeted language functions (narrating, giving instructions, comparing advantages and disadvantages, and stating an opinion) were transcribed and analyzed.

4.2 *The OPI*

The OPIs were also administered at the end of the semester to the same individuals who took the practice SOPI tests. The testees were asked questions that would elicit the same language functions of narrating, giving instructions, comparing advantages and disadvantages, and stating an opinion. The particular stimuli that targeted the functions are also listed in the Appendix. While the paired tasks in the two types of tests are not exactly the same, they were matched as closely as possible in function.[3]

Each of the testees was interviewed separately by the investigator entirely in Spanish for approximately 30 minutes. They were asked other questions besides those targeted for analysis, and each topic and related topics were discussed until conversation seemed to be exhausted. The testees were aware that they would also receive a grade for their performance in the interviews.

Since the OPI was administered entirely in Spanish, this format differed from that of the SOPI. This format was followed because it was believed that switching back and forth from English to Spanish during conditions that were supposed to simulate a conversation would be too confusing for most learners.

4.3 *Testees*

Unlike Shohamy's studies, this investigation involves a population schooled in taking oral proficiency tests, because the testees were ten students in a course designed to prepare them to take a SOPI, specifically the TOPT. The investigator of this study was their instructor. The testees were randomly chosen from a total of 36 students, most at the Intermediate-High and Advanced levels, and it is believed that they were representative of the typical population of students, predominantly female, who take the course. Each student was screened for an approximate proficiency level and other background factors (e.g., true intent to take the TOPT) by the instructor before being allowed to register for the course. Typically, about one-third of the class are Hispanic-American students who grew up hearing Spanish. These students, however, are not very fluent or are limited in the domains about which they can converse, and they are not very confident about their ability to express themselves in Spanish. The other students are usually native speakers of English who are completing four years of Spanish study at the university and who have, for the most part, spent some time studying abroad. As shown in Table 1, this group of testees included one learner estimated by the investigator to be at the Intermediate-Mid level, three estimated to be at the Intermediate-High level, and six estimated to be at the Advanced level. These estimations were made after the students had finished the course and after reviewing the test tapes they had made since the midpoint of the course.[4] The data from the ten testees were not divided according to proficiency level, since the objective of the study was to see what was produced by a typical group of learners who were preparing to take the SOPI.

The course in which these students were enrolled focuses on helping learners prepare for the TOPT by working on rhetorical structure, grammar, organizational skills, and, most of all, by practicing the language functions and the format of the test. Students typically are motivated to work hard in the class and take the testing procedures seriously since they need to pass the TOPT in order to qualify for a teaching job.

4.4 *Data Collection and Analysis*

Most of the features selected for analysis were chosen because they reflect two general areas of concern to this study. The first group of features reflects management strategies, those strategies and techniques that speakers consciously or subconsciously use to manage or maintain control over their speech production. Such strategies include pauses, fillers, false starts, self-correction, rising intonation, and switches to English. Also included as management strategies are turn-taking and possible turn signals. It is important to note, though, that since the interviewer may control the turns that occur turn-taking is not always a technique that the testee controls. The interviewer in this study, however, was the same person in all cases and consciously made an effort to wait until the testee appeared to give up the floor before taking a turn. Turn-taking is, nevertheless, a strategy employed by many speakers to avoid having to talk as much and to allow the interviewer to guide the conversation.

Table 1. Background of Testees

Testee	Gender	Ethnic group	Estimated proficiency
Deb	F	Anglo-American	Intermediate-Mid
Marty	F	Anglo-American	Intermediate-High
Juana	F	Hispanic-American	Intermediate-High
Sue	F	Anglo-American	Intermediate-High
Nona	F	African-American	Advanced
Al	M	Hispanic-American	Advanced
Jenn	F	Hispanic-American	Advanced
Mary	F	Anglo-American	Advanced
Grace	F	Hispanic-American	Advanced
Jana	F	Anglo-American	Advanced

Each informant's discourse produced on each of the four tasks in both the SOPI and the OPI was transcribed and analyzed for the following management strategies. They were measured in terms of frequency of occurrence.

Pauses. The frequency of pauses, as well as the length of the pauses (less than one second, one second, or two or more seconds in length), were noted.

Possible turn signals. Any pauses one second or more in length were recorded, since they are considered to be possible signals to the interviewer that the testee would be willing to give up the turn at that point.

Fillers. The number of fillers in each context was counted. Fillers included words such as *uh, um, este, eh*, and discourse markers such as *bueno* "well" and *y* "and." It is acknowledged that fillers were used for many functions and were included for analysis since they show a break in the flow of communication, whatever the intent may be (e.g., to fill in gaps, to retain the floor).

Turns. The number of turns it took for the testee and interviewer to complete the task to the apparent satisfaction of the interviewer in the direct test was counted. The number of turns in the SOPI, of course, remained constant at one turn.

Self-correction. The total number of self-corrections (without assistance from the interviewer) made by the testee was noted. The type of self-correction was also recorded as grammatical, lexical, or phonological.

Rising intonation. The number of times the testee ended an utterance with a rising intonational contour marked in the transcripts by "?," where the utterance was not a question, syntactically speaking (e.g., *And then the man hit the dog? And then the dog bit him?*), was counted. These instances were subcategorized as to whether the intent of the intonational rise appeared to be to confirm that the interviewer had understood the communication, or to confirm that a lexical item was appropriately used.[5]

False starts. The number of false starts in expressing ideas was counted (e.g., *And then the man started to... Oh, the woman ran up and grabbed the bag*). They differ from self-corrections in that the testees interrupt their speech to add a new proposition instead of doing so to correct an error. False starts in expressing lexical items were not included (e.g., *reversa — reserver — reverserv —* to express *reservación*).

Switches to English. The number of times the testee switched from Spanish to English in the discourse was counted. Proper names pronounced with English pronunciation were not included.

The second area under examination comprises structural components used by the testees in the discourse. These components include propositions and supporting statements, speech acts, and the use of direct or indirect quotes. It is expected that these components reveal different aspects of the organization of the discourse.

Propositions/supporting statements. The number of main ideas and elaborations or supporting statements of those ideas were counted (e.g., main idea: *Bicycles are better for the environment*; support: *They don't pollute the air and use no natural resources*). In the narrative tasks, the data were also examined for the presence of an orientation section (e.g., *There was this old man, who had a house in the woods*), actions, and an evaluative comment that expressed some emotional reaction to the events (e.g., *I was really scared after that*; see Labov 1972).

Quotations. The number of direct or indirect quotations included in the discourse was counted. Quotations were considered because, especially in the narrative context, they suspend the sequence of action momentarily to emphasize the thoughts or feelings of the protagonists in the story being recounted and thus serve as a structural device.

Speech acts. The total numbers of various speech functions were recorded (e.g., an apology, a request for assistance, elaborative comments). Also included under this heading are other functions that do not have a conventional meaning, such as elaborating a point. The speech acts were labeled by examining the function they played in the testees' replies.

Uncorrected errors. The single category for analysis that does not fit under the headings of management strategies or structural components is uncorrected errors, which are included mainly to provide an idea of differences in accuracy under the two test modalities. The number of uncorrected errors in the three categories of grammar, lexicon, and pronunciation was counted. The results of the two kinds of

Table 2. Comparisons of Discourse Features Between the OPI and SOPI

Discourse feature	OPI M	OPI SD	SOPI M	SOPI SD	t	p
Management Strategies						
Pauses	17.1	5.97	20.8	12.90	−1.1	0.276
Possible turn signals	7.0	4.37	8.2	6.86	−0.8	0.405
Fillers	94.7	29.90	108.0	25.70	−2.4	0.035*
Turns	18.4	5.85	3.9	0.32	7.9	0.000*
Self-correction	10.2	4.13	13.2	7.48	−1.2	0.239
Rising intonation	7.9	6.14	8.1	6.24	−0.0	0.929
False starts	4.1	2.89	5.2	3.71	−0.8	0.421
Switches to English	1.9	1.66	0.6	0.84	3.6	0.006*
Structural Components						
Propositions/supporting statements	39.2	5.20	36.2	6.55	1.8	0.110
Quotations	0.6	0.70	0.1	0.32	3.0	0.015*
Speech acts	17.1	5.80	12.0	2.91	2.9	0.016*
Accuracy						
Uncorrected errors	31.3	12.96	36.8	13.30	−1.3	0.227

Note. Number of pairwise comparisons = 10; *p < 0.05

samples were compared using the Analysis of Variance component of the SPSS statistical program, specifically the t-test for matched pairs.

5 Analysis of Results

5.1 *General Comparison of the Two Contexts*

Significant differences in the discourse by test type were found in five of the twelve variables examined, as shown in Table 2. In the OPI, testees took significantly more turns, quoted more, used more speech acts, and switched into English more often than in the SOPI. On the other hand, testees in the SOPI used more fillers than those in the OPI. The greater use of fillers in the SOPI may be an indication of greater stress and attempts to fill in gaps under this condition. The switches indicate that either the testee lacked the appropriate lexical item in Spanish, or there was a momentary lapse of concentration and the testee slipped in an occasional word in

English (e.g., *So*), or the speaker was relying on shared knowledge of English with the interviewer. The greater use of turns, switches, and speech acts in the OPI seems to reflect the interactive nature of this test. In general, the direct test results suggest an increased awareness of and response to the presence of a live interviewer and a greater willingness to utilize the linguistic resources of that person.

The greater use of quotes in the OPI reflects the more informal, conversational nature of the OPI, but it can also be attributed to specific elements of the tasks or to the way the testees framed particular tasks, an issue that is discussed below.

5.2 *Results by Task*

A closer look at the results by task in Table 3 reveals that, of the twelve variables examined in the discourse, there were actually very few significant differences between the speech samples in the two tests. In the comparison of advantages and disadvantages, the only significant difference is the greater number of turns in the OPI, while in the opinion task, differences are noted in the greater number of pauses in the SOPI and turns in the OPI. In the task of giving instructions, differences are seen in the greater number of turns, speech acts, and propositions and supporting statements in the OPI. The greatest number of differences is found in the narrative task, in the increased use of turns and speech acts in the OPI and fillers and uncorrected errors in the SOPI. Thus there is a relationship between the type of task and the results.

We can discount the difference in turns, seen in all the tasks, as an inherent difference in the nature of the two tests. The SOPI allows only one turn, while the OPI permits any number of turns on a given topic. The greater use of pauses in the SOPI opinion task indicates a greater hesitancy, due perhaps to the greater difficulty of the SOPI question over the OPI (why one should stay in a hotel in Mexico in the SOPI vs. adolescent marriage in the OPI). Moreover, the SOPI question asks the testee to give an opinion to a group of people, a task that would be considered at the Superior level if the testee gave and supported an opinion and also if the matter were hypothetical or in the future and not immediate and concrete. On the other hand, the OPI stimulus is framed more in terms of giving advice, given the role of the testee as a teacher. These inherent differences in the stimuli could cause testees in the SOPI to have more difficulty expressing themselves, simply because they might push the task very close to the Superior level.

In giving instructions, the testees in the OPI produced more varieties of speech acts and also more propositions and supporting ideas. The first supports the hypothesis that the interactive nature of the OPI lends itself to a greater range of

Table 3. *Comparisons of Discourse Features Between the OPI and SOPI by Task (Significant Differences Only)*

Discourse feature	OPI		SOPI		t	p
	M	SD	M	SD		
Task 1. Comparing Advantages and Disadvantages						
Turns	3.4	2.01	1.0	0.00	3.77	0.004*
Task 2. Narration						
Fillers	19.8	10.90	27.4	9.98	−3.00	0.015*
Turns	4.1	2.08	0.9	0.32	5.24	0.001*
Speech acts	3.7	1.34	1.4	0.52	4.87	0.001*
Uncorrected errors	5.8	3.36	10.7	4.35	−3.80	0.004*
Task 3. Giving Instructions						
Turns	5.9	2.23	1.0	0.00	6.94	0.000*
Propositions/ Supporting statements	9.4	1.58	7.3	2.06	2.91	0.017*
Speech acts	4.6	1.17	3.4	1.78	2.25	0.051*
Task 4. Giving and Supporting an Opinion						
Pauses	5.1	3.21	9.0	4.71	−2.80	0.021*
Turns	5.0	2.71	1.0	0.00	4.67	0.001*

Note. Number of pairwise comparisons = 10; *$p < 0.05$

speech acts, mirroring more closely conversational interaction. The fact that testees expressed more ideas in the OPI may be a function of the specific topic: the OPI stimulus required them to describe the process involved in getting a driver's license, while the SOPI stimulus led them to enumerate steps for using a computer terminal in the library. The latter topic is more difficult in terms of specific technical vocabulary, which prevented many testees from saying a great deal.

The narrative task gave the most significantly different results. The greater number of speech acts and turns again reflects the interactive, conversational nature of the OPI. The greater frequency of fillers and uncorrected errors in the SOPI suggests more stress and more concentration on communicating the message than on the form of the message. The low number of uncorrected errors in the OPI is perhaps attributable to the fact that the narrative told was a personal experience. It may be assumed that the testees had more control over the grammar and vocabulary because the narrative was based entirely on their own experiences. The narrative requested in the SOPI was an accident that they had experienced or witnessed, and most chose to recount a third-person experience. Therefore, it may be that the more personal the questions, the more control testees have over their production in terms of grammar, vocabulary, and pronunciation. It is interesting that no testees inserted dialogue into their narratives in the SOPI and very few gave evaluative or emotional comments external to the story line, showing that: (a) the narrative in the SOPI was given more as a report of an event, whereas in the OPI it was more a personal story; and (b) the time constraint in the SOPI probably affected the inclusion of an evaluative comment external to the story, which usually is given after the entire narrative is told. This evaluative comment also appears in most narratives after the listener expresses some emotional reaction to the narrative, such as a gasp or an interjection, which primes the speaker to add to the emotional intensity and impact of the story. Given that the testees often did not complete their narratives before time was up and that there was no actual listener present, it is not surprising that they did not make such a comment.

In summary, the testees' discourse in the two tests varied according to the stimuli for many of the variables examined. It appears that familiarity with the topic to be discussed allows testees to control their production to a greater extent while also concentrating on communicating meaning. The difficulty of the topic itself or other relevant factors might also have influenced their production.

5.3 *Specific Categories of Discourse Features*

In order to gain a finer perspective on the data, some discourse features are examined here in detail. These include errors, propositions and supporting statements, and range of speech acts.

5.3.1 *Errors*

Looking more closely at self-corrected and uncorrected errors by categories of grammatical, lexical, and pronunciation errors, only one significant difference was found. The narrative task elicited more uncorrected *grammatical* errors in the SOPI ($M = 7.33$, $SD = 2.40$) than the OPI ($M = 3.89$, $SD = 1.90$), $t(10) = -4.86$, $p = .001$. These results may be due again to how the narrative was presented in the two tests (report vs. story, respectively). As seen earlier, however, the propositions category shows that testees expressed about the same number of ideas in their narratives in both tests. The highest means of errors in all contexts and tasks were grammatical errors, and the lowest were pronunciation errors. Most of the grammatical errors

Table 4. Models of Propositional Organization for Task 1 (Comparing Advantages and Disadvantages)

Listing Strategy	Contrastive Strategy
1. Topic sentence	1. Topic sentence
2. Advantage 1 of X (Support)	2. Advantage 1 of X (Support)
3. Advantage 2 of X (Support)	3. Advantage 2 of X (Support)
4. Disadvantage 1 of X (Support)	4. Disadvantage 1 of Y (Support)
5. Disadvantage 2 of X (Support)	5. Disadvantage 2 of Y (Support)
6. Advantage 1 of Y (Support)	6. Advantage 1 of Y (Support)
7. Advantage 2 of Y (Support)	7. Advantage 2 of Y (Support)
8. Disadvantage 1 of Y (Support)	8. Disadvantage 1 of X (Support)
9. Disadvantage 2 of Y (Support)	9. Disadvantage 2 of X (Support)
10. Conclusion	10. Conclusion

were in adjective or definite/indefinite article and noun agreement, showing that at these higher levels of proficiency, agreement has not been mastered.

5.3.2 Propositions and Supporting Statements

I now discuss some of the data from a qualitative perspective to see what propositions and supporting statements the learners actually produced in their samples and how they organized them. As a basis for comparison I have outlined in Table 4 two models of how a logical, top-down organizational structure of propositions and supporting statements might appear in the task of comparing advantages and disadvantages. These models were compiled from an overall impression of how several Advanced testees organized their samples for the same task. The first shows a listing strategy in which the testee lists several advantages and disadvantages of a given referent before doing the same for the second referent. Supporting statements in parentheses indicate possible examples and other elaborations of those points. The second model is a strategy in which the advantages of a referent are given, followed by a contrastive statement of the disadvantages of the other referent. Then the advantages of the second referent are stated, followed by another contrastive statement of the disadvantages of the first referent. In each model the paradigm of giving both advantages and disadvantages is completed, followed by a statement of the testee's opinion as to which referent is perceived as better. One can assume that the more testees who complete the paradigm in a logical progression, giving several points and supporting at least some of them with examples and other elaborations, the more complete and well-presented the discourse might be. One can also assume that the ability to do this is linked to proficiency in the target language.

Let us take a closer look at how three of the testees actually structured their answers. Grace's comparison of advantages and disadvantages given in the OPI and SOPI are shown in Excerpts 1 and 2, respectively. An English translation is provided in the notes at the end of this chapter (*IR* is the interviewer).[6]

(1) Grace's comparison of advantages and disadvantages in the OPI[7]

```
1   G.:  Pues, tsk, (0.5) creo que tienen muchas aventajas y
2        desventajas. Una: (0.3) >desventaja de una escuela
3        grande<, es que, te puedes perder. Si, como si
4        estás, sufriendo mucho en una ⌈clase⌉, a lo mejor
5        no sabes adonde puedes ir, que hay alguien que te
6        ayude. Y, en una escuela chiquita eso no es un
7        problema porque, no hay tanta gente en la clase y
8        el maestro te puede ayudar, mejor, uno a uno. Pero
9        (0.5) uh, en una universidad grande (0.5), pienso
10       que hay muchos más oportunidades que en una escuela
11       pequeña, tienen más que ofrecerte porque son tan
12       grande, y, y pueden, ser, muy diversos en las
13       clases que te ⌈dan.⌉ Y, si necesitas ayuda en una
14       escuela grande, lo puedes encontrar pero,
15       solamente, la diferencia entre la escuela grande y
16       la chiquita es que, en la chi—en la grande tienes
17       que buscar la ayuda y, pienso que en una escuela
18       chiquita la ayuda está más, um (1.0)
19  IR:  Accesible.
20  G.:  Accesible.
```

(2) Grace's comparison of advantages and disadvantages in the SOPI[8]

```
1   G.:  Pienso que, usando una bicicleta o una motocicleta
2        los dos tienen, aventajas y desventajas. Una mayor,
3        aventaja para la bicicleta pienso es que, la
4        bicicleta es muy bien para el ambiente. El
5        bicicleta no, no, sale, no: saca humo ni nada y es,
6        eso es muy bien. Y pienso que también la bicicleta
7        es bien para, para hacer ejer⌈cicios.⌉ Uh, una:
8        aventaja para la motocicleta, será, sería que,
9        ((sniff)) es muy pequeña, y no, nece—no: (0.5)
10       tiene, no es tan grande como un carro. Pero una
11       desventaja de: la motocicleta es que no es bien
12       para el ambiente. Y las motocicletas hacen mucho
```

```
13          ruido. Pienso yo, que, la mejor idea sería usar una
14          bicicleta porque, la bicicleta >pienso que tiene<
15          más, aventajas, que la, que la motocicleta. >La
16          bicicleta te puede dar< ejercicios, (0.5) te puede
17          llevar a muchos lugares una, una desventaja de la
18          bicicleta a lo mejor sería que, el tiempo, que en
19          una motocicleta llegarías en un lugar como en diez
20          minutos, pero por bicicleta a lo mejor, (0.5)
21          neces—vas a necesitar más tiempo, para llegar
22          adonde necesitas llegar y, a lo mejor si hace mucho
23          calor afuera, vas a sudar y, a lo mejor eso no es,
24          no es una manera de, de, transportación para Ud.
25          So: pienso que a lo mejor la motocicleta será, una:
26          (.03) teng—tenga una aventaja para las personas que
27          necesitan llegar a lugares, con aprisa o no, o no
28          necesita—o no tienen que, no tienen el tiempo para,
29          para gastar en una bicicleta.
```

Table 5 shows an analysis of Grace's propositional organization in both tests. Numbers represent the order in which the main propositions appeared, while the words in parentheses represent elaborations or supporting statements. Although Grace gave a general, organizing statement at the beginning of both the OPI and the SOPI, it can be seen that she performed better in the SOPI than in the OPI in terms of expressing many ideas, since she gave several advantages and disadvantages for both bicycles and motorcycles, contrasting positive and negative points, and several supporting statements. She was also able to make a summarizing statement in her final sentence in the SOPI (lines 25–29). On the other hand, in the same task in the OPI she repeated the same idea twice (i.e., you can't get help easily in a big university; lines 2–6 and 16–18), she did not list the disadvantages of a small school, and she did not give any kind of concluding statement. Grace's SOPI discourse approximates the model given in Table 4 of a contrastive strategy for comparing advantages and disadvantages.

Another testee, Mary, is not so proficient a speaker as Grace. As Excerpts 3 and 4 illustrate, her discourse in both the OPI and the SOPI on the same task is not as complete in structure as Grace's, although numerically she supported her opinions well. Qualitatively speaking, however, her samples, although better than those of most other testees, are not as well structured as Grace's samples.

Table 5. *Comparison of Grace's Propositional Organization on Task 1 (Comparing Advantages and Disadvantages) of the OPI and SOPI*

OPI	SOPI
1. Topic sentence: They have many advantages and disadvantages 2. Disadvantage 1 of big school: You can get lost (You don't know where to go) 3. Advantage 1 of small school: Not a problem to get lost (Not so many people) (Teacher helps you) 4. Advantage 1 of big: More opportunities (More to offer you) (They are so big) (They can be so diverse) 5. Disadvantage 2 of big: You must seek help (repeats) 6. Advantage 2 of small: Help more accessible (repeats) 7. Conclusion: —	1. Topic sentence: Both have advantages and disadvantages 2. Advantage 1 of bicycles: Don't emit smoke 3. Advantage 2 of bicycles: Good for doing exercise 4. Advantage 1 of motorcycles: Small (Not like a car) 5. Disadvantage 1 of motorcycles: Not good for the environment 6. Disadvantage 2 of motorcycles: Noisy 7. Topic sentence 2: Bicycles have more advantages 8. Advantage 3 of bicycles: Good for doing exercise (repeats) 9. Advantage 4 of bicycles: Takes you to many places 10. Disadvantage 1 of bicycles: Take time (You need more) 11. Advantage 2 of motorcycles: Faster 12. Disadvantage 2 of bicycles: You are going to sweat 13. Conclusion: Motorcycle is better for those who have no time

(3) Mary's comparison of advantages and disadvantages in the OPI[9]

```
 1 Mary:  Las ventajas, (0.7) las ventajas serían, que, (1.0)
 2        los estudiantes, y el racio? el racio de los
 3        profesores a las, a los estudiantes es más, uh, más
 4        bajo? Y, entonces los estudiantes pueden recibir
 5        más atención personal, de, los, profesores? Um, no
 6        es, uh, >no es algo que<, los estudiantes en la
 7        universidad, universidad muy pública muy grande
 8        pueden recibir. Pero, um, (0.3) en la universidad
 9        uh, muy grande, las las clases de, (0.3) el español
10        y del, del inglés y, las matemáticas um son muy más
11        o menos pequeñas para la atención personal. Um—pero
```

```
12          en la universidad ((laugh)) (1.0) en la universidad
13          uh, muy grande las clases de, uh psicología y uh
14          biología, las ciencias, son muy grandes con, °uh °
15          trescientos personas, y es, uh, es °difícil para
16          recibir la atención personal.° Pero, um, creo que,
17          uh, las ventajas en la univers—, universidad grande
18          es que, o son que, una persona, un estudiante? °uh
19          ° aprende? má:s de, (1.0) más información, que, uh,
20          (0.5) que reciben en las, el cuarto de clase? Uh,
21          porque, en las clases grandes? con trescientas
22          personas 1—el estudiante aprende cómo, uh, cómo
23          (1.0) cómo ir a su profesor, uh, ↑solo. Y (0.5) no
24          ↓sé. Pero, pero el estudiante, el estudiante en la
25          universidad grande tiene que: uh, tiene que,
26          desa:rrollar una independencia? y, uh, y . . l:os
27          profesores aquí dependen de los estudiantes para
28          (0.5) uh, para buscar a ellos, para ayudar, o para
29          ↑ayuda. Y, entonces, es, uh, una persona aquí es
30          más (0.5), es más independiente.↓ Yo creo.
31    IR:   ¿Es una desventaja?
32 Mary:    No, es una ventaja.
33    IR:   Es una ventaja.
34 Mary:    Sí, sí.
35    IR:   ¿Para ti o para el profesor?
36 Mary:    Para, para ambos. ((laugh)) Pero, um, es, es (1.0)
37          un requisito que, todas las personas necesitan,
38          tener para, crecer. Y para sobrevivir en el mundo
39          real.=
40    IR:   Exacto.
41 Mary:    =El mundo real muy frío.
```

(4) Mary's comparison of advantages and disadvantages in the SOPI[10]

```
1 Mary:    Ento:nces, uh, >mis amigos<, creo que, uh, la
2          bicicleta es, es la solución, uh, mejor, para el
3          problema de viajar. Porque, uh, creo que la
4          bicicleta? uh, no da, uh más palus—, polución, a la
5          ciudad, en México, y, um el, la, motocicleta, sí,
6          um, da, la, polución, um, el. Aunque la bi- la
7          motocicleta es, es más rápido, um, para viajar, la
8          ↑bicicleta↓ no requiere, uh, no requiere tiempo o
9          dinero, o demasiado tiempo o dinero para arreglar y
10         para segurar que, uh, está funcionada, uh, todo el
11         tiempo. Um (0.5) uh, (0.5) m— me gusta la bicicleta
```

Table 6. *Comparison of Mary's Propositional Organization on Task 1 (Comparing Advantages and Disadvantages) of the OPI and SOPI*

OPI	SOPI
1. Topic sentence: —	1. Topic sentence: The bicycle is the best solution
2. Advantage 1 of small school: Lower ratio, students get more personal attention	2. Advantage 1 of bicycle: Bicycles don't create more pollution
3. Disadvantage 1 of big: No [personal attention]	3. Disadvantage 1 of motorcycle: Motorcycle does make pollution
4. Advantage 1 of big: Small Spanish and math classes	4. Advantage 1 of motorcycle: Motorcycle is faster
5. Advantage 2 of big: One learns more outside of class (You learn how to go to the professor) (Develop an independence) (Professors depend on students to seek them)	5. Advantage 2 of bicycle: Bicycle doesn't require time or money (repeats)
	6. Conclusion (?): I like (bicycles) more, the best choice
6. Advantage 3 of big: They learn to survive	7. Advantage 3 of bicycle: Bicycle gives more exercise
7. Conclusion:—	8. Disadvantage 2 of motorcycle: Motorcycle doesn't give exercise

```
12      más, uh, >creo que< la bicicleta uh, es, la, uh, es
13      la selección, uh, mejor para una ciudad como ésa?
14      uh. Y, um, (2 sec.) Y uh, necesitamos pensar en
15      que, uh, en que más razones para eso. Um, ((laugh))
16      uh, la polución y la arreglación, um, y uh. También
17      la bicicleta da más ejercicio, um, a la persona que
18      monta? que lo monta?. La monta. Um, y la
19      motocicleta no da, uh, ejercicio porque en la
20      motocicleta, uh, solamente uh, solamente: una
21      persona se sienta, en eso.
```

In the OPI Mary gives no general statement to organize her answer but begins with two advantages of small schools. She then implies one disadvantage of large schools and elaborates further on this implied idea. She lists two advantages of large schools, elaborating extensively on one statement (namely, that one learns more outside of class—lines 21–38). She never gives the disadvantages of small schools; thus she does not fill in the whole structure, but she does support her points fairly well, as seen in Table 6. Mary's SOPI sample is formulated more in terms of stating and supporting an opinion than listing advantages and disadvantages, and shows more repetition, very little elaboration, no disadvantages given for bicycles, and no concluding statement.

If one looks at the way in which Mary changed the task to that of giving and supporting an opinion, however, it is evident that she was aware that she needed to support her opinion with reasons (lines 14–15). In other words, she demonstrates her knowledge of an organizational structure, albeit for a different task, but has trouble filling it in. Thus, although Mary was on task and had more to say in the OPI, it appears that she actually performed better in organizational structure under the conditions of the SOPI.

Excerpts 5 and 6 from Deb, a much less proficient speaker than the other two, illustrate more fragmented and less cohesive structures, as seen in Table 7.

(5) Deb's comparison of advantages and disadvantages in the OPI[11]

```
1   Deb: Okay. Um, bueno. (1.0) Las, las para ↑mí, ↓las
2        ventajas, ↓son, más grandes que las desventajas,
3        porque: soy de [another state] y: y, escogí a: a
4        esa universidad. Y, bueno, las ven tajas son, son
5        que: toda la gente aquí pueden, pueden decidir,
6        qué, quieren estudia, estudiar, aquí. Si, una
7        persona, no le gusta: uh, Business, puede estudiar
8        otra cosa de: de: len— de: bueno, de: Engineering.
9        Engeniero.=
10  IR:  Ingeniería.
11  Deb: =Engeniería. Y: hay muchas opciones y, que no están
12       en una: una escuela más pequeña. Pero, la, los
13       niveles aquí de: de: de administración son más
14       grandes, y es una pro↑blema, ↓para, para mucha
15       gente aquí, por, >mucha la gente<, porque: uh,
16       >bueno<, cuesta mucho tiempo? para, para (0.5)
17       decidir cosas. Si: si una persona necesita
18       financial aid, o dinero para, para ir a la escuela,
19       es más difícil en una escuela más grande, que en
20       una escuela pequeña. Y: porque hay mucha gente que
21       necesitan, necesita decir, "bueno, estoy de
22       acuerdo o no estoy de acuerdo," y todo. Y, pero
23       creo que es más importante? hacer, o abtener, todas
24       sus opciones, en frente, de ↑ti.↓
25  IR:  Entonces casi ninguna desventaja.
26  Deb: Bueno, la—los niveles administrativas, son
27       ((laugh)) malísimas.
```

(6) Deb's comparison of advantages and disadvantages in the SOPI[12]

```
1   Deb:  Bueno (1.0). Hay dos, dos cosas. Uno es que, que,
2         la gente debe montar, a una: bicicleta, para: para:
3         trans—la transporta│ción,↓ uh, y: otro es, los
4         motocicletas son mejores, o mejor manera, una me—
5         jor, una mejora manera, de, de, de (0.5) transpor—
6         te, de transportación. Y, y creo que, que, los, las
7         bicicletas son más sanas para el ambiente. Y, y: no
8         hacen, humo, ni nada en en el aire. Y, eso es una,
9         buen característica porque: estamos en Mej—en la
10        ciudad de México, donde: el humo y todo de: de la
11        industria es, (0.5) uh, malísima. Y: los
12        motocicletas, uh, tienen, tienen, ventajas? y
13        desventajas también. Las ventajas son que: que es
14        una: (0.2) un, un tipo, una tipa de transportación
15        más rápida, y toda la gente puede: puede uh, (0.5)
16        movar o, o, (0.5) sí, más rápida. Más rápido. Y,
17        la, la otra cosa es que: la gente no suda, cuando,
18        cuando monta una motocicleta. En, en una bicicleta
19        sí, todos sudan. Y ésa es una, una, buen, buena
20        aventaja, para todos los que trabajen.
```

Deb's OPI comparison of advantages and disadvantages begins with a personal opinion, implying that the advantages outweigh the disadvantages and that is why she chose to go to a big university. Although the statement reveals her stance toward the question, it does not serve to organize her answer. She gives only one advantage and one disadvantage of a large school (lines 5–8, 13–15, and 15–20, respectively) and one disadvantage of a small school (lines 13–15). She has few supporting statements and she concludes with an opinion about knowing one's options, but it is not entirely clear what she refers to in this statement.

Deb begins her SOPI excerpt with two general statements that were probably intended to contrast with each other but do not do so (lines 1–6). They seemingly organize the answer by stating the two points she wants to elaborate on. She does give more details on why people should ride bicycles (lines 6–12), but instead of elaborating on why motorcycles are a better means of transportation, she goes on to say that they have advantages and disadvantages (lines 12–13). She states only the advantages, however. She shows more of a notion of structure in her SOPI reply, but the content of her answer interferes with the unity of the sample, making it difficult to follow. Thus Deb's two samples are weak in both test modalities.

Table 7. *Comparison of Deb's Propositional Organization on Task 1 (Comparing Advantages and Disadvantages) of the OPI and SOPI*

OPI	SOPI
1. Topic sentence: Advantages are greater than the disadvantages (I am from [another state], I chose that university)	1. Topic sentence: There are two things: (a) People should ride a bicycle for transportation, (b) Motorcycles are a better means of transportation
2. Advantage 1 of big school: All can decide what they want to study (Example) (Many options)	2. Advantage 1 of bicycles: Better for the environment (Don't make smoke) (Good because we are in Mexico City)
3. Disadvantage 1 of small: Not many options	3. Topic sentence #2: Motorcycles have advantages and disadvantages, too
4. Disadvantage 1 of big: Big levels of administration (Takes time to decide things) (Example) (Lots of people to be in agreement)	4. Advantage 1 of motorcycles: Fast form of transportation (People can move quickly) (People don't sweat riding motorcycles)
5. Conclusion (?): Better to get all the options in front of you	5. Disadvantage 1 of bicycles: Everyone sweats
	6. [Referring to #4]: This is a good advantage for those who work
	7. Conclusion: —

In sum, these three examples illustrate how different testees vary with respect to organizational structure according to several factors, including test modality and proficiency level. Grace, an Advanced-level speaker, produced a very well organized and complete answer for the SOPI question as compared with the same OPI task. Mary, a less competent but still quite proficient speaker, showed that structure was important to her as she struggled to produce a SOPI sample, even though her answer did not match the task elicited because she interpreted the task incorrectly. Her SOPI answer was better organized than the one she gave in the OPI. Finally, Deb, a much less proficient speaker than the other two, shows that a weakness in proficiency level can interfere with the organization of an answer regardless of test modality. These samples indicate that Advanced-level speakers are able to make "a coherent presentation of a number of utterances tied together by an overall message-intent, such as narration of an event, or description or comparison of a set of circumstances" (Buck, Byrnes, and Thompson 1989:2.7–2.8). It appears that more advanced speakers can produce topic sentences and support them with detail and elaborations, and seem to do so better in the context of the SOPI than in that of the OPI. The results suggest that the SOPI conditions focus testees on structuring their answers somewhat more tightly, especially for more proficient speakers. One must keep in mind, however, that an OPI answer could be shaped differently by a perceptive interviewer who could ask leading questions so that the testee completes the entire structure and elaborates as much as possible.

5.3.3 Range of Speech Acts

The data were also categorized into speech acts found in the OPI and SOPI replies. If the range of speech acts that a testee can use appropriately and correctly during a test is a measure of proficiency, then the data indicate that the OPI elicits a wider range of speech acts than the SOPI in all the tasks except one, as seen in Table 8. The table shows that in the task of giving and supporting an opinion, testees used the same number of speech acts in both tests, although they were not entirely the same ones. Testees used a significantly wider range of speech acts in the OPI narrative than in the SOPI. The data indicate that the task greatly affects the production of speech acts. Moreover, the data show that testees stayed more on task in the SOPI, using a narrow range of acts, while in the OPI they used many more speech acts that reflect an interaction with the interviewer, such as asking for assistance, making jokes, and reassuring the listener. These findings support those of Shohamy (1994).

Table 8. Comparisons of Speech Acts Used in OPI and SOPI by Task

OPI	SOPI
\multicolumn{2}{c}{Task 1. Comparing Advantages and Disadvantages}	
make statement/give opinion	make statement/give opinion
elaborate point	elaborate point
make joke	make contradiction
give anecdote	think thought aloud
seek help	
make analogy	
answer question	
make conjecture	
give examples	
\multicolumn{2}{c}{Task 2. Narration}	
narrate	narrate
seek help	make conjecture
give opinion	make description
elaborate point	make comment
make emotional comment	

make comparison
answer question
make correction
give description
make clarification
make joke

Task 3. Giving Instructions

give instructions	give instructions
seek help	give opinion
give reassurance	give orientation
make joke	give description
make hedge	give confirmation
give excuse	answer (invented) question
make guess	give advice
make disclaimer	make conjecture
give description	elaborate point
give confirmation	make apology
give anecdote	
give opinion	
answer question	
give advice	
make conjecture	
make comparison	

Task 4. Giving and Supporting an Opinion

give opinion	give opinion
elaborate point	elaborate point
ask question	make apology
make joke	give option
give advice	make suggestion
answer question	make conjecture
give anecdote	make disclaimer
make comparison	give reassurance
give reaction	offer help

6 Conclusions

The conclusions that can be drawn from these findings in answer to the research questions proposed at the beginning of this chapter are as follows.

1. The significant differences between the discourse drawn from the SOPI and the OPI are not numerous, and most can be traced to the task type and specific topic

rather than the test modalities themselves. These findings do not support claims of Shohamy (1994) that test modality is a more important factor than the stimuli.

2. The test modalities, however, did influence the use of particular strategic and discourse factors. The OPI yielded results that reflected the interactive nature of the test, while the SOPI testees tended to produce a more formal and somewhat more awkward discourse, using more fillers to fill in gaps and correcting themselves to a greater extent. That does not mean they did not communicate well in the SOPI; on the contrary, testees tended to produce more ideas with better organization and stayed more focused on the specific task in the SOPI.

3. Regarding management strategies and structural components, the data again showed no conclusive findings. In general, the use of the management strategies of pauses, fillers, false starts, self-correction, and switches to English varied in both test conditions and according to task and topic. The data on the structural components of use of quoted speech, speech acts, and propositions show some interesting features. Quoted speech really appeared only in the OPI samples, reflecting again the more conversational nature of the exam as opposed to the monologic format of the SOPI. The greater range of speech acts in the OPI also supports the same conclusion. While this has been acknowledged by Stansfield and Kenyon (1992) and others, it should also be acknowledged that FL classrooms today are fostering a communicative, interactive type of discourse. Monologues put the focus on the individual speaker and induce more stress; if there is not ample practice for this kind of discourse, testees probably suffer more anxiety and may not do as well in the SOPI. Also, the fact that the SOPI does not ask many questions of a personal nature again suggests that testees may perform better overall when allowed more opportunities to speak about personal experiences.

Examining the results by task, the propositions given—especially in the task of giving instructions—were far fewer in both the OPI and the SOPI than in the other tasks. In quantitative terms, the propositions expressed in the other three tasks did not appear to vary much according to test type. Looking at some samples qualitatively, however, there are indications that the SOPI may elicit better organized talk than the OPI, in which the testee is more focused on the task. Nevertheless, one must keep in mind that in the OPI, the interviewer may lead the testee to elaborate on the initial response over the course of a few turns. One question that arises in this regard is whether individuals structure their discourse in their native language in the same way. If so, then perhaps the structuring of ideas and supporting statements should not enter into assessment at all, unless it is a goal of FL educators that learners should come away from the FL learning experience with a better command of rhetorical structures in the FL than in the L_1.

Finally, two further implications can be drawn from the analysis of these data.

4. If the ability to perform a number of functions at a given level is a sign of proficiency, oral proficiency testers need to test a range of types of tasks on the SOPI to obtain a range of functions, as Shohamy (1993) points out. Testers should test for both monologic and interactive discourse in order to assess a testee's overall communicative ability. Moreover, as Young (1995) states, these findings call into question the use of rigid-format exams like the SOPI as the only basis on which to make an assessment of overall competence.

5. The study also suggests the need to examine management strategies and propositional organization in the assessment of OPI and SOPI samples and, perhaps, to include a description of them in the criteria for assessment.

It is hoped that the findings and suggestions of this investigation can lead to a better understanding of the discourse elicited in these tests, and can also lead to improvements in the tests and testing procedures involved.

Appendix: *OPI and SOPI Test Stimuli*

Prompts are presented in the language(s) in which they were presented in the tests. See notes for English translations of Spanish stimuli.

Task 1. Comparing Advantages and Disadvantages

OPI: ¿Cuáles son las ventajas y desventajas de ir a una universidad grande como la Universidad de Tejas, en vez de una pequeña como Huston-Tillotson?[13]

SOPI: While talking with some of your friends in Mexico, one of them says that people should use bicycles as their major means of transportation, while another friend says that motorcycles would solve many problems. Then the others present turn to you. Present your position logically by comparing advantages and disadvantages of the bicycle/motorcycle issue. (20 sec. pause) ¿Y qué piensas tú?[14]

Task 2. Narration

OPI: ¿Puede contarme la experiencia que más le haya asustado en la vida?[15]

SOPI: Describe in most vivid terms an accident that you were in or have witnessed. Your audience is made up of your colleagues of this class. (20 sec. pause) ¿Qué pasó ese día?[16]

Task 3. Giving Instructions

OPI: Yo soy nueva aquí, soy profesora en mi país, y no sé cómo se consigue una licencia de manejar en Tejas. ¿Me puede Ud. explicar lo que tengo que hacer?[17]

SOPI: An educator from South America who has come to study at UT asks you how to use the computer terminals in the library to locate a book he must read. Tell him what he must do. (20 sec. pause) ¿Me puede Ud. explicar lo que tengo que hacer?[18]

Task 4. Giving and Supporting an Opinion

OPI: Me llamo Alicia, soy una alumna en su clase de español avanzado, y sólo quería decirle que estoy pensando en casarme con mi novio. El quiere que nos casemos ahora, en vez de esperar hasta después de graduarnos. Ya que tengo sólo catorce años, y él dieciséis, tengo unas dudas. ¿Qué le parece esta idea?[19]

SOPI: You are in charge of a tour group from Texas who came to Ixtapa, Mexico, to spend a week at the Sheraton and enjoy sun and fun at the beach. When you arrive there, you find that your hotel reservations were changed to a second-class hotel in a neighboring town, Zihua, and all the tour members are angry. Half of them want to go right back to Texas, and the other half want to go to the Sheraton to demand rooms. Take a position on the matter. (20 sec. pause) Pues, ¿qué debemos hacer?[20]

Acknowledgments

I thank Judith Liskin-Gasparro for her insightful comments on an earlier version of this study, and Richard Young and Agnes He for their help in finalizing it. All errors, however, are my own.

Notes

1. According to the *ACTFL Guidelines* (ACTFL 1986), the differences between the Intermediate-High and Advanced-level speakers are as follows:

Intermediate-High: Able to handle successfully most uncomplicated communicative tasks and social situations. Can initiate, sustain, and close a general conversation with a number of strategies appropriate to a range of circumstances and topics, but errors are evident. Limited vocabulary still necessitates hesitation and may bring about slightly unexpected circumlocution. There is emerging evidence of connected discourse, particularly for simple narration and/or description. The Intermediate-High speaker can generally be understood even by interlocutors not accustomed to dealing with speakers at this level, but repetition may still be required.

Advanced: Able to satisfy the requirements of everyday situations and routine school and work requirements. Can handle with confidence but not with facility complicated tasks and social situations, such as elaborating, complaining, and apologizing. Can narrate and describe with some details, linking sentences together smoothly. Can communicate facts and talk casually about topics of current public and personal interest, using general vocabulary. Shortcomings can often be smoothed over by communicative strategies, such as pause fillers, stalling devices, and different rates of speech. Circumlocution that arises from vocabulary or syntactic limitations very often is quite successful, though some groping for words may still be evident. The Advanced-level speaker can be understood without difficulty by native interlocutors.

2. The TOPT comprises the following sections: (1) a warm-up consisting of personal questions; (2) questions asking informants to give directions, usually in reference to a map shown to them; (3) a picture stimulus requiring a detailed description; (4) a sequence of pictures eliciting a story in different tenses; (5) various topics requiring an ability to address specialized content and use different discourse strategies; and (6) situations that present a specific problem, to which testees must respond appropriately.

3. It should be noted here that, unlike those in the ACTFL OPI, the questions were not tailored to each individual learner; that is, all the questions were asked in the same way for all testees. There were also two role-play situations involved in the tests described here, whereas in the ACTFL OPI there is usually only one.

4. As a matter of fact, four of the six estimated at the Advanced level went on to take the TOPT in the months subsequent to the course and passed at the Advanced level. I do not know the fate of the other two estimated at the Advanced level, but I do know that two of the students estimated at the Intermediate-High level did not pass at the Advanced level.

5. The intent of the intonational rise was determined by considering factors such as hesitation before using a word or expression and trouble with pronunciation, in which case it was deemed to signify a question regarding the appropriateness of a lexical item. If the rise appeared at the end of a phrase or after a very commonly used word, then it was considered to signal a confirmation check.

6. The transcript notation used in the examples is that outlined in Atkinson and Heritage (1984:ix–xvi).

7. Grace: Well, tsk, I think that they have many advantages and disadvantages. One disadvantage of a big school, is that, you can get lost. If, like if you are, suffering a lot in a class, probably you don't know where you can go, that there is someone that can help you. And, in a small school that is not a problem because there aren't as many people in a class and the teacher can help you, better, one on one. But, uh, in a big university, I think that there are many more opportunities than in a small school. They have more to offer you because they are so big and, and, they can, be, very diverse in the classes that they give. And, if you need help in a big school, you can find it but, only, the difference between the big school and the small one, in the sm—in the big one you have to look for help and, I think that in a small school the help is more, um
   IR: Accessible.
   Grace: Accessible.

8. Grace: I think that, using a bicycle or a motorcycle the two have, advantages and disadvantages. A most important, advantage for the bicycle I think is that, the bicycle is very good for the environment. The bicycle doesn't—doesn't go out, doesn't let off smoke or anything and it is, that is very good. And I think that also the bicycle is better for, for doing exercise. Uh, an, advantage for the motorcycle will be, would be that, it is very small, and doesn't nee—doesn't have, isn't as big as a car. But a disadvantage of, the motorcycle is that it isn't good for the environment. And motorcycles make a lot of noise. I think that the better idea would be to use a bicycle because, the bicycle I

think that has more, advantages than the, than the motorcycle. The bicycle can give you more exercise, can take you to more places a, a disadvantage of the bicycle probably would be, the time, that on a motorcycle you would arrive at a place like in ten minutes, but by bicycle probably, you nee —, you are going to need more time to get to where you need to get and, probably if it is very hot outside, you are going to sweat and, probably that isn't, isn't a kind of, of transportation for you. So, I think that probably the motorcycle will be, may have an advantage for the people that need to get to places in a hurry or don't, don't need, or don't have to, don't have the time to, to waste on a bicycle.

9. Mary: The advantages, the advantages would be, the students, and the ratio, the ratio [incorrect word] of the professors to the students is more, uh, lower. And so the students can receive more personal attention from, the professors. Um, it isn't, uh, it isn't something that the students in the university, very public very big university can receive. But, um, in the uh, very big university, the the classes of, Spanish and of, of English and, math um are very more or less small for personal attention. Um. But in the university (laugh) in the very big university the classes of, uh psychology and uh biology, the sciences, are very big with, uh, 300 people. And it is, uh, it is difficult to receive personal attention. But um, I think that, uh, the advantages in the universi— big university is that, are that a person, a student, uh, learns more from, more information, than uh they get in the, the classroom. Uh, because in the big classes with 300 people the student learns how, uh, how, how to go to his professor alone. And, I don't know. But, but the student, the student in the big university has to, uh, has to develop an independence and uh, and ... the professors here depend on the students to look for them, to help, or for help. And then it is, uh, a person here is more, is more independent. I think.
IR: Is it a disadvantage?
Mary: No, it is an advantage.
IR: An advantage.
Mary: Yes, yes.
IR: For you or for the professor?
Mary: For both, I think. But um, it is, it is a requirement that all people need to have to, grow. And to survive in the real world.
IR: Exactly.
Mary: The very cold real world.

10. Mary: So, uh, my friends, I think that uh, the bicycle is, is the, uh best solution for the problem of traveling. Because, uh, I think that the bicycle, uh, doesn't give, uh, more pollution, to the city in Mexico, and um, the motorcycle, does give pollution, um, the. Although the bi— the motorcycle is, is faster, um, to travel, the bicycle doesn't require, uh, doesn't require time or money, or too much time or money to fix and to be sure that, uh, it is functioned, uh, all the time. Um, uh, I like the bicycle more, uh, I think that the bicycle is, the, uh is the best choice for a city like that one, uh. And um. And uh, we need to think more about, uh, about more reasons for that. Um, uh, the pollution and the repair, um, and uh. Also, the bicycle gives more exercise, um, to the person that rides, that rides it. Rides it. Um, and the motorcycle doesn't give, uh,

exercise because on the motorcycle, uh, a person only, uh, only sits, on that.

11. Deb: Okay, um, well. The, the for me, the advantages are, greater than the disadvantages, because, I am from [another state] and, and, I chose this, this university. And, well, the advantages are, are that, everyone here can, can decide, what, they want to study, study here. If, a person, doesn't like, uh, Business, he can study something else of, of, len- of, well, of Engineering. Engineer.
    IR: Engineering.
    Deb: And, and there are many options that, that aren't in a, a smaller school. But, the, the levels here of, of, of administration are larger, and it is a problem, for, for a lot of people here, for, a lot of people because, uh, well, it takes a long time, to, to decide things. If, if a person needs financial aid, or money to, to go to school, it is more difficult in a larger school, than in a small school. And, because there are a lot of people who need, need to say, "well, I agree or I don't agree," and all. And, but I think that it is more important, to do, or obtain, all their options, in front of you.
    IR: So almost no disadvantage.
    Deb: Well, the, the administrative levels, are, really bad.

12. Deb: Well. There are two, two things. One is that, that, people should ride a bicycle for, for, trans—transportation, uh, and, the other is, the motorcycles are better, or a better way, a better, a better way of, of, of transport, transportation. And, and I think that, that, the, the bicycles are healthier for the environment. And, and, they don't make, smoke, or anything in in the air. And, that is a good characteristic because, we are in Mex, in the city of Mexico, where, the smoke and all of, of the industry is, uh, really bad. And, the motorcycles, uh, have, have, advantages, and disadvantages also. The advantages are that, that it is a, a kind, a kind of faster transportation, and all the people can, can uh, move or, or, yes, more quickly. More quickly. And, the, the other thing is that, people don't sweat, when, when they ride a motorcycle. On, on a bicycle yes, everyone sweats. And that is a, a good, good advantage, for all those who work.

13. What are the advantages and disadvantages of going to a large university like the University of Texas, instead of a small one like Huston-Tillotson? (Huston-Tillotson is a very small local college in Austin, Texas.)

14. And what do you think?

15. Can you tell me about the experience that most frightened you in your life?

16. What happened that day?

17. I am new here, I am a professor in my country, and I don't understand how to get a driver's license in Texas. Can you explain to me what I need to do? (*Licencia de manejar* is the term used most frequently in colloquial language in Texas to denote "driver's license," although the Texas Department of Public Safety uses the term *licencia de conducir* in their Spanish manuals. For purposes of this test I decided to use the colloquial term to avoid having to translate for any of the testees.)

18. Can you explain to me what I need to do?

19. My name is Alicia, I am a student in your advanced Spanish class, and I just wanted to tell you that I am thinking about getting married to my boyfriend. He wants us to get married now, instead of waiting until after we graduate. Since I am only fourteen, and he is sixteen, I have some doubts. What do you think of this?

20. Well, what should we do?

References

American Council on the Teaching of Foreign Languages. 1986. *ACTFL Provisional Proficiency Guidelines*. Yonkers, NY: Author.

Atkinson, J. Maxwell, and John Heritage, eds. 1984. *Structures of Social Action: Studies in Conversation Analysis*. Cambridge: Cambridge University Press.

Buck, Kathryn, Heidi Byrnes, and Irene Thompson, eds. 1989. *The ACTFL Oral Proficiency Interview Tester Training Manual*. Yonkers, NY: American Council on the Teaching of Foreign Languages.

Clark, John. 1986. "Development of a Tape-Mediated, ACTFL-ILR Scale-Based Test of Chinese Speaking Proficiency." In *Technology and Language Testing*, ed. by Charles Stansfield, 130–145. Washington, DC: Teachers of English to Speakers of Other Languages.

Labov, William. 1972. *Language in the Inner City*. Philadelphia: University of Pennsylvania Press.

Shohamy, Elana. 1994. "The Validity of Direct Versus Semi-Direct Oral Tests." *Language Testing* 11.99–123.

Shohamy, Elana, Claire Gordon, Dorry Kenyon, and Charles Stansfield. 1989. "The Development and Validation of a Semi-Direct Test for Assessing Oral Proficiency in Hebrew." *Bulletin of Higher Hebrew Education* 4.4–8.

Shohamy, Elana, Smadar Donitsa-Schmidt, and Ronit Waizer. 1993. "The Effect of the Elicitation Mode on the Language Samples Obtained on Oral Tests." Revised version of a paper presented at the Language Testing Research Colloquium, Cambridge, England.

Stansfield, Charles. 1993. "An Approach to Performance Testing of Oral Language Proficiency for Bilingual Education Teacher Certification." In *Proceedings of the Third National Research Symposium on Limited English Proficiency Student Issues: Focus on Middle and High School Issues*, vol. 1, 187–215. Washington, DC: U.S. Department of Education.

Stansfield, Charles, and Dorry Kenyon. 1992. "Research on the Comparability of the SOPI and the OPI." *System* 20.347–364.

Young, Richard. 1995. "Conversational Styles in Language Proficiency Interviews." *Language Learning* 45.3–42.

Part 2

Turns and Sequences in Language Proficiency Interviews

Answering Questions in LPIs: A Case Study

Agnes Weiyun He
State University of New York at Stony Brook

1 LPI Interaction: Focusing on Questions and Answers

As has been observed by many researchers (Lazaraton 1992, Riggenbach 1991, Ross and Berwick 1992, van Lier 1989, Young 1995), a significant portion, if not all, of the talk in language proficiency interviews (LPIs) consists of questions by the examiner and answers by the language learner. Hence, to a large extent, the question of how well the learner fares in the LPI can be translated into the question of how well he/she answers the examiner's questions.

Question-answer is prototypical of the kind of paired utterances called adjacency pairs (Sacks 1992; Sacks, Schegloff, and Jefferson 1974) that are deeply interrelated with the turn-taking system as a method of locally managing the selection of a next speaker in conversation. The most important interactional consequence of the notion of adjacency pair is that given the first part of a pair (e.g., a question), a second part (e.g., an answer) becomes immediately relevant and expected. In other words, given a question, there is a "conditional relevance" (Schegloff 1972) for an answer to occur. If an answer fails to occur, it is noticeably absent.

From a conversation-analytic point of view (see, among others, Drew and Heritage 1992), talk in LPIs is a describable domain of interactional activity exhibiting stable, orderly properties that are specific and analyzable achievements of students and examiners. An answer is something that is jointly produced by the participants (Button 1987). For example, if a learner who has been answering a question stops speaking and if there is no uptake by the examiner (evidenced by either a period of silence or a blank stare if visual information is available as well), then we can say that there exists an interactional need for the learner to elaborate on his/her response.

In analyzing a variety of educational test instruments used in face-to-face assessments of L_1 children's scholastic abilities, Marlaire and Maynard (1990) and Maynard and Marlaire (1992) argue that the results of these tests are collaborative productions by both the children and the examiners. The giving and receiving of interview prompts depends upon interactional systematicity and orderly modes of collaborative behavior. Test results are "accountable" (Maynard and Marlaire 1992:178) in that they are dependent upon an organization of concerted practical actions that constitutes the participants' interaction. Drawing on videotapes and transcripts of actual exam episodes, Maynard and Marlaire show that each part of a testing sequence is assembled in the socially organized interaction between the examiner and the examinee. Marlaire and Maynard (1990) and Maynard and Marlaire (1992:193) highlight the interactional substrate of the interview, i.e., the interactional skills that examiners and learners use to arrive at accountable answers to interview questions. The interactional substrate outlined by Maynard and Marlaire (1992) consists of such practical activities as prompting with test items, answering, initiation repair, correction of prompts and answers, doing the repair and correction, acknowledging, evaluating, and engaging in other vocal and nonvocal practices that constitute the test as an official and valid enterprise.

Recent studies of interaction in LPIs have begun to pay attention to the design of interview questions, not only as enacted scripts but also as resources that guide the examiner's and the learner's behavior and through which the examiner and the learner negotiate meanings. Several researchers have investigated the question dimension of the Q-A adjacency pairs. For example, Lazaraton (1992) examined the examiner's question design and the interactively co-constructed nature of the assessment of the learner's language ability. Ross and Berwick (1992) analyzed how the examiner accommodated his/her questions to the discourse behavior of the learner. As a result of this work, it is now known that poor question design (e.g., problems of question relevance and meaning) can impair comprehension of questions and cause interactional problems. Answers in the question-answer pair, however, have received limited attention.

2 An Interactional Approach to Answers

In an earlier study that concerned ESL learners taking the Cambridge First Certificate in English oral interview (He 1994), I found that high proficiency learners gave longer answers in response to a sequentially preceding question. Low proficiency learners often used falling intonation, gave short (often one- word/phrase) answers, used long pauses, paused at turn-transition-relevant places (TRPs), and repeated much information. Consequently, examiners used many probing questions, continuers, and pauses between turns. When their efforts failed, they gave up pursuing further response from the learner and moved on to the next question. High proficiency learners often volunteered elaboration. To keep the floor, they resorted to rising intonation, pauses between turn-constructional units, multiple utterances, and terminal overlaps. The interactional upshot was that examiners usually joined these high proficiency learners in their construction of an elaborated response. I attributed the differences in the manner of elaboration in part to learners' different perceptions regarding the goals of the LPI activity.

The purpose of this chapter is to provide a more comprehensive examination of answer-related interactive features, particularly those that contribute to failure in LPIs. Focusing on one specific LPI session whose goal is to assess the oral proficiency level of a prospective international teaching assistant (ITA), this chapter describes aspects of discourse competence specific to the speech activity of a LPI, and suggests that discourse competence and grammatical competence are inseparable from each other.

Most of the previous work related to ITAs' discourse (Anderson-Hsieh and Koehler 1988; Bailey, Pialorsi, and Zukowski/Faust 1984; Davies, Tyler, and Koran 1989; Madden and Myers 1994; Pica, Barnes, and Finger 1990) has tended to quantify grammatical and/or pronunciation errors and has examined the relationship between number of errors and ratings of teaching effectiveness. Textbooks on problems that face ITAs (Byrd, Constantinides, and Bennington 1989; Smith, Meyers, and Burkhalter 1992) tend to view problems in ITA oral communication as local ones that can be solved through more precise and rigorous methods such as elaborate training manuals and multivariate statistical analyses. ITAs' problems are seen as resulting primarily from the lack of proficiency in phonology and lexicogrammar, not as problems faced by non-native speakers in talking with and understanding native speakers in the process of interactive meaning construction.

Recent research on non-native communicative abilities in general (Bachman 1990) and on ITA training in particular (Hoekje and Linnell 1994) is beginning to recognize that discourse features affect communicative competence. Rounds (1987) notes that ITAs frequently do not adequately elaborate the key points of their presentations, name important steps, or make cohesive links between ideas. Tyler (1992) suggests that ITAs misuse various lexical, syntactic, and prosodic cues, and that they fail to signal the relative importance of ideas. Similarly, Williams (1992) points to the importance of explicit marking of discourse structure in ITAs' speech. Although this limited body of literature on discourse aspects of ITAs' language use has gone beyond discrete phonological and morphosyntactic analysis, it has focused exclusively on ITAs' speech production without considering the effects of input from their native English-speaking interlocutors in the context of face-to-face interaction.

The present study differs from previous research in its focus on the interactionally situated nature of language use, an area that has been largely overlooked in the past. Many conversational features identified in this chapter (e.g., the length and placement of a pause, the ways in which turn-taking is organized, the ways in which speech errors, misunderstanding, and not-understanding are dealt with) create problems in communication only when they are considered in their sequential and situational contexts. The present study differs also in its interactional approach, in which language forms are not divorced from the conversational, sequential contexts in which they occur. In this view, language is an interactive phenomenon and a form of action fully embedded in the social world. Linguistic activities are situated practices with interactional, conversation-structural expectations and preferences. To be proficient in a language means in part to be able to satisfy these expectations and preferences.

This chapter details the ways in which one particular ITA copes with LPI questions, and suggests causes of his failure in the interview.

3 Data and Methods

The data presented in this chapter are drawn from twenty English LPIs for international graduate students who applied for a teaching assistantship in their academic departments at an American university. These interview sessions were audiotaped during fall 1994 and spring 1995. Each of the interviews involved four participants: the candidate (coded as ITA in data excerpts) and three examiners—a representative from the Center for English as a Second Language (coded as A), a representative from the Graduate School (coded as B), and a representative from the prospective ITA's home department (coded as C).

Talk in these interview sessions was generally broken down into three parts. Examiner A began with general topics such as cultural differences, educational systems, food, and the weather. Examiner B continued with queries regarding the candidate's educational background and career objectives. And examiner C ended with questions directly related to specific classroom activities as well as the subject matter that the ITA would teach. Thus the candidate was engaged in verbal interaction with one examiner at a time.

The interviews took place during the beginning weeks of the semester. At the time of the interviews, the candidates had already been offered a probationary teaching assistantship prior to arrival at the university and had been performing their teaching duties for a couple of weeks. According to the Graduate School guidelines, their final contracts would not be signed until their oral English was determined to be adequate. It was for the purpose of making this determination that these twenty interviews were conducted.

The audio recordings of these interviews were transcribed according to the conventions developed by conversation analysis (Sacks, Schegloff, and Jefferson 1974:731–733; Atkinson and Heritage 1984:ix–xiii).[1] Names that identify individuals or institutions of the research site have been changed to ensure anonymity. Due to the fact that it was not possible to collect video data, analyses that required such data have been avoided.

One particular candidate was chosen for analysis in this chapter as he was the only one out of the twenty who failed the LPI exam and who was denied a graduate teaching assistantship. This candidate was a male organic chemistry major who had come from China to the U.S. four weeks before the interview. All of his examiners were native speakers of American English. Examiners *A* and *B* were females, and Examiner *C* was male. All three examiners had at least five years of experience conducting this type of interview.

4 Problems in Answers

This section presents two interrelated dimensions of this ITA's answers to LPI questions: his use of *yeah*, and the character of the ITA's turn immediately following the examiner's question.

4.1 *"Yeah" Exhibiting Not-understanding*

Yeah is used in English conversation as a continuer (Schegloff 1982) or a receipt token or a backchanneling device (Tao and Thompson 1991). Its primary function in native English discourse is to acknowledge understanding and exhibit cooperation.

This ITA's use of *yeah* often suggests that he does not understand what the examiner has said or done, whether it concerns questions, repairs of questions, grammatical units, or turn-constructional units.[2] Below are some illustrative examples.

(1) Not understanding a question

```
120     A:   So what was your concentration=
121→  ITA:   =Yeah
122     A:   in China?
123→  ITA:   Yeah.
124     A:   What con- what did you concentrate on=
125   ITA:   =Physical chemistry.
```

Yeah in line 121 of Excerpt 1 acknowledges *A*'s turn in 120. The fact that the ITA latches his *yeah* to the end of *A*'s first recognizable turn-constructional unit (TCU) shows that he understands either the construct of TCU and/or the last lexical item *concentration*; later examples will show that it is more likely the latter. *A* provides an increment (*in China*, line 122) to her TCU in the next turn, thereby completing her question. The ITA's *yeah* in 123 acknowledges that *A* has taken a turn, but exhibits no understanding of the character of *A*'s turn as a question. In other words, if *yeah* in 121 is ambiguous, *yeah* in 123 clearly shows that the ITA does not understand that a question has been posed to him. This is certainly how *A* interprets him, as in the immediate next turn she recasts her question (line 124).

In several instances, the ITA exhibits understanding of the question form of the examiner's original question but fails to understand the repair of the question (for a specification of the repair mechanism, see Egbert 1998; Schegloff, Jefferson, and Sacks 1977). Excerpt 2 is a case in point.

(2) Not understanding a repair of a question

```
271     C:   Okay which ones are used? ((ones=tests))
272   ITA:   Mm (1.0) you means- uh- the student have a
273          test?
274     C:   >No no no< not examination as in writing but
275          (.) CHEmically.
276→  ITA:   Yeah.
277     C:   Performing a chemical test on the unknown.
278→  ITA:   Umm.
279     C:   Uh what sort o:f (.2) what sort of (.2)
280          functional group tests are performed on the
281          compound?
282   ITA:   Mm (have no idea)
```

Here, the ITA apparently recognizes that a question has been asked in 271, as in line 272 he provides a next turn repair initiation. But his *yeah* in 276 suggests that he does not realize that *C* has repaired his initial question in 274, and *Umm* in 278 suggests that he does not comprehend that *C*'s utterance in 277 is yet another clarification of 274, continuing to elicit an answer from him. *C* then once again redesigns his question in 279, and it is only after *C*'s turn beginning from line 279 that the ITA responds to *C*'s question. We may speculate at this stage that the ITA's not understanding of *C*'s repair may have to do with two factors. The first is the nature of the repair initiation: the ITA hears and understands the words in the original question but has trouble determining the referent of *ones [tests]* (line 271). The second factor is the absence of the explicit question form (e.g., a *wh-* item) in *C*'s clarification.

By contrast, in instances such as Excerpt 2a where the reason for repair initiation (line 37) is not specified and the examiner repeats the original question with a fullfledged question form (line 38), the ITA exhibits no comprehension problems (line 40).[3]

```
(2a)   Contrast with (2)

035      A:   Mhum. How did you hear about this
036           university?
037      ITA: Mhm?
038      A:   How did you HEAR about this
039           university?
040→    ITA: Mmm I:: (.2) I know the university fro:m uh
041           (.) my friend.
```

The ITA's use of *yeah* further suggests that he has difficulty deciphering what constitutes a meaningful grammatical unit and what constitutes a turn-constructional unit. In Excerpt 3, the ITA uses *yeah* primarily to register recognition of individual lexical items, thereby disrupting the flow of interaction.

```
(3)    Not understanding turn-constructional units

179      C:   Three forty five is your only assignment this
180           semester?
181      ITA: Yeah.
182      C:   So you are working at Dr. Gatsby's?
183      ITA: Yeah.
184      C:   And is the: (.2) is <that course designed>
185→    ITA: ye ⌈ah
186      C:      ⌊in such a way that students are simply
187           given unknowns=
188→    ITA: =Yeah unknowns
189      C:   and they spend the entire semester=
```

```
190→  ITA:  =Yeah
191     C:  trying to: determine the identity=
192→  ITA:  =Yeah identity
193     C:  and then make derivatives
194   ITA:  Yeah, yeah
```

*Yeah*s in 185 and 190 are placed within turn-constructional units and thus appear to exhibit understanding of words but not the meaning (grammatical or interactional) of *C*'s utterances. This becomes salient in *yeah* tokens in 188 and 192, in which cases the ITA appends the lexical items (*unknowns* and *identity*) to *yeah*, thus specifying of what his *yeah* is an acknowledgment. Taken together, these four instances of *yeah* strongly suggest that the ITA uses *yeah* to exhibit word recognition (often the examiner's last word to which his *yeah* is adjacent). His *yeah* usage shows that he does not understand what constitutes a meaningful grammatical unit or what constitutes a turn-constructional unit.

4.2 *Problematic Next Turn After the Question*

In the turn immediately following the examiner's initial question, the ITA often exhibits the need for the examiner either to ask a follow-up question or to repeat or recast her/his question. The need for a follow-up question is exhibited through short, often one-word responses and silences immediately following the question. The need for the examiner to repeat or recast the question is primarily shown in two ways: through an explicit repair initiation made by the ITA and through a problematic answer that the ITA supplies.

4.2.1 *Elicited Elaboration*
Like learners of low proficiency level in the First Certificate in English oral interviews (He 1994), the ITA often provides short, one-word responses to the examiners' questions and leaves long pauses immediately following the examiners' questions.

```
(4)   One-word response

138     A:  Did you WRITE a thesis u:h (.2) when you
139         finished your (.) your studies in China?
140→  ITA:  Yeah.
141     A:  Can you tell me about it?
142   ITA:  Ummm (.3) mm (.2) I forget I think it's only
143         (.2) it's a prob- u:h (.3) uh:: (.3)
```

```
144             (challenge) iron uh (.2) effects effections
145             on (.8) a (reeled) electro-optic (electro
146             object).
```

(4a) A variation of (4) with a different examiner

```
157     B:    Okay uh (.2) do you know what your assignment
158           is as a TA?
159→   ITA:   Yeah.
160     B:    What what've you been doing?
161    ITA:   Mm an hour of ( ) with intro uh (.2) er if a
162           student have any questions I will tell you
163           how to do and (tell) your (partner) how to
164           start up the (.) uh instrument (.2) and if
165           you (.) during an experiment if a student
166           have any questions such as about uh if she uh
167           adds some agent agents and (.) he don't know
168           uh re- don't know the result and I will (.)
169           try to (.2) figure out the the construction
170           (.) conclusions with the student.
```

In both (4) and (4a), the ITA has a one-word response (*Yeah*, lines 140 and 159) to the examiner's question. In both instances, the examiner follows up in the immediate next turn with another question (lines 141 and 160). The fact that the ITA produces a considerable amount of talk in response to the follow-up question in both cases (lines 142–146 and 161–170) seems to suggest that his brevity in 140 and 159 has more to do with the lack of understanding of an interactional necessity to elaborate than with anything else (see also Ross 1998).

Pauses, together with scant responses, also contribute to the examiner's further elicitation of elaborations, as can be seen in (5).

(5) Pauses

```
223     C:    Right. Do they do qualitative tests as well?
224→          (.2)
225     C:    U:h (.) ⎡functional group tests?
226    ITA:          ⎣((clears throat))
227    ITA:   Yeah.
228     C:    Which ones?
229→          (.2)
230     C:    Give me an example (.) one or two of
231           qualitative test.
232→          (.6)
```

233   ITA: I'll try which function?

In this case, following *C*'s question in 223, there is no uptake by the ITA (line 224). *C* further specifies his question in 225, to which the ITA gives yet another one-word response (*Yeah*, 227). *C* then asks for elaboration in 228, which is followed by another pause with no uptake by the ITA (line 229). *C* finally changes his strategy in line 230 and asks instead for an example, using an imperative rather than an interrogative. A longer pause ensues (line 232). This is certainly not an isolated instance in this interview session; rather, this is indicative of a general tendency.

4.2.2 *Problematic Responses*

The difficulty of this interview session also manifests itself in terms of the amount of repetition the examiners make. As remarked earlier, several reasons contribute to the examiners' repetition of their questions. Excerpts 6–9 provide examples for each. Excerpt 6 is an example of examiners having to repeat themselves due to the ITA's indication of an unspecified trouble source.

```
(6)    Unspecified trouble in understanding

136       A:   Okay, .hh c:an uh (.2) did you write a thesis?
137→   ITA:   Uhm?
138       A:   Did you WRITE a thesis u:h (.2) when you
139               finished your (.) your studies in China?
```

Here, the ITA puts forth a next-turn repair initiation (NTRI) in line 137 (*Uhm?*), the kind of NTRI that fails to identify the trouble source (Drew 1995). In other words, this NTRI gives no indication about which part of the question in line 136 the ITA does not understand or hear; nor does it provide any clue as to whether the problem has to do with comprehension or hearing. This NTRI thus requires that *A* repeat her original question, which she does in line 138 and to which she adds an increment (lines 138–139) to make the question more specific.

Excerpts 7 and 8 show that the ITA not only explicitly makes requests for repetition but also gives answers so problematic that the examiner has to repeat the question. In these instances, the ITA himself does not exhibit any orientation to problems in interaction; it is the examiner who identifies and redresses problems on the basis of the ITA's initial uptake of the interview question.

```
(7)    Wrong answer

047       A:   A:nd uh did your friend uh how had your
```

```
048            friend heard about the this university?
049→  ITA:     About (.2) two year.
050    A:      HOW had she heard about this (.) this
051            university?
```

(8)   Undecipherable answer

```
195    C:      and what sort of compounds are given out from
196            unknowns what types of compounds?
197→  ITA:     Uh as about u:h (.3) >all of this is about
198            uh< ((some chemical elements))
199    C:      Uhm I'm sorry uh what functional groups are
200            are used? Esters, acids, alcohols, aldehydes
201            what (.) what types of compounds?
```

In Excerpt 7, the ITA clearly mistakes the question word *how* to mean *how long* (line 49), which leads *A* to repeat her question, stressing *HOW* (line 50). In (8), the ITA's response in 197 is undecipherable—not only unintelligible to the analyst but also, and more importantly, not comprehensible to *C*, as indicated by *C*'s design of his turn beginning from line 199, which prefaces the repetition of the original question (line 201) with an apology for misunderstanding (*Uhm I'm sorry*, 199), a reframing of the question (*what functional groups are used?*, 199–200), and a list of possible candidate answers (*Esters, acids, alcohols, aldehydes*, 200).

Excerpt 9 is perhaps the most troubling instance of all. In this case, the ITA provides answers that conflict with his own previous statement and that are contradictory to each other.

(9)   Contradictory answers

```
067    ITA:    ⌊She she's a a classmate.
068    A:      So you studied together?
069→  ITA:     NO.
070    A:      No?
071→  ITA:     Hhuhu all right she uh he is a classmate in
072            (   ) University.
073    A:      She was your classmate there=
074    ITA:    =Yeah.
075    A:      Did you take the same classes?
076→  ITA:     Yeah.
```

In line 69, the ITA gives an emphatic negative answer (stressed *NO*) to *A*'s question in 68. This answer clearly contradicts his earlier statement in line 67. *A* pursues the question in line 70; the ITA reiterates that *she is a classmate* in 71 and confirms the fact in 74. At this point, *A* transforms her question from *So you studied together?* (line 68) to *Did you take the same classes?* (line 75). To the latter the ITA replies with *Yeah* (line 76). What appears to be the issue here is that the ITA's semantic scopes of *classmate* and *study* differ from those of *A*'s. To the ITA, a classmate is someone with whom one takes classes but not studies; to take the same classes does not mean to study together.

5 Concluding Remarks

The ITA in this interview exhibits many deficiencies in all areas of language, including syntax, lexicon, and pronunciation. This chapter has focused on conversation-analytic features that helped contribute to his not passing the oral interview and thus not being granted a teaching assistantship. It has situated ITA language proficiency interviews in the context of human interaction as well as language learning and language assessment. It has examined the ITA's oral production vis-à-vis the replies and responses he receives from his native English-speaking interlocutors. It has considered the sequentially grounded and interactionally constructed understandings of interviews as particular types of speech activities through which the ITA's L_2 oral proficiency is exhibited.

The notion of communicative competence has undergone numerous refashionings since its inception in the 1970s. I submit that it is high time now to detail what discourse competence entails. As can be seen in the data presented in this chapter, to be a competent participant in language proficiency interviews means in part to exhibit understanding of questions, repairs, and turn-constructional units; to elaborate responses; to strategically position pauses in between speech; and to specify trouble source in the case of difficulty in communication. More generally, this study suggests that it is fruitful to examine discourse competence in the context of specific speech activities. Different activities with their different goals, agendas, and speech roles may have different discourse/interactional mandates for their participants. Further research is necessary to investigate which aspects of discourse and interaction are common to all activity types and which ones are activity-specific.

This study also highlights the necessity of considering grammatical competence and the kind of discourse competence this chapter has addressed as inseparable from each other. For example, reluctance in elaboration may have to do with not only the ITA's perception concerning the goals of the LPI activity (Levinson 1979, He 1994) or his culture-specific conversational styles (Young 1995); it can also be construed as a kind of avoidance strategy due to the ITA's limited linguistic resources.

Similarly, pauses following the interview question and the problematic uses of discourse markers such as *yeah* point to the lack of comprehension of grammatical as well as interactional structures. Wrong and undecipherable responses suggest limitations in language skill areas of listening and speaking, in the sense these terms have conventionally been used in the teaching of second/foreign languages.

Acknowledgments

I gratefully acknowledge a Special Research Grant from Southern Illinois University, that helped make this research possible. I thank Alice Morris for assistance with data collection, and Shinichi Izumi and Snezha Tsoneva for assistance with data transcription. I am grateful to Richard Young, Sheila Brutten, and Rita Moore for comments and feedback. Remaining deficiencies are mine alone.

Notes

1. Transcription symbols:

CAPS	emphasis, signaled by pitch or volume
.	falling intonation
,	falling-rising intonation
°	quiet speech
[ ]	overlapped talk
-	cutoff
=	latched talk
:	prolonged sound or syllable
(0.0)	silences roughly in seconds and tenths of seconds (measured more according to the relative speech rate of the interaction than to the actual clock time)
(.)	short, untimed pauses of one-tenth of a second or less
( )	undecipherable or doubtful hearing
→	turn(s) focused for analysis
(( ))	additional observation
X:	at the beginning of a stretch of talk, identifies the speaker
> <	rapid speech
< >	slow speech

2. Sacks, Schegloff, and Jefferson (1974) proposed that speaking turns in conversation consist of turn-constructional units (TCUs) that enable the speaker to project the shape of interaction and to allocate rights and obligations in talk. They suggested that TCUs are syntactic units (e.g., phrases, clauses, sentences) and invited linguists to contribute to the understanding of the nature of these units. Recent work by Ford and Thompson (1996) addresses this issue by taking into consideration not only syntactic structures but also intonation and conversational pragmatics.

3. The question of modification of speech on the part of both the native speaker and the non-native speaker in NS-NNS interaction has been addressed extensively by researchers such as Gass and

Varonis (1985), Long (1983), and Pica (1988) under the rubric of negotiation of meaning or negotiation of comprehensible input. It is important to point out, however, that interaction itself is negotiated and collaboratively accomplished and that each moment in interaction is a moment of negotiation of meaning.

References

Anderson-Hsieh, Janet, and Kenneth Koehler. 1988. "The Effect of Foreign Accent and Speaking Rate on Native Speaker Comprehension." *Language Learning* 38.561–613.

Atkinson, J. Maxwell, and John Heritage, eds. 1984. *Structures of Social Action: Studies in Conversation Analysis*. Cambridge: Cambridge University Press.

Bachman, Lyle. 1990. *Fundamental Considerations in Language Testing*. Oxford: Oxford University Press.

Bailey, Kathleen M., Frank Pialorsi, and Jean Zukowski/Faust. 1984. *Foreign Teaching Assistants in U.S. Universities*. Washington, DC: National Association of Foreign Student Advisors.

Button, Graham. 1987. "Answers as Interactional Products: Two Sequential Practices in Interviews." *Social Psychology Quarterly* 50.160–171.

Byrd, Patricia, Janet Constantinides, and Martha Bennington. 1989. *The Foreign Teaching Assistant's Manual*. New York: Collier MacMillan.

Davies, Catherine E., Andrea Tyler, and John J. Koran, Jr. 1989. "Face-to-face with English Speakers: An Advanced Training Class for International Teaching Assistants." *English for Specific Purposes* 8.139–153.

Drew, Paul. 1995, February. "'What?' A Sequential Basis for an Open Form of Repair Initiation in Conversation (and Some Implications for Cognitive Approaches to Interaction)." Paper presented at the Georgetown Linguistics Society Conference, Washington, DC.

Drew, Paul, and John Heritage, eds. 1992. *Talk at Work*. New York: Cambridge University Press.

Egbert, Maria M. 1998. "Miscommunication in Language Proficiency Interviews of First-Year German Students: A Comparison with Natural Conversation." In *Talking and Testing: Discourse Approaches to the Assessment of Oral Proficiency*, ed. by Richard Young and Agnes W. He, 147–169. Amsterdam and Philadelphia: Benjamins.

Ford, Cecilia E., and Sandra Thompson. 1996. "Interactional Units in Conversation: Syntactic, Intonational, and Pragmatic Resources for the Management of Turns." In *Interaction and Grammar*, ed. by Elinor Ochs, Emanuel A. Schegloff and Sandra Thompson, 134–184. Cambridge: Cambridge University Press.

Gass, Susan M., and Evangeline M. Varonis. 1985. "Variation in Native Speaker Speech Modification to Non-Native Speakers." *Studies in Second Language Acquisition* 7.37–57.

He, Agnes W. 1994, March. "Elicited vs. Volunteered Elaboration: Talk and Task in Language Proficiency Interviews." Paper presented at the annual conference of the American Association for Applied Linguistics, Baltimore, Maryland.

Hoekje, Barbara, and Kimberly Linnell. 1994. "'Authenticity' in Language Testing: Evaluating Spoken Language Tests for ITAs." *TESOL Quarterly* 28.103–126.

Lazaraton, Anne. 1992. "The Structural Organization of a Language Interview: A Conversation Analytic Perspective." *System* 20.373–386.

Levinson, Stephen C. 1979. "Activity Types and Language." *Linguistics* 17.365–399.

Long, Michael H. 1983. "Native Speaker/Non-Native Speaker Conversation and the Negotiation of Comprehensible Input." *Applied Linguistics* 4.126–141.

Madden, Carolyn G., and Cynthia L. Myers, eds. 1994. *Discourse and Performance of International Teaching Assistants*. Alexandria, VA: TESOL.

Marlaire, Courtney L., and Douglas W. Maynard. 1990. "Standardized Testing as an Interactional Phenomenon." *Sociology of Education* 63.83–101.

Maynard, Douglas W., and Courtney L. Marlaire. 1992. "Good Reasons for Bad Testing Performance: The Interactional Substrate of Educational Exams." *Qualitative Sociology* 15.177–202.

Pica, Teresa P. 1988. "Interlanguage Adjustments as an Outcome of NS-NNS Negotiated Interaction." *Language Learning* 38.45–73.

Pica, Teresa P., Gregory A. Barnes, and Alexis Finger. 1990. *Teaching Matters: Skills and Strategies for International Teaching Assistants*. New York: Newbury House.

Riggenbach, Heidi. 1991. "Towards an Understanding of Fluency: A Microanalysis of Nonnative Speaker Conversations." *Discourse Processes* 14.423–441.

Ross, Steven. 1998. "Divergent Frame Interpretation in Oral Proficiency Interview Interaction." In *Talking and Testing: Discourse Approaches to the Assessment of Oral Proficiency*, ed. by Richard Young and Agnes W. He, 333–353. Amsterdam and Philadelphia: Benjamins.

Ross, Steven, and Richard Berwick. 1992. "The Discourse of Accommodation in Oral Proficiency Interviews." *Studies in Second Language Acquisition* 14.159–176.

Rounds, Patricia L. 1987. "Characterizing Successful Classroom Discourse for NNS Teaching Assistant Training." *TESOL Quarterly* 21.643–672.

Sacks, Harvey. 1992. *Lectures on Conversation*, vols. 1 and 2. Cambridge, MA: Blackwell.

Sacks, Harvey, Emanuel A. Schegloff, and Gail Jefferson. 1974. "A Simplest Systematics for the Organization of Turn-taking for Conversation." *Language* 50.696–735.

Schegloff, Emanuel A. 1972. "Notes on a Conversational Practice: Formulating Place." In *Studies in Social Interaction*, ed. by David Sudnow, 75–119. New York: Free Press.

Schegloff, Emanuel. A. 1982. "Discourse as an Interactional Achievement: Some Uses of 'Uh Huh' and Other Things that Come Between Sentences." In *Georgetown University Roundtable on Languages and Linguistics*, ed. by Deborah Tannen, 71–93. Washington, DC: Georgetown University Press.

Schegloff, Emanuel A., Gail Jefferson, and Harvey Sacks. 1977. "The Preference for Self-correction in the Organization of Repair in Conversation." *Language* 53.361–82.

Smith, Jan, Colleen M. Meyers, and Amy J. Burkhalter. 1992. *Communicate: Strategies for International Teaching Assistants*. Englewood Cliffs, NJ: Prentice Hall/Regents.

Tao, Hongyin, and Sandra Thompson. 1991. "English Backchannels in Mandarin Conversations: A Case Study of Superstratum Pragmatic 'Interference'." *Journal of Pragmatics* 16.209–223.

Tyler, Andrea. 1992. "Discourse Structure and the Perception of Incoherence in International Teaching Assistants' Spoken Discourse." *TESOL Quarterly* 26.713–729.

van Lier, Leo. 1989. "Reeling, Writhing, Drawling, Stretching, and Fainting in Coils: Oral Proficiency Interviews as Conversation." *TESOL Quarterly* 23.489–508.

Williams, Jessica. 1992. "Planning, Discourse Marking, and the Comprehensibility of International Teaching Assistants." *TESOL Quarterly* 26.693–711.

Young, Richard. 1995. "Conversational Styles in Language Proficiency Interviews." *Language Learning* 45.3–42.

Framing the Language Proficiency Interview as a Speech Event: Native and Non-Native Speakers' Questions

Carol Lynn Moder and Gene B. Halleck
Oklahoma State University

1 Interviews and Conversation

Language proficiency interviews and, in particular, the American Council on the Teaching of Foreign Languages Oral Proficiency Interview (ACTFL OPI), have been the subject of some debate concerning the extent to which they can adequately represent a student's communicative competence (Bachman and Savignon 1986, Kramsch 1986). Those who have taken the position that the OPI is not an authentic communicative situation have done so largely on the basis of intuitive comparisons between the situations involved in informal conversation and those involved in the OPI, suggesting that the OPI measures language in a situation that is not representative of those in which non-native speakers will typically communicate (Clark 1972, Clark and Clifford 1988, Lantolf and Frawley 1985, Raffaldini 1988, van Lier 1989). One example is the approach of van Lier (1989), who suggests that although the OPI has the potential to elicit conversational language, it does not often do so. He contrasts "existing interviewing practices" with "interaction in genuine conversation" (p. 500), suggesting that the two are not only different, but that "it is so difficult to attain conversation in the formal context of an OPI" (p. 501). Standing in opposition to the work of those critiquing the OPI is the discourse analytic approach of Ross and Berwick (1992:160), who characterize the OPI as "a hybrid of interview and conversational interaction." This research and that of Ross (1992) highlight the features of face-to-face interactions that do occur in the OPI, with a particular focus on various forms of linguistic accommodation.

The difficulty with trying to determine whether the OPI can be viewed as an instance of conversation is the ambiguity with which that term has been used by researchers. If we consider conversation in its broadest terms to be equivalent to any kind of talk-in-interaction (Stenstrom 1984, Orestrom 1983), then the OPI is a clear instance of conversation. The alternative view is to categorize conversation as one type of speech exchange system and to categorize meetings, debates, and interviews as distinct types (Sacks, Schegloff, and Jefferson 1974). If we adopt this latter view, the OPI is clearly not a conversation. Indeed, it was not designed to mirror conversation; it was designed to take place within the context of a distinct speech event, the interview. As Bragger (1985:44) points out, although the OPI "may seem like an unstructured, informal conversation," it is in fact a highly structured instrument with four distinct phases developed to elicit a wide range of linguistic tasks.

But the fact that the ACTFL OPI does not measure proficiency in an informal conversational context does not establish that it is an inadequate measure of communicative competence. In fact, we may well question whether it would be more appropriate as a language test if it were an informal conversation. Researchers who have critiqued the OPI as not authentically conversational have assumed that conversation is the primary speech event in which learners participate and have typically taken informal, non-purposive conversation as their model. But informal conversation is only one type of speech event in which communication takes place, and it is probably no more representative of the events in which non-native speakers participate than other speech events. For many non-native speakers, the majority of their interactions in English may occur in contexts where there is an institutionally based power discrepancy between participants and where the interaction is purposive. As Hymes (1972) has indicated, communicative competence encompasses the ability to interact in a wide variety of sociolinguistic situations, among which informal conversation is just one type of speech event. Other speech events, and the interview in particular, are not only common but also have significant consequences, making them more critical for the participants. Thus, in this paper, rather than focus on the extent to which the OPI mirrors informal conversation, we address the OPI within the context of the interview frame (Goffman 1974, 1981; Schiffrin 1994). Since a second major concern of those critiquing the OPI is the lack of native speaker norms for interaction, we focus first on the parameters of the interview frame as it is used by native speakers and on the findings of studies of native speakers' behavior in interviews. Following this discussion, we compare the use of the interview frame in the OPI by native speakers and non-native speakers.

Interviews are a critical part of everyday life. Many encounters in institutional settings involve interviews of one type or another, running the gamut from brief service encounters to job interviews. Furthermore, these encounters are likely to involve significant consequences for the participants, determining access to services or occupational opportunities. Thus an understanding of the structure of expectations relevant to the interview—the interview frame—is a crucial part of a speaker's communicative competence. Although the specific expectations relevant to interviews vary across contexts, the majority of interviews share certain important features. These features typically include an institutional setting in which two participants—an interviewer and an interviewee—interact for a particular institutionally relevant purpose. There is usually an asymmetry in the positions of the participants, either because of the power of one participant to make decisions concerning the other or because of an asymmetry in the information held by the participants. The interview frame also constrains the interactional roles of the participants in the interview. It gives the interviewer the power to control the interaction, determining how it will be conducted and the topics to be discussed, and it constrains the interviewee to respond to the interviewer's questions and provide information to be evaluated (Akinnaso and Ajirotutu 1982, Gumperz and Cook-Gumperz 1982, Fiksdal 1989).

On the other hand, the way in which the interview frame is realized depends to a large extent on the specific context in which it occurs. One pervasive type of interview, which has distinctive characteristics, is the job interview. Akinnaso and Ajirotutu (1982:120) define the frame of the job interview as "an interrogative encounter between someone who has the right or privilege to know and another in a less powerful position who is obliged to respond, rather defensively, to justify his/her action, to explain his/her problems, to give him/herself up for evaluation." As this definition suggests, they describe the interviewer's questions as the focus of the speech event. Furthermore, they indicate that interview questions are often indirect, requiring the interviewee to infer the type of answer that is appropriate. They analyze job interviews with two African Americans, one with previous experience with job interviews and the other without. The less experienced interviewee used strategies more characteristic of informal conversations, and often failed to infer the requirements of the question; the more experienced interviewee correctly inferred the types of responses required by the situation. This study suggests that the use of questions in interviews may be distinct from their use in less purposive communicative settings.

Two other types of interview—the library reference desk interview and the sociolinguistic interview—were examined by Schiffrin (1994). She found that the framework of each type of interview had an effect on the speech acts performed. By using Hymes's (1972) taxonomy for encoding speech events, she showed that two elements—the participants and their respective ends—had an effect on the discourse, most specifically on the number and types of questions the participants asked.

According to Schiffrin's analysis, the reference interview takes place at the librarian's desk and usually involves two participants, the library patron and the reference librarian. In a reference interview the participants share a common end: the resolution of the patron's problem or inquiry. Given the asymmetric distribution of the knowledge necessary to resolve the problem, the participants' use of questions is also asymmetric. The librarian makes offers, the patron issues queries, and both request clarification. The result is a short, focused encounter in which question-and-answer sequences are used collaboratively to reach the shared goal.

The sociolinguistic interview, on the other hand, exhibits a different participant framework and different ends according to Schiffrin. The sociolinguistic interview usually occurs in the interviewee's home and involves at least two participants, the researcher and the interviewee. The researcher's goal is to gather information on specific language patterns, social practices, and attitudes of the interviewee. While the interviewee is usually aware of the general interests of the researcher, he or she is not aware of the more specific patterns the researcher hopes to elicit. Furthermore, some of the covert goals of the sociolinguistic researcher—such as avoiding question-and-answer patterns and eliciting a variety of styles and types of talk—are at odds with the general interview frame. Thus there may be a discrepancy between the interviewer's frame for the interview and that of the interviewee.

Schiffrin found that the asymmetrical roles and ends of the participants in the sociolinguistic interview led to a difference in the amount and type of questions they used. The interviewees asked many fewer questions than the interviewer. Schiffrin's analysis divides questions into three communicative types: information-seeking, information-checking, and clarification. *Information-seeking* questions are those in which the speaker lacks knowledge and attempts to gain it by posing a question to the hearer. Information-seeking questions take a variety of forms and may seek information on either general or specific topics. They may nominate a new topic or be related to the topic of prior discourse. In Schiffrin's interviews, information-seeking questions were almost exclusively asked by the interviewer. On the few occasions when such questions were used by the interviewee, Schiffrin (1994:165) reports that the interchanges "seemed less like interviews than conversations."

The second type of question is *information-checking*. These questions differ from information-seeking questions in that they do not seek unknown information; instead, they check whether the hearer has adequately processed a referent or proposition in the ongoing talk. By posing such questions, the speaker gives the hearer an opportunity to acknowledge the reception of the proposition or referent.

As defined by Schiffrin (1994:169), information-checking questions take many forms, including all typical interrogatives as well as particles with rising intonation like *see?*, *really?*, *oh?*, *right?*, and *you know?*. Information-checking questions were used by both types of participant in Schiffrin's interviews, but they were used in different ways. The interviewer used these questions to verify or acknowledge information in the interviewee's preceding utterance; the interviewee used them to check whether the interviewer had identified a referent or proposition in the speaker's utterance. The interviewer's use of information-checking questions had the additional effect of encouraging the interviewee to continue or take back the speaking turn.

The third type of question, *clarification*, occurs when a hearer has not heard or understood all or part of a previous utterance and asks the speaker to clarify it. These questions typically take the form of either a repetition of all or part of a previous utterance or a general question like *Pardon me?* or *What's ___?* (Schiffrin 1994:175). Clarification questions were used by both types of participants in the sociolinguistic interviews. The researcher usually asked for clarification of an answer from the interviewee, whereas the interviewee usually sought clarification of a question from the interviewer. Thus the use of questions clearly reflects one of the elements of the interview frame: it is the role of the interviewer to ask questions and the role of the interviewee to answer them adequately and appropriately.

Schiffrin's study clearly demonstrates that the participant framework and the ends of the participants are reflected in their use of language in the interview. Both types of interviews examined by Schiffrin may be considered atypical with respect to the relative power of the interviewer and interviewee. This is due in part to the fact that the ultimate outcome of these interviews will have little effect on the life of the interviewee. As a result, he or she is under no obligation to answer all the questions posed. This was clearly not the case with the job interviews studied by Akinnaso and Ajirotutu (1982), where the potential consequences of the interview for the interviewee were great and thus the obligation to answer the questions appropriately was also great.

The nature of the interview frame in the OPI shares many of the characteristics common to these other interview types. The OPI usually takes place in an institutional setting with two participants: an interviewer and an interviewee. The roles of the participants are constrained: the interviewer controls the interaction and the topics discussed, and the interviewee responds and provides information, which the interviewer will evaluate. Unlike the reference interview or the sociolinguistic interview but like the job interview, the OPI has important consequences for the interviewee, constraining him or her to respond in the most appropriate and contextually relevant manner. One way in which the OPI may be distinct from these other interview types is that it requires the interviewer to more stringently evaluate the language of the interviewee's responses. The language a candidate uses in a job interview is evaluated to some extent, but it is not typically the main focus of the interview. In the reference interview, the form of the utterances is not at all a focus as long as the communicative goal is attained. In the sociolinguistic interview, the language used by the interviewee is of particular interest to the interviewer, but, as we have discussed above, this goal is not usually known by the interviewee.

By contrast, in the OPI not only is the form of the utterances significant but their linguistic evaluation is also an overt goal, known to both participants. In this respect the OPI shares characteristics with other language proficiency interviews (Young 1995, Young and Milanovic 1992). Unlike those language proficiency interviews which script the questions to be asked, however, the OPI prescribes neither specific questions nor the content of the answers the interviewee must provide. The more spontaneous nature of the OPI makes it closer to other interview events. Furthermore, it should be noted that the OPI's goal of language evaluation is neither inauthentic nor communicatively inappropriate in the context of an interview, since the general participant framework of an interview already includes an evaluative goal on the part of one participant. The linguistic evaluation does not represent a distortion of the interview event but rather expands on its basic framework. In this sense the interview frame is a much more appropriate context in which to test language than is a conversation frame.

As we have seen, both Schiffrin's (1994) study and Akinnaso and Ajirotutu's (1982) highlight the centrality of the use of questions as an indicator of the roles of the participants in interview discourse. This chapter reports an investigation of the extent to which an OPI interviewer and native or non-native English-speaking interviewees conform to the general interview frame as indicated by the frequency and types of questions they use. If the language evaluation goal of the OPI significantly skews the interview frame, we would expect a different frequency and distribution of communicative question types in the OPIs as compared to those found in other interviews. We might also expect to find differences in the way the frame is interpreted in interviews with native and non-native English speakers, since the native speakers are presumably not as greatly affected by the language examination frame in their interviews. If, on the other hand, the OPI occurs within the same frame as other interviews, we would expect the question patterns to be similar for native and non-native speakers.

2 Methods: Turns and Questions

In recent years large corporations and universities have been turning to language tests for help in evaluating bilingual applicants for positions. As a result, the ACTFL OPI has been used not only for academic purposes but also as a job screening device in industry. The interviews analyzed in this paper were conducted for the purposes of screening the English language proficiency of applicants for positions both in the academic and corporate worlds.

We analyzed the ACTFL OPIs of twenty subjects. Ten were native speakers of English (NSs) and ten were speakers of English as a second language (NNSs). Within each group, five interviewees were female and five were male. The NNSs' language backgrounds include the following: Amharic (N = 1), Farsi (N = 1), Polish (N = 2), Tamil (N = 2), Telugu (N = 2), Tigrinya (N = 1), and Urdu (N = 1). The proficiency levels of all twenty interviewees were at the Advanced level or higher as defined by the ACTFL OPI guidelines (American Council on the Teaching of Foreign Languages 1986).[1]

Twelve of the interviews were conducted by telephone by the second author, an ACTFL-certified interviewer, as part of a screening process for bilingual positions at a large U.S.-based company. All of the NSs and two of the NNSs (the Polish candidates) were interviewed for these positions by telephone. The other eight interviews were conducted by the same ACTFL-certified interviewer as part of a pre-semester screening process to determine which international teaching assistants (ITAs) would be eligible to do classroom teaching at a large public university.

Interviews were tape-recorded and then transcribed and divided into turns. We considered each time a speaker held the floor to be a single turn. The subsequent turn began when the other participant took the floor. Instances in which the listener provided a backchannel cue like *uh-huh* or *yeah* that did not interrupt the current speaker's discourse or cause the speaking turn to shift were not counted as separate turns. We provide an example in Excerpt 1, taken from an interview with a NNS. In this and all subsequent examples, the interviewee is represented by the initial of his/her first name and the interviewer is indicated by the letter *I*. In (1) the interviewer has the first turn, in which she poses an information-seeking question. This results in a turn transition and *V*'s response begins a new turn. During *V*'s turn the interviewer provides several backchannel cues, which are shown in parentheses. None of these cues interrupts the flow of *V*'s discourse and his turn continues until he reaches the completion point of his response, *back to San Antonio*. The interviewer acknowledges the information in a new turn with the phrase *No kidding?*. This response, unlike her previous ones, receives an explicit acknowledgment from *V, yeah*, which begins his subsequent turn. Thus Excerpt 1 consists of four turns.

```
(1)   Turn segmentation

   I: If you had a choice would you want to live in New York
      again?
   V: Uh not really (I: Uh huh) I've gotten so used to San
      Antonio now (I: Yeah) that I've been back to home maybe
      about six years ago (I: Uh huh) and I was supposed to be
      there for two weeks and after one week I went to get
      back to San Antonio
   I: No kidding?
   V: Yeah, cause I- I was uh not used to all the noise, all
      the rush rush anymore . . .
```

We then identified all the questions in each turn of the interviewer and interviewees. Although researchers focusing on questions in discourse often include all interrogative speech acts regardless of the linguistic form of the utterance (Blakemore 1992, Tsui 1992, Weber 1993), in this study we counted as questions only those utterances that formally marked the interrogative, either syntactically or intonationally. We chose to count only the overtly marked questions for two reasons. First, counting questions in this manner requires fewer subjective judgments about the intentions of the speakers in the interaction and, therefore, makes the results more easily replicable. The second reason was that this method was employed by Schiffrin in her study, and we were interested in comparing the trends in our data with those in hers. It should be noted, however, that with this method our analysis undercounts interrogative speech acts, given that indirect marking is common and that, in an interview frame, the relevance conditions of the context imply that such utterances should typically be interpreted as requests for information. Examples of the types of indirect interrogative speech acts that were not counted as questions in our study are provided in Excerpts 2 and 3 below.

```
(2)   Indirect interrogative

      I: . . . You know President Bush's big war. Did you think
         we belonged there and we were doing the right thing?
      A: America has a very large stake in the Middle East. Not
         necessarily America but most of westernized nations
         are heavily dependent on oil. Oil is the basic
         ingredient of our economic growth and development.
```

>   Our economies is run by it. All the goods that are
>   shipped from manufacturers to the consumers are done
>   by truck. And it's very important part our economic
>   growth and I think that uh the policy that uh the
>   previous government followed was the correct one.
> → I: So what you're saying is that we were there because of
>   the oil. We weren't there because Saddam Hussein did
>   something wrong.
>   A: Well, Saddam Hussein has done a lot of things wrong
>   and we have never paid attention to it. It it there
>   were reports of atrocities against the Kurds in the
>   North as early as 81, 83 and we have done nothing
>   about it . . .

In (2), the highlighted turn indicated by the arrow explicitly summarizes the interviewer's understanding of the implications of A's previous turn. In the context of the interview, this utterance functions as an invitation for the interviewee to elaborate. Such an utterance can be viewed in the context as an indirect interrogative. In this study such utterances were counted as questions only if they were uttered with rising intonation (indicated in the transcripts with a final "?") and were not counted if they were uttered with falling intonation (indicated with a final ".").

(3) Indirect interrogative

>   D: . . . The life life here is really easy I mean
>   everything is made much simple but I can see there is
>   no family bonding which is very much back home. And I
>   really miss that.
> → I: Okay. I think you need to explain to me what you mean
>   by family bonding.
>   D: ah I can see here that eh the children especially
>   after they get into their teens the parents kind of
>   accept that their children are going through a phase
>   . . .

In Excerpt 3, the interviewer's highlighted utterance asks explicitly for D to clarify her previous utterance, but since it is syntactically formed as a declarative it was not counted as a question in this study.

After identifying all the explicitly marked questions in the transcripts, we categorized them according to Schiffrin's (1995) taxonomy into three communicative types: information-seeking, clarification, and information-checking. Examples from our data of each question type are provided below. The first question type, information-seeking, is illustrated in Excerpts 4 and 5. The questions relevant to each example are indicated with an arrow. In these excerpts, the speaker lacks information and asks the information-seeking question in order to gain it.

(4) Information-seeking question

      S: I can never be loyal to U.S. one hundred percent.
→   Don't count it. (laughs) Okay, it does, it does, does it go to CIA?
      I: No it's for my research.
      S: Okay. I don't think I will ever be because my parents . . .

In Excerpt 4 the NNS interviewee, *S*, having revealed potentially incriminating information about himself, interrupts his narration to find out what the interviewer will do with his audiotape. In the next turn the interviewer supplies this information, which the interviewee acknowledges before continuing.

(5) Information-seeking question

→   I: Does that make the quality of your life quite different, having Ethiopian colleagues?
→   T: Well sure. Have you been out of the United States?
      I: Yeah.
→   T: Did you live, I mean, not as a tourist?
      I: Uh huh.
      T: Oh, well, okay. Well then you can think how you know, the sense of an American, you know . . .

In Excerpt 5 the interviewer begins the exchange with an information-seeking question. The NNS, *T*, answers the question and follows it with a sequence of two of his own information-seeking questions, each of which is answered by the interviewer.

The second type of question, clarification, is illustrated in Excerpts 6 and 7.

(6) Clarification question

      W: . . . My aim is not to become a big shot. If I become (. . .) I'll be very happy.
      I: Well, why do we go to graduate school then if not to be a big shot?
→   W: Sorry?

I: What's the purpose of going to graduate school if you
   don't want to be a big shot. Just to learn?

In Excerpt 6 the interviewer asks an information-seeking question in response to *W*'s prior utterance. Before answering the question, *W* responds with a general clarification question, *Sorry?*, which elicits a rephrasing of the previous question by the interviewer.

A second subtype of clarification question sequence appears in (7), where the interviewee, *K*, poses a clarification question by repeating part of the previous utterance, *the best?*, and then proceeds without waiting for a response from the interviewer.

(7) Clarification question

    I: Could you tell me which city you like the best?
→ K: The best? Oh I can't tell you, you know, because . . .

The third main question type, information-checking, is exemplified in Excerpts 8 and 9. In (8) the non-native-speaking interviewee, *F*, introduces the topic of the movie, *Tron*, and then poses an information-checking question to verify the interviewer's familiarity with this referent. Following the interviewer's negative response, *F* goes on to provide background details.

(8) Information-checking question

    I: Can you tell me about one movie whi- which had some
   technology in it that was good?
    F: Well, the latest one that I've see- wasn't . . . it's
   kind of an older movie, but I, found it
→   interesting. It was um a movie called *Tron*. and
→   I don't know if you're familiar with that at all?
    I: *Tron*?
    F: *Tron*, yeah.
    I: No, I never heard of it.
    F: It was kinda more like uh, it was uh, an animated type
   show . . .

In Excerpt 9 the NNS interviewee, *W*, poses the information-checking question *You know?* within his own narration. The purpose of such questions is to verify that the listener has adequately received the proposition that preceded it and is following the flow of the discourse. Although in many cases such questions do not elicit an explicit answer, they do provide an opportunity for the listener to acknowledge receipt of the information either verbally or nonverbally.

(9) Information-checking question

```
I:   . . . .but we didn't get him out of Iraq. Should we
     have done more?
W:   Well, I think that is for the Iraqis to do that. I
     mean, you have no, I mean moral or political right to
     dislodge other peoples from their own country. I mean
     that's — he's an Iraqi and if the people don't like
     him, kick him out. Sometimes,
→    maybe they might need some help. You know?
```

3 Results

In order to address whether the OPI conforms to the general interview frame, we consider in this section whether the pattern of the distribution of questions we found in the OPIs was similar to that found by Schiffrin. In order to address the extent to which NS and NNS interviewees interpret the interview frame similarly in the context of the OPI, we compare first their general turn distribution patterns and then their patterns of question use. For each between-group comparison we examine the medians and the range of variation and, where appropriate, report the Mann-Whitney U statistic to determine whether the differences are significant at the $p < .05$ level.

3.1 *Distribution and Length of Turns*

Although all the interviews lasted between twenty-five and thirty minutes, there was some variation in the number and length of turns in each interview. Table 1 shows the median number of turns each interviewee took during the interview and the median number of words in each turn. The NNSs took significantly fewer turns than the NSs, as indicated by the Mann-Whitney U statistic ($U = 18, p < .05$). The difference in the number of turns each interviewee takes is related to the length of his or her turns. The NNS turns were significantly longer than the NS turns ($U = 76, p < .05$). The longer turns of the NNSs suggest that they interpret the interview as a situation that requires them to display more, while the NSs do not place as much importance on displaying in English, even though they are in a testing situation.

Table 1. Comparisons of NS and NNS Interviewees' Turns per Interview

Interviewees	Number of turns		Words per turn	
	Median	Range	Median	Range
NS	112	61–128	26	20–67
NNS	69	55–118	45	22–92
U	18		76	
p	<.05		<.05	

Given that the interviews were restricted to a specific length of time, the longer turns of the NNSs led to their interviews having fewer turns overall.

Table 2 shows the number of turns taken by the interviewer with NS and with NNS interviewees. As expected in an interview context, the interviewer's number of turns is either the same as the number for the interviewee or one turn greater, if her turns begin and end the interview. Thus the interviewer takes significantly more turns in interviews with NSs than in those with NNSs ($U = 18, p < .05$). On the other hand, the length of the interviewer's turns did not differ with the native language of the interviewee ($U = 48, p > .05$).

Table 2. Comparisons of Interviewer's Turns per Interview with NS and NNS Interviewees

Interviewer	Number of turns		Words per turn	
	Median	Range	Median	Range
NS	112	61–129	13	10–18
NNS	69.5	55–118	12	9–22
U	18		48	
p	<.05		n.s.	

The results of the analysis of the distribution and length of turns reflect the asymmetry typically found in interviews. One participant, the interviewer, strictly limits the length of her turns, while the interviewee produces much longer turns. This asymmetry was found in interviews with both NSs and NNSs, even though the actual length of the interviewees' turns differed. The typical turns of the NS interviewees were twice as long as those of the interviewer, while the turns of the NNSs were three times longer than the interviewer's.

As we have discussed above, one important aspect of the interview frame is the constraints it puts on the question-asking behavior of both the interviewer and interviewees. If the NSs and the NNSs are both drawing on the general interview frame, we would expect there to be a similarity in the frequency and types of questions used by the participants.

3.2 *Question Frequency*

If we consider the number of questions asked by the interviewees, we find a significant difference between NSs and NNSs. As shown in Table 3, the NS interviewees asked a median of 10.5 questions per interview, while the NNSs asked a median of only 5 questions per interview ($U = 22, p < .05$). The median number of questions asked by the interviewer is slightly higher with NSs than with NNSs, but this difference is not significant ($U = 25, p > .05$). The number of questions asked—like the number of turns—may be affected by the length of the turns each interviewee takes. Since, as we discussed above, the NSs take shorter turns, they have more opportunities to ask questions than NNSs. Therefore it is not clear whether the difference in the number of questions asked by the interviewees is due to a significant difference in their interpretations of the interview frame or simply to a difference in their overall number of turns.

Table 3. Median Number of Turns per Interview with Questions for Interviewees and Interviewer

Interviewee	Median	Range	Interviewer	Median	Range
NS	10.5	2–19	NS interviewee	51.5	20–61
NNS	5.0	0–11	NNS interviewee	37.0	20–54
U	22			25	
p	< .05			n.s.	

We controlled for the length of the interviews by considering the percentage of turns in which a question was asked in a given interview. Table 4 shows that there is a similar percentage of turns in which the interviewee asks questions, with NSs asking questions in 7% of their turns and NNSs asking questions in 10%. This difference is not significant ($U = 32, p > .05$). The percentage of the turns in which the interviewer asks questions of NS and NNSs interviewees is also similar, 49% and 46% respectively. Again, the difference is not significant ($U = 59, p > .05$).

Both NS and NNS interviewees restrict the percentage of turns in which they ask questions, while the interviewer exercises her role as the participant responsible for posing questions and thereby also selecting topics. These percentages strongly support the participants' use of the interview frame to determine their roles. Were

Table 4. Percentage of turns per interview with questions for interviewees and interviewer

Interviewee	Percent	Interviewer	Percent
NS	7%	NS	49%
NNS	10%	NNS	46%
U	32		59
p	n.s.		n.s.

the interview frame not in operation, we might have expected the interviewees to ask more questions or the interviewer to have asked fewer, thereby conforming more to a conversational frame. This was clearly not the case in these interviews. Furthermore, although the NSs ask more questions overall than the NNSs, this difference seems to be related to their shorter turn length and the corresponding increase in their number of turns.

3.3 Interviewees' Question Types

The overall percentages of turns in which questions are asked may be similar, but the types of questions used may have been distributed quite differently. In order to check this, we examined the distribution of the three types of questions: information-seeking, clarification, and information-checking.

Table 5. Distribution of Interviewees' Question Types per Interview

	Information-seeking		Clarification		Information-checking	
Interviewee	Median	Range	Median	Range	Median	Range
NS	2	0–6	3	1–12	3	1–25
NNS	1	0–4	2	0–5	1	0–5
U	33.5		30		20.5	
p	n.s.		n.s.		<.05	

Table 5 shows that the median number of questions asked by NS and NNS interviewees is similar across all three questions types. There are, however, differences in the number of questions of each type asked by the interviewees. The first question type is the information-seeking question. Both the NSs and the NNSs asked a very limited number of these questions, ranging from 0 to 6 per interviewee in the entire 30-minute interview. The difference between the two groups was not significant ($U = 33.5, p > .05$). Thus all the interviewees show an understanding of their role in the interview frame: to provide answers to information-seeking questions, not to ask them.

The second type of question, clarification, occurred more frequently. The NNSs asked slightly fewer clarification questions than NS interviewees, who asked between 1 and 12 clarification questions per interview, as indicated in Table 5. This difference is also not significant ($U = 30, p > .05$). The lack of difference in the number of clarification questions used is surprising, given that we might typically expect NNSs to require greater clarification of utterances than NSs. We will examine this issue further in section 3.3.2.

The third major type of question, information-checking, was significantly more frequent in the discourse of NS interviewees. Table 5 shows that the NSs asked a median of 3 information-checking questions per interview, whereas NNS interviewees asked a median of 1. The NSs also showed a wider variation, ranging from 1 to 25 per interview, whereas the NNSs had a more limited range, from 0 to 5 information-checking questions per interview. The difference in the number of information-checking questions used by the two groups of interviewees was significant ($U = 20.5, p < .05$). Thus we have found that while NSs and NNSs do not differ in the number of information-seeking and clarification questions they ask during the OPI, they do differ significantly in their number of information-checking questions.

In order to provide further insights into this difference and into the ways in which the interviewees' use of questions defines the interview frame, in the following section we examine the contexts in which each of the three question types occurred.

3.3.1 *Information-seeking Questions in Context*

The contexts we examined suggested that the information-seeking questions could be divided into three subtypes, based on the ways in which they were used. Examples of these are shown in Excerpts 10, 11, and 12.

The first subtype appears in many of the interviews conducted by telephone, where the information-seeking questions were asked in order to establish contextual features relevant to the interaction. An example of this appears in Excerpt 10. *F*, a NS, asks the interviewer about her location, information that would have been obvious in a face-to-face encounter. This question is relevant to the discourse since the interviewee has heard background noises over the telephone, which he has attempted to use to identify the interviewer's setting. Such questions occurred occasionally in the interviews conducted by phone but were not necessary in the face-to-face interviews.

(10) Information-seeking questions by the interviewee

```
    I: Uh huh oh that's really great yeah. They are lucky.
 → F: Are you at home or in an office?
    I: I'm in an office
    F: Oh okay
```

In Excerpt 11 the second subtype occurs in response to the interviewer's explicit invitation, which gives *R* permission to ask a question. This is within the prerogative of the interviewer, since part of the interview frame gives her control of the format of the interaction. In our data, such invitations from the interviewer occurred only in the phone interviews, and then only occasionally. Both the NS and NNS interviewees responded to these invitations by asking information-seeking questions. The majority of the information-seeking questions asked by the interviewees fell into the two subtypes shown in (10) and (11).

(11) Information-seeking question by the interviewee

```
    I: Hum and on that positive note I think our interview is
       just about over. So unless you have any questions for
       me (R: No) we've done everything we have to do.
 → R: No. Do you know anybody named ***** here in Corpus?
    I: No I don't
    R: Oh I h-have a temporary job and-and we have somebody
       Tom *****.
    I: Oh really?
 → R: And why- I wondered if you're related?
    I: No. Well we probably . . .
```

Questions of the third subtype, exemplified in Excerpt 12, were extremely rare. In the part of the interview that preceded this excerpt, the interviewer had asked a series of questions about movies that *J*, a NS, liked. After providing responses to these questions over several turns, *J* took control of the questioning by posing the highlighted question, which temporarily broke the normal interview frame and evoked a more conversational style. In our interviews only two NS and two NNS interviewees asked such questions, and even in those cases such questions were restricted to only one portion of their interviews. The remainder of their interviews conformed to the interview frame.

(12) Information-seeking question by the interviewee
[previous discussion prompted by the interviewer's question
about movies J has seen and actors he likes]

    J: The voices of course. (I: uh huh) he has so many
       different voices
    I: Hum
→ J: What type of movies do you like to see?
    I: Well, I like Mrs. Doubtfire
    J: Did ya?
    I: Yeah I mean he- he is really good.

Thus the interviewees in the context of the OPI rarely used information-seeking questions, and then only in restricted contexts. These questions were typically prompted either by the need for contextual information missing because of the unusual setting of the phone interviews or by the interviewer's giving the interviewee permission to ask them. As was the case in Schiffrin's sociolinguistic interviews, the interviewees in the OPI rarely asked a true information-seeking question. Thus they revealed an understanding of their role as participants in the interview frame.

3.3.2 *Clarification Questions in Context*

In examining the frequency of clarification questions, we found that there was no significant difference between NSs and NNSs. Based on the findings of previous research, we might have expected the NNSs to require more clarification, owing to a lack of familiarity with certain linguistic features of the discourse. But if we look at the functions for which clarification questions are used in these interviews, we find that they do not typically focus on linguistic problems. We also find that there are some differences in the contexts in which NS and NNS interviewees use them.

Clarifications of the subtype shown in Excerpt 13 represent the most typical function of these questions.

(13) Clarification questions asked by interviewee

    I: Okay do you think America did the right thing by
       pulling out when it did?
→ H: Pulling out?
    I: Instead of . . .
→ H: For who? the people of region or United States?
    I: Well tell me either one

The interviewee asks the question *Pulling out?* to elicit verification of his understanding of the interviewer's prior question. It could be assumed that *H* asks the question because he does not understand the interviewer's phrase. With his follow-up questions, however, he does not ask for an explanation of the phrase, rather he asks for further specification of the scope of the interviewer's question. These follow-up questions lead us to conclude that the interviewee's clarification questions focus not on the linguistic form of the interviewer's question but on its intention. This was typical of the clarification questions in our data. Furthermore, the majority of the clarification requests by both NS and NNS interviewees were of this first subtype.

The second subtype of clarification question is illustrated in Excerpt 14. In this excerpt, *R* asks the clarification question but then proceeds to respond without waiting for an answer from the interviewer. This subtype was used more frequently by NSs than by NNSs, accounting for their slightly larger number of clarification requests. Approximately 30 per cent of the NSs' clarification questions were of this subtype, while the NNSs never used these. It is not clear whether this difference is due to distinctive interactional styles of individual participants or to a different interpretation of the interview frame itself.

(14)   Clarification question asked by interviewee

    I: . . . what do you like to do in your free time?
→ R: in my free time? Um I like to work in my yard. I have-
       I have over a hundred rose bushes.

Clarifications of the subtype shown in Excerpt 15 were very infrequently asked by the interviewees. The question from the interviewee, *It's not enough?*, is a break in the interview frame, since the interviewee, a NS, is not clarifying a question from the interviewer but rather is verifying an assertion the interviewer made. In this case, it could be argued that in her comment, *Yeah but two years of Japanese is not enough*, the interviewer broke the frame herself, taking on the role of information giver rather than information seeker. Since the interviewer is responsible for determining the format of the interaction in the interview, such shifts in participant role on the part of the interviewer may invite the interviewee to make the corresponding role shift.

(15)   Clarification question asked by interviewee

    V: I took two years, two years of Japanese.

```
I: Uh huh. Have you ever been to Japan?
V: No ma'am. I'd like to go there one of these days.
I: Yeah but two years of Japanese is not enough.
→ V: It's not enough?
I: No. I went to Japan with oh at least two years of
   Japanese and I couldn't say much at all.
```

Thus we find that both NSs and NNSs typically use clarification questions to verify their understanding of the interviewer's questions. In addition, NSs also use clarification questions as a preface to their own answers. Neither group of interviewees uses clarification requests frequently to verify an assertion made by the interviewer. These results, like those for information-seeking questions, parallel those of Schiffrin and support the interviewee's use of a general interview frame.

3.3.3 *Information-checking Questions*

In Table 5 we saw that NSs asked significantly more information-checking questions than NNSs. Examining the specific contexts in which the interviewees used questions of this type makes the nature of this difference clearer.

The information-checking questions fell into two subtypes. The first subtype is illustrated in Excerpt 16. In the prior discourse *J*, a NS, has talked about horror movies and books that she likes. The interviewer then asks her whether she is interested in a recent murder case. *J* indicates that she is not, giving the reason that begins Excerpt 16, followed by the information-checking question *You know what I mean?*. This question is posed by *J* in order to verify that the interviewer has received the proposition in the preceding utterance. The interviewer does not respond to this question. *J* then makes a stronger assertion of the same proposition and follows it with another information-checking question, *You know?*. This time the interviewer does acknowledge receipt of the proposition. This subtype of information-checking was very frequent among the NSs, but occurred only occasionally with NNSs.

```
(16) Information-checking questions by interviewee

→    J: that's too too too much real life (I: Oh) You know
        what I mean? That's such a reality that it could
        happen to anybody.
→       You know?
     I: Uh huh.
```

The second subtype of information-checking question appears in Excerpt 17. In this example, also from *J*'s interview, *J* asks the information-checking question in order to verify whether the interviewer has identified the referent on which her discourse will focus. After receiving a negative response, she continues, providing necessary background information. The interjection of this type of question was not common in the interviews; it appeared in only two NS and two NNS interviews.

(17) Information-checking question by interviewee

```
    I: Tell me about a scary book that you read. I don't like
       scary books. I don't really read them so I can learn
       vicariously through you
 →  J: Okay. Amityville Horror. I don't know if you've ever
       saw that movie?
    I: No I didn't
    J: Okay I saw the movie and I saw the book. Believe me
       the book is much better.
```

Thus information-checking questions, unlike the other two types, were used significantly more frequently by NS than by NNS interviewees. This is primarily due to the NSs' greater use of questions like *you know?* to involve the listener and monitor the information flow. It is possible that the increased use of this subtype of information-checking question by NSs indicates that they are taking a more informal approach to interaction within the interview frame. On the other hand, they may simply be employing an interactional style that they use more frequently than NNSs across various speech events.

In general, the use of questions by both NSs and NNS interviewees shows striking similarities to that found by Schiffrin in sociolinguistic interviews. Interviewees typically restrict their questions to those appropriate to their role as information givers rather than seekers. They ask few information-seeking questions, more typically using clarification and information-checking questions. The main functions for which they use these two questions are to assure that their answers are appropriate and that they are adequately understood and acknowledged by the interviewer. One distinctive finding of our study is the higher use of checking questions by NS interviewees. It is unclear, however, whether this increased use reflects a difference in interpretation of the interview frame. We turn now to an examination of the use of these three question types by the interviewer.

3.4 Interviewer's Question Types

The profile of the interviewer's questions also reflects the expectations typical in the interview frame. As shown in Table 6, information-seeking questions were overwhelmingly the most frequent type, followed by information-checking and then clarification questions.

Table 6. Distribution of Interviewer's Question Types per Interview

Interviewee	Information-seeking		Clarification		Information-checking	
	Median	Range	Median	Range	Median	Range
NS	45	17–58	2	0–9	9	5–17
NNS	34	17–54	1	1–4	2	0–5
U	29		38		50	
p	n.s.		n.s.		< .05	

The interviewer asked more information-seeking questions of the NS interviewees than of the NNSs, but this difference was not significant ($U = 29, p > .05$). The high frequency of information-seeking questions in interviews with both sets of interviewees highlights the main roles of the interviewer: to control the discourse by nominating topics, and to elicit a language sample for evaluation. This role was interpreted similarly whether the other participant was a NS or a NNS.

Unlike those of the interviewees, the interviewer's information-seeking questions were all of one subtype: they were true information-seeking questions of the type illustrated for the interviewees in Excerpt 12. Given the pervasiveness of the interviewer's use of this subtype of information-seeking question, such questions can be found in virtually all the examples we have previously discussed. They are especially prominent in the interviewer's first turns in Excerpts 1, 5, 7, 8, 9, 13, and 14.

The interviewer uses the second type of question—clarification—very infrequently in all interviews, as the figures in Table 6 illustrate. There was no significant difference in her use of clarification questions with the two groups of interviewees ($U = 38, p > .05$). As was the case with the question types used by the interviewees, the interviewer's interpretation of the interview frame can be further elucidated by examining the contexts in which she used these clarification questions.

Whereas the interviewees used clarification questions primarily to gain understanding of the purpose of the questions posed to them, the interviewer used them primarily to clarify the interviewee's response. The use of clarification questions most typical for the interviewer is exemplified in Excerpt 18.

(18) Clarification questions by interviewer

    G: My husband is also an artist uh I mean not all in the photography but he's a paint . . . he's painter uh painting artist. He paints and he makes films uh . . .
→   I: He makes films?
    G: Films yeah I mean uh some kind of artistic movies.

In (18), *G* describes her husband as an artist and then goes on to mention something about making films. The interviewer appears not to be sure that she has correctly understood exactly what *G*'s husband does. She repeats a portion of *G*'s utterance in an attempt to have her clarify this, which *G* does in the following utterance.

The third type of question—information-checking—occurs significantly more frequently in interviews with NSs than it does with NNSs $(U = .50, p < .05)$. If we view the primary function of an information-checking question to be verifying the interviewer's understanding of the interviewees' utterances, their greater frequency in interviews with NSs is surprising. But an examination of the contexts in which the questions occur shows that this is not their typical function in our data.

The two most common functions of the interviewer's information-checking questions appear in Excerpts 19 and 20.

(19) Information-checking question by interviewer

    R: And basically that's what makes it funny he's always playing jokes on his co-host and uh
→   I: So it's a comedy?
    R: Yes.

In (19), the interviewer draws an inference based on the previous response and prefaces it with *So*. This utterance serves as an invitation for the interviewee to elaborate. This subtype of information-checking question constituted 60 percent of the information-checking questions addressed to NS interviewees but only 40 percent of those addressed to NNSs. The larger number of this subtype of information-checking questions addressed to NNSs may be the result of a difference between the NNSs' conceptions of the interview frame and the interviewer's. As we discussed above, the NSs tended to have shorter turns, and therefore the interviewer made more attempts to draw them out with these questions.

The example in (20), *Really?*, is a more general response to the interviewee's previous utterance, but it also functions as a request for elaboration. This subtype was also more frequently addressed to NSs than to NNSs. Both of these subtypes of information-checking question conform to the interview frame, since they represent attempts by the interviewer to encourage more elaborate responses from the interviewees.

(20) Information-checking question by interviewer

```
     R: there's a lot of um movies that we like to watch when
        they're talking about uh child abuse or uh runaways
        and stuff like that. Me and my wife like to have the
        children sit down and watch those movies.
  →  I: Really?
     R: Yes, so they if they ever have problems . . .
```

The third subtype of information-checking question, when used by the interviewer, indicates a break in the interview frame. The example of this subtype in Excerpt 21 is a continuation of the excerpt previously illustrated in (12), in which the interviewee broke the frame by asking an information-seeking question. Since the interviewer is now the participant providing information rather than the one seeking it, she asks the information-checking question, *Did, did you see Shadowlands?*, in order to verify the hearer's familiarity with a focused referent. This question serves the same function as the information-checking question of the interviewee exemplified in Excerpt 17: it attempts to determine whether the hearer has adequately identified a focused referent. In using such questions, the interviewer temporarily adopts the role of interviewee and the subtype of information-checking question typical of that role. In only two interviews did the interviewer use such information-checking questions, and in both cases the interviewees were NSs.

(21) Information-checking question by interviewer

```
     J: What type of movies do you like to see?
     I: Well I like Mrs. Doubtfire.
     J: Did ya?
     I: Yeah, I mean he — he is really good. I saw
  →     Shadowlands. Did, did you see Shadowlands?
     J: No I haven't seen that one.
```

```
I:  It's about, yeah, an- a writer about two writers
    actually . . .
```

As we have seen, the interviewer's use of the three question types is more narrowly focused than that of the interviewees. The interviewer overwhelmingly uses information-seeking questions, which elicit information on a topic from the interviewee. This question type is complemented by the use of information-checking questions, which invite the interviewee to elaborate on a previous utterance. Such information-seeking questions were used more frequently with NS interviewees than with NNSs. Occasionally the interviewer uses the third type of question—clarification—to ask the interviewee to rephrase or explain an utterance. Breaks in the interview frame, indicated by a deviation from the use of these question types in these specific functions, occurred very rarely but did occur with both native and non-native interviewees.

As we have seen, the interviewer's use of the various question types is more restricted than the interviewees'. The interviewer elicits information initially with information-seeking questions and invites elaboration with information-checking questions. The use of information-checking questions to elicit elaboration was more frequent in the interviews with NSs, largely because of their shorter responses. Only occasionally does the interviewer ask either a NS or NNS interviewee for clarification of a previous utterance. The interviewer's use of all three question types conforms to the patterns that Schiffrin found in the sociolinguistic interviews, suggesting that the interviewer in the OPI conforms to the participant roles of the general interview frame. Furthermore, the use of these questions indicates a similar interpretation of the frame irrespective of whether the interviewees are NSs or NNSs. The one exception to this is the interviewer's greater use of information-checking questions with NSs. This use is also consistent with the interview frame, however, since she uses these questions primarily to encourage elaboration on the part of the interviewee. Since the appropriate length of an interviewee's turn varies with the specific context in which the interview frame is used, such cooperative attempts to negotiate an appropriate turn length may be a typical feature of the frame.

4 Discussion

This study investigated the use of questions by an interviewer and interviewees in the OPIs of NSs and NNSs of English in order to determine whether they interpreted the frame of the interview in similar or in distinct ways.

Our analysis of the number and length of the turns taken by the interviewees showed significant differences: the NSs took more turns and used fewer words in each turn than the NNSs. This may suggest a difference in the way these speakers interpret their role. The NSs were more willing to give short, unelaborated answers, which required the interviewer to use various strategies to elicit greater detail. In contrast, the NNSs clearly understood the expectation for more detailed answers. This difference may be due to their greater experience in interview settings. In our sample the NNSs, in particular those being screened for university teaching positions, had a higher level of education than the NSs, most of whom were not college graduates. This may have resulted in a greater familiarity with the nature of formal interview settings on the part of NNSs. As Akinnaso and Ajirotutu (1982) found, even for NSs, experience in formal interview settings made a great difference in the response strategies of interviewees. An alternative explanation may be that the NNSs were more familiar with the display requirements of a language proficiency test. Young (1995) has shown that advanced learners of English are aware of the requirements of the language proficiency interview, in which a question requires not only a content answer but one that specifically displays the language competence of the interviewee. Such knowledge may not have been part of the native speakers' frame for the interview.

Based on Schiffrin's study, we expected to find a discrepancy in the number and types of questions asked by the interviewer and interviewees. This expectation was confirmed. The question type used most often by the interviewer was the information-seeking question, the primary function of which is to nominate a topic and elicit a response from the interviewees. Her other major question type was the information-checking question, which functioned primarily to elicit elaboration on a previously nominated topic. The interviewer used this question type much less frequently overall than the information-seeking question. Her least frequent question type was the clarification question, which clarifies ambiguous or unclear information in the interviewee's previous utterance.

The interviewees, in contrast, asked many fewer questions overall, and these were distributed more evenly over the three question types. The vast majority of their uses of these questions reflects their role within the interview frame. They most frequently asked clarification questions, the focus of which was the interviewer's prior question. Questions of this sort may have two types of focus: the interviewee may be asking for a clarification of either the linguistic content of the interviewer's questions or the interviewer's communicative intention in asking it. In his study of OPIs conducted with interviewees whose proficiency levels ranged from high-intermediate to superior, Ross (1992) found the former: the interviewees' use of clarification requests was primarily a result of misunderstanding the language of the question. In our interviews, such linguistically based misunderstandings were rare, possibly due to the higher proficiency level of our interviewees. What is most notable in our study is that both the NSs and NNSs typically used clarification questions to verify their understanding of the interviewer's focus in asking the question, indicating that they were attempting to provide an answer that was optimally relevant in the context (cf. Sperber and Wilson 1995). This is strong evidence that the OPI involves one of the fundamental principles underlying communicative competence.

The interviewees' use of information-checking questions gives evidence of their sensitivity to the co-constructed nature of the discourse. These questions are primarily used to judge the background knowledge of the interviewer in order to gauge the appropriate amount of information that must be provided in an optimally relevant response. This use was common to both NS and NNS interviewees. In addition, some interviewees, most of whom were NSs, used information-checking questions like *you know?* in order to get acknowledgment from the interviewer of the receipt of a referent or proposition and to monitor her involvement in the discourse. Although this use of these questions was found in many of the interviews, the frequency with which it occurred varied widely across individuals. The frequency difference may indicate that some NNSs adopt a more informal style in the interview frame, or it may reflect a general difference in the personal interaction style of the interviewee. Thus the interviewees' use of information-checking questions suggests that they are all sensitive to the need for co-constructing the discourse but some of them use these questions to monitor involvement more overtly.

Finally, the limited use of information-seeking questions on the part of the interviewees is a clear indication that they understand and accept that their role as participants is not to seek information or nominate topics. They use these questions to fill in necessary contextual information as needed to tailor their responses to the situation. Only occasionally do they ask such questions in a way that breaks the interview frame.

5 Conclusions

The results of this investigation of the questions asked in the OPI strongly support the operation of the general interview frame in this context. The comparison of the interviews of NSs and NNSs indicates that the frame is interpreted similarly, suggesting that the examination frame does not override the communicative frame of the event. This suggests that the OPI can be viewed as an authentic instance of talk-in-interaction. It is not an informal conversation, but it does sample the communicative behavior of interviewees in an authentic speech event. If we accept the OPI as an instance of a speech event distinct from informal conversation, we may then ask which aspects of communicative competence are sampled in such a frame. It is clear that some aspects of communicative competence highlighted in informal conversations are not highlighted in the interview frame. These would include nomination and control of topic by the interviewee, as well as other aspects of turn-taking relevant to situations in which turns are not tightly controlled. As Young (1995) has suggested, language proficiency interviews, particularly the structured interviews he examined, provide little opportunity for interviewees to show their abilities to obtain and keep the conversational floor. Our study confirms this. While there were occasional frame breaks in which interviewees briefly took control of turn allocation, such occurrences are not part of the general interview frame and are not common in the OPI. But many other aspects of talk-in-interaction are involved in interviews. Previous studies by Ross (1992) and Ross and Berwick (1992) have provided ample evidence that linguistic accommodations necessary to various communicative settings do occur in the OPI. In our study we have highlighted other aspects of communicative behavior, in particular, questioning strategies involved in the co-construction of discourse and the interpretation and formation of utterances that are optimally relevant in the context.

If we wish to determine the validity of the OPI as a test of communicative competence, we must carefully examine the behaviors that occur in the interview frame and consider how representative these behaviors are of those in which the interviewees typically engage. Such studies must be based on an analysis of the actual communicative needs and behaviors of speakers, not on intuitions or introspection alone. Further discourse-based studies of the nature of the language used in the interview frame will allow us to more productively assess the representativeness of the communicative behavior sampled in the OPI.

Note

1. The ACTFL guidelines (American Council on the Teaching of Foreign Languages 1986) define the competence of the Advanced-level speaker as follows:

> Able to satisfy the requirements of everyday situations and routine school and work requirements. Can handle with confidence but not with facility complicated tasks and social situations, such as elaborating, complaining apologizing. Can narrate and describe with some details, linking sentences together smoothly. Can communicate facts and talk casually about

topics of current public and personal interest, using general vocabulary. Shortcomings can often be smoothed over by communicative strategies, such as pause fillers, stalling devices, and different rates of speech. Circumlocution that arises from vocabulary or syntactic limitations very often is quite successful, though some groping for words may still be evident. The Advanced-level speaker can be understood without difficulty by native interlocutors.

References

Akinnaso, F. Niya, and Cheryl Seabrook Ajirotutu. 1982. "Performance and Ethnic Style in Job Interviews." In *Language and Social Identity*, ed. by John J. Gumperz, 119–144. Cambridge: Cambridge University Press.

American Council on the Teaching of Foreign Languages. 1986. *ACTFL Proficiency Guidelines*. Hastings-on-Hudson, NY: Author.

Bachman, Lyle F., and Sandra J. Savignon. 1986. "The Evaluation of Communicative Language Proficiency: A Critique of the ACTFL Oral Interview." *Modern Language Journal* 70.380–390.

Blakemore, Diane. 1992. *Understanding Utterances: An Approach to Pragmatics*. Cambridge, MA: Blackwell.

Bragger, Jeannette. 1985. "The Development of Oral Proficiency." In *Proficiency, Curriculum, Articulation: The Ties that Bind*, ed. by Alice Omaggio, 41–75. Middlebury, VT: Northeast Conference on the Teaching of Foreign Languages.

Clark, John L. D. 1972. "Measurement Implications of Recent Trends in Foreign Language Testing." *ACTFL Review of Foreign Language Education* 4.219–257.

Clark, John L. D., and Ray T. Clifford. 1988. "The FSI/ILR/ACTFL Proficiency Scales and Testing Techniques: Development, Current Status, and Needed Research." *Studies in Second Language Acquisition* 10.129–147.

Fiksdal, Susan. 1989. "Framing Uncomfortable Moments in Crosscultural Gatekeeping Interviews." In *Variation in Second Language Acquisition*, vol. 1: *Discourse and Pragmatics*, ed. by Susan Gass, Carolyn Madden, Dennis Preston, and Larry Selinker, 190–207. Philadelphia: Multilingual Matters.

Goffman, Erving. 1974. *Frame Analysis*. New York: Harper and Row.

Goffman, Erving. 1981. *Forms of Talk*. Philadelphia: University of Pennsylvania Press.

Gumperz, John J., and Jenny Cook-Gumperz. 1982. "Introduction." In *Language and Social Identity*, ed. by John J. Gumperz, 1–21. Cambridge: Cambridge University Press.

Hymes, Dell. 1972. "Towards Ethnographies of Communication: The Analysis of Communicative Events." In *Language and Social Context*, ed. by Pierpaolo Giglioli, 21–43. Harmondsworth, Middlesex: Penguin.

Kramsch, Claire. 1986. "From Language Proficiency to Interactional Competence." *Modern Language Journal* 70.366–372.

Lantolf, James P., and William Frawley. 1985. "Oral Proficiency Testing: A Critical Analysis." *Modern Language Journal* 69.337–345.

Orestrom, Bengt. 1983. *Turn-taking in English Conversation* (= *Lund Studies in English*, 66). Malmo, Sweden: CLK Gleerup.

Raffaldini, Tina. 1988. "The Use of Situation Tests as Measures of Communicative Ability." *Studies in Second Language Acquisition* 10.197–216.

Ross, Steven. 1992. "Accommodative Questions in Oral Proficiency Interviews." *Language Testing* 9.173–186.

Ross, Steven, and Richard Berwick. 1992. "The Discourse of Accommodation in Oral Proficiency Interviews." *Studies in Second Language Acquisition* 14.159–176.

Sacks, Harvey, Emanuel A. Schegloff, and Gail Jefferson. 1974. "A Simplest Systematics for the Organization of Turn-taking in Conversation." *Language* 50.696–735.

Schiffrin, Deborah. 1994. *Approaches to Discourse*. Cambridge, MA: Blackwell.

Sperber, Dan, and Deidre Wilson. 1995. *Relevance: Communication and Cognition* (2nd ed.). Cambridge, MA: Blackwell.

Stenstrom, Anna-Brita. 1984. *Questions and Responses in English Conversation* (= *Lund Studies in English*, 68). Malmo, Sweden: CLK Gleerup.

Tsui, Amy. 1992. "A Functional Description of Questions." In *Advances in Spoken Discourse Analysis*, ed. by Malcolm Coulthard, 89–110. NY: Routledge.

van Lier, Leo. 1989. "Reeling, Writhing, Drawling, Stretching, and Fainting in Coils: Oral Proficiency Interviews in Conversation." *TESOL Quarterly* 23.489–508.

Weber, Elizabeth G. 1993. *Varieties of Questions in English Conversation*. Amsterdam and Philadelphia: Benjamins.

Young, Richard. 1995. "Conversational Styles in Language Proficiency Interviews." *Language Learning* 45.3–42.

Young, Richard, and Michael Milanovic. 1992. "Discourse Variation in Oral Proficiency Interviews." *Studies in Second Language Acquisition* 14.403–424.

Miscommunication in Language Proficiency Interviews of First-Year German Students: A Comparison with Natural Conversation

Maria M. Egbert
University of Texas at Austin

1 Introduction

The goal of language proficiency interviews (LPIs) is to evaluate how well a language learner might function in conversation with native speakers of the target language.[1] Oral interviews are needed as language proficiency tests because "it is not feasible to follow learners around to see how well they perform in non-instructional settings" (van Lier 1989:494). Hence LPIs are implemented in imitation of natural conversation in order to evaluate a learner's conversational proficiency. Bachman points out that "one of the main preoccupations in language testing for the past quarter of a century (at least) has been a sincere concern to somehow capture or recreate in language tests the essence of language use, to make our language tests 'authentic'" (Bachman 1990:300). This desideratum presupposes that we should study language use in natural conversation in order to be able to simulate it in LPIs. But the LPI was implemented without ever establishing whether LPIs can actually simulate conversation or exactly what specific characteristics they might share with conversation.

Although recent studies in discourse analysis have examined speech in oral language tests (Bennett and Slaughter 1983, Fiksdal 1990, Lazaraton 1991, Lazaraton 1997, Young 1995), systematic comparisons of LPIs with natural conversation are needed. Bachman states the need to gain an understanding "of the nature of communicative language use" as one of the fundamental needs in test development (1990:8). Likewise, van Lier (1989:492) proposes that "we need detailed discourse studies of language—interlanguage—use in action, and this involves taking stock of current work in sociology, particularly conversation analysis, as well as microethnographic studies of our language learners at work using the second language in different situations—classrooms, OPIs, and other settings." The present study is an investigation of how exactly the two participation frameworks of the LPI and natural conversation differ. It focuses on one particular mechanism underlying talk-in-interaction—that of other-initiated repair, that is, how interactants deal with trouble in hearing or understanding one another's talk.

Using conversation analysis (CA) in the tradition of Sacks, Schegloff, and Jefferson (1974), this study examines how both the language learner and the interviewer orient through the talk used in repair sequences to the participation framework of the LPI. CA, or the study of talk-in-interaction, is an empirical research methodology with the goal of understanding the social structure underlying interaction. It is data driven and examines naturally occurring instances of social interaction in conversation or institutional interaction. "The central goal of conversation analysis research is the description and explication of the competencies that ordinary speakers use and rely on in participating in intelligible, socially organized interaction" (Atkinson and Heritage 1984:1). CA studies not only ordinary or everyday conversation but also interaction in institutions. Given that everyday conversation is "a primordial site of sociality" (Schegloff 1992:1296), interactions in institutional settings are analyzed to determine how "participants' institutional or professional identities are somehow made relevant to the work activities in which they are engaged" (Drew and Heritage 1992:4).

Methodologically, this paper's conversation analytic study of repair in LPIs with German students presents a complex task. Ideally, we need a complete analysis of repair in the following settings: (1) repair in everyday German conversation as a benchmark; (2) repair in a variety of interview settings to compare how LPIs show similarities and differences with other types of interviews; (3) repair in dyadic interactions between native German speakers and learners of German with about two semesters of classroom instruction in the language (the talk of the native speakers and the talk of the learners have to be distinguished from each other); and (4) repair in everyday American conversation because learners might transfer repair strategies from their first language. Such background knowledge would enable us to pinpoint in the German LPIs exactly what differences from ordinary conversation result from the different aspects of the participation framework—the interview setting or the interaction of a native speaker with a learner.

Some but not all of this knowledge is available. The organization of repair has been described in detail for American English (Schegloff 1979, 1987a, 1987b, 1987c, 1990–1993, 1992, 1997; Schegloff, Jefferson, and Sacks 1977). A replication with German data suggests that "the same machinery of repair is at work" in English and in German (Egbert 1996). But there have been no conversation analytic studies of repair in German interview settings or between native and non-native speakers of German. This shortcoming limits the interpretation of the findings of this paper. While it will be demonstrated that repair in LPIs differs qualitatively and quantitatively from ordinary conversation in the talk of the non-native-speaking interviewee as well as in the talk of the native-speaking interviewer, the interpretation of these results has to await further studies of interaction in interviews and between native speakers of German with American learners of German.

The talk of the interviewer and the interviewees in LPIs departs from everyday conversation in the following three ways. First, while native speakers of a language are usually unaware of the underlying mechanisms of repair, some aspects of the organization of repair in LPIs are explained metalinguistically and exemplified by the interviewer. In all the LPIs analyzed, before the testing phase of the interview begins, the interviewer explicitly establishes the rules for repair by explaining the rules in English and by giving examples in German. The forms the interviewer provides for other-initiated repair do not occur in natural German conversation, and, conversely, the interviewer does not provide most forms used among native speakers.[2] Second, five types of repair initiations can be observed in ordinary American English conversation (Schegloff et al. 1977) and in German conversation (Egbert 1996). In contrast, in the LPIs examined in this chapter, students not only use the types of repair they have been instructed to use, they also produce other types. Finally, in the native German interviewer's response to student-initiated repair, deviations from everyday conversation can be observed in the sequence structure. In contrast to the sequence structure of ordinary conversation—where the response to the repair initiation is designed to resolve the trouble as swiftly as possible—we observe in LPIs that the interviewer orients to certain types of student-initiated repair as a request first and then as a display of trouble in hearing or understanding. Thus a more elaborate sequence and turn structure is observable.

This study makes use of two data sets. The first is a collection of twenty videotaped and transcribed LPIs. A week before the actual interviews, students were informed of the purpose of the present study and asked for written permission to be videotaped; all of them gave their consent. In these dyadic interviews, a language instructor and trained interviewer—a native German—interviewed American college students at the end of their first year of instruction in German. In each interview the student is asked to take on different roles, such as talking in German with siblings, classmates, and students from Germany. The format of the interview was developed by Donahue (1989) as an adaptation of the ACTFL Oral Proficiency

Interview (OPI). The principles of the proficiency movement are applied to a communicatively oriented curriculum. Based on a description of the performance criteria of the ACTFL OPIs, students after the first year of instruction in this curriculum would probably perform between the 0+ and 1+ ratings on the ACTFL proficiency scale, with the lower 25% in the 0+ to 1– range, the middle 50% with a 1 rating, and the upper 25% at the 1+ rating (Donahue, personal communication).[3]

The second data set consists of 26 hours of naturally occurring everyday conversation among a total of 41 adult native speakers of German, 23 male and 18 female, from 10 different cities in northern and central Germany. The data were collected in Germany in the summers of 1991 and 1992. The participants are middle-class Germans, ranging in age from 25 to 58 years of age. In most cases, interactants are acquaintances, friends, or family members who have gathered around a table for coffee or dinner. Since only one camera was available for filming in Germany, its viewing frame was enhanced with a wide angle lens. The camera was set up prior to the participants gathering around the table; the camera angle was adjusted to capture all seated participants. Persons leaving the room disappear from the camera frame, although they might still be visible and audible to some of the seated participants. Oral consent prior to filming an event was obtained from the host or hostess of the gathering, who then informed the guests.

Before turning to the analysis, other-initiated repair will now be defined and some background information relevant to the upcoming analysis will be briefly reported. When a listener has trouble hearing or understanding the current speaker's talk, he or she can indicate this trouble in the next turn. The speaker usually addresses this trouble with an attempt to resolve it, and thus, reestablishes mutual understanding (Schegloff et al. 1977). Excerpt 1 exemplifies the sequence structure of other-initiated repair. The repair-initiation turn is indicated by an arrow (→).[4] The repair initiation *welcher* (which, line 3) targets *der Stu:hl* (cha:ir, line 1), as repairable in the preceding turn.

(1) Other-initiated repair by native speakers of German

1   H: Boh äj der Stu:hl hat aber gelitten.
        Wow the cha:ir has suffered.

2   (1.0)

3→ M: Welcher.
        Which.

```
4   H:  Dieser hier
        This one here
```

Schegloff et al. (1977) found that other-initiated repair turns in English vary in specificity in identifying the trouble source, ranging from displaying non-specified trouble, such as *huh?*, *what?*, *sorry?*, or *pardon?*, to more specified turns, such as candidate understandings of the trouble-source turn.[5] Excerpt 2 features a repair initiation turn of the type known as candidate understanding at line 2, indicated by an arrow (→).

```
(2)   Candidate understanding from Schegloff et al.
      (1977:368)

1    A:  Why did I turn out this way.
2→   B:  You mean homosexual?
3    A:  Yes.
```

Since a parallel organization of repair initiation turns is documented for German (Egbert 1996), repair initiations in LPIs can be compared to ordinary conversation of native speakers of German.

2 Analysis

The analysis starts with a condensed description of the sequence structure of the LPIs under investigation, which offers the reader an insight into the data. A more detailed description and analysis is offered for the second phase of the interview, where the interviewer establishes the rules for repair and exemplifies how the interviewee may initiate repair. The types of other-initiated repair subsequently used by interviewees to initiate repair are analyzed. The focus of the last part of the analysis is the interviewer's response to students' repair initiations.

2.1 *Sequential Structure of the LPIs*

All twenty interviews analyzed follow the same sequential development of five phases. In Phase 1, the interviewer opens the encounter in English. In Phase 2, the interviewer instructs the student on proper conduct in the interview—including how to initiate repair, as will be shown below. After these administrative and organizational tasks, the testing period starts. In Phase 3, the interviewer describes situations in English and the student provides speech samples in German appropriate to the given situation. The interviewer outlines in English a communicative situation to the student and then tells the student to produce talk in German appropriate for the particular situation. The situations are designed to elicit talk in which the interviewee (1) asks informal questions (e.g., the student meets an exchange student from Germany at a party on campus), (2) gives informal commands to an individual person (e.g., the student is babysitting his little nephew and tells him what to do to get ready for bed), and (3) gives informal commands to a group of persons (e.g., the student tells his brothers and sisters what to do shortly before the guests arrive for a surprise party). In Phase 4, the interviewer poses questions in German and the student responds in German. The questions might include, for instance, to whom did the student write a letter recently, what did he or she write, and what did he or she do during spring break. After completion of the last question/answer sequence, the interviewer closes the encounter in Phase 5.

2.2 *Instructions for Repair*

As mentioned above, the second phase of the interview—after the opening—is of crucial importance to repair. Here the interviewer instructs the learner how to initiate repair, both as a means of self-correction and as a ways of repairing others' talk. The interviewer attends in much detail to the proper place and manner for self-repair and in what way the student is expected to display trouble in hearing or understanding the interviewer's talk, i.e., other-initiated repair. Excerpt 3 presents a typical Phase 2. The German used by the interviewer at line 48 is translated in the line beneath it.[6]

```
(3)    Interviewer instructs student on how to repair

32     I:    Have you been in an oral interview before here
33           in the department?
34           (.)
35 S10:      m hm [five oh six.
36     I:         [five oh six.
37           So you know the format of the exam that I'm
38           gonna ask you a bunch of nosy questions and
39           you're supposed to answer them during the
40           interview at any point in time and ehm if you-
41           you made a mistake, feel free to correct
42           yourself even if it's at the very end, and you
43           wanna correct something that you said at the
44           beginning that's absolutely fine. Also if you
45           don't understand what I'm saying because I speak
46           too fast or because I mumble or something like
```

```
47         that then you can always ask me Wiederholen Sie
48         bitte Sprechen Sie langsamer or whatever.
           Repeat Please speak more slowly
49         Okay?
50 S10:    Okay.
51  I:     Do you have any questions? Before we start?
52 S10:    I don't think so.
53  I:     Okay right. Let's get them over with then.
```

After making sure that the interviewee is familiar with the general format of the interview (lines 32–40), the interviewer proceeds to instruct the student on the rules for self-repair (*during the interview at any point in time and ehm if you- you made a mistake, feel free to correct yourself even if it's at the very end, and you wanna correct something that you said at the beginning that's absolutely fine*, lines 39–44). The interviewer states the same rules for self-repair that have been found for American conversation (Schegloff et al. 1977) and for German conversation (Egbert 1996). In everyday conversation, self-repair is usually initiated in the same turn as the repairable utterance but can also be initiated from positions more distant from the trouble source. In stark contrast to everyday conversation, where rules for repair are not stated explicitly, in these LPIs the interviewer states that the student is allowed to self-repair and that the student may self-repair at any point in the interview. Here, then, the interviewer orients in her talk to the participation framework of the interview.

The explicitly stated rules for repair in these LPIs can be identified as a characteristic in which the oral interview deviates from conversation. In ordinary conversation, participants are not aware of the rules for repair, nor do they instruct their conversational partners on how to initiate repair. The fact that the interviewer needs to state the rules for self-repair shows that these rules are not self-evident, although they are the same as in everyday conversation. The interviewer's explication of the rules for self-repair are a materialization of the participation framework of the LPI in a second respect. In all the LPIs analyzed, it is the interviewer who states the rules for the conduct of the interviewee. This is one way in which the roles of the participants and a power asymmetry are established. The interviewer not only opens and closes the encounter and assigns a grade, she also sets the rules for interactional conduct pertaining to the mechanism of repair.[7]

The same orientation to the participation framework of the LPI becomes apparent in the interviewer's ensuing explication of other-initiated repair. She states the rules for other-initiated repair by explaining, *also if you don't understand what I'm saying because I speak too fast or because I mumble or something like that then you can always ask me Wiederholen Sie bitte Sprechen Sie langsamer or whatever* (lines 44–48; the German phrase here means repeat please speak more slowly). With these instructions the interviewer informs the student of the rules for how he or she should properly initiate repair when there is trouble in hearing or understanding. The interviewer then provides the examinee with two examples in German of how the student can initiate repair. The interviewer is so specific that she even provides the particular lexical resources the student could use, namely *Wiederholen Sie bitte* (Repeat please, lines 47–48) and *Sprechen Sie langsamer* (Speak more slowly, line 48). These examples are not only lexical resources, they are turns to be used as repair initiators. As we will see later in this chapter, repair initiation turns in everyday conversation are not selected arbitrarily but rather according to an organizing principle. In connection with this observation, I will show that on the one hand, the interviewer instructs the student to use language not found among native speakers of German, and that on the other hand, students make use of a much larger variety of turn types for other-initiated repair. As observed for the instructions for self-repair, the explication for other-initiated repair shows an asymmetrical power distribution between the interviewer and interviewee.

These observations of the explicitness of rules tie in with Irvine's (1984) discussion of formality. Irvine cautions against a dichotomy of the categories formal and informal, and proposes that a social situation may have certain characteristics that can make it more or less formal. One of the characteristics discussed by Irvine is "some greater elaboration of rules" and "explicitness" of rules. As the analysis in this section shows, this characteristic is quite distinct in the LPIs analyzed. Hence LPIs can be characterized as a more formal type of interaction than everyday talk.

The analysis also indicates places in the interview where the roles of the interviewer and interviewee manifest in the talk. As Ross and Berwick (1992:162) note, "A key characteristic of all interviews, including OPIs, seems to be the allocation of rights to the interviewer to control the encounter." In this particular set of interviews, the interviewer orients to her role by opening and closing the encounter, by setting sequential boundaries throughout the interview, and by establishing the rules of conduct for the student, as well as through other actions. This shapes many aspects of the interaction, and is of central concern in this paper for the organization of repair. While much more could be said about the differences between LPIs and natural conversation—for instance, in the area of turn-taking and sequence structure—it is already observable that in these LPIs, the mechanism of repair differs drastically from everyday conversation. How repair is actually carried out in the testing phase of the interview will be examined next.

2.3 Types of Other-Initiated Repair Used by Learners

In the sequential analysis above we noted that the interviewer instructs the learner on how to initiate repair and provides the learner with two turns to use, namely by saying *Wiederholen Sie bitte* (Repeat please) and *Sprechen Sie langsamer* (Speak more slowly.) We will now examine what types of repair initiations the learner actually employs in the testing period of the interview.

In the twenty interviews examined, a total of 46 instances of student-initiated repair occur. These repair initiations will now be categorized according to Schegloff et al.'s (1977) typology of repair initiations established for English and by Egbert's (1996) typology for German. We will refer to six types of repair initiation: the five types found in ordinary conversation, and an additional type—requests for repetition—found only in these LPIs. Table 1 below shows the number of occurrences for each of these six categories of other-initiated repair in the LPIs. The ensuing analysis will explain the results summarized in this table.

The oral output from the students must be interpreted in light of the input they have received. We have already analyzed the input during the LPI in section 2.2 above. Input on repair was also available from the instructional materials. In the workbook of the instructional materials (Donahue and Watzinger 1990:3), students are taught the following German forms together with their English translations.

Wiederholen Sie!	Repeat.
Wiederholen Sie das, bitte.	Repeat that please.
Sagen Sie das noch einmal, bitte.	Say that again please.
Noch einmal! (or) *Noch 'mal!*	Once again.
Wie bitte?	How's that please?

We have no record of other input that students have been exposed to, such as classroom data. It is conceivable that teachers use all kinds of repair initiations and students thus acquire them subconsciously. In addition, students may have had exposure to or interaction with native speakers' usage of repair.

As Table 1 shows, although students are taught to initiate repair by requesting a repetition, and they use this form relatively frequently (with 10 instances it is the second largest category of repair initiations), they also make extensive use of other types of repair initiations. Three points will be made in comparing the students' repair initiations with those used by native speakers: (1) In the categories of understanding-checks and partial repeats, no difference between non-native speaker and native speaker usage could be found. (2) The linguistically more challenging

Table 1. Types and Frequency of Student-Initiated Repairs

Type of repair	Number of occurrences in 20 LPIs
Understanding-checks	9
Partial repeats	25
Partial repeats with question word	2
Interrogatives	0
Non-specified trouble	0
Requests for repetition	10

categories of partial repeat with question words and interrogatives are either very infrequent or not used at all. (3) Among the non-specified trouble repair initiations, no form used by native speakers was found in the non-native speaker talk; non-native speakers use requests for repetition quite frequently, but they used the form they were instructed to use, which is not found in the talk of native speakers.

2.3.1 *Understanding-Checks and Partial Repeats*
Although students are not taught to initiate repair by means of understanding-checks or partial repeats, these types are used most frequently. Line 222 in Excerpt 4 exemplifies a student-initiated partial repeat, and lines 240–241 in Excerpt 5 show a student-initiated candidate understanding.

```
(4)     Student-initiated partial repeat

219     I:  Okay. und ehm sa:gen Sie mir wem Sie das
            Okay. and uhm te:ll me to whom you wrote a

220         letzte Mal einen Brie:f geschrieben haben,
            letter the last time,

221         und was Sie geschrieben haben.
            and what you wrote.

222→S7:     .hhh ich habe ehm letztes Mal?
            .hhh I have ehm last time?

223     I:  Mhm,
            Uh huh,
```

```
224   S7:  Habe ich meinem- (.) meinen (.) eh meiner
           I wrote to my- (.) my (.) uh to my

225        Schwester geschrieben,
           sister,
```

(5) Student-initiated candidate understanding

```
237   I:   Beschreiben Sie Ihr Zimmer zu Hause (.) e:h
           Describe your room at home (.) u:h

238        was ist in Ihrem Zimmer wo steh::t alles
           what is in your room where is everything
239        in Ihrem Zimmer=
           in your room=

240→S6:    =Mein- mein Schlafzimmer oder mein Wohnzimmer,
           =My- my bedroom or my living room,

241→S6:    od[e:r,
           o:r,
              [
242   I:      [Wie Sie möchten
              As you like
```

One reason why repair initiations in these two categories are used so extensively by students may be because a partial repeat and a candidate understanding are relatively simple strategies that can be transferred from English. Note that neither of these strategies is part of the instructions for repair at the beginning of the interview, nor is either one mentioned in the textbook.

Students' use of repair initiations seems to indicate that they have an interactive need to employ a wider range of repair initiations than they have been taught. This need may be the force driving students to transfer English strategies into German. It would be an interesting endeavor to find students with different first languages who use different other-initiated repairs, in order to examine whether transfer of strategies can result in an interlanguage use of repair initiations.

2.3.2 Interrogatives and Partial Repeats with Question Words
Sometimes a listener has trouble in properly hearing or understanding a particular portion of the trouble-source turn, but understands it well enough to target the trouble-source with a particular question word. In this case, interrogatives used as

repair initiations in the native-speaker German data set are *wer?* (who), *was?* (what?), *wo?* (where?), *welcher?* and *welchen?* (which —marked for nominative and accusative case), and *wann?* (when?). In the LPI data set, not a single interrogative used as repair initiation by students could be located. But a very small number— a total of two instances—of partial repeats with question words are produced by students. One of these is displayed in Excerpt 6.

```
(6)    Student-initiated partial repeat with question word

59     I:    Beschreiben Sie Ihr Zimmer zu Hause. Was ist
             Describe your room at home. What is

60           in Ihrem Zimmer, und wo stehen die Sachen
             in your room, and where the things are located

61           in Ihrem Zimmer.
             in your room.

62→S19:      Ehm we:lches Zimmer,? Any Zimmer?
             Uhm whi:ch room,? Any room?

63     I:    Egal.
             Doesn't matter.
```

Why are these types of repair initiation so rarely used by students? Interrogatives and partial repeats with question words require a combination of cognitive, linguistic, and interactive skills, for example, a fair amount of analysis of the trouble-source turn, the immediate retrieval of the appropriate interrogative, and, with inflected question words, linguistic knowledge about case, number, and gender. For example, in Excerpt 6 the interrogative *welches* (which) needs to be marked for case, number, and gender in order to agree with the subsequent noun. Such linguistic production under the pressure of time and performance may not be highly developed in first-year German students, and this may be one reason why they resort to other types of repair-initiations.

2.3.3 *Non-Specified Trouble*

In everyday German conversation, the repair initiations *hm?* (huh?), *bitte?* (pardon?), and *was?* (what?) are used to initiate repair on the entire preceding turn. This category is called non-specified trouble because these repair initiations do not specify what exactly in the preceding turn is troublesome. These non-specified trouble repair initiations usually yield a repetition of the trouble-source turn, as exemplified in everyday conversation by Excerpts 7 and 8.

(7) Non-specified trouble repair initiations with *häh?* — native speakers of German

```
1    D:  Ist dir nicht zu kàlt?
         Are you not too cold?

2        (0.5)

3→   P:  Häh?
         Huh?

4    D:  Ist dir nicht zu kalt?
         Are you not too cold?
```

(8) Non-specified trouble repair initiations with *was?* — native speakers of German

```
1    H:  Stefan stell dein Auto jetz weg.
         Stefan put your car away now.

2        (0.5)

3→   S:  Wa:s?
         Wha:t?

4    H:  Stell dein Auto jetz weg.
         Put your car away now.
```

In the LPIs analyzed, no occurrence of these non-specified trouble repair initiations could be located. This is conspicuous since *hm?* and *was?* are cognates of English huh? and what?, and *bitte?* is a simple lexical item that is already part of these students' vocabulary.[8] A different type of repair initiation, however, similar to the non-specified category, is used by students quite frequently; with 12 instances it is the second largest category. This type is an explicit request for repetition. It is similar to the non-specified category in that it can also yield a repetition of the trouble-source turn as response. The request for repetition takes one of following three formats. The first format is displayed in Excerpt 9, where the student initiates repair at line 197 by asking the interviewer to repeat that please.

(9) Request for repetition (simplified)

```
195     I:  Was durften Sie als Kind ni:cht machen.
            What were you no:t allowed to do as a child.

196         (1.5)

197→S1:     °ehm° (0.5) tch! (1.0) Wiederhole[n, Sie das bitte?
            °uhm° (0.5) tch! (1.0) Repeat that please?
                                             [
198     I:                                   [ja:a
                                             ye:es

199     I:  Natürlich. .hh Was durften Sie als Kind nicht
            machen
            Of course. .hh What were you not allowed to do as a
            child
```

The rationale for this non-native usage is quite straightforward; as shown earlier in this paper, with repair initiations such as *Wiederholen, Sie das bitte?* (Repeat that please?) the student uses a format that the interviewer explicitly instructed him or her to employ to initiate repair. Recall that in Phase 2 of the interview the interviewer tells the student, *"If you don't understand what I'm saying because I speak too fast or because I mumble or something like that then you can always ask me Wiederholen Sie bitte."* In addition, the textbook teaches students to use such forms.

Another request for repetition, in this case one not put forth by the interviewer but included in the textbook, is shown in Excerpt 10. At line 207, the student halts the sequence with *Entschuldigung* (Excuse me) and when the interviewer signals compliance (line 208), the student launches the request for repetition (line 209).

(10) Request for repetition

```
200     I:  Ich kenne Austin nicht gu:t ich bin neu hier.
            I do not know Austin we:ll I am new here.

201         (0.2) tch! Sa:gen Sie mir was man hier machen
            (0.2) tch! Te:ll me what one can do here

202         kann wenn man sich amüsieren will.
            when one wants to amuse oneself.

203         (0.5)
```

```
204         ja,? .hhh wohin kann man gehe:n:, wann ist die
            yes,? .hhh where can one go:, when is the

205         beste zei:t dorthin zu gehen was kann man dort
            best ti:me to go there and what can one

206         machen, wie komm ich dorthin und so weiter
            do there, how do I get there and so on

207→S6:     a::h e:hm (2.0) ahm Entschuldigung
            a::h u:hm (2.0) uhm Excuse me

208   I:    Mhm.
            Uh huh.

209→S6:     u:h Können Sie das noch einmal sa:gen,?
            u:h Could you sa:y that once more,?

210   I:    natürlich. ja, ich kenne Austin nicht gut.
            of course. yes, I don't know Austin very well.

211         sa:gen Sie mir was man hier machen ka:nn, wenn
            te:ll me what one ca:n do here, if

212         man sich amüsieren will, wenn man spa:β haben
            one wants to amuse oneself, when one wants to have
            fu:n,

213         will, tch! °ne,?°
            tz! °right,°
```

In this excerpt, the student prefaces his repair initiation with the apology *Entschuldigung* (Excuse me). After he halts the flow of the talk, he launches his request for repetition (line 209). In the everyday German data set, no example was found of a native German speaker using *entschuldigung* (excuse me) as a preface to a repair initiation. As in Excerpt 9, the repair initiation in Excerpt 10 is an explicit request for repetition—in this case the student does not use a form previously provided by the interviewer but rather a phrase listed in the textbook. Similarly, in line 39 of Excerpt 11, the student uses a request for repetition not mentioned by the interviewer but included in the textbook.

(11) Request for repetition

```
36      I:    Was hat Ihnen dieses Semester im Deutschkurs
37            ni:cht gefallen
              What did you no:t like this semester in your German
              course.

38            (1.5)

39→S17:       No:ch einmal?
              O:nce more?

40      I:    Mhm tch! Was hat Ihnen dieses Semester
              Uh huh tz! What did you not like this semester

41            im Deutschkurs ni:cht gefallen.
              in your German course.
```

Just as the native-speaker forms of non-specified trouble repair initiations may yield a repetition of the trouble-source turn, the students' more explicit requests for repetition are successful in that, in all cases, the interviewer complies with the student's request and repeats the entire trouble-source turn. All three types of request for repetition employed by these American students of German are non-native usages not found in the data set of repair initiations by native German speakers. These non-native types have in common the fact that they are comparatively long turns to achieve what a much shorter lexical item like *hm?*, *bitte?*, or *was?* accomplishes in native-speaker usage.

To sum up the examination of the categories of repair initiations, we note that these American students of German make use of repair initiations they are instructed to use and others that the interviewer does not mention. The students' exposure to the interviewer and to the textbook account for why we observe repair initiations in a format not found in non-native-speaker interaction. The way students are taught is limited to requesting a repetition of the trouble-source turn. Apparently interviewees feel a need for a larger variety of repair initiations, and thus they use some repair initiation strategies that they may have transferred from English. The linguistically more challenging repair initiations such as interrogatives or partial repeats with question words either do not occur or occur very infrequently.

2.4 Interviewer's Response to Student-Initiated Repair

The student-initiated requests for repetition discussed in the previous section are of interest because of another deviation from the repair sequence found in interaction between native speakers. In native-speaker interaction, the response to the repair initiation is usually a repetition of the trouble-source turn—see Excerpts 7 and 8 above. In all twelve requests for repetition launched by learners of German, the interviewer responds with a compliance token before she repeats the trouble-source turn. These tokens are indicated by arrows in the next two excerpts. In Excerpt 12, the interviewer first responds with the compliance token *ja:a natürlich* (ye:es of course, lines 198–199) and then proceeds with a repetition of the trouble-source turn.

(12) Interviewer's compliance token

```
197  S1:   °ehm°  (0.5) tch! (1.0) Wiederhole[n, Sie das bitte?
           °uhm°  (0.5) tch! (1.0) Repeat, that please?
                                              [
198→ I:                                       [ja:a
                                              ye:es
199→       Natürlich. .hh Was durften Sie als Kind nicht
           machen
           Of course. .hh What were you not allowed to do as a
           kid
```

In Excerpt 13, the compliance token is *mhm* (uh huh, line 39), followed by a repetition of the trouble-source turn.

(13) Interviewer's response to student's repair initiation

```
35   I:    Was hat Ihnen dieses Semester im Deutschkurs
           What did you no:t like this semester in the

36         ni:cht gefallen
           German course.

37         (1.5)

38   S17:  No:ch einmal?
           O:nce more?
```

```
39→  I:    mhm tch! Was hat Ihnen dieses Semester im
           uh huh tch! What did you no:t like this semester in

40         Deutschkurs ni:cht gefallen.
           the German course.
```

In response to a student's request for repetition, the interviewer first orients to this type of turn as a request by displaying her compliance with the request. She then regularly responds to the repair initiation component of the student's turn by repeating the trouble-source turn. Thus all responses to a student's request for repetition consist of two turn-constructional units, the first one a compliance token to the request, the second one the actual compliance with the request.

The interviewer's responses to these repair initiations—unlike those in ordinary conversation—are expanded by the element of displaying compliance. There are several conceivable explanations for this difference from everyday native-speaker conversation: an orientation to the participation framework of the interview or an orientation to the non-native proficiency level of the interviewee. Such expansions by the interviewer may have pedagogical value in that they may make the interviewee feel more at ease about having displayed trouble. Yet in everyday conversation such elements do not occur; the speaker who uttered the trouble-source turn may simply repeat the turn. If used in naturally occurring conversation with native German speakers, such expansions can mark the language learner as a non-native speaker. The learner is disadvantaged by having to use a cumbersome form and also because he or she is side-tracked from learning the proper form.

3 Summary and Conclusions

The goal of the language proficiency interview is to simulate natural conversation or at least to capture elements of it. This study was motivated by previous research comparing language use in conversation with language use in language proficiency interviews. As part of the broader study of language use in language proficiency interviews, the present study attempted to find out how in other-initiated repair—the central mechanism for dealing with interactional breakdowns in mutual understanding—LPIs of twenty American students of German as a foreign language differ from everyday German conversation.

Three main results are reported. First, the organization of repair in LPIs is explained explicitly by the interviewer; in natural conversation participants usually do not engage in metatalk pertaining to the mechanism of repair. This explicitness could be an aspect of the formality of the interview. Second, the language learners in this study initiate repair by means of forms taught to them that are not found in native-speaker interaction, students also use some native-speaker forms that they have not been taught. The repair initiations used by students that differ from everyday conversation derive from the input students receive from their textbook and from the interviewer in the LPI. The forms students use that are like those found in everyday native-speaker conversation may derive from repair strategies transferred from the students' first language. Deviation from everyday native-speaker conversation is also found in the interviewer's talk. When she responds to student-initiated requests for repetition, she orients both to the request character of the turn and to the repair initiation character, resulting in a more elaborate turn structure than is observable in everyday interaction among native speakers.

These results have implications for pedagogy, evaluation, language learning, and research methodology. From a pedagogical point of view, students are instructed to initiate repair in a comparatively cumbersome way. Should students use these forms in less formal contexts than the LPI, they would be marked as non-native speakers, or at least some awkwardness could be detected in their talk. It would be very easy to teach students of German to initiate repair via *hm?*, *was?* or *bitte?*; these are small words that would save the student from having to memorize long phrases. In addition, it would be empowering for learners to know that when they have problems with only part of the trouble source, they can specify the trouble and thus give the trouble-source turn speaker more help in removing the trouble. Students who are instructed to initiate repair in the same fashion as native speakers may feel more confident in handling their trouble in hearing or understanding when they know that their problem is not unique to language learners but also happens regularly in native-speaker interaction.

This study also suggests implications for evaluation. While I agree with Bachman and Savignon (1986:385) that it is a mistake to clearly identify native speakers as a standard of language performance for second language learners, I would like to propose that for many conversational mechanisms, as shown here for the organization of other-initiated repair, there is a describable native-speaker mechanism that can be taught and tested. In evaluating language learners, we can judge interviewees' handling of their trouble in hearing or understanding. This includes two distinct tasks for the evaluator. First, students' repair initiations may reveal gaps in their knowledge of the target language. While such gaps can be used to help diagnose the students' level of proficiency, ratings should be positively influenced if interviewees initiate repair in a native-speaker-like fashion. Studies like this could then meet one of Bachman's (1990:297) proposals that "for both theory and practice, the challenge is thus to develop tests that reflect current views of language and language use."

One of the foremost reasons for studying LPIs is to examine learners' language use. Even though learners' performances may be distorted by the context of the LPI, their talk may be a window on the development of their conversational skills—for example, the acquisition of ways of initiating repair. We have observed in the usage of the first-year American students of German in this study that linguistically challenging repair types (interrogatives and partial repeats with question words) are almost never used. This raises the question of how repair as an interactional and linguistic system is acquired. Is there an order in which different types of repair initiations are acquired? Is there transfer from the first language? What is the relationship between input and acquisition of repair initiations?

In terms of research methodology, this conversation analytic study has shown that a comparison of LPIs with ordinary conversation among native speakers yields new insights into the interaction between interviewer and interviewee. While it is necessary to examine LPIs by means of multiple methods, conversation analysis seems particularly apt for the analysis of interactional structures displayed in the talk, especially since language proficiency interviews constitute social encounters that are quite complex at the microanalytical level.

Acknowledgments

This research was partially funded by a Special Research Grant from the University Research Institute at the University of Texas at Austin. I wish to thank the participating students and the interviewer for allowing me to videotape their interactions. I am most grateful to Frank Donahue for permission and support to collect data in his program, and to Carmen Taleghani-Nikazm for helping with transcription. I also wish to express my gratitude to Agnes He and Richard Young for helpful comments.

Notes

1. By *conversation* I mean ordinary talk-in-interaction in contrast to interaction in institutional settings. For a discussion of the differences between everyday conversation and institutional interactions, see Drew and Heritage (1992:22).

2. The ideas put forth in this paper are not meant in any way to be critical of this particular interviewer or the German program in which the data were collected. Since there are so few conversation analytic studies of everyday German conversation, textbook writers and instructors face the difficult task of teaching German conversation without being able to rely on an empirical description of the conversational features of German.

3. The following ACTFL numerical and descriptive scales are equivalent.

Novice-Low	0–
Novice-Mid	0
Novice-High	0+
Intermediate-Low	1–
Intermediate-Mid	1
Intermediate-High	1+
Advanced	2–
Advanced-High	2
Superior	2+

4. Conversation analysis entails the preparation of a detailed transcript of the talk according to specific notations devised by Jefferson (1983, 1985) that represent characteristics of speech delivery, pauses, and overlaps. See appendix in Sacks, Schegloff, and Jefferson (1974) for an early description of the transcription notation, and Atkinson and Heritage (1994:ix–xvi) for a more detailed version. The translation of data is prepared according to Egbert (1993). The first line of transcript is the original speech in German, the second line (in italics) the English translation.

5. *Candidate understanding* is a technical term in CA referring to a specific type of other-initiated repair; it should not to be confused with the term *candidate* referring to the interviewee.

6. To protect participants, speakers are identified by codes rather than by names. Codes for students identify students as *S1* through *S20*. The code for the interviewer is *I*.

7. See Young and Milanovic (1992) for a discussion of dominance in language proficiency interviews.

8. For an analysis of the distinct usage of *bitte?* see Egbert (1996). Drew's (1997) analysis of a set of non-specified trouble repair initiations in British English reports on important sequential environments in which this type of repair initiation is used.

References

Atkinson, J. Maxwell, and John Heritage. 1984. *Structures of Social Action*. Cambridge: Cambridge University Press.

Bachman, Lyle F. 1990. *Fundamental Considerations in Language Testing*. Oxford University Press.

Bachman, Lyle F., and Sandra Savignon. 1986. "The Evaluation of Communicative Language Proficiency: A Critique of the ACTFL Oral Interview." *Modern Language Journal* 70.380–390.

Bennett, Adrian, and Helen Slaughter. 1983. "A Sociolinguistic/Discourse Approach to the Description of the Communicative Competence of Linguistic Minority Children." In

An Ethnographic/Sociolinguistic Approach to Language Proficiency Assessment, ed. by Charlene Rivera, 2–26. Clevedon, Avon: Multilingual Matters.

Donahue, Frank. 1989. "Oral Achievement Testing in the First-Year German Program: A Model." Paper presented at the annual conference of the American Association of Teachers of German, Boston, MA, November.

Donahue, Frank, and Johanna Watzinger. 1990. *Deutsch Zusammen: A Communicative Course in German*. New York: Macmillan.

Drew, Paul. 1997. "'Open' Class Repair Initiators in Response to Sequential Sources of Troubles in Conversation." *Journal of Pragmatics* 28. 69-101.

Drew, Paul, and John Heritage. 1992. "Analyzing Talk at Work: An Introduction." In *Talk at Work: Interaction in Institutional Settings*, ed. by Paul Drew and John Heritage, 3–65. Cambridge: Cambridge University Press.

Egbert, Maria M. 1993. *Schisming: The Transformation from a Single Conversation to Multiple Conversations.* Unpublished Ph.D. dissertation, University of California, Los Angeles.

Egbert, Maria M. 1996. "Context-sensitivity in Conversation: Eye Gaze and the German Repair Initiator *Bitte?*." *Language in Society* 25.587–612

Fiksdal, Susan. 1990. *The Right Time and Pace: A Microanalysis of Cross-cultural Gatekeeping Interviews*. Norwood, NJ: Ablex.

Irvine, Judith T. 1984. "Formality and Informality in Communicative Events." In *Language in Use: Readings in Sociolinguistics*, ed. by John Baugh and Joel Sherzer, 211–228. Englewood Cliffs, NJ: Prentice Hall.

Jefferson, Gail. 1983. "Two Explorations of the Organization of Overlapping Talk in Conversation." (= *Tilburg Papers in Language and Literature*, 28.). Tilburg, The Netherlands: Tilburg University.

Jefferson, Gail. 1985. "An Exercise in the Transcription and Analysis of Laughter." In *Handbook of Discourse Analysis*, ed. by Teun A. van Dijk, 25–34. New York: Academic Press.

Lazaraton, Anne L. 1991. *A Conversation Analysis of Structure and Interaction in the Language Interview*. Unpublished Ph.D. dissertation, University of California, Los Angeles.

Lazaraton, Anne L. 1997. "Preference Organization in Oral Proficiency Interviews: The Case of Language Ability Assessments." *Research on Language and Social Interaction* 30.53–72.

Ross, Stephen, and Richard Berwick. 1992. "The Discourse of Accommodation in Oral Proficiency Interviews." *Studies in Second Language Acquisition* 14.159–176.

Sacks, Harvey, Emanuel A. Schegloff, and Gail Jefferson. 1974. "A Simplest Systematics for the Organization of Turn-taking for Conversation." *Language* 50.696–735.

Schegloff, Emanuel A. 1979. "The Relevance of Repair to Syntax-for-Conversation." In *Syntax and Semantics*, vol. 12: *Discourse and Syntax*, ed. by Talmy Givón, 261–288. New York: Academic Press.

Schegloff, Emanuel A. 1987a. "Between Micro and Macro: Contexts and Other Connections." In *The Micro-Macro Link*, ed. by Jeffrey C. Alexander, Bernhard Giesen, Richard Münch, and Neil J. Smelser, 207–234. Berkeley, CA: University of California Press.

Schegloff, Emanuel A. 1987b. "Some Sources of Misunderstanding in Talk-in-Interaction." *Linguistics* 25.201–218.

Schegloff, Emanuel A. 1987c. "Recycled Turn Beginnings." In *Talk and Social Organization*, ed. by Graham Button and John R. E. Lee, 70–85. Clevedon, Avon: Multilingual Matters.

Schegloff, Emanuel A. 1990–1993. "Conversational Structures and Repair." Lectures given in the Department of Sociology, University of California, Los Angeles.

Schegloff, Emanuel A. 1992. "Repair After Next Turn: The Last Structurally Provided Defense of Intersubjectivity in Conversation." *American Journal of Sociology* 97.1295–1345.

Schegloff, Emanuel A. 1997. "Third-turn Repair." In *Towards a Social Science of Language: Papers in Honor of William Labov*, vol. 2, ed. by Gregory R. Guy, Crawford Feagin, Deborah Schiffrin, and John Baugh., 31–40. Amsterdam and Philadelphia: Benjamins.

Schegloff, Emanuel A., Gail Jefferson, and Harvey Sacks. 1977. "The Preference for Self Correction in the Organization of Repair in Conversation." *Language* 54.361–382.

van Lier, Leo. 1989. "Reeling, Writhing, Drawling, Stretching, and Fainting in Coils: Oral Proficiency Interviews as Conversation." *TESOL Quarterly* 23.489–508.

Young, Richard. 1995. "Conversational Styles in Language Proficiency Interviews." *Language Learning* 45.3–42.

Young, Richard, and Michael Milanovic. 1992. "Discourse Variation in Oral Proficiency Interviews." *Studies in Second Language Acquisition* 14.403–424.

Part 3

Knowledge and Communication in Language Proficiency Interviews

Part I

Acknowledged Communication in
Language Production Activities

Knowledge Structures in Oral Proficiency Interviews for International Teaching Assistants

Bernard Mohan
The University of British Columbia

The aim of this chapter is to examine oral question-and-answer interaction in interviews as co-construction of knowledge structures. In so doing I will raise questions about the assessment of the oral proficiency of second language learners for academic contexts.

The data for this chapter are drawn from a group of oral proficiency interviews (OPIs) administered to international teaching assistants (ITAs). The ITA's job includes the oral presentational work of lecturing and the oral interactional work of laboratory assignments and office hours. Madden and Myers (1994:154) suggest that interaction outweighs presentation in the language needs of ITAs: "Answering questions is a far more typical task than lecturing." The nature of ITA-student communication is reportedly problematic (Madden and Myers 1994, Tyler 1992, Williams 1992), which motivates an interest in the study of ITA performance during the OPI as a potential window on the ITA's capacity to undertake subject matter instruction for undergraduates. The OPI does not, of course, replicate the specific conditions of laboratories and office hours but it does provide access to relevant performances by the candidate.

How can the oral construction of knowledge be analyzed? My analysis of interview discourse explores a knowledge structure approach. It speaks to the lack of viable approaches to academic discourse assessment of language proficiency interviews. Drawing on the perspective of systemic functional linguistics, I address issues of knowledge, or "field," particularly issues of knowledge structures. I will show how ITAs use discourse to order the experiential world and to construct different structures of knowledge. An analysis of the discourse semantics and lexicogrammar of the texts will show how the speakers use their linguistic resources to build sequences of action or to build principles such as rules or empirical generalizations. These are knowledge structures—structures of the field of discourse. I will show too how the speakers differentiate in discourse semantics and lexicogrammar between types and subtypes of knowledge structures, between, for example, the ingredients of productive procedures and the time framing of schedules, or between analytic rules and empirical generalizations.

I will also show that the interviewer is doing much more than simply eliciting a ratable sample of discourse from the ITA. To account for these interviews as interviews, we need to account for the knowledge structures within them. The interviewer leads into a knowledge structure on a topic. The ITA constructs the knowledge structure. And the interviewer probes and follows up on the knowledge structure. In other words, the interviewer and the ITA co-construct the knowledge structure. The use of a knowledge structure analysis enables us to account more adequately for the contingencies between the interviewer's contributions and the ITA's contributions as a joint construction over an extended discourse. It also helps us show how the interviewer's strategies differentiate between types and subtypes of knowledge structures.

In what follows I will begin with a discussion of knowledge structures and then relate knowledge structures to theoretical and empirical work in systemic functional linguistics. Next I will briefly review criticisms of the OPI as a measure of oral proficiency in academic contexts, considered as an elicitation and as an interview. This will set the stage for an analysis of the interview data with respect to two main knowledge structures—sequence and principles—exploring how knowledge structure analysis can examine the processes of knowledge co-construction in discourse and illuminate the assessment issues at stake. Finally, conclusions will be discussed concerning data analysis, data explanation, oral discourse in educational contexts, and assessment.

1 Knowledge Structures

A framework for knowledge structures is illustrated in detail in Mohan (1986), and relevant research is reviewed in Mohan (1990). In this framework, an activity type (situation type, social practice, frame) includes action knowledge and background knowledge (practice and theory). Action knowledge includes the knowledge structures of *description, sequence,* and *choice*; background knowledge includes the knowledge structures of *classification, principles,* and *values*. These six are a core group, chosen as a working hypothesis because they seem to be fairly general and a good place to begin. There are no doubt others. These knowledge structures (KSs) are broad, general patterns of the organization of information at a fairly high level of abstraction. They show up as structures of discourse, but they also show up as structures in the mind that people use to process discourse.

Examples of action KSs are usually fairly frequent and obvious in narratives. A narrative will typically contain one or more descriptions of a particular person, place, or thing. The story line will include a time sequence of events or actions, or states, and it will often explore a choice, decision, or dilemma of one of its characters.

In academic texts at college and university, there is often a pattern of linking practice and theory, relating action KSs and background KSs that helps the reader see them more clearly. A description of a particular person, place, or thing may be related to a classification or set of general concepts; a particular time sequence of states, events, or actions may be related to general principles (social rules or cause-effect relations) that link one state to another; and a particular choice or decision may relate to general values.

Excerpts 1 and 2 are examples of classification and description: a classification of lakes is followed by a description of a particular lake, Loch Coruisk. Textbook headings are indicated by bolding and capitalization.

(1) Classification (From Monkhouse 1960:155)

Classification of Lakes. Lakes may be most conveniently classified according to the mode of origin of the hollows which contain their waters. The most important categories are produced by erosion, by deposition, and by earth movements and volcanic activity.

(2) Description (From Monkhouse 1960:159)

LAKE-HOLLOWS PRODUCED BY EROSION. (i) **Glaciation** . . . Most striking of all is Loch Coruisk in the Isle of Skye (Fig. 72). The loch is about 1.5 miles in length and some 600 yards wide and lies in a rock basin almost divided in two by a ridge from which a few rocky islets reach the surface.

The role of classification in helping the student organize detailed information in this physical geography textbook is explicitly pointed out by the author in the preface (Monkhouse 1960:viii): "Wherever possible, classifications, with careful headings and sub-headings, have been used in order to bring some system and ordered relationship into the mass of material with which we are confronted." All of the other KSs are used in textbooks for the same purpose of bringing order into the mass of academic material.

Excerpts 3 and 4 are examples of choice and value, and are taken from a section entitled *Methods: The Choices and the Trade-Offs* in a psychology research methods textbook. Excerpt 3 details the decisions (i.e., choices) the personality researcher must make. Excerpt 4 mentions the contrasting subjective/objective interests (i.e., contrasting values) that enter into one of the decisions.

```
(3)   Choice  (From Lewin 1979:209)

Good personality research, however, is difficult. The
personality researcher must come to a decision about each of
five different issues. And, as we shall see, each issue is
surrounded by controversy. These critical issues may be
stated in question form as follows:
1.    Shall I study single cases, or large groups of people?
2.    Shall I adopt a grand theory and attempt to test it, or
      shall I try open-minded empiricism?
3.    Shall I focus on subjective and unconscious variables, or
      on objective and overt variables?

(4)   Values  (From Lewin 1979:210)

Subjective and Unconscious Variables versus Objective and
Overt Variables: The subjective versus objective issue has
caused more argument than almost any other within
personality research. Those who are interested in a
subject's inner world and in underlying or latent meanings
are sometimes called "subjective" researchers. The
"objective" psychologist, on the other hand, seeks easily
observed data requiring minimal interpretations.
```

In this chapter I will use the remaining KSs of sequence and principles (considered individually, not as linked theory and practice) to analyze oral interviews. While all KSs apply to academic discourse, sequence and principles provide a contrast that can be examined within the limited space of the chapter. It is doubtful whether any academic discipline could avoid these KSs and do without either schedules or procedures, rules or cause-effect relations, for example. Excerpts 5 and 6 indicate in a preliminary way the general issues that I will deal with. These are both examples of sequence (a series of events in time), where the interviewer (IN) asks about a teaching assistant's (TA) educational history (specific details have been trivially changed to protect identities).

Knowledge Structures in Oral Proficiency Interviews 177

(5) Sequence

```
1 IN:  Tell me about your educational background.
2 TA:  I graduated from the Department of Mathematics in
       Canton University in 1982. In 1986 I went to
       university to get my master's degree in statistics. I
       got my graduate degree in 1986 in Beijing, and after
       that I go to Beijing and work in the XX university as
       a professor and I taught mathematics and statistics,
       and after that I came to Calgary.
3 IN:  So you've been here about three years?
4 TA:  About two and a half.
```

(6) Sequence

```
1 IN:  How long have you been at Western University?
2 TA:  Almost three years. I came here in the fall of '91.
3 IN:  From?
4 TA:  From Edmonton. I came from Shanghai originally and I
       did two years in the program at the University of
       Edmonton.
5 IN:  What's your background in China?
6 TA:  I did a Bachelor's degree in applied math in Xiamen
       and I did two years of a master's program.
```

The first issue concerns the interview as an elicitation of TA discourse. What knowledge structure is the TA constructing? In both excerpts the TAs are building a knowledge structure of sequence of events, giving an account of their educational history—their educational curriculum vitae. The reader is able to recognize the similarity of the examples and the parallel with a written curriculum vitae by recognizing that they are examples of a sequence KS. Both are a sequence of events in time. But how is this done through the resources of discourse? The reader notices but is not confused by the fact that Excerpt 5 goes from early time to later time, but Excerpt 6 goes, more or less, from later to earlier. Nor is the reader confused by the fact that Excerpt 5 is closer to monologue and Excerpt 6 to a balanced dialogue. These matters of textual order would be highly important for an analysis of the interviews as a genre, but they are not relevant to the sequence of events.

The second issue concerns the interview as an interview, as an interaction between interviewer and TA. What role is the interviewer playing in the co-construction of knowledge? In both examples, the sequence of events is built jointly by the TA and the interviewer. The knowledge structure is co-constructed through discourse. The interviewer plays an active role, and the questioning strategies vary between the two interviews. In Excerpt 5, the initial question successfully unlocks most of the timeline of events. The last question makes an inference from the time line. In Excerpt 6, several questions trace the timeline. What role is the interviewer playing in the co-construction of knowledge?

2 Systemic Functional Linguistics

My development of KSs draws on the perspective of systemic functional linguistics (SFL) but is an independent creation. So first I will review those aspects of SFL that act as background to my KS analysis below; then I will say how KS analysis relates to recent work in SFL.

SFL has a number of important orientations (see Halliday and Martin 1993:22–23). It is oriented to the description of language as a resource for meaning rather than a system of rules, and it is oriented to what speakers can mean, rather than on constraints on what they can say. SFL is concerned with texts rather than sentences, and treats grammar as the realization of discourse—hence the notion of functional grammar. SFL is oriented to texts in social contexts rather than texts as decontextualized entities. SFL is concerned with language as a meaning-making system rather than a meaning-expressing one; it views language as a system for construing meaning rather than a conduit through which thoughts are poured.

In SFL's model of text-context relations (Halliday and Hasan 1989), a text relates to its context through *field*, the subject matter of the text or the socially recognized activity that is taking place at the time; through *tenor*, the social relationships that hold among the various participants in the interaction; and through *mode*, the role of language in the interaction. *Register* is the configuration of meanings that are typically associated with a particular situational configuration of field, mode, and tenor. *Genre* is a staged, goal-oriented social process realized through register (Martin 1992:505).

This model of text/context relations and its associated functional grammar has been used by scholars in SFL as part of the process of making explicit the discourses constituting different subjects across the curriculum. Specifically, as Christie, Devlin, Freebody, Luke, Martin, Threadgold, and Walton (1991:186–187) state, it has been used to:

1. Recognize the different genres used to package knowledge in different disciplinary areas (genre);
2. Interpret the ways in which technical language is used to construct knowledge in a discipline (field);

3. Understand the role of abstract language in organizing text and defining technical terms (mode); and
4. Appreciate the role of impersonal documentation and argumentation, with a view to teaching critical reading (tenor).

Genre work on the language and literacy demands of high school subjects provides examples of the kind of sophisticated functional analyses of discourse in educational contexts that research on the OPI needs to take into account. Building on a considerable body of earlier research, the *Write It Right Project* (Write It Right 1992) has covered genre analysis of all major curriculum areas including English, geography, history, science, math, visual arts, and media studies. Publications from this project appear in the series *Write It Right: Resources for Literacy and Learning*, and include volumes on literacy in school English and literacy in school science.

An approach to spoken and written second language assessment particularly influenced by genre and more generally by the SFL text/context model has been developed by the New South Wales Adult Migrant English Service in its' Certificates in Spoken and Written English (see New South Wales Adult Migrant English Service/National Centre for English Language Teaching and Research 1993). In addition, Hood (1996) explores detailed genre analyses of benchmark student performances.

Genre analysis should be carefully distinguished from field analysis. An example of field analysis is provided by Martin's (1985) deconstruction of secondary school physical geography textbooks from the perspective of field, in which discourse created an un-commonsense perspective on the world, where physical entities were organized by taxonomies and processes were organized by implication sequences. Martin shows that taxonomies and implication sequences can be generalized across the physical and biological sciences, and that they show up in two main genres used to construct un-commonsense knowledge—report (used to build up taxonomies) and explanation (used to build up implication sequences). He shows how taxonomies, as semantic structures, are distinctively reflected in the lexicogrammar (i.e., the lexicon and the grammar) of the discourse, and does the same for implication sequences (Halliday and Martin 1993:134–135).

Genre and field analysis differ considerably. As noted above, genre is a staged, goal-oriented social process realized through register and is associated with a particular situational configuration of field, tenor, and mode. Field analysis concentrates on one component of genre: field—the subject matter of text—so that it has the potential to reveal commonalities across differences of tenor (e.g., informal versus formal) and mode (e.g., spoken versus written). More exactly, in the example above, field analysis concentrates on the structures of field, on the taxonomies and implication sequences rather than the entities and processes. In my terms, it concentrates on knowledge structures rather than knowledge. Field analysis shows how these structures underlie genres. It analyzes a structure as a semantic structure and examines its reflection in the lexicogrammar. By contrast, genre analysis deals with the stages of a text process (i.e., with the textual order of the text) and with the lexicogrammar of the whole situational configuration.

Knowledge structure analysis is essentially similar in its goals to field (structure) analysis (but see Mohan 1987 for qualifications). It examines a knowledge structure as a semantic structure and explores how it is distinctively reflected in the lexicogrammar of discourse. Martin's terms "taxonomy" and "implication sequence" are labeled *classification* and *cause-effect relation* in knowledge structure terms, and the six knowledge structures, taken as a whole, underlie a large number of genres of educational discourse. One consequence of this is that it shows the relation of the present study to genre work on educational discourse. A further consequence is that my treatment of the lexicogrammar of knowledge structures is able to lean heavily on the resources provided by earlier analyses of genre in the SFL tradition. The general pattern of a KS analysis will appear in my analysis of the discourse data below: I will discuss a knowledge structure in semantic terms and examine its reflection in the lexicogrammar.

These discourse data are, of course, spoken dialogue. The body of work on genre and Martin's work on taxonomies and implication sequences have shown the importance of knowledge structures in written discourse in textbooks. There is a corresponding need for work on the role of knowledge structures in the oral discourse of teaching and learning. Fortunately, one of the advantages of an analysis based on field or knowledge structures rather than genre is that it can reveal commonalities across differences of written and spoken mode and across differences of textual order within dialogues and between dialogue and monologue.

Significant work on the oral strategies of teaching and learning was done in the 1960s at the University of Illinois by a group of educational philosophers (Smith, Meux, Coombs, Nuthall, and Precians 1967). This work indicates a direction of analysis that has been generally neglected by language researchers. It presents categories of analysis that are logically described, based on the empirical study of classroom interaction, and supported by definitions and discourse examples, thus providing evidence for the viability of these categories. Many of these categories correspond closely to the knowledge structures given above, as follows, with the KSs given in upper case and the categories given in lower case: CLASSIFICATION: concepts; PRINCIPLES: rules, cause-effect; EVALUATION: evaluations;

DESCRIPTION: particulars; SEQUENCE: procedures; CHOICE: reason-action. All of these categories have types of conversational moves associated with them; for instance, *rules* has moves such as rule formulation and range of application. Several of these categories and moves will be helpful in enriching the knowledge structure statements in my analysis below.

3 The OPI

My KS analysis of the interview data needs to be seen against the backdrop of criticism of the Oral Proficiency Interview. Two aspects of the OPI that have received criticism are the OPI as an elicitation and the OPI as an interview. The OPI involves an elicitation of a sample of speech from the examinee and a rating of that sample for oral proficiency. The rating scale used in the OPI is based on a functional view of discourse and language, but it lacks a basis of theory and research. It fails to draw on available resources such as SFL.

From its inception, the OPI was intended to match the functional abilities to perform communicative tasks with linguistic abilities. This later resulted in the functional trisection, in which performance is evaluated for three factors: functions, contexts (i.e., range of topics and situations), and linguistic accuracy (Clark and Clifford 1988). Functions include "give instructions, describe, report and provide narration about current past and future activities ... provide explanations ... offer supported opinions and hypothesize." At the highest level of proficiency, Level 5, the trisection states: "Functions equivalent to an educated native speaker" (Educational Testing Service 1982:22). Quite clearly, the OPI is based on a functional view of discourse and language and aims to assess oral proficiency in academic contexts across all subject areas.

The OPI fails to achieve its aims. In a fundamental condemnation of the OPI, Lantolf and Frawley (1985, 1988) observe that the definitions of proficiency in the OPI are not linked to any observation of natural communication or to any theory of communication; they are instead arbitrary lists of characteristics presumed to be in the repertoire of a proficient native speaker. Nor is the OPI an isolated case. Cummins (Cummins 1984, 1991) argues that a major reason for the confused state of language proficiency assessment in bilingual programs stems from the failure to develop an adequate theoretical framework for relating language proficiency to academic achievement.

Valdman (1988:126) refers to the "Achilles' heel of the OPI: overemphasis on sentence-level linguistic features. The disproportionate attention given to grammatical structure results in the neglect of central constituents of communicative behavior, particularly discourse coherence spanning the entire dyadic interaction." To put it more specifically, the OPI's grammar is not functional and is not related to the OPI's functional categories; the functional categories are not adequately defined, and in any case they are not operative in assessment. By contrast, in my analysis of candidates' discourse, I will present knowledge structure categories, discuss them in semantic terms, relate them to discourse realizations in functional lexicogrammar, and do so within the general theoretical framework of SFL, which provides a functional view of language and discourse and a sophisticated analysis of discourse in educational contexts.

I now turn to the OPI as interview. The aim of this section is to explore the interviews as the co-construction of knowledge structures, as epistemic interactions for building knowledge. Knowledge structures have not been examined in recent research that has reviewed the OPI as an interview. Nevertheless, this research provides helpful orientation. This body of work has examined language proficiency interviews from the standpoint of power and control in dyadic interaction and as instances of extended asymmetric discourse (Ross and Berwick 1992, van Lier 1989, Young and Milanovic 1992). It has shown rather clearly that language proficiency interviews are not the transparent collection of a sample of discourse from a candidate, and that the interview process can produce threats to both the validity of the interview and the validity of the subsequent rating process. Similarly, in the data below, knowledge structure analysis of interviewing will also show evidence of validity threats.

Work that throws unexpected but valuable light on the application of knowledge structures to interviews is the tradition of anthropological fieldwork interviewing drawn together by Werner and Schoepfle (1987). In this tradition, the ethnographer tries to obtain the cultural knowledge of the natives in epistemic (knowledge-seeking) interviews, and elicitation of information for an ethnography proceeds from the general to the particulars of an individual's knowledge. The individual's cultural knowledge is understood to be organized in knowledge structures. Consequently the interviewer uses careful and systematic questioning techniques that consciously draw on knowledge structures such as taxonomies, part-whole relations, time sequences, decisions, causal chains, and values. For example, questions about time schedules are fundamental because all people act in temporal sequences. Ethnographers often ask the informant a general question about the activities or schedule of a recent day. Then more specific questions may be asked about the activities mentioned as part of the day, such as eating a meal or herding the sheep. Thus the general question is based on time sequence and the specific questions are systematically based on the part-whole relations of the schedule (Werner and Schoepfle 1987:

Chapters 9 and 10). Of course, ethnographic interviews are different from OPI interviews, and OPI interviewers are not necessarily systematic questioners. Nevertheless, there are parallels between epistemic ethnographic interviews that aim to elicit knowledge via discourse and epistemic language interviews that aim to elicit discourse via the discussion of knowledge. For instance, as we will see below, the OPI interviewer in my data asks the ITA about the schedule of a day, using questions that elicit time sequences and set the activities of the day within the time frame of the whole day. There are also parallels between epistemic ethnographic interviews and those forms of scaffolding in classroom interaction where a teacher asks a series of questions that elicit and support a learner's construction of a discourse (Cazden 1988:101). I am not acquainted, however, with any studies of the scaffolding of knowledge structures.

With the epistemic interview in mind, I will use the model of dyadic interaction from the power and control studies of the OPI as a baseline comparison for my analysis of knowledge co-construction. The model developed in these studies to analyze the discourse structure of OPIs uses two dimensions: goal orientation and contingency (Jones and Gerard 1967). Goal orientation reflects the goals of each speaker separately, while contingency reflects how participants react to each other. Young and Milanovic (1992: 405), who develop this model further, define a contingent utterance as "one in which the content and often the form of the utterance depend in some way on a previous utterance." Berwick and Ross (1996:39) further elaborate the idea of contingency in their discussion of control strategies. In their analysis the goal of the interviewer is to obtain a ratable sample of speech through the mandated examination procedures. This goal is reflected in interviewer control strategies, which include:

> interviewer moves to nominate new topics in the discourse, to abandon previously nominated topics when they generate insufficient interviewee talk, to extend and alter the interviewer's immediately preceding utterance in order to shape the interviewee's next turn and to reformulate the propositional content of topics to which there has been an apparent underelaboration provided by the interviewee. All of these moves converge on the interviewer's compelling need to obtain a ratable sample of speech and form the core of strategies intended to advance the interview.

Berwick and Ross draw particular attention to the ways in which interviewers lead up to a probe over a series of turns. For example, the interviewer may negotiate a series of information resources about the interviewer's recent experience and then commit the interviewee to deal with an aspect or implication of the established resource. Or the interviewer may successively build up the propositional content of a coming probe through turns and then launch the probe.

In the interview excerpts I will examine, I have chosen as a unit of analysis the interviewer's probe plus the teaching assistant's response plus any lead-ins or follow-ups, plus closure if it occurs verbally. This can be represented schematically as:

(Lead-ins) + Probe + Response + (Follow-ups) + (Closure)

If we use the dyadic model above as a baseline comparison, we can assume that: the interviewer's goal is to launch a successful probe that is answered by the candidate with a ratable discourse response; the interviewer will use lead-ins as a strategy to increase the chances of a successful probe; the interviewer will also use follow-ups as a strategy to elaborate the TA's response. We can also assume that the candidate's goal is to provide a discourse response that adequately displays the his or her abilities.

The analysis below will show that we have to go beyond this baseline in a knowledge structure analysis. For example, in Excerpt 7 the interviewer leads in by trying to establish that the ITA knows how to cook. Then the interviewer gives a probe that asks the ITA to give a recipe. The ITA gives an incomplete recipe, so the interviewer asks for the part that is missing. Thus it is not enough to say that the probe requests a ratable sample of speech and that the probe and response are similar in topic. Rather, the probe requests a recipe, that is, it requests the ITA to construct a particular kind of knowledge structure in discourse. Because the probe request assumes that the ITA knows the recipe, the interviewer tries to establish this in the lead-in. Because the probe request is not fulfilled or satisfied by the incomplete recipe, the interviewer tries to secure this in the follow-up.

More generally, the pattern of explanation is: the probe requests the candidate to respond with a recipe, a schedule, a rule, a causal generalization. The interviewer uses lead-ins to support the assumptions of the probe, considered as a speech act. The interviewer uses follow-ups to fulfill the satisfaction conditions of the response, considered as a speech act. Since all the responses imply certain knowledge structures, the follow-ups are likely to reflect those knowledge structures.

The pattern is an elaboration of a model for strategic discourse interaction outlined in Mohan (1974). The model uses speech-act theory and practical reasoning theory to account for strategies in dyadic discourse. In brief it says: if a speaker intends to perform a speech act whose intended perlocutionary effect (IPE) requires certain belief conditions to be the case, s/he will consider whether these beliefs are mutually shared with the addressee, and if this is not known, s/he will try to find out about or will try to establish these beliefs if possible, using further speech acts. Three kinds of belief conditions are: the felicity conditions of the speech act, the presuppositions of the proposition of the speech act, and the satisfaction conditions for the response requested. The model applies both to the interviewer and to the candidate. The model relates goal-orientation to the intentionality of speech acts, contingency to elements of speech acts, and strategy to practical reasoning. Formal models of a number of aspects of strategic discourse interaction are available in the growing body of research work on discourse planning by specialists in computer science and artificial intelligence (e.g., Hovy 1988).

4 Knowledge Structure Analysis

The four interview excerpts analyzed in this chapter were taken from eight OPIs administered, audiotaped, and rated at the beginning of the 1993-4 academic year by a single, trained interviewer (IN), the transcriptions of which were examined for the use of knowledge structures during probes. The unit of analysis includes the probe, which is indicated by an arrow (→), plus the response of the international teaching assistant (TA), whose OPI rating is given at the beginning of the excerpt. The four excerpts contrast two subtypes each of two knowledge structures—sequence (schedules, procedures) and principles (rules, cause-effect generalizations). The aim of the analysis is to show how these knowledge structure contrasts influence functional grammar and to relate elicitation and interaction aspects of the OPI as knowledge construction: They reveal themselves both at the micro level of the lexicogrammar of the clause and at the macro level of the whole excerpt, and they reveal themselves in the talk by the individual TA and in the interaction between the interviewer and the TA. In each excerpt I will discuss first the interview as an elicitation of discourse by the TA, and second, the interview as an interaction between the interviewer and the TA.

4.1 *Sequence as a Knowledge Structure*

Sequence can be defined as actions (and/or events) in time order. One type of sequence is a schedule, such as a person's schedule for a day, a week, or a year. Another type of sequence is a procedure. There is a whole-part relation between a schedule and its constituent actions or events and between a procedure and its constituent actions or events.

4.1.1 Schedule

A schedule is a sequence of actions within, and limited by, a time frame, such as a day. The actions can be by one person or a number of persons. Even in the case of one person on one day, there need be no connection between the actions other than that they are done by that person on that day, so the time frame is an important source of unity. The time frame also goes beyond sequence of time and brings in time-when (location in time), relative to clock and calendar. Schedules are not discussed in Smith et al. (1967), but they do receive attention under the heading of "plans" in Werner and Schoepfle (1987 vol. 2:121–122). In ethnographic interviews, the day and its activities form a popular temporal unit and getting up and going to bed at night offer well-defined boundaries, since the human activity-day is clearly not identical with the astronomical day or the 24-hour day (Werner and Schoepfle 1987 vol. 1:329).

4.1.2 Procedures

Smith et al (1967:47–50) define procedures as follows.

> A venture of this type discloses a sequence of actions by which an end may be achieved. The sequence of actions may be related to solving a problem, making a product, or bringing about a certain type of event.... Sometimes by "procedure" is meant nothing more than the sequence of actions that took place or will be taking place. The term "performance" will be used to convey this sense. On the other hand, "procedure" is often used to refer to an abstract structure, or set of ideas, which determines the sequence to be performed on a particular occasion. It is to this abstract conception that we refer by the term "procedure."
>
> Our example procedure is about cooking, where the sequence of actions is about making a product, for example a meal. The performance/procedure distinction is clear in the data. *What might you prepare for this evening's meal?* is a question about a performance; *Tell me how to make it* is a request for a procedure. When the TA comments about this request: *I'm not expert at cooking*, he is saying that talking about cooking procedures requires expertise, not just experience. Cooking frequently is not the same as cooking expertly.

Three of the moves described by Smith et al. (1967:52) will be used in the data analysis:

Summary of Steps. The steps in a procedure are summarized in a schematic or point-like fashion, either generally or in terms of the particular problem dealt with in the venture.

Characterization of Performance. A performance is described, discussed, explained, carried out, or evaluated.

Discussion of Procedure. Description, explanation, discussion, or evaluation of the procedure itself is given.

Lexicogrammatical features. Actions/events appear mainly through action verbs (in SFL terms, material process transitivity) but also through lexis (e.g., *What would be your normal routine or activity?*). If the text deals with specific occasions, tense may be simple past or simple future. If the text deals with a generic procedure, the tense may be timeless—for instance, the simple present—and the agent may be nonspecific (*one, you*). Procedures often state what should be done, and may therefore include modal verbs, whereas accounts of specific occasions usually describe what actually happened. Time order often appears through linking items (*then*), time-when through circumstances of time (*on Monday*).

Both Excerpts 7 and 8 have sequence in common. But there are important differences between schedules and procedures that are also reflected in the excerpts. As noted above, there need be no connection between actions in a schedule, other than the time frame. The actions in the sequence are semantically related to the time frame. In Excerpt 7 we will accordingly see the importance of time frame references to time-when. By contrast, there is a very close connection between actions in a procedure, since a procedure is a sequence of actions by which an end may be achieved, and thus forms a unified whole. The actions in the sequence are semantically related to the end. In Excerpt 8 we will see the importance of this unity, which appears through the way actions process ingredients into a final product and constitute important parts of the whole process. A further contrast between schedules and procedures is that while a procedure typically requires expertise and experience, a schedule does not. Your schedule is simply what you do, given that you work to a timetable. Here it would make no sense for the TA to say *I'm not an expert* and it would make no sense for the interviewer to attempt to establish TA's experience in the lead-in of the schedule text.

```
(7)  Sequence — Personal schedule. TA's OPI rating: 3.
     Arrows indicate probe.

1 IN: Let's imagine a situation for next week.
2 TA: Um.
3 IN: Okay. It's Monday morning about 9 o'clock and what
      would be your normal routine or activity?
→     What could be a schedule for that Monday,
→     starting about 9 o'clock?
```

```
4  TA:  Okay. I think I'll be getting up at that time and I
        naturally go to the PC lab, do one hour of work as a
        teaching assistant. And after that, I'll have a half
        an hour break, and then later I'll be going to another
        class for one-and-a-half hour. And then I'd have my
        lunch. And then after that I'll be staying for a
        while. And then at 3:30 I'll be having another class
        for one hour. And then I'll decide whether I want to
        study or go to see a movie.
5  IN:  Hah, on Monday.
6  TA:  Uh, huh.
7  IN:  Wonderful.
```

4.1.3 *TA Talk*

IN's probe in turn 3 can be paraphrased: *What could be a schedule* (= your normal routine or activity) *for that Monday* (= next week) *starting about 9 o'clock* (= in the morning)? In turn 4 the TA responds appropriately with his imagined schedule of action for the day.

In turn 4 the TA constructs the schedule as a sequence of actions. In the schedule the verbs are mainly action verbs (*get up, go, do*) in the future tense and the agent is always the specific *I*. (I treat *I have a class/break/lunch* as equivalent to the action verb *I go to class;* see Halliday 1994:147). Time sequence is usually explicitly marked (*after that, then later, and then*). Since this is a schedule, where actions are within and limited by the time frame given by IN, the TA not only constructs a sequence of actions, he relates the actions to the time frame. The TA locates actions with time-when references (*at that time, at 3:30*) and with how-long references that are roughly anchored to the time frame via the time-when references (*one hour, half an hour, for one-and-a-half hour, for a while, for one hour*). The listener, and the interviewer in particular, can use these time references to assess the presentation of the schedule. Is the day filled? Are there gaps?

4.1.4 *Interviewer's Interaction with TA*

IN uses two lead-ins in turns 1 and 3, then gives the probe in turn 3, then gives a follow-up in turn 5 and a closure in turn 7. In the lead-ins, IN takes pains to establish the time frame on which the probe crucially depends. First IN gives a broad time-when reference in turn 1, *a situation for next week*, then a specific one in turn 3, *it is Monday morning about 9 o'clock*. Finally, in the probe itself, IN makes it clear that Monday is the time frame limit of the schedule and that 9 a.m. is the start of the schedule. Just as the probe depends crucially on the specific time frame, it also depends crucially on the TA's general understanding of *schedule*. To convey that he

Knowledge Structures in Oral Proficiency Interviews 189

is asking for a schedule (and not just *What will you do on Monday?*), IN leads in with a paraphrase, *your normal routine or activity*. This seems to succeed, for the TA does describe his actions, as we have seen, not just in time sequence but in time-when and how-long, namely, in relation to a time frame or timetable.

When TA stops listing his actions, his schedule for that Monday, it is not clear that the schedule is complete. Since the TA starts his schedule with getting up, it is a reasonable expectation that he will go to bed within the time frame. IN follows up in turn 5 with a mild prompt for completeness by mentioning again the time frame limit of the schedule: *On Monday*. This is some evidence that IN has been tracking the progress of the schedule against the time frame. TA indicates in turn 6 that there is nothing more to offer, and IN accepts this gracefully with a positive evaluative closure in turn 7. Thus the interactions of the IN and the TA are linked not only by sequence but particularly by the notion of the time frame of a sequence of events.

(8) Sequence — Production procedure (cooking). TA's OPI rating: 1. Arrow indicates probe.

```
1   IN:  Okay. Do you live by yourself?
2   TA:  Yes.
3   IN:  Do you cook for yourself?
4   TA:  Yes.
5   IN:  What might you prepare for this evening's meal, do
         you think?
6   TA:  Just some Chinese food. Some rice and some
         vegetables and some meat.
7   IN:  Sounds good.
→        Tell me how to make it.
8   TA:  You mean, just cook it first with fried little
         meat, then we cut little vegetable and we put it
         into an oven. And I put it in pan. And then I think
         you have to put them in wok, into it and some sauce,
         sometime some sugar. I'm not expert at cooking.
9   IN:  And is that all? Do you have any rice or anything
         like that?
10  TA:  I think cooking the rice is very simple. Just some
         water and some rice.
11  IN:  Okay. All right.
```

4.1.5 *TA Talk*

The probe in turn 7 can be paraphrased: *Tell me how to make it* (= the Chinese food you might prepare for this evening's meal). The TA responds appropriately with a generalized procedure. In terms of the moves of Smith et al. (1967), the TA's response is a summary of steps (of a procedure), and the probe is a request for a summary.

The TA constructs the generalized procedure as a sequence of actions/events, using standard grammatical resources. In the procedure in turn 8, the verbs are action verbs (*cook, cut, put*) in the timeless simple present and the agents are mainly nonspecific (*you* meaning *anyone doing this procedure*). Time sequence is indicated explicitly (*first, then, then*) and implicitly (*and* meaning *and then*). But beyond being a sequence, this is a procedure for making something; its end is a product, a meal. The listener can track this developing product or end, and IN does track it, by tracking the ingredients. The TA refers to ingredients (*meat, vegetables, sauce, sugar*) being put into utensils/receptacles (*oven, pan, wok*) and cumulatively processed as a combined *it* until *it* becomes the meal. In this sense, the ingredients, as they flow through the separate actions into a product, are an important unifying element binding the parts of the procedure into a whole and an important source of clues to the completeness of the procedure. A problem with the procedure occurs in turn 8, *cook it*, where *it* has no clear reference.

4.1.6 *Interviewer's Interaction with TA*

IN asks three lead-in questions (turns 1, 3, 5), then gives the probe (turn 7), then asks a follow-up question (turn 9), and then provides closure (turn 11). In terms of moves, turn 3 is a request for a characterization of performance, and one is provided by turn 4; turn 5 is again a request for a characterization of performance, and one is provided by turn 6. Here in turns 3 and 5, IN is clearly asking about TA's performance on particular occasions: *What might you prepare for this evening's meal*. The probe, however, is asking about a procedure, asking *how to make it* rather than *how you make it*. At the end of turn 8 the TA makes a Discussion of Procedure move, *I'm not expert at cooking*, referring at a metalevel to the procedure. IN's follow-up question in turn 9 is also a discussion of procedure, *And is that all?*.

IN evidently intends the lead-in questions to establish a basis for the probe. For example, turns 5 and 6 establish what TA will be cooking that evening and turn 7 asks how to cook it, the assumption being that if you cook it, you know how to cook it. As I have noted, however, turns 5 and 6 deal with performances while turn 7 deals with a procedure. IN has miscalculated. The TA points to this gap at the end of turn 8 with the disclaimer *I'm not expert at cooking*. His experience with cooking is not the same as expertise.

By giving this disclaimer at the end of turn 8, the TA signals that his statement of the procedure is finished. But in the follow-up question in turn 9, IN queries the completeness of the procedure and asks about the preparation of rice, a missing ingredient and a missing part of the procedure. This harks back to turn 6, where TA volunteers that rice will be one of the parts or ingredients of the meal. IN apparently has been monitoring the quality of TA's statement of the procedure by tracking the ingredients and making sure that the procedure has all its parts. Here IN and TA co-construct by sharing a structure of knowledge: The TA specifies parts of the procedure and the interviewer asks about a missing part.

From the standpoint of the OPI rating it is likely to be important that the TA's discourse is inconsistent when stating the procedure in turn 8. In *cook, we cut, we put, I put,* and *you have to put,* the agents vary and are internally inconsistent. *I put* is appropriate to an account of personal performance; *you have to put* is appropriate to official procedure. Superficially, an evaluator might judge the *I* to be an inconsistency on the part of the TA alone; an examination of the co-construction of the interview suggests that the TA's performance/procedure inconsistency in turn 8 might derive from IN's performance/procedure inconsistency between turns 5 and 7. The TA's most frequent structural inaccuracy is the omission of articles (five cases), but this does not appear to affect the interpretation of the procedure.

4.2 *Principles as a Knowledge Structure*

I will consider two types of principle: cause-effect relations and rules (as in rules of games). Both share the element of conditions (whether necessary or sufficient or otherwise), conditions for a rule to apply or conditions for an effect to take place. This central element can be given a basic definition: state of affairs A is necessary and/or sufficient for state of affairs B (Mohan 1986:40). "Necessary and sufficient" is understood more broadly to include weaker relations like "contributes to." "State of affairs" is understood very broadly to include changes of state (i.e., events) and actions.

4.2.1 *Rules*

For rules, state of affairs A represents the condition(s) necessary and/or sufficient for the rule to apply in state B. As Smith et al. (1967:42–44) put it,

> The term "rule" as it is used here refers to conventional ways of doing things and to analytic relationships which may be used to guide actions. Thus rules include such things as rules of grammar, rules for playing a game, laws of a state, mathematical equations. A rule is a conventional guide or regulation for action . . . rules are not reports of empirical investigations.

Four of the verbal moves identified by Smith et al. (1967:45) will be used in the data analysis:

> *Rule Formulation.* A rule governing actions or decisions about alternative actions of a given type is stated or described.
> *Range of Application.* The range of a rule is explicitly noted or discussed independently of the rule formulation.
> *Case Explication.* A particular situation or type of situation is presented and explicated in terms that indicate how the rule is to be applied.
> *Term Explication.* The meaning of one of the terms in the rule formulation is noted or discussed.

4.2.2 Cause-Effect Relations

For cause-effect relations, state of affairs A represents the condition(s) necessary and/or sufficient for the effect(s) in state B. As Smith et al. (1967:20 ff) say,

> The primary cognitive import of this kind of venture is the identification, description, or discussion of events, agents, or characteristics of events or agents which are said to cause, generate, or facilitate the occurrence of a particular phenomenon or class of phenomena. . . . The most important thing to note is that a cause-effect relationship is, in one important sense, empirical. . . . The truth or falsity of a statement of a cause-effect relationship is determined by empirical evidence.

It is important to note that this definition does not limit itself to the familiar image of billiard-ball causation; it includes correlations such as cross-cultural comparisons, as in the excerpt below, where *being in Canada* or *being in China* might be the facilitating (or inhibiting) conditions, and individuals' behaviors are the effects.

Three of the verbal moves identified by Smith et al. (1967:23–24) will be used in the data analysis:

> *Cause Identifying.* A condition or set of conditions is either (a) identified as a cause, or (b) identified as something that produces or contributes to the production of a given effect.
> *Causation Instancing.* An instance of a class of things that has been cited as a cause is shown to occur in conjunction with an instance of a class of things that has been cited as an effect.
> *Concomitant Variation.* It is noted that, when different causal conditions occur, or when the context surrounding the causal conditions is changed, the effect is different, or does not occur.

Lexicogrammatical features. Cause-effect generalizations cover actions and events, so they typically involve action verbs in the timeless or indefinite present with generic participants. Rules can be similar, though relational processes and nonspecific participants are more likely to appear in rules. Conditions for rules and conditions for effects may appear in conditional clauses and circumstantial phrases, among other possibilities. Cases and examples to which rules and generalizations apply may be contrasted with cases and examples to which they do not apply. The example relation and the contrast relation may be realized in a variety of ways.

In Excerpts 9 and 10 we see the similarities and differences between these two types of principle flow through the discourse, from the micro level of the grammar to the larger patterning of the interaction strategies. Conditions will be very salient in the rule excerpt, less salient but still important in the cause-effect excerpt; application to cases will appear in both; the empirical/non-empirical contrast will have consequences.

(9) Principles − Rules. TA's OPI rating: 1+. Arrow indicates probe.

```
1    IN:  How would you describe the programs you see on
          Channel 30?
2    TA:  My most favorite sport is soccer. Every Saturday
          from 11:30 is the soccer Saturday program.
3    IN:  Do you also play soccer?
4    TA:  Yes.
5    IN:  Let me ask you a question about soccer.
6    TA:  Okay.
7    IN:  One thing I've never understood is what it means to
          be offside.
8    TA:  Offside?
9→   IN:  Yeah. Could you explain that to me?
10   TA:  Okay. I think − how to conduct player who is in the
          front. Because when you play soccer, you always has
          three level of, first is so-called front, and is
          the middle, and the defense. So there's a − I
          cannot − if there's a − it's very hard to explain.
11   IN:  Well you probably need a board.
12   TA:  Yeah, maybe the board, something like that.
13   IN:  How about going up to the front. You can still
          probably do the recording. Just give us a big
          voice.
14   TA:  Okay. So here is the player. [TA begins to draw a
          case of a soccer state of play on the blackboard]
15   IN:  Uh huh.
```

```
16  TA:  So have two teams. And here is the gate. And here is
         some people, belongs to this team we call A.
17  IN:  Yes.
18  TA:  And this there, if they stand there, so they forms
         a line like this, this is defense, and if ball is
         still in here, and a player from team B exceeds
         this line, we call the base line, that is called
         offside.
19  IN:  Have you ever been offside?
20  TA:  Oh yes! [Laughter]. Because sometimes you think
         "Okay, let's run," and — I don't know —
21  IN:  Okay.
```

4.2.3 *TA Talk*

The probe in turn 9 can be paraphrased as *Concerning soccer, could you explain to me what it means to be offside?*. It is a request for the conditions under which the offside rule applies. TA states these conditions in turn 18.

The TA constructs a response using four moves. In turn 10, TA begins with a range-of-application-of-the-rule statement (Smith et al. 1967:45); *how to conduct player who is in front* is an attempt to say which players the rule applies to. Then in turn 10 the TA explains the term *front* in a term explication move. The TA then tries to produce an explanation, but breaks down: *It's very hard to explain*. At this point the rule explanation stops while the breakdown is repaired. In turns 11–13, IN suggests using the blackboard and TA takes up the suggestion. Returning to the explanation, in turns 14–16 the TA uses the blackboard as an aid to describe a case of a soccer state-of-play, giving a case-explication. In the case explication, the processes are relational, and in the immediate present, and the participants specific (*the gate, this team*). Finally, in turn 18, the TA gives a rule formulation, specifying a constitutive rule. In the rule formulation, the processes are mainly relational (*is, is called*), and there is a switch toward timelessness with the participants typically nonspecific (*a player*), but the switch from case-explication is not complete. The conditions under which the rule applies are specified by *if*-clauses, and the constitutive nature of the rule (what constitutes or counts as offside) appears in *is called offside* (compare the eliciting question *what it means to be offside*). Thus, despite difficulties, TA manages an explanation of *offside* that includes a number of the elements noted by Smith et al. (1967).

4.2.4 *Interviewer's Interaction with TA*

IN is active in the lead-in to the probe and, after the probe, helps TA repair the breakdown. IN is relatively passive in follow-up but actively provides closure and some humor. In turns 1–2, IN learns of the TA's interest in soccer, and in turns 3–4 establishes that the TA is a soccer player, and thus probably has expertise in the rules of the game. In turns 5 and 7, IN leads up to the probe in turn 9, announcing the topic—soccer—the specific topic—the offside rule—and then requesting an explanation. By speaking of *what it means to be offside*, IN signals that an expert analytical explanation is requested, not an empirical generalization about personal experience. After TA's breakdown at the end of turn 10, IN suggests using the blackboard. IN appears to be merely supplementing the role of verbal discourse with visual communication (a shift in mode of communication), but in fact it is a shift in field also, since the TA uses the blackboard to present a case-explication, when what the probe requested was a general rule rather than a specific case. IN does no further follow-up, though IN could have queried TA further by asking, for example, about the contrasting condition where the player receives the ball direct from a corner kick; however, IN does not do so, presumably because of a lack of knowledge of soccer. Thus IN is given an example by the TA without prompting, but IN fails to prompt TA for contrast where contrast was possible. In turns 19–20, IN provides closure and relaxes the level. Interestingly, this is managed in turn 19 *Have you ever been offside?*, by switching the question under consideration from expert rule to personal experience, a shift in the construction of the topic, which is received with laughter.

(10) Principles – Cause-effect. TA OPI rating: 3. Arrows
     indicate probe.

(Earlier probe and response three minutes prior to line 1:
     IN: How would you compare the way statistics is done in
          your university in China and in Canada?
     TA: Actually, not much different. The only difference I
          found in schools back in China and in Canada is you
          can drink and eat in the class.
     IN: In Canada?
     TA: In Canada, right)

→1 IN: When you go out into the general world, I mean
→   outside of the university, what are some of the
→   things that you have discovered over the last
→   few years that you think are a little unusual
→   or different from what you were used to back
→   home?
 2 TA: Oh it seems to me, it still seems like the
        Canadians are doing outrageous things.
 3 IN: Pardon me?

4	TA:	It used to seem to me and it still seems to me that Canadians do lots of outrageous things.
5	IN:	Okay. For example. Course, I agree with you but I'm
6	TA:	For example, um, okay. For example, some of them dye their hair green.
7	IN:	Uh huh.
8	TA:	And pull their hair like a hork, hawk, H-A-W-K.
9	IN:	Right.
10	TA:	And they wear their rings everywhere.
11	IN:	You mean not only on the finger but some other places?
12	TA:	Some unspeakable places. Hah, hah, hah.
13	IN:	You mean to tell me, comparing your understanding of Chinese society, there're no odd people in China?
14	TA:	At least they don't feel PROUD in doing them. People are more keen to keep the same as the rest of the crowd. They feel safer to be hurt in a crowd. Not standing up.
15	IN:	So the key difference here is whether they're PROUD of their difference?
16	TA:	They will be shamed of the difference while Canadians is very proud and showing off the difference.
17	IN:	Does that cause trouble sometimes, do you think?
18	TA:	I think I'm open-minded enough to all these different things. But myself, I wouldn't do it. It's other people's business.
19	IN:	It's okay for other people, but you have your own way. I understand.

4.2.5 *TA Talk*

The probe question can be paraphrased: *What things outside the university are different in Canada from China?*. Like the earlier probe, this probe asks for a contrast between Canada and China. The probe assumes that the different circumstances or conditions in Canada and China give rise to other differences, and it asks what these other differences are. IN expresses these conditions through circumstantial phrases (*in China, in Canada, back home*). TA expresses them through agents (*Canadians* = people in Canada).

TA's reply (2–16) is in four moves and in four parts, responding to IN's questions. Turns 2–4 form a cause-identifying move: under the condition of being in Canada rather than in China, people do outrageous things. Turns 6–12 form a causation-instancing move, providing examples of the causal statement given in turns 2–4. *Canadians do outrageous things* is a generic agent causation structure (agent X causes event A), as appears most clearly in *they dye their hair green*, that is, Canadians dye their hair causing their hair to become green. Action (*Canadians do, some of them dye, (they) pull, they wear*) is realized in the verb as actions by groups of agents at a generic time, and the tense is typically timeless present. In the causation-instancing move, turns 6–12, the TA gives three examples. The example relation is verbally marked or realized, obviously enough, by *for example*, but it also appears in the verbs in the lexical taxonomy pattern of DO: *dye, pull, wear*. We also get examples within examples. The three examples of Canadian action are themselves generic. Consequently the interviewer probes the third one—*they wear their rings everywhere*—for examples of *everywhere* (*not only on the finger but some other places? Some unspeakable places*). Here a taxonomy relation is established between *everywhere* (=all places), *on the finger, other places*, and *unspeakable places*.

Responding to IN's challenge in turn 13, turn 14 is a concomitant variation move (see definition above), where it is noted that in China people act differently from Canada, that is, when there is a contrast in causal conditions, the effect is different. The contrast relation is realized in the responses by the negatives *don't* and *not*, by the comparatives *more keen* and *safer*, by the contrast between *in a crowd* and *standing up* and later on by the contrast between Chinese being *shamed* while Canadians are *proud and showing off*.

Turn 16 is another cause-identifying move: under the condition of being in China rather than in Canada, people who do outrageous things are ashamed of their differences. This is a reworking of the original effect claimed. Attitudes to action are thus mentioned (*they will be shamed*, parallel with the earlier *they don't feel proud in doing that*), often with a verb of mental process like *feel*. There is an implication here that Chinese society constrains this type of behavior, which makes it clearer that we are dealing with cause-effect relations rather than with a simple comparison of inconsequential differences between societies.

4.2.6 *Interviewer's Interaction with TA*

IN does not give any lead-ins to the probe but uses another approach, relying on prior context. The probe itself is carefully crafted to support its response, and is very actively followed up. Closure is initiated by the TA and confirmed by IN.

The earlier probe is similar to the present probe in turn 1, though the comparison is between university worlds rather than general worlds. In turn 1, IN appears to reference this earlier probe and response as a prior context, by the phrase *outside of the university*. Apart from this, the probe in turn 1 is without lead-ins. But turn 1 does have built-in qualifications. It lays stress on TA's personal experience and opinion as the basis for the generalization required in the response: *when you go out, you have discovered, you think, you were used to*. This marks the generalization as an empirical generalization (by contrast with the analytical rule in the other principle example), but an empirical generalization about personal experience that the TA has privileged access to, and IN does not, rather than a sociological generalization.

Of IN's follow-up questions, turns 5 and 11 explore the example relation, and are causation-instancing questions. Turn 13 explores the contrast relation and is a concomitant variation question. TA's reply that *Canadians do outrageous things* implies that people do not do outrageous things in China. The interviewer takes the opportunity to challenge this contrastive claim: *there're no odd people in China?*. Then, since what TA says in turn 14 is apparently inconsistent with what TA said in turn 4, IN asks for a restatement of the new claim in turn 15. Like the original probe, this is a cause-identifying question. In turn 17, IN asks a supplementary cause-identifying question. TA's response in turn 18 does not extend the contrastive generalization about Canada and China but switches to a statement of TA's personal position. The topic is maintained, but the probe's construction of the topic is abandoned. This switch from public to personal treatment of the topic heralds a closure, for IN supportively paraphrases that personal position in turn 19, accepting closure of the exploration of the probe. In sum, IN has helped TA construct the topic of social behavior in Canada and China as an empirical causal generalization based on personal experience with examples and a clear and consistent contrast.

5 Conclusions

I will discuss conclusions concerning data analysis, data explanation, oral discourse in educational contexts, and assessment.

5.1 *The OPI as Elicitation*

How can the oral construction of knowledge be analyzed? In my analysis of TA discourses I explored the potential of a knowledge structure approach to this issue. I have shown how the TAs are using discourse to order the experiential world and to construct different structures of knowledge. An analysis of the discourse semantics and lexicogrammar of the texts shows how the speakers use their linguistic resources to build sequences of action and principles such as rules or empirical generalizations. These are knowledge structures, structures of the field of discourse. I have shown too how the speakers differentiate in discourse semantics between subtypes of knowledge structures, between the ingredients of productive procedures and the time framing of schedules, between analytic rules and empirical generalizations. And I have shown how these differentiations are reflected in the lexicogrammar of these discourses.

My analysis went beyond mere description to provide explanation. My data analysis was located in the general framework of systemic functional linguistics. Within that general framework I addressed issues of field (i.e., topic or knowledge), particularly issues of the structure of field (i.e., knowledge structures), with a view to the analysis of the construction of knowledge in oral discourse. In my analysis I used the semantic relations of knowledge structures to mediate between the broadly cognitive or logical categories of Smith et al. (1967) and Werner and Schoepfle (1987) on the one hand, and the lexicogrammatical categories of Halliday (1994) on the other. My hypothesis was that knowledge structures were important macro features of discourse. I defined them in semantic terms, and then showed them to correspond to the lexicogrammatical evidence at the micro level of discourse. In this sense, a knowledge structure at the macrolevel accounts for a variety of features at the micro level.

Accounting for these features of discourse is fundamental to exploring the question of evaluating learner's abilities in oral discourse in relation to the cognitive and communicative demands of education. Within the knowledge structures I worked with, procedures, rules, and cause-effect generalizations were related to categories that had been established for the analysis of oral interaction in teaching and learning by the work of Smith et al. (1967). Various forms of the KSs of sequence and principles underlie a number of the genres central to higher levels of literacy, which have been the target of a large body of Australian work in the systemic linguistic tradition. It is hard to see any justification for ignoring such features any longer.

The discourse analysis of knowledge structures has major implications for the theory and practice of assessment of academic oral proficiency. Although the OPI aims at a functional view of language and discourse, and at oral proficiency in academic contexts, it fails to achieve this. Ultimately this failure can be traced to the failure of the OPI to take advantage of theoretical and empirical work based on a functional view of language. The OPI's conception of grammar as accuracy should be replaced by the richer functional conception of language as a resource for meaning. This has immediate implications for raters. They must move beyond the assessment of grammar for its own sake and a cursory and unconnected judgment of the functional quality of the discourse. They must begin to see how the wording of discourse plays a role in the larger patterns of meaning in discourse, and they must develop a sharpened appreciation of those larger patterns. An alternative to the design of the OPI would be a test that provides a systematic exploration of knowledge structures as larger patterns of discourse.

5.2 The OPI as Interview

The OPI is not merely an elicitation, it is an interview. Hence we are not dealing merely with the construction of knowledge, we are dealing with the interactional co-construction of knowledge. The TA is not a lone builder: the interviewer is a co-worker on the building site. What they are jointly building are knowledge structures.

In these data, a probe by IN does not merely request that the TA talk about a particular topic or field; the probe indicates a speech act and a knowledge structure for that topic—the TA is asked to talk about a sequence (a procedure, a schedule) or a principle (a rule, an empirical generalization). Turning to probe lead-ins, IN leads in to the probe not only by progressively narrowing the topic and by establishing that TA knows something about the topic but also, on occasion, by trying to establish that TA knows enough to construct a given knowledge structure on that topic. The TA likes soccer, but is he a soccer player and therefore likely to know the rules? In speech act terms, this is the difference between the more general "Does TA have the knowledge to answer the probe?" and the more specific "Does TA have the expertise to explain a procedure, or to explain a rule, or have the personal experiences to make a generalization contrasting China and Canada?" IN follows up probes not merely to request more information on the topic but to request information that completes the knowledge structure for the topic. A cooking procedure is given, but there is an ingredient missing; a schedule is given but there is activity remaining to be accounted for; a generalization is given, but without examples, and an implied contrast needs to be made explicit. In speech act terms, this is the difference between the more general "Has TA answered the question satisfactorily?" and the more specific "Has TA replied with a reasonably complete schedule, procedure, rule, or contrastive generalization?" IN can even close a knowledge structure on a topic by switching from *rule about the topic* to *personal experience of the topic*, thereby lightening the tone. The topic remains the same but the development of the rule knowledge structure has been closed.

To account for these interviews, we need to account for knowledge structures as well as topic, and for speech acts as well as talk. IN leads in to, and probes, the knowledge structure of a topic. TA constructs a knowledge structure with that topic. And IN follows up on the knowledge structure of the topic. In other words, IN and TA co-construct field, topic, or knowledge structure. The use of a knowledge structure analysis enables us to account more adequately for the contingencies between IN's contributions and TA's contributions as a joint construction over an extended discourse.

I employed speech act theory and practical reasoning, in a model that built on Mohan (1974), to pick out the goal orientations of IN and TA. IN's target is a probe that is intended to elicit extended discourse from TA. TA's target is an extended discourse. IN's lead-ins to the probe can generally be accounted for as strategies to help the probe work, to help ensure that the felicity conditions and presuppositions of the probe will not fail. Similarly, IN's probe follow-ups are strategies intended to monitor, support, and acknowledge closure of the satisfaction conditions of TA's extended discourse. As I have argued, IN's probes specify the KS of a topic, and it is particularly the KS of the topic that I have used to draw the connections between IN's discourse work and TA's discourse work.

How is this analysis an explanation rather than a mere description? Prior research has analyzed the OPI as an interview using the variables of goal orientation, contingency, and strategy. This model relates goal-orientation to the intentionality of speech acts, contingency to the elements of speech acts, and strategy to principles of practical reasoning applied to speech acts. Speech act theory is the central place in linguistic theory where intentions and goals have been discussed. It allows us to talk about contingency and strategy, not in ad hoc terms but in linguistic terms that illuminate the data and extend the theory.

Accounting more adequately for the interviewer's role as co-constructor of knowledge has implications for the analysis of teaching/learning interactions. A better account of co-construction in interviewing can support a better account of co-construction in the classroom. For example, accounts of scaffolding can begin to make finer distinctions, such as those between scaffolding a genre and scaffolding a knowledge structure.

The analysis has implications for the theory and practice of assessment of academic oral proficiency. The evidence shows that the interviewer is doing much more than simply eliciting a ratable sample, and is engaging in a complex of co-construction strategies, though this is not to say that the interviewer is eliciting knowledge structures in the conscious, systematic, and thorough ways described by Werner and Schoepfle (1987). Interviewers' co-construction strategies dovetail with candidate performance and can produce threats to the validity of the OPI interview and the subsequent rating. My data suggest that when the interviewer co-constructs knowledge structures with the interviewee, fine variations in knowledge structure and lexicogrammar resonate across both. In Excerpt 8, for instance, the interviewer's uncertainty between performance and procedure may have led to grammatical uncertainty on the part of the TA. The OPI rating would not take this into account. Thus future research needs to clarify this situation. Interviewers need to be alerted to their role in co-constructing the interview and the need to develop consistent and empirically based interview strategies, and raters need to become conscious of the ways these matters affect candidate performance. On the other hand, there are positive possibilities in this picture. Future work on the assessment of academic oral proficiency could well consider developing conscious and systematic interviewer strategies for the purposes of exploring the discourse of knowledge construction.

My aim in this chapter has been to move to a position where the assessment issues at stake can be illuminated though the data of discourse. Not the least of the failings of the OPI is that the ratings it makes are not sufficiently explicit and open to scrutiny. This chapter has argued that knowledge structures provide a way of analyzing oral dialogue that illuminates questions of the construction of knowledge and the contributions of the participants in extended co-construction.

Acknowledgment

I wish to give special thanks to Rick Berwick, who generously drew on his expert knowledge of the OPI and provided essential, in-depth support for this paper in many different ways, including extended critical discussion of ideas and insightful comments and suggestions on drafts. He is not, of course, responsible for errors that remain.

References

Berwick, Richard, and Steven Ross. 1996. "Cross-Cultural Pragmatics in Oral Proficiency Interview Strategies." In *Studies in Language Testing,* vol. 3: *Performance Testing, Cognition and Assessment,* ed. by Nick Saville and Michael Milanovic, 34–54. Cambridge: Cambridge University Press.

Cazden, Courtney B. 1988. *Classroom Discourse.* Portsmouth, NH: Heinemann.

Christie, Frances, Brian Devlin, Peter Freebody, Allan Luke, James R. Martin, Terry Threadgold, and Christine Walton. 1991. *Teaching English Literacy.* Canberra: Department of Employment, Education and Training, Commonwealth of Australia.

Clark, John L. D., and Ray T. Clifford. 1988. "The FSI/ILR/ACTFL Proficiency Scales and Testing Techniques: Development, Current Status, and Needed Research." *Studies in Second Language Acquisition* 10.129–148.

Cummins, Jim. 1984. *Bilingualism and Special Education: Issues in Assessment and Pedagogy.* Clevedon, Avon: Multilingual Matters.

Cummins, Jim. 1991. "Conversational and Academic Language Proficiency in Bilingual Contexts." *AILA Review* 8.75–89.

Educational Testing Service. 1982. *ETS Oral Proficiency Testing Manual*. Princeton, NJ: Author.
Halliday, Michael A. K. 1994. *An Introduction to Functional Grammar* (2nd ed.). London: Edward Arnold.
Halliday, Michael A. K., and Ruqaiya Hasan. 1989. *Language, Context and Text: Aspects of Language in a Social-semiotic Perspective*. Oxford: Oxford University Press.
Halliday, Michael A. K., and James R. Martin. 1993. *Writing Science*. London: Falmer Press.
Hood, Susan. 1996. "Systemic Functional Linguistics and ESL Pedagogy." Paper presented at the annual conference of the American Association for Applied Linguistics, Chicago, March 23–26.
Hovy, Eduard. 1988. *Generating Natural Language Under Pragmatic Constraints*. Hillsdale, NJ: Erlbaum.
Jones, Edward E., and Harold B. Gerard. 1967. *Foundations of Social Psychology*. New York: Wiley.
Lantolf, James P., and William Frawley. 1985. "Oral Proficiency Testing: A Critical Analysis." *Modern Language Journal* 69.337–345.
Lantolf, James P., and William Frawley. 1988. "Proficiency: Understanding the Construct." *Studies in Second Language Acquisition* 10.149–164.
Lewin, Miriam. 1979. *Understanding Psychological Research*. New York: Wiley.
Madden, Carolyn G., and Cynthia L. Myers. 1994. *Discourse and Performance of International Teaching Assistants*. Alexandria, VA: Teachers of English to Speakers of Other Languages.
Martin, James R. 1985. *Factual Writing: Exploring and Challenging Social Reality*. Victoria: Deakin University.
Martin, James R. 1992. *English Text*. Amsterdam and Philadelphia: Benjamins.
Mohan, Bernard. 1974. "Do Sequencing Rules Exist?" *Semiotica* 12.75–96.
Mohan, Bernard. 1986. *Language and Content*. Reading, MA: Addison-Wesley.
Mohan, Bernard. 1987. "The Structure of Situations and the Analysis of Text." In *Language Topics: Essays in Honour of Michael Halliday*, ed. by Ross Steele and Terry Threadgold, 507–522. Amsterdam and Philadelphia: Benjamins.
Mohan, Bernard. 1990. "LEP Students and the Integration of Language and Content: Knowledge Structures and Tasks." In *Proceedings of the First Research Symposium on Limited English Proficient Students' Issues*, ed. by Carmen Simich-Dudgeon, 113–160. Washington, DC: Office of Bilingual Education and Minority Languages Affairs.
Monkhouse, Francis J. 1960. *Principles of Physical Geography*. London: University of London Press.
New South Wales Adult Migrant English Service/National Centre for English Language Teaching and Research. 1993. *Certificate in Spoken and Written English* (2nd ed.). Surry Hills, NSW: Author.
Ross, Steven, and Richard Berwick. 1992. "The Discourse of Accommodation in Oral Proficiency Interviews." *Studies in Second Language Acquisition* 14.159–176.

Smith, B. Othanel, Milton Meux, Jerrold Coombs, Graham Nuthall, and Robert Precians. 1967. *A Study of the Strategies of Teaching*. Champaign, IL: University of Illinois Bureau of Educational Research.

Tyler, Andrea. 1992. "Discourse Structure and Perception of Incoherence in International Teaching Assistants' Spoken Discourse." *TESOL Quarterly* 26.713–729.

Valdman, Albert. 1988. "Introduction." *Studies in Second Language Acquisition* 10.121–128.

van Lier, Leo. 1989. "Reeling, Writhing, Drawling, Stretching, and Fainting in Coils: Oral Proficiency Interviews as Conversation." *TESOL Quarterly* 23.489–508.

Werner, Oswald, and G. Mark Schoepfle. 1987. *Systematic Fieldwork*. Newbury Park, CA: Sage.

Williams, Jessica. 1992. "Planning, Discourse Marking, and the Comprehensibility of International Teaching Assistants." *TESOL Quarterly* 26.693–711.

Write It Right. 1992. *Quarterly Report No. 5*. Sydney, Australia: New South Wales Department of School Education, Metropolitan East Region, Disadvantaged Schools Program.

Young, Richard, and Michael Milanovic. 1992. "Discourse Variation in Oral Proficiency Interviews." *Studies in Second Language Acquisition* 14.403–424.

The Use of Communication Strategies in Language Proficiency Interviews

Yumiko Yoshida-Morise
Teachers College, Columbia University

1 Introduction

Since Selinker (1972) first proposed the notion of communication strategies as one of the five learning processes for second language (L_2) learners, research into second language acquisition (SLA) has increasingly emphasized these processes. In addition, Hymes's (1972) elucidation of the concept of communicative competence has prompted L_2 teachers and SLA researchers to be concerned with the development of integrated linguistic and sociolinguistic competencies. Furthermore, Canale and Swain (1980:25), by referring to communication strategies as strategic competence and including it as one of the components of communicative competence, broadened its definition. They describe strategic competence as:

> ... strategies that speakers employ to handle breakdowns in communication: for example, how to deal with false starts, hesitations, and other performance factors, how to avoid grammatical forms that have not been mastered fully, how to address strangers when unsure of their social status—in short, how to cope in an authentic communicative situation and how to keep the communicative channel open.

The inclusion of strategic competence in the framework of communicative competence and the increasing importance accorded to the development of communicative language skills has prompted attempts to define communication strategies and led to several studies on the use of communication strategies in communicative situations (Færch and Kasper 1980, 1983a; Paribakht 1985; Poulisse 1987, 1990; Tarone 1977, 1980).

Færch and Kasper (1983b), for example, claim that to some extent, all L_2 speech production involves various types of problem solving or decision making due to speakers' limited amount of L_2 knowledge. L_2 speakers may express their intended meanings by employing words from their native language, by paraphrasing particular L_2 lexical items, or by creating L_2-like words. In order to achieve communication goals, L_2 speakers resort to various communication strategies in L_2 production. This seems to suggest that communication strategies play an important role in compensating for the inadequacy of L_2 resources in L_2 use.

The key questions are, then, what communication strategies do L_2 learners use in interaction situations and how do they use them? Additionally, do individual learners possessing varying amounts of L_2 knowledge employ communication strategies differently, and, if so, how? Since the use of communication strategies is assumed as one aspect of communicative ability, the answers to these questions are important for a better understanding of language proficiency interviews in which L_2 learners' communicative skills are assessed.

The study reported here aimed at examining the use of communication strategies by setting two main goals. First and foremost, this study attempted to identify the nature and number of communication strategies in the speech production of adult Japanese L_2 speakers of English in oral interview situations in which their level of proficiency was rated. Second, the study sought to explore the relationship between the use of communication strategies and level of proficiency. The specific interview used was the Oral Proficiency Interview (Educational Testing Service 1982), an updated version of the Foreign Service Institute Oral Proficiency Interview designed by Educational Testing Service to assess communicative language ability (Lowe 1987).

2 Definition of Communication Strategies

While there are various theoretical approaches to the definition of communication strategies (Bialystok 1990; Poulisse 1990; Tarone 1980, 1981), from the psycholinguistic perspective, Færch and Kasper (1980:81) define communication strategies as "potentially conscious plans for solving what to an individual presents itself as a problem in reaching a particular communicative goal." According to Færch and Kasper (1983b), communication strategies are placed in a processing model of speech production during the stages of goal formation, planning, and execution. The use of communication strategies during speech production is illustrated in Figure 1.

Speech-production processing begins with the establishment of communication goals appropriate to situations and proceeds to the organization of linguistic plans,

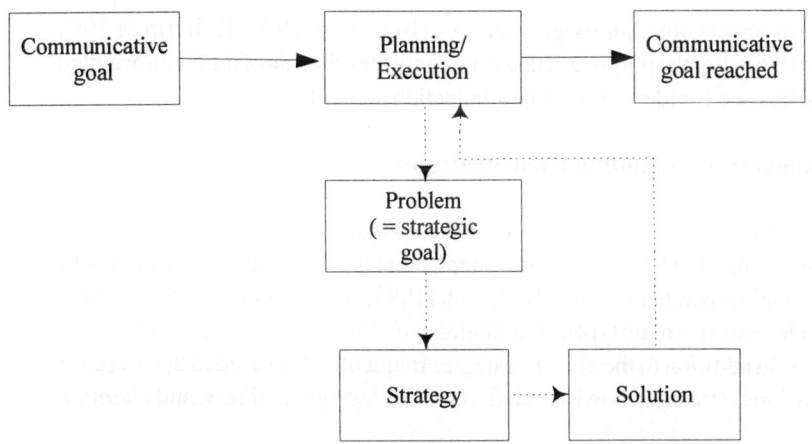

Figure 1. Strategic Planning (Faerch and Kasper 1983b:33). Reprinted by permission of Addison Wesley Longman Ltd.

which are then executed. In the case of L_2 communication, L_2 speakers with insufficient L_2 resources may make modifications to their intended goals during the planning processes to compensate for gaps between what would be required to accomplish their intended goals and what they can actually do. Incomplete processes may also result from automatized first language (L_1) processing and the resulting L_1 to L_2 transfer (McLaughlin 1987; McLaughlin, Rossman, and McLeon 1983; Poulisse and Bongaerts 1994). L_2 speakers attempt to solve various problems they encounter in L_2 communication by employing strategies that best convey their intended meanings. Færch and Kasper note, however, that communication strategies are characteristic not only of L_2 speech production but also of L_1. In situations where L_1 speakers are conversing with L_2 learners, the L_1 speakers also need strategies, such as paraphrasing in order to make their utterances easier for their interlocutor to comprehend.

On the basis of this processing model, Færch and Kasper offer two criteria for identifying communication strategies: *problem-orientedness* and *consciousness*. The primary criterion, problem-orientedness, "presupposes a distinction between goals which the individual experiences no difficulty in reaching and goals which present themselves to the individual as 'problems': only plans that relate to the latter type of goals will be considered strategies" (Færch and Kasper 1983b:32). The secondary criterion, consciousness, is referred to as "always" or "sometimes" (p. 36) conscious attention to the problems that L_2 speakers perceive or problem-solving processes. For all practical purposes, however, consciousness is impossible to indicate in observable language behavior (Bialystok 1990, Kellerman 1991, Poulisse 1990). For the purpose of this study, only the criterion of problem-orientedness will be used for identifying communication strategies.

3 A Taxonomy of Communication Strategies

The taxonomy used in the present study is based mainly on those of Tarone (1977, 1980) and Færch and Kasper (1983b), supplemented by strategies presented in the work of other researchers such as Bialystok (1983), Corder (1983), and Paribakht (1985). There are two main types of strategies, *reduction strategies* and *achievement strategies*. In addition to the above strategies frequently discussed in the literature, four additional strategies are included: *repair, telegraphic, fillers*, and *change of role*.

3.1 Reduction Strategies

Learners employ reduction strategies when they try to solve problems in communication by abandoning or reducing their intended meanings. These comprise topic avoidance, message abandonment, and semantic avoidance (Corder 1983; Færch and Kasper 1983b; Tarone 1977, 1981).

3.1.1 *Topic Avoidance*
Remaining silent or changing an intended goal completely is a strategy of topic avoidance. In Excerpt 1, for example, S5 stops talking, and the NS in response changes the topic.

(1) Topic avoidance[1]

```
NS:  Why did you decide Spanish.
S5:  Spanish. ah . . . there is no reason, but my parents
     recommend to take a . . Spanish course because . . now
     . . . Spanish . . is . . . popular, so . . . I just took
     it. (laugh)
NS:  Spanish is popular in . . Japanese schools?
S5:  Ummm . . . um . . . not . . I don't think so, (laugh)
     but . . .
NS:  Okay. Tell me a little bit about your trip to the
     States and where you went.
```

3.1.2 *Message Abandonment*

Learners sometimes abandon their attempt to express an intended meaning in the middle of the sentence rather than employ an alternative strategy. Message abandonment may also be used when problems occur in retrieving certain items in a constructed verbal plan. An example of this strategy can be seen in Excerpt 2, in which S5 attempts to explain *crater* but cannot achieve her goal.

```
(2) Message abandonment

    NS:  Ummm . . why is it called Crater Lake.
    S5:  Why . . called?
    NS:  Why is it called Crater Lake.
    S5:  Ah . . . I'm not sure but . . the . . maybe in the first
         . . . um . . . crater means the . . . ah . . . I don't
         know how to explain.
```

3.1.3 *Semantic Avoidance*

Learners change their intended message slightly rather than abandoning. Learners may reduce the scope of the message, resulting in rather general or vague meanings within the context. Excerpt 3 seems to indicate such semantic reductions.

```
(3) Semantic avoidance

    S6:  What what kind of cost is this and . . this is the ah .
         . . and ah . . . actually, they . . do the ah . . same
         eh thing they ah . . wrote in. . write in the ah . . ah
         . . application . . and . . they do the, actually they
         do the, they do the same thing . . abroad.
    NS:  Uh huh.
    S6:  And I check their . . on the . . just on the paper.
```

3.2. *Achievement Strategies*

Learners employ achievement strategies to fill in gaps between their IL knowledge and the competence required to reach communication goals. Achievement strategies can be divided into six main categories: approximation, paraphrase, interlingual transfer, restructuring, cooperative strategies, and non-linguistic strategies (Bialystok 1983, Færch and Kasper 1983b, Paribakht 1985, Tarone 1981).

3.2.1 *Approximation*

Learners substitute items that they assume convey semantic meanings related to their intended goal. The following three strategies are classified under this category.

Lexical Substitution: substitution of words that share coordinate semantic features

```
S8:   My father . . is ah . . president (= "principal") of eh
      . . junior high school,
```

Generalization: substitution of words that are superordinate to intended meanings

```
S1:   Eh . . . I . . . went (= "sailed") to:: uh . . Mikuni
      port to Oki island, ah!, we need two days.
```

Exemplification: substitution of words that are subordinate in relation to intended meanings

```
S6:   So, it is good way for the sport ah . . sports ah. . .
      people to ah . . . eat ah . . bread or rice or spaghetti
      . . . something like that. (= "carbohydrates")
```

3.2.2 *Paraphrase*

Learners build up images of target words by describing them in other linguistic forms, through circumlocution, word coinage, or morphological creativity.

Circumlocution: expressing properties of intended items, such as their physical or functional descriptions. Excerpt 4 shows a physical description strategy. S3 attempts to explain his work involving surface-mount techniques for building electronic components by describing the surface of circuit boards as composed of very fine or narrow lines.

```
(4) Circumlocution

NS:   What kind of work.
S3:   Oh, oh . . I was working now eh . . . develop and . .
      fine-line pattern, . . . uh . . . circuit board, like
      circuit board. . very fine. (= "surface-mount
      technology")
```

Word Coinage: creating new words or compound words related to the original intended meaning, such as:

```
S2:    . . . in total we have we are . . we stayed . . . two . .
       . sleep . . . s::leep days (= "two nights") in the
       mountain.
```

Morphological Creativity: creating words by applying L_2 morphology (Poulisse 1987, 1990), such as:

```
S6:    ah . . . we have to uh . . . uh . .
       internationalization, but . . before . . before that
       we have uh . . been internationaliza-,
       internationalizated.
```

In this excerpt S6, not knowing the verb form of *internationalization*, first uses the unmodified form with a problem indication and, in the second attempt, creates a verb form by using his knowledge of English morphology.

3.2.3 *Restructuring*
Learners change their plans in the middle of the sentence upon realizing their limitations and try to construct an alternative plan (Færch and Kasper 1983b). Excerpt 5 seems to show that S4 has restructured the sentence because she identified the incorrect use of *more* or lacked an appropriate lexical item that could follow the word *more* in order to express her intention.

```
(5) Restructuring

NS:    Why why did you NOT decide to go to Hawaii like
       everyone else?
S4:    Ah . . . I've ever been to Hawaii . . so . . but so ah .
       . many Japanese there.
NS:    . . . of course, the number of Japanese who are going
       to Canada for their honeymoon is increasing too. So
       you may not be alone.
S4:    . . . But Hawaii is more . . . but Canada is . . bigger
       than Hawaii.
```

One problematic aspect of restructuring strategies is distinguishing them from reduction strategies (Bialystok 1990), as illustrated below.

```
S11:    Ah!, I was born in A prefecture, and . . I have . . I
        had been here until I was 19, and . . I . . my gra-. .
        my . . university was situated in B, so I spent I had
        spen- I have spent . . . four years in . . . B.
```

In this excerpt S11 may have started to say a sentence only to change his intended goal. Or he may have simply changed the structure of the sentence so that he could successfully express the intended meaning. As long as the speaker's turn continues and the language use is relevant in context, such cases are considered an attempt by the learner to continue his or her speech, that is, restructuring strategies.

3.2.4 *Interlingual Strategies*

Learners rely on their L_1 (or other foreign languages) in L_2 communication in the strategies of borrowing, foreignizing, and literal translation.

Borrowing: use of L_1 items in place of L_2 words or phrases

```
S6:     Japanese say eh . . . yakimono. (= "pottery")
```

Foreignizing: use of L_1 utterances adjusted to L_2 phonology and/or morphology. The word *department* in the sample below can be interpreted as a combination of a Japanese loan word, *depaato*, modified from the English word, and the L_2 suffix, *-ment*, and pronounced like English.

```
S7:     and when I . . when I did a . . part-time job at . . a
        department. (= "department store")
```

Literal Translation: use of L_1 words and expressions translated literally into L_2. In Excerpt 6, S6 talks about living in a building that houses a *bag shop*. The literal Japanese translation of this phrase refers to a store where items such as handbags and suitcases are sold. In addition, the choice of the word *bag* may have derived from the fact that it is also an English loan word in Japanese. On the syntactic level, the expression in English also requires additional explanation; for example, *I live behind (next to or above) the bag shop that my parents own.*

```
(6) Literal translation

S6:     Ya, ah . . I live in . . the my house, that is the ah .
        . bag shop.
NS:     . . .
```

```
S6:  BAG.
NS:  Bag shop
```

Note that some L_2 usages may be influenced by L_1 language and cultural patterns of learners (Beebe, Takahashi, and Uliss-Weltz 1990; Kumaravadivelu 1988; Richards and Sukwiwat 1983; Scarcella 1983). The following excerpt seems to indicate S11's sensitivity to a direct negative expression (cf. Loveday 1986, 1988).

```
S11: But I'm not I'm . . to tell the truth, I don't, I'm
     sorry I don't know so much about this.
```

In this case, the same topic was discussed for about four minutes until the learner indirectly asked the NS to change the topic.

3.2.5 Cooperative Strategies
Learners signal their interlocutor for help in solving communication problems by asking for an L_2 usage that they do not know or by indicating that they cannot explain.

```
S9:  Umm . . . it's very hard for me to answer.
```

Although this may not be an intended outcome, unsuccessful speech may also result in a cooperative strategy as in Excerpt 7, due to the fact that in such cases, interlocutors tend to be drawn into assisting learners.

```
(7) Reduction strategy becomes a cooperative strategy

NS:  What's Bunkyo-ku.
S8:  Bun-
NS:  Oh, that's that's ah . . .
S8:  Tokyo . . . no . . . (Japanese no = "of")
NS:  Geographical area?
S8:  Ya.
```

3.2.6 Non-linguistic Strategies and Multiple Strategy Use
Learners also use gestures, mime, and sound-imitations in lieu of linguistic forms or to supplement L_2 speech (e.g., Færch and Kasper 1983b). In addition, several strategies may be used simultaneously (Ellis 1985; Færch and Kasper 1983b; Kellerman 1991; Kellerman, Bongaerts, and Poulisse 1987; Poulisse 1987, 1990; Tarone 1981). For example, one utterance may have two or more explicit strategies

such as *It's big like ah . . . zoo* ([zo:], a Japanese word for "elephant"). In this sentence, both paraphrase and borrowing strategies are evident.

3.3 Other Strategies

3.3.1 Repair Strategies
According to Tarone (1980:425 citing Schwartz 1977; see also Morrison and Low 1983), the strategic use of repairs occurs "primarily when the speaker perceives that the first-attempt utterance contains a linguistic or sociolinguistic structure that does not communicate an intended meaning X closely enough to ensure that there will be shared meaning." If learners change an utterance, yielding what could be considered better communication, the modified segment is identified as a *repair strategy*. Excerpt 8 shows an example of this strategy.

```
(8) Repair strategy

    NS:  How old is your son?
         . . .
    NS:  Uh . . . and how about the next one, you want a girl?
    S1:  Ah . . . I . . . ya I . . . next year, ah . . . we have .
         . new . . members.
    NS:  Ahh.
    S1:  Ah . . I hope ah . . . man . . . ah . . I hope son.
```

3.3.2 Telegraphic Strategies
Telegraphic strategies refer to cases in which, despite a message reduction, the speaker clearly conveys the intended meaning, as in Excerpt 9.

```
(9) Telegraphic strategy

    S2:  and we go to Mount . . Shirouma . . . we go to eh . . .
         we . . in . . . in night, we get on . . the train . . .
         at . . B . . B station,
    NS:  Uh huh.
    S2:  and . . . Shi- . . . Shirouma, Shirouma station.
         (= "arrived at")
```

This excerpt shows that S2 has a problem in expressing his intention but attempts to successfully communicate instead of giving up. Although this may represent a semantic avoidance strategy, the above example seems to show the speaker's attempt, according to Grice's (1975) Cooperative Principle, to enable the hearer to infer the speaker's intention from the context (Poulisse 1990), and to achieve the communication goal. Such utterances are categorized as *telegraphic*.

3.3.3 Fillers
Færch and Kasper (1983b) refer to the use of fillers as a strategic device. An example of a *filler* appears below.

```
S9:   So, I think, I hope ne (Japanese backchannel) at least
      . . nanteyuukana . . four go- gold medals.
      (= "How do you say?")
```

3.3.4 Change of Role
Wagner (1983) identified a strategy used to change the questioner and respondent roles of the speakers in a communication situation. This type of strategy, categorized as *change of role*, is shown in Excerpt 10.

```
(10)  Change of role

S4:   but . . I am the . . . between . . new generalization
      and old people? so called old people.
NS:   How do you mean between.
S4:   Un . . cause . . . (pause) ah . . . I thi- . . . What's
      what's the new generation's idea, do you think?
```

4 Communication Strategies and Proficiency

There have been several studies of the communication strategies of L_2 speakers of English in which subjects have been assigned different tasks such as concept identification tasks (Paribakht 1985), picture description tasks (Bongaerts, Kellerman, and Bentlage 1987; Tarone 1977; Tarone and Yule 1989) and interviews or conversations (Haastrup and Phillipson 1983, Labarca and Khanji 1986, Poulisse 1990). These previous studies suggest the following factors may affect the communication strategies used by L_2 speakers: personality (Tarone 1977), learning situation or instructional differences (Haastrup and Phillipson 1983, Labarca and Khanji 1986), L_1/L_2 speaker differences (Bongaerts et al. 1987; Kellerman, Ammerlaan, Bongaerts, and Poulisse 1990; Paribakht 1985; Poulisse 1990; Tarone and Yule 1989), task differences (Poulisse 1990), and proficiency level (Paribakht 1985, Poulisse 1990).

The study conducted by Paribakht (1985) relates the use of communication strategies to the level of proficiency. Persian subjects learning English were instructed to describe concrete and abstract items to an interlocutor. These tasks limited the problems that each subject needed to solve; however, they enabled the identification of communication strategies used to solve particular problems they faced. The subjects' proficiency levels were measured by the Michigan Test of English Language Proficiency and the International Education Achievement Test of Proficiency. The study revealed a directional relationship between proficiency level and communication strategies. Advanced learners used more approximation strategies than lower-level learners. The less competent learners were found to rely more on their world and paralinguistic knowledge.

Poulisse (1990) investigated the use of achievement strategies, or "compensatory strategies," by Dutch learners of English by focusing only on lexical items. The subjects were selected based on their years of tuition in English, school-report/exam marks, teacher judgments, and scores on a cloze test. No assessment of interactional communicative skills of the subjects was conducted. Four different tasks were assigned to each subject: (a) a concrete picture description task, (b) an abstract figure description task, (c) a story retelling task, and (d) an oral interview. Tasks (a), (c), and (d)—ranging from more to less controlled—were used in order to investigate the relationship between the strategic behaviors and task variation as well as the level of proficiency. Task (b) was assigned to the subjects in both Dutch and English, in order to compare their strategic use in L_1 and L_2 speech production.

Poulisse's major research findings were threefold. First, the number of strategies used by the subjects varied in relation to their proficiency level. The lower proficiency subjects used more achievement strategies than the higher proficiency subjects. Poulisse interprets this as resulting from the limited L_2 vocabulary that could be controlled by the low-proficiency subjects to cope with the problems. By contrast, she suggests that the greater number of holistic strategies (or approximation) used by the high-proficiency subjects reflected their greater capacity to deal with a larger number of L_2 lexical items. Second, the type of compensatory strategies used was found to be highly task-specific, depending on the degree of task demands required to achieve the intended communication goal. Poulisse (1990:153) suggests that the type of strategy that "is necessary depends largely on the task demand and the context, while what is possible depends on the knowledge shared with the interlocutor and the amount of time available." Third, the comparison between the strategies used in English (L_2) and Dutch (L_1) performances on task (b) revealed that the subjects' use of communication strategies in both languages is similar. This finding, according to Poulisse, suggests the application of L_1 strategic competence to an L_2 context.

Although these studies and many others discuss the strategic utterances of L_2 speakers, the majority are limited to particular communicative situations in which the subjects were given specific problems to solve in their L_2. In situations such as L_2 conversation, however, the assumption can be made that L_2 speakers, having limited L_2 resources, will face varying problems that they must overcome in order to achieve their communication goals. Therefore, the strategies of L_2 speakers in such interactional situations need to be investigated. Furthermore, as previous studies indicate a directional relationship between the use of communication strategies and level of proficiency, it is necessary to investigate whether such a relationship also applies to an interview situation in which learners' proficiency is being tested. Further inquiry into the relationship between the use of communication strategies in interview situations and proficiency levels will help us gain a better understanding of the development of communication strategies along the IL continuum. The following sections will discuss a study designed to investigate these issues.

5 The Study

In this study, twelve recorded interviews, which were rated in accordance with the Oral Proficiency Interview rating scale (Educational Testing Service 1982), were analyzed to identify the types of communication strategies used by interviewees. Two questions addressed in this study were:

1. What types of strategies and how many strategies do adult Japanese speakers of English as a second language employ in oral interview test situations?
2. To what extent is there a link between the use of these strategies and the proficiency level of the speakers as determined by the interview ratings?

5.1 *Methodology*

5.1.1 *Oral Proficiency Interview Test*
The Oral Proficiency Interview (OPI) of Educational Testing Service (ETS) was used to assess level of proficiency. The OPI, formerly referred to as the FSI Oral Proficiency Interview, was first developed by the Foreign Service Institute and later was used for academic purposes by ETS. The OPI is an integrative, direct test that aims to test an L_2 speaker's ability "to use the language effectively and appropriately in real-life situations" (ETS 1982:7). The OPI involves a face-to-face interaction between a trained interviewer and an interviewee. The interview is carefully

structured in four phases in order to successfully define the boundaries of interviewees' proficiency: warm-up, level check, probes, and wind-down. The interviewer is responsible for initiating and controlling the discourse of the interview. Thus it can be said that there is an asymmetrical relationship between speakers in such an interview situation that is unlike the relationship between speakers in informal conversations (cf. van Lier 1989, Young 1995, Young and Milanovic 1992).

Each interview takes between 10 and 30 minutes, depending on the interviewee's proficiency level. The OPI's topics vary for each interviewee, mainly based on his or her capability in communication and background knowledge. Interviewers attempt to discuss a variety of topics with individual interviewees in order to discover "the highest level at which the candidate sustains most of his or her speech during the test" (ETS 1982:11). The OPI rating scale ranges from "0 (for no practical ability to function in the language) to 5 (for ability equivalent to that of an educated native speaker) with plus ratings for strong performance within a level" (ETS 1982:1), yielding a total of 11 skill levels. Each level of proficiency is described broadly "to include both weaker and stronger performances over a significantly wide range" (ETS 1982:1). The reliability of ratings has proven to be significantly high (Clark 1975, Lowe 1987).

5.1.2 *Samples*

The tape-recorded interviews used in this study were conducted as part of the oral proficiency testing system of a language institute in Japan. The subjects were adult Japanese who had graduated from two- or four-year post-secondary programs in Japanese colleges or universities. They were students of English at the language institute at the time of the interviews.

Each interview was rated by certified OPI interviewers with two other certified testers reviewing the tape. Because proficiency level is a critical variable in this study, the interview samples chosen were limited to those in which all three raters agreed on the levels of proficiency. In order to have equal numbers for analysis, three samples from each level, 1+, 2, 2+, and 3, were selected for a total of twelve. Speakers in levels 1+ and 2 were assumed to possess some creativity in L_2 use but limited competence in dealing with various kinds of discourse function and topics (Magnan 1988). The assumption was that various communication strategies would be required in order to overcome the limitations at these levels.

5.2 Procedures

5.2.1 Identification Procedure

I transcribed the twelve interviews (see Appendix 1 for the transcription conventions). On the basis of the interviewees' behaviors that seemed to indicate difficulty in conveying intended meanings, I identified communication strategies by using three kinds of indicators described by Færch and Kasper (1983c:230): "implicit signals of uncertainty, explicit signals of uncertainty, and direct appeals for assistance." Implicit signals of uncertainty are behaviors such as filled and unfilled pauses, false starts, marked intonation, repair, repetition, drawls, laughs, and sighs. Explicit signals of uncertainty are verbally indicated expressions such as gambits, *what's it called?*, and *you know*. Direct appeals for assistance are those in which the L_2 speakers ask the interlocutors for help by saying, for example, *How do you say yakimono in English?*

With regard to the identification of the communication strategies, certain strategies are not observable. For example, competent speakers may have a large amount of automatized L_2 knowledge that reduces the processing load (McLaughlin et al. 1983). Problem-solving may then become much easier for them than for less competent speakers and may not be exhibited overtly in their L_2 communication (Færch and Kasper 1983c, Poulisse 1990). But since this study was restricted to the analysis of observed behaviors in the interview samples, strategic utterances without any problem indications were practically impossible to distinguish from nonstrategic behaviors (Færch and Kasper 1986, 1989; Kellerman 1983; Poulisse and Bongaerts 1994). Thus they were not counted as strategies, and the number of strategies identified in this study can be considered fewer than those actually present.

One additional procedure that should be mentioned here is that the identification process was, in many cases, supported by context. For example, the repetition of strategic utterance after an interval such as in the following excerpt varies considerably depending on the context.

```
S8:   My father . . is ah . . president of eh . . junior high
      school, and . . my mother is a president of
      kindergarten. (= "principal")
```

The first *president* preceded by a pause seems to have solved S8's problem, and no hesitation is identified in the second part. In such cases, only the former was treated as a strategy. By contrast, the following case demonstrates that a problem persists and was counted as two strategies.

```
S4:    but . . my . . younger . . younger . . students . .
       don't . . don't devote in studies and club activities
       like . . my elder students.
       . . .
       I can't . . I can't agree . . my young . . younger stu-
       . . my younger students. (= "my junior")
```

Finally, with regard to the identification process, there were quite a large number of Japanese conversational fillers such as *anoh, eh, eeto,* and *ah!*.[2] Due to the fact that Japanese interactions tend to be more fragmented by frequent use of fillers and backchannels than English (Maynard 1989, Takahashi 1989), and the studies on the use of fillers in L_2 speech indicating L_1 transfer (Raupach 1980, Scarcella 1983, Takahashi 1989), special care was necessary in identifying problem indicators.

5.2.2 Classification Procedure

Based on an initial analysis of the samples, the following points were taken into account in the classification of communication strategies. First, this study dealt only with speech production, not comprehension. Thus samples such as *Pardon me? Ah .. I can't catch*, a cooperative strategy derived from a perception problem, were not included in the study. Second, problems that seemed strictly phonological and grammatical such as *I writed: . ah. . . wrote* were not included in the study. Third, because the interview samples were audiotaped, non-linguistic strategies such as gestures were not included (although some such responses may be inferred from phrases such as *this big*).

The rest of the classification procedures need to be discussed mainly with respect to this study's reliance on observable language behaviors. First, strategies may be used simultaneously or may be embedded within other strategies. Such covert strategic utterances, which may have been employed by the interviewees, were not included in the study. Second, certain reduction strategies, such as topic avoidance or replacement of a particular meaning, could only be identified if there was an inappropriate change of topic attempted by the interviewee or if the interviewee stopped conversing without an interruption by the interviewer, as in Excerpt 11.

```
(11) Message abandonment

    NS:   so . . you still live at home now?
    S6:   Yes, I . . . yes.
    NS:   Ummm . . What did you study at A?
```

5.2.3 Classification of Communication Strategies

The communication strategies investigated in this study included 14 types taken from the previous research and four additional types included in this study (see Appendix 2).

On the basis of the procedures, I, a native speaker of Japanese (*J*), classified the types of communication strategies in the twelve samples. Two native speakers of English checked the appropriateness of English utterances in the samples. In order to test the reliability of the classification, one sample from each level of proficiency, yielding a total of four samples, was randomly selected and analyzed by a native speaker of English (*E*). Inter-rater reliability was studied in the four samples. The subjectivity of the analysis was expected to be reduced by conducting two analyses on the same data.

But the inter-rater reliability was a low 64%, mainly due to the discrepant classification of Japanese L_1-based strategies, that is, borrowing, foreignizing, and literal translation, and other types of L_2-based strategies. When these discrepant strategies were removed from the total, the agreement between researchers greatly improved, averaging 90%. A crucial point that needs to be discussed here is that researcher *J* classified strategies based mainly on her NS knowledge of Japanese, while researcher *E*, with very little knowledge of Japanese, relied on his English-based knowledge and/or his experiences in ESL/EFL teaching. Some strategic utterances such as *yakimono*, "pottery," were so obvious that both identified them as borrowing. Researcher *E*, however, interpreted utterances for which he could not infer the intention from context as L_1-based strategies or ambiguous. In a few instances he had difficulty inferring expressions, such as in Excerpt 12.

```
(12) Ambiguous strategies

NS:  Okay . . so you went drinking last night, eh?
S1:  Ya . . . ah . . . about ah . . . 12 o'clock, eh . . we
     are . . . we were drinking uh . . . near K city.
NS:  Uh huh. Weren't you ah . . weren't you worried about
     today's interview?
S1:  Ya . . . a . . . I was very worried, but eh . . my boss .
     . let's go drinking . . . uh . . . next next next next.
NS:  Ummmm . . .
S1:  eh . . he said to me, don't worry.
```

Researcher *E* categorized the underlined segment as ambiguous, after first considering it an example of topic avoidance. But researcher *J* interpreted it as a paraphrase to express barhopping, which is an important form of socializing among

Japanese businessmen. Such examples seem to confirm that the identification of strategic behaviors involves sociocultural knowledge.

The following excerpt shows another instance of discrepant classification. This utterance could be classified in at least four ways: a literal translation of the word *floor*, which includes a knowledge of the L_2 possessive marker (*three floors' building*), a word coinage (*three floors building*), a lexical substitution (*story* replaced by *floors*), or a grammatical error (*three-floor-building*).

```
S4:    That's . . . three three building. Ah . . three floors
       building.
```

Since there is no distinction between *floor* and *story* in Japanese, researcher *J* categorized it as a literal translation, while researcher *E*, after considering these four possible interpretations, classified it as ambiguous.

Another example attesting to the complexity of strategy classification can be seen in the following excerpt.

```
S12:   I mean the all . . of the people in the world can enjoy
       the: more . . cheaper . . products, or ah . . more . .
       better quality products
```

Researcher *E* interpreted the underlined segments as a repair, while researcher *J* classified the use of *more* and *more better* as borrowing derived from a Japanese loan word *moa bettaa*. In fact, S12 used *cheaper* correctly in other contexts, while he consistently used *more better*, leading to the conclusion that both interpretations seem possible.

Although researcher *J* had problems classifying some strategies, she ultimately categorized many cases as L_1-based strategies. One interview with subject S4 was then analyzed by another Japanese native speaker to examine the reliability between Japanese native speakers. The second Japanese rater's classification agreed 95.5% with that of researcher *J*. Thus the discrepancies between raters *J* and *E* seem to indicate a bias caused by the researchers' language knowledge.

Due to the fact that the inter-rater reliability of classification, after excluding L_1/L_2 disagreements, increased to 90%, the classification was considered to be reliable. Researcher *J* reanalyzed all the samples, focusing on strategies involving L_1. Those strategies that could be classified as L_1-based or other alternative strategies were excluded from the study.

6 Results and Discussion

The discussion of results is divided according to two major issues: the relationship between the use of communication strategies and level of proficiency, and methodological implications. The latter is included since a number of procedural and analytical issues emerged during the study that seem to have an important bearing on future studies dealing with communication strategies and interview discourse.

6.1 Proficiency-Related Differences in the Use of Communication Strategies

6.1.1 Overall Frequency of Strategy Use

The data were first summarized by counting the number of each type of strategy used by each subject. Due to the varying lengths of the interviews and, more importantly, differences in speech rate among speakers, the speech of each subject in each interview was divided into t-units (Hunt 1966). The procedures for counting the t-units were established by the researcher, taking into consideration the fragmented nature of interactive discourse, especially involving L_2 learners (see Yoshida 1991 for details). For example, there were subjectless units such as *ah.. ah.. find.. find ... no problem*. Preposing, postposing, and embedding of a segment of a unit, such as *my work.. eh.. I don't like*, were also typical features identified in the samples. Any clause-like unit that could be reconstructed by the researcher was counted as a t-unit.[3]

Frequency of occurrence of each type of communication strategy in each sample was calculated by dividing the number of strategies by the number of t-units. Table 1 summarizes the frequency of occurrence of the communication strategies used by each subject.

The results indicate the greatest difference between the three higher levels (3, 2+, and 2), and level 1+. Low-proficiency subjects (level 1+) used more strategies than the rest of the subjects in order to compensate for their insufficient L_2 knowledge. There is not a great deal of difference among the mean frequency levels of the top three groups (levels 3, 2+, and 2).

Note, however, that in all three of these levels there was a certain degree of variance. In particular, while gender was not addressed as a research issue in the study, an extreme instance can be observed in the scores of two female subjects, S4 and S5, in comparison to a male subject, S6, in the same level. Furthermore, S5 was the only subject who was interviewed by a female interviewer, and this subject used fewer strategies than any other subject at any level of proficiency. In their study of

Table 1. Frequency of Occurrence of Communication Strategies

Level	Subject	(A) No. of t-units	(B) No. of strategies	(B ÷ A) Strategies per t-unit	Average frequency
1+	S1	102	46	0.45	
	S2	65	29	0.45	0.54
	S3	75	55	0.73	
2	S4 (F)	123	27	0.22	
	S5 (F)	144	27	0.19	0.28
	S6	188	75	0.40	
2+	S7 (F)	125	29	0.23	
	S8	92	22	0.24	0.27
	S9	145	48	0.33	
3	S10	131	45	0.34	
	S11	130	41	0.32	0.29
	S12	126	27	0.21	

Note. (F) indicates a female subject

interactional behaviors in relation to topic initiation and ratification between speakers in L_2 interviews, Young and Milanovic (1992) found significant differences according to gender, particularly in interviews between female speakers. Thus gender may have had some effect on strategy use or on interactional performances. Since there were only three subjects in each level of proficiency and few female subjects, it is difficult to generalize variables from the sample but the results indicate an area for further investigation.

6.1.2 *Percentages of Different Strategies*

To test the relationship between the use of communication strategies and level of proficiency, the strategies identified in each sample were first grouped into 11 categories according to the major groups of reduction, approximation, paraphrase, interlingual, restructuring, cooperative strategies, repair, telegraphic, fillers, change of role, and those strategies that could not be assigned to one of these specific categories (labeled *ambiguous*). The percentage of each category used by subjects at each level of proficiency is shown in Table 2. The chi-square statistic was used to examine whether there is a significant relationship between the two variables: the frequency of a particular communication strategy and the level of proficiency (Hatch and Lazaraton 1991).

Table 2. *Percentage of Communication Strategies Used at Each Proficiency Level*

Strategy		1+	2	2+	3	Chi-square	p
Reduction		2.3	16.3	7.1	6.2	15.07	0.002
Achievement:							
	Approximation	20.0	18.6	21.2	21.2	0.23	ns[1]
	Paraphrase	25.4	17.8	9.1	11.5	9.60	0.022
	Interlingual	8.5	1.6	4.0	0.9	—[2]	0.015
	Restructuring	12.3	19.4	24.3	21.2	4.14	ns
	Cooperative	0.8	0.8	2.0	1.8	—	ns
Others:							
	Repair	12.3	11.6	18.2	33.6	15.83	0.000
	Telegraphic	13.8	4.6	4.0	0.9	17.17	0.000
	Fillers	3.1	3.1	8.1	0.0	—	0.014
	Change of role	0.0	1.6	0.0	0.0	—	ns

Note. Chi-square was calculated on raw data.
1. *ns* means that the value of chi-square or Fisher's Exact Test did not reach the criterial value for alpha = .05.
2. No value in the chi-square column refers to cell frequencies that fell below 5. In such cases, Fisher's Exact Test was used to calculate the value of *p*.

Before proceeding with further discussion, it is necessary to note that the final number calculated for certain strategies such as interlingual, cooperative, fillers, and change of role was very small. In particular, as mentioned earlier, almost all interlingual type of strategies first identified were excluded from the data, resulting in a very small number of L_1-based strategies. These factors may need to be taken into consideration when interpreting the results.

As can be seen in Table 2, six out of eleven strategies showed significant differences according to level. Further examination of the figures does indicate three distinct groups of strategies: group 1, a relative increase in percentage as the level of proficiency increases for the repair strategy; group 2, a relative decrease in percentage as the level of proficiency increases for the paraphrase, interlingual, and telegraphic strategies; and group 3, an increase in percentage in intermediate levels for reduction and fillers.

In group 1, subjects in level 3 used more repair strategies than those in levels 1+, 2, and 2+. This finding seems to indicate highly proficient subjects' ability to control and monitor their language utterances. Their well-automatized L_2 knowledge may have reduced the cognitive load and enabled them to identify their problems more easily than less proficient subjects. A greater L_2 knowledge may also have enabled high-level subjects to repair what they had said in order to get their messages across better.

In contrast, in group 2, a decrease in the use of telegraphic, paraphrase, and interlingual strategies was evident as the level of proficiency increased. The telegraphic strategy indicated a clear directional tendency. This seems to be related to insufficient lexical and syntactic L_2 knowledge on the part of subjects at lower levels, especially at level 1+. Due to limited L_2 resources, the less proficient subjects may have simply listed words in order to convey their intentions. In addition, the less proficient subjects attempted to compensate for their insufficient L_2 knowledge by paraphrasing intended meanings, by creating L_2-like words, and by resorting to their L_1 linguistic knowledge.

In group 3 there was an increase in the use of reduction strategies and fillers at the intermediate levels. Reduction strategies were used more often by subjects in level 2 than by those in levels 1+, 2+, and 3. This result appears to reflect the U-shaped language behavior of L_2 learners (Kellerman 1979, Lightbown 1985, Magnan 1988). Subjects in level 2 can be assumed to be at the developmental stage in which they begin to use L_2 creatively, as illustrated by their increasing use of various syntactic forms. The structure of the interview, then, requires interviewers to attempt to discuss topics calling for more complex language use from interviewees at level 2 than from those at level 1+. The limitation of their L_2 knowledge, however, may lead to difficulties in controlling a variety of topics and discourse functions and constructing alternative plans to achieve their original goals. As a result, they resort to reducing and abandoning their intended meanings.

By contrast, a decrease in reduction strategies in the upper levels reflects greater L_2 resources, which can be manipulated by these highly proficient subjects to solve communication problems in varying topics and discourse functions. Topics that the interviewer chooses for subjects at level 1+ are less difficult than those at higher levels, although they may be relatively as demanding as those at upper levels. Within their existing resources, therefore, lower proficiency subjects attempt to express their intended meanings by employing such strategies as telegraphic, paraphrase, and L_1-based strategies. This seems to suggest that the use of reduction strategies is one critical factor that leads interviewers to determine the proficiency level of interviewees.

It is worth noting that the study of Ross and Berwick (1992) on OPI interviewers' accommodative behaviors revealed a greater variance in how interviewers accommodated to their interviewees in interviews at levels 2 and 2+ than at levels 1+ and 3. This evidence may be an indication of interviewers having difficulties in adjusting their speech to the interviewees' level of communicative skill. At one point in an interview, intermediate-level interviewees may demonstrate better command of L_2 communicative skills. Yet at another point, they may reduce and abandon their communication goals. Thus interviewers may readjust their speech as shown by Ross and Berwick.

Fillers also showed significant differences across proficiency levels. This seems to have resulted from particular individuals who frequently used the strategy of fillers at each of levels 1+, 2, and 2+. Due to inconsistent use among subjects at the same level of proficiency, this particular type of strategy does not seem to be related to the level of proficiency.

At this point it should be noted that individual differences were also evidenced in a number of strategy categories. For example, subject S8 in level 2+ and subject S11 in level 3 used more reduction strategies than the other subjects in the same levels. Subject S3 in level 1+ and subject S12 in level 3 used paraphrase strategies much more often than other subjects at the same levels of proficiency. Subject S12 in level 3 used repair strategies much less often than the other two subjects, while subject S2 in level 1+ and subject S4 in level 2 used them much more than other subjects at the same levels of proficiency.

Strategies that showed no statistically significant difference along proficiency levels also reflected individual differences. For example, subject S2 in level 1+ and subject S4 in level 2 used far fewer approximation strategies than the rest of the subjects at the same proficiency levels. Subject S5 in level 2 and subject S10 in level 3 used restructuring strategies much less often than the rest of the subjects at the same levels. Subject S8 in level 2+ used no restructuring strategies, while others used them frequently.

Two points can be discussed here in relation to individual variation identified in the results. First, individuals' personalities may have some effect on their choice of strategy. For example, if L_2 speakers are highly motivated to communicate with their interlocutors in their L_2, they may try various kinds of strategies until they can achieve mutual understanding between speakers. By contrast, speakers who tend to be hesitant to speak in their L_2, especially when they encounter problems expressing themselves, may reduce their language in form and message content.

The second point is related to the OPI rating scales. In this study the subjects' level of proficiency was assigned by an interviewer, and each assigned level was confirmed by two other raters. This does not necessarily mean, however, that subjects at the same proficiency level show identical L_2 oral skills. Differences among subjects at the same level of proficiency may be due to the fact that during certain parts of the interview, an individual's performance may exceed, or fail to meet, the requirements of the level descriptors. Proficiency ratings are ultimately determined by the highest sustained level of performance. In other words, each individual within a given proficiency band may have a different distribution of particular skills. One subject's proficiency level in level 3 may be closer to level 2+, while other subjects in the same level may be closer to level 3+. Although no conclusive evidence is available at this moment, we may assume that these two factors—individual differences and a broad band of proficiency in the OPI rating scales—may have had some effect on strategic behaviors identified in this study and produced individual variation in the research findings.

Finally, this study dealt with only twelve subjects. This, together with the various methodological issues identified in the study, limits the generalizability of the findings. Further studies on the use of communication strategies in various types of communicative situations are necessary in order to investigate factors that cause differences in the use of communication strategies. In addition, this study identified three distinct tendencies in the use of communication strategies according to level. As learners become able to manipulate increasingly complex L_2 forms, they resort to different types of strategies in order to solve communicative problems. Further study on the use of communication strategies should be conducted by using various types of language proficiency interviews; these studies should be compared with the results of this study in an attempt to illuminate the relationship between strategic utterances and proficiency levels.

6.2 Methodological Implications

This section first summarizes the methodological issues involved in the identification and classification of communication strategies by focusing on three factors identified as needing close attention in their analysis. The remaining discussion will explore the potential implications drawn from the study in relation to studies on language proficiency interview discourse.

In this study, as mentioned earlier, inter-rater reliability turned out to be unexpectedly low. The main problem contributing to low inter-rater reliability was disagreement in classifying L_1-based strategies. While this issue has been addressed by Bialystok (1990) and Poulisse (1990), it does not seem to surface in most other studies. Poulisse, for example, reported that the researchers had a 93% agreement on the classification task. Three factors can be suggested for this discrepancy:

classification approach, the degree of analysts' shared language knowledge (particularly knowledge of the L_1 of the subjects), and language-specific differences.

First, this study dealt only with observed behaviors of the subjects; classification was conducted by inferring intended meanings that the subjects seemed to be trying to convey from interactions between the speakers. Although in many cases context supported the interpretation of speakers' intentions, this approach made it difficult to achieve agreement. Poulisse (1990) emphasizes that retrospective data obtained from the subjects' comments clarified the interpretation of strategic behaviors. The lack of retrospection in the present study may have influenced the identification and classification. Although some questions can be raised concerning the quality and reliability of comments obtained from subjects (McLaughlin 1990), the combination of classification and retrospection seems a promising technique for improving the analysis of communication strategies (Færch and Kasper 1987).

Second, the two researchers classified the strategies from the perspective of their own language knowledge, especially researcher J who had the same L_1 background as the subjects in this study. It should also be noted that since this study dealt with interactional behaviors, culture-specific knowledge affected the interpretation of strategic utterances. Given this, both researchers' classifications could possibly be accurate. The question becomes, then, to what extent must researchers and subjects in this type of study have shared language knowledge? The results of the inter-rater reliability rating seem to show that the degree of shared language knowledge particularly influences the classification task. While Bialystok (1983:107) and other researchers discuss the topic of who uses which communication strategies, this study raises the additional question of who does the analysis of the communication strategies in L_2 speech.

The inability to achieve high inter-rater reliability in the case of L_1-based strategies leads to the third and perhaps most significant issue: the effect of subjects' L_1 backgrounds on the use of communication strategies. The fact that Japanese speakers were used in this study and speakers of European languages were used in many previous studies may have affected the types of strategic utterances identified. If the assumption can be made that Japanese and English are considerably different not only linguistically but also in the social rules that govern them, this would strongly increase the likelihood of discrepancies between the results of studies using subjects with varying L_1 backgrounds. Pragmatic differences between Japanese and English may also have posed additional difficulties in the classification task of the present study.

Kellerman (1977, 1979, 1983, 1986) claims that the distance that learners perceive between their L_1 and L_2 influences what they actually transfer. Since significant typological differences exist between Japanese and English, Japanese learners of English may perceive a large distance between English and Japanese. If it can be assumed that they perceive the L_1 not transferable to English contexts, they would be less likely to employ L_1 forms directly in L_2 speech. On the other hand, L_2 learners whose L_1 and L_2 are closely related may perceive less language distance. They may perceive their L_1 transferable to L_2 and apply their L_1 overtly in L_2 speech (see also Ringbom 1978). According to Poulisse (1990), for example, 17.8% of all strategic utterances used by Dutch learners of English in the interview task were borrowing (7.9%) or foreignizing (9.9%), which involved the use of Dutch words. Furthermore, these were used rather consistently by all the subjects. In the present study, only 3% of all the strategies were classified as borrowing and none as foreignizing (borrowing and foreignizing made up 6.4% of the strategies in the initial analysis conducted by researcher J). These figures appear to indicate that Japanese learners used many fewer L_1 items in L_2 speech than Dutch learners in order to overcome communicative difficulties. The tendency observed instead is that Japanese learners attempt to express their intention within the available L_2 linguistic resources. Due to the methodological differences between previous studies and the present one, no further comparisons or conclusive discussion can be made at this point. Further research using subjects with various L_1 backgrounds is needed in order to provide a clearer picture of the effect of L_1 background on the use of communication strategies in L_2 speech production.

Turning the discussion to the analysis of communication strategies in language proficiency interview situations, two additional factors may need to be taken into consideration. First, in this study the data were obtained from language proficiency interviews in which L_2 learners' oral skills were assessed and learners had to demonstrate their L_2 communicative skills. Although interviews show evidence of asymmetrical relationships between speakers, several situations, such as Excerpt 13, seem to give evidence that not only interviewers but also interviewees initiate conversation (see also Young 1995, Young and Milanovic 1992):

```
(13) Interviewee initiates

    S6:  but ah . . it is the . . ah . . it it depend the person
         how to ah . . . level up their ah . . power.
    NS:  Umm I see. So, maybe it's ah . . . Japanese coaches
         that . .
    S6:  that ya . . and . . ya . . Do you . . . what what kind of
         sport do you like?
    NS:  Ice hockey.
```

```
S6:  Ahhh, ya, ice hockey . . ya, how how long uh . . do . .
     you play ice hockey?
NS:  Uhhh . . . for . . . I guess about twenty . . years.
S6:  Twenty years, ah . . . I can . . skate but ah . . I di-
     I can't ice hockey.
NS:  There is ah . . .
S6:  Is it dangerous?
```

This conversation continued on the same topic for about seventeen additional turns between the speakers, S6 always taking the role of questioner.

On the other hand, some L_2 speakers in interview situations may experience a high degree of anxiety as exemplified in Excerpt 14.

```
(14) Interviewee expresses anxiety

NS:  Ahh . . how long have you been working for A.
S11: Yes, I entered this mon- . . this country eh . . this
     April, so . .
NS:  This April,
S11: Yes, so I have been in this company for half . . about
     half an hour.
NS:  Half.
S11: Half an hour.
NS:  HALF AN HOUR!
S11: Yes . . . ah!, sorry, half an year half a year . .
NS:  Half a year . . I see. .
S11: So . . I'm a little nervous. (laugh)
```

As can be seen, S11 first answers an interrogative question by saying *yes*, that is a common response from Japanese L_2 learners of English. He then does not notice that he said *country* and *half an hour*. This situation seems to indicate that anxiety may have influenced speakers' performance in the samples used for this study. Additionally, note that S11 in the above example continued to answer questions with a formal *yes*, but never an informal *yeah* or *ya*. Such utterances as *yes* seem to show a rather formal and polite interactional management in the interview, which could be said to be derived from his L_1 habits (Hinds 1978; Loveday 1986, 1988). Thus it seems necessary to emphasize that this study showed strategic utterances of L_2 speakers in particular interview testing situations. The effect of situational differences on the use of communication strategies needs to be explored further in direct vs. indirect oral proficiency testing situations and in testing vs. non-testing situations.

Second, in this study the interviewers who conducted the interviews in Japan had some knowledge of Japanese as well as experiences living and teaching in Japan and interviewing Japanese L_2 learners. Although the interviewers were trained in OPI interviews, detailed analyses of some situations in the samples seemed to show different reactions to Japanese-oriented expressions spoken by the interviewees as in Excerpts 15a and 15b.

```
(15a) Interviewer's response to Japanese expressions
S8:   And I will eh . . help my mother and father eh . . . to
      do mochitsuki. (= "rice cake making")
NS:   Ah ha.
S8:   Eh . . in eh thirty of . . Dec- eh, thirty . .
      thirtieth, December.
```

But compare Excerpt 15a with 15b:

```
(15b) Interviewer's response to Japanese expressions
S1:   Ah . . . B make eh . . . many . . eh tree [túri] pot,
      many many tree [túri] pot.
      (= "flower pot")
NS:   What's that.
S1:   Ah . . .
NS:   What are those.
S1:   Chi-, Chini-?, Chini-? . . eh . . . I'm sorry I don't .
      . . eh . . .
```

As shown in these excerpts, the interviewers' knowledge of Japanese may have influenced their comprehension of what the interviewee tried to convey. The interviewers' understanding of L_1 items may lead interviewees to resort to their L_1. On the other hand, lack of mutual understanding may increase the strategic performances of L_2 speakers. For example, if the NS in Excerpt 15a had acted as if he did not understand what *mochitsuki* meant, the subsequent interaction may have consisted of S1 trying to explain what he meant by *mochitsuki*. Or if the NS in (15b) had responded to S1 as in (15a), S1 would not have experienced difficulty in expressing what he meant by *tree [túri] pot*. Thus there may have been influences derived from differences among interviewers' reactions that affected the subsequent use of communication strategies. It seems critical, therefore, to examine the effect of interlocutor differences on the use of communication strategies as these differences may affect the speech performance of L_2 speakers as well as the interviewers' perceptions of their communicative skills.

In sum, with respect to the methodological issues, the following factors were suggested: classification approach, researchers' shared language knowledge, subjects' L_1 backgrounds, situational differences, and interlocutor differences. As an increasing number of studies have reported variable factors identified in interviews, taking these factors into consideration in further investigations on the effects of strategic behaviors in language proficiency interviews will provide better understanding of interview discourse across proficiency levels.

Acknowledgments

This study is based on a master's thesis submitted to Southern Illinois University at Carbondale (Yoshida 1991). I would like to express my gratitude for the guidance and advice received at SIUC from Paul Angelis, Kyle Perkins, and Richard Young, and for comments and suggestions from Clifford A. Hill at Teachers College, Columbia University, and the editors of this volume. Also, I am thankful to Joe Greenholtz for his valuable feedback. Finally, Margaret Cosgrove's suggestions and encouragement helped me refine my writing.

Notes

1. The conversation examples cited in the paper were taken from the sample data used in the study. Each sample was numbered S1 through S12. Subjects S1–S3 were asserted at LPI level 1+, S4–S6 at level 2, S7–S9 at level 2+, and S10–S12 at level 3. For transcription conventions, see Appendix 1. The first three periods at the beginning of the turn indicate the omission of the first part of the speech.

2. In four samples, one from each proficiency level, an average of 31% of all the filled pauses observed were typical Japanese fillers, and only 1% typical English fillers such as *uhm, uh- huh, oh, okay,* and *well.*

3. Independent clauses that followed dependent clauses that included more than one clause conjoined by *and* or *or* were counted as two separate t-units. Optional dependent clauses that could stand by themselves as clauses were counted separately from their independent clauses. Self-repetition of a t-unit was counted as another t-unit. Repetition of any interlocutor's speech segments, however, was considered to be a filler, thus not a t-unit. Direct quotes, if preceded by a main clause, were counted as one t-unit.

Appendix 1. Transcription Conventions (adapted from van Lier 1988 and Maynard 1989)

NS : interviewer (native speaker of English)

Sn	: interviewee, subject n (Japanese L_2 learner of English)
?	: rising intonation, not necessarily a question
!	: strong emphasis with falling intonation
.	: a period unseparated from the preceding word indicates falling intonation
,	: a comma indicates low-rising intonation, suggesting continuation
:	: one or more colons indicate lengthening of the preceding sound (drawls)
-	: a hyphen indicates an abrupt cutoff, with level pitch
[ ] :	square brackets indicate phonetic transcription, particularly "Japanized" or pronounced in such a way that may cause misunderstanding
'	: stress is assigned only when needed to emphasize its incorrectness
..	: unfilled pause
...	: longer unfilled pause
( )	: (a) unintelligible, unclear, probable word or words, (b) comments such as pause and laugh
CAPS :	a word in upper case indicates marked prominence

When proper nouns appear in the data, either random initials or names are used.

Appendix 2. List of Communication Strategies

1. Reduction strategies
    a. Topic avoidance
    b. Message abandonment
    c. Semantic avoidance
2. Achievement strategies
    a. Approximation
        i. Lexical substitution
        ii. Generalization
        iii. Exemplification
    b. Paraphrase strategies
        i. Circumlocution
        ii. Word coinage
        iii. Morphological creativity
    c. Interlingual strategies
        i. Borrowing
        ii. Foreignizing
        iii. Literal translation
    d. Restructuring
    e. Cooperative strategies
3. Other strategies
    a. Repair
    b. Telegraphic
    c. Fillers
    d. Change of role
    e. Others

References

Beebe, Leslie, Tomoko Takahashi, and Robin Uliss-Weltz. 1990. "Pragmatic Transfer of ESL Refusals." In *Developing Communicative Competence in a Second Language*, ed. by Robin C. Scarcella, Elaine S. Andersen, and Stephen D. Krashen, 55–73. New York: Newbury House Publishers.

Bialystok, Ellen. 1983. "Some Factors in the Selection and Implementation of Communication Strategies." In *Strategies in Interlanguage Communication*, ed. by Claus Færch and Gabriele Kasper, 100–118. New York: Longman.

Bialystok, Ellen. 1990. *Communication Strategies: A Psychological Analysis of Second Language Use*. Oxford: Basil Blackwell.

Bongaerts, Theo, Eric Kellerman, and Andy Bentlage. 1987. "Perspective and Proficiency in L_2 Referential Communication." *Studies in Second Language Acquisition* 9.171–200.

Canale, Michael, and Merrill Swain. 1980. "Theoretical Bases of Communicative Approaches to Second Language Teaching and Testing." *Applied Linguistics* 1.1–47.

Clark, John L. D. 1975. "Theoretical and Technical Considerations in Oral Proficiency Testing." In *Testing Language Proficiency*, ed. by Randall L. Jones and Bernard Spolsky, 10–28. Arlington, VA: The Center for Applied Linguistics.

Corder, S. Pit. 1983. "Strategies of Communication." In *Strategies in Interlanguage Communication*, ed. by Claus Færch and Gabriele Kasper, 15–19. New York: Longman.

Educational Testing Service. 1982. *ETS Oral Proficiency Testing Manual*. Princeton, NJ: Author.

Ellis, Rod. 1985. *Understanding Second Language Acquisition*. Oxford: Oxford University Press.

Færch, Claus, and Gabriele Kasper. 1980. "Processes and Strategies in Foreign Language Learning and Communication." *Interlanguage Studies Bulletin* 5.47–118.

Færch, Claus, and Gabriele Kasper. 1983a. *Strategies in Interlanguage Communication*. New York: Longman.

Færch, Claus, and Gabriele Kasper. 1983b. "Plans and Strategies in Foreign Language Communication." In *Strategies in Interlanguage Communication*, ed. by Claus Færch and Gabriele Kasper, 20–60. New York: Longman.

Færch, Claus, and Gabriele Kasper. 1983c. "On Identifying Communication Strategies in Interlanguage Production." In *Strategies in Interlanguage Communication*, ed. by Claus Færch and Gabriele Kasper, 210–238. New York: Longman.

Færch, Claus, and Gabriele Kasper. 1986. "Cognitive Dimensions of Language Transfer." In *Crosslinguistic Influence in Second Language Acquisition*, ed. by Eric Kellerman and Michael Sharwood Smith, 49–65. Oxford: Pergamon.

Færch, Claus, and Gabriele Kasper. 1987. *Introspection in Second Language Research*. Clevedon: Multilingual Matters.

Færch, Claus, and Gabriele Kasper. 1989. "Transfer of Production: Some Implications for the Interlanguage Hypothesis." In *Transfer in Language Production*, ed. by Hans W. Dechert and Manfred Raupach, 173–193. Norwood, NJ: Ablex.

Grice, H. Paul. 1975. "Logic and Conversation." In *Syntax and Semantics: Speech Acts*, ed. by Peter Cole and Jerry L. Morgan, 41–58. New York: Academic Press.

Haastrup, Kirsten, and Robert Phillipson. 1983. "Achievement Strategies in Learner/Native Speaker Interaction." In *Strategies in Interlanguage Communication*, ed. by Claus Færch and Gabriele Kasper, 140–158. New York: Longman.

Hatch, Evelyn, and Anne Lazaraton. 1991. *The Research Manual: Design and Statistics for Applied Linguistics*. New York: Newbury House Publishers.

Hinds, John. 1978. "Conversational Structure: An Investigation Based on Japanese Interview Discourse." In *Problems in Japanese Syntax and Semantics*, ed. by John Hinds and Irwin Howard, 79–121. Tokyo: Kaitakusha.

Hunt, Kellogg W. 1966. "Recent Measures in Syntactic Development." *Elementary English* 43.732–739.

Hymes, Dell. 1972. "On Communicative Competence." In *Sociolinguistics*, ed. by John B. Pride and Janet Holmes, 269–293. Harmondsworth, Middlesex: Penguin.

Kellerman, Eric. 1977. "Towards a Characterization of the Strategy of Transfer in Second Language Learning." *Interlanguage Studies Bulletin* 2.58–145.

Kellerman, Eric. 1979. "Transfer and Non-transfer: Where Are We Now?" *Studies in Second Language Acquisition* 2.37–57.

Kellerman, Eric. 1983. "Now You See It, Now You Don't." In *Language Transfer in Language Learning*, ed. by Susan M. Gass and Larry Selinker, 112–134. Rowley, MA: Newbury House Publishers.

Kellerman, Eric. 1986. "An Eye for an Eye: Crosslinguistic Constraints on the Development of the L_2 Lexicon." In *Crosslinguistic Influence in Second Language Acquisition*, ed. by Eric Kellerman and Michael Sharwood Smith, 35–48. Oxford: Pergamon Press.

Kellerman, Eric. 1991. "Compensatory Strategies in Second Language Research: A Critique, a Revision, and Some (Non-)Implications for the Classroom." In *Foreign/Second Language Pedagogy Research*, ed. by Robert Phillipson, Eric Kellerman, Larry Selinker, Michael Sharwood Smith, and Merrill Swain, 142–161. Clevedon, Avon: Multilingual Matters.

Kellerman, Eric, Ton Ammerlaan, Theo Bongaerts, and Nanda Poulisse. 1990. "System and Hierarchy in L_2 Compensatory Strategies." In *Developing Communicative Competence in a Second Language*, ed. by Robin C. Scarcella, Elaine S. Andersen, and Stephen D. Krashen, 163–178. New York: Newbury House.

Kellerman, Eric, Theo Bongaerts, and Nanda Poulisse. 1987. "Strategy and System in L_2 Referential Communication." In *Second Language Acquisition in Context*, ed. by Rod Ellis, 100–112. London: Prentice-Hall International.

Kumaravadivelu, B. 1988. "Communication Strategies and Psychological Processes Underlying Lexical Simplification." *International Review of Applied Linguistics* 26.309–319.

Labarca, Angela, and Rajai Khanji. 1986. "On Communication Strategies: Focus on Interaction." *Studies in Second Language Acquisition* 8.68–79.
Lightbown, Patsy M. 1985. "Great Expectations: Second-Language Acquisition Research and Classroom Teaching." *Applied Linguistics* 6.171–189.
Loveday, Leo J. 1986. *Japanese Sociolinguistics*. Philadelphia: John Benjamins.
Loveday, Leo J. 1988. "Communicative Interference: From Japanese to English." In *Interlanguage Studies*, ed. by Dietrich Nehls, 135–151. Heidelberg: Julius Groos.
Lowe, Pardee, Jr. 1987. "Interagency Language Roundtable Oral Proficiency Interview." In *Reviews of English Language Proficiency Tests*, ed. by J. Charles Alderson, Karl J. Krahnke, and Charles W. Stansfield, 43–47. Washington, DC: TESOL.
Magnan, Sally S. 1988. "Grammar and the ACTFL Oral Proficiency Interview: Discussion and Data." *The Modern Language Journal* 72.266–276.
Maynard, Senko K. 1989. *Japanese Conversation: Self-contextualization through Structure and Interactional Management*. Norwood, NJ: Ablex.
McLaughlin, Barry. 1987. *Theories of Second-Language Learning*. London: Edward Arnold.
McLaughlin, Barry. 1990. "'Conscious' vs. 'Unconscious' Learning." *TESOL Quarterly* 24.617–634.
McLaughlin, Barry, Tammi Rossman, and Beverly McLeon. 1983. "Second Language Learning: An Information-Processing Perspective." *Language Learning* 33.135–158.
Morrison, Donald M., and Graham Low. 1983. "Monitoring and the Second Language Learner." In *Language and Communication*, ed. by Jack C. Richards and Richard W. Schmidt. New York: Longman.
Paribakht, Tahereh. 1985. "Strategic Competence and Language Proficiency." *Applied Linguistics* 6.132–146.
Poulisse, Nanda. 1987. "Problems and Solutions in the Classification of Compensatory Strategies." *Second Language Research* 3.141–153.
Poulisse, Nanda. 1990. *The Use of Compensatory Strategies by Dutch Learners of English*. Dordrecht: Foris.
Poulisse, Nanda, and Theo Bongaerts. 1994. "First Language Use in Second Language Production." *Applied Linguistics* 15.36–57.
Raupach, Manfred. 1980. "Temporal Variables in First and Second Language Speech Production." In *Temporal Variables in Speech*, ed. by Hans W. Dechert and Manfred Raupach, 263–270. The Hague: Mouton.
Richards, Jack C., and Mayuri Sukwiwat. 1983. "Language Transfer and Conversational Competence." *Applied Linguistics* 4.113–125.
Ringbom, Håkan. 1978. "The Influence of the Mother Tongue on the Translation of Lexical Items." *Interlanguage Studies Bulletin* 3.80–101.
Ross, Steven, and Richard Berwick. 1992. "The Discourse of Accommodation in Oral Proficiency Interviews." *Studies in Second Language Learning* 14.159–176.

Scarcella, Robin C. 1983. "Discourse Accent in Second Language Performance." In *Language Transfer in Language Learning*, ed. by Susan Gass and Larry Selinker, 306–326. Rowley, MA: Newbury House.

Schwartz, Joan. 1977. *Repair in Conversations Between Adult Second Language Learners of English*. Unpublished M.A. thesis, University of California, Los Angeles.

Selinker, Larry. 1972. "Interlanguage." *International Review of Applied Linguistics* 10.209–231.

Takahashi, Tomoko. 1989. "The Influence of the Listener on L_2 Speech." In *Variation in Second Language Acquisition: Psycholinguistic Issues*, ed. by Susan Gass, Carolyn Madden, Dennis Preston, and Larry Selinker, 245–279. Clevedon, Avon: Multilingual Matters.

Tarone, Elaine. 1977. "Conscious Communication Strategies in Interlanguage." In *On TESOL '77*, ed. by H. Douglas Brown, Carlos A. Yorio, and Ruth C. Crymes, 195–203. Washington, DC: TESOL.

Tarone, Elaine. 1980. "Communication Strategies, Foreigner Talk, and Repair in Interlanguage." *Language Learning* 30.417–431.

Tarone, Elaine. 1981. "Some Thoughts on the Notion of Communicative Strategy." *TESOL Quarterly* 15.285–95.

Tarone, Elaine, and George Yule. 1989. *Focus on the Language Learner*. Oxford: Oxford University Press.

van Lier, Leo. 1988. *The Classroom and the Language Learner*. New York: Longman.

van Lier, Leo. 1989. "Reeling, Writing, Drawing, Stretching, and Fainting in Coils: Oral Proficiency Interviews as Conversation." *TESOL Quarterly* 23.489–508.

Wagner, Johannes. 1983. "Dann du Tagen Eineeeee—Weisse Platte—An Analysis of Interlanguage Communication in Instructions." In *Strategies in Interlanguage Communication*, ed. by Claus Færch and Gabriele Kasper, 159–174. New York: Longman.

Yoshida, Yumiko. 1991. *The Use of Communication Strategies by Adult Japanese Speakers of English as a Second Language in Language Proficiency Interviews*. Unpublished M.A. thesis, Southern Illinois University at Carbondale.

Young, Richard. 1995. "Conversational Styles in Language Proficiency Interviews." *Language Learning* 45.3–42.

Young, Richard, and Michael Milanovic. 1992. "Discourse Variation in Oral Proficiency Interviews." *Studies in Second Language Acquisition* 14.403–424.

Meaning Negotiation in the Hungarian Oral Proficiency Examination of English

Lucy Katona
The State Foreign Languages Examination Board, Hungary

Since the 1970s extensive research has been conducted into the interlanguage communication process. The term interlanguage was coined by Selinker in 1972 to refer to foreign language learners' developing language system, which can be viewed as an approximation to the target language. Selinker (1972) was also the first to posit strategies of second-language communication as one of the central processes for language learning, and the first empirical study into this area was conducted only a year later by Váradi (1973). Although there is still no clear-cut and generally accepted definition, the term communication strategies is commonly used to refer to the (extra)linguistic resources non-native speakers resort to in case of actual or potential communication breakdown. These strategies may include the processes of lexical simplification, substitution, and approximation, as well as the impact of the mother tongue on learners' L_2 utterances (Bialystok 1983).

Apart from investigating learners' interlanguage performance in instances of problematic communication, several researchers have examined foreigner talk—the linguistic and conversational adjustments native speakers make when they interact with non-native speakers. Most of the research, however, has focused on one participant at a time—either on the learner or on the native-speaking interlocutor—and thus relatively little research has been done into the communicative procedures that both participants follow when they want to negotiate meaning.

This chapter reports the results of a research project conducted into negotiated communication between Hungarian interviewers and interviewees during the English Oral Proficiency Examination (OPE). The question the project set out to address was whether familiarity with the interlocutor (known or unknown examiner) caused any significant differences in the different types of meaning negotiation that took place between the participants. On the basis of previous research and the findings of this investigation, a partly new taxonomy is presented where communication strategies are incorporated into a more general, interactional framework. This analytic framework has been developed by taking a more integrated approach to studies of second language interaction, as proposed by Yule and Tarone (1991:170), who argue that "the key moves by both the learner and the interlocutor within this interaction can be effectively described within a communication strategy framework that can be applied to both sides of the transcription" (Yule and Tarone 1991:167). The present study describes the results of such an investigation into the negotiated interaction of the Hungarian subjects in testing conditions. It investigates oral test discourse in the OPE in instances of problematic communication, with special emphasis on what linguistic means candidates use to solve their communication problems and how interviewers try to help them achieve mutual understanding.

The chapter begins with a review of the previous research literature, which is followed by background information relevant to the project. After detailed description of the methods employed in the present study, a taxonomy of communication strategies is presented; then the analytic framework based on the results of the qualitative analysis is described. Within this framework the observed negotiation sequences and exchanges are analyzed and some emerging patterns are established. Finally, conclusions are drawn about the generalizability of the findings, and some areas of further research are suggested.

1 Review of Previous Research

1.1 *Communication Strategies*

Communication strategies (CSs) are thought to be manifestations of underlying strategic competence, one of the basic components of communicative competence as posited by Canale and Swain (1980). Canale (1983:10–11) defines strategic competence as follows:

> This component is composed of mastery of verbal and nonverbal communication strategies that may be called into action for two main reasons: (a) to compensate for breakdowns in communication due to limiting conditions in actual communication (e.g., momentary inability to recall an idea or grammatical form) or to insufficient competence in one or more of the other areas of communicative competence; and (b) to enhance the effectiveness of communication (e.g., deliberately slow and soft speech for rhetorical effect).

In other words, CSs can be used in instances of problematic or successful communication by both native speakers and learners of a given language. Most of the research to be reviewed in this section deals with the first area, since, as Tarone and Yule (1987) point out, very little systematic investigation has been conducted into the second one.

There have been several attempts to define CSs in greater detail. Perhaps the two best known are by Tarone (1980, 1981) and Færch and Kasper (1983a). These definitions reflect two different approaches to the concept; Tarone's is based on an interactional perspective, whereas Færch and Kasper's conceptualization draws on a psycholinguistic approach (cf. Færch and Kasper 1984). For Tarone (1981:288), CSs relate to "a mutual attempt of two interlocutors to agree on a meaning in situations where requisite meaning structures do not seem to be shared." Thus she emphasizes their cooperative nature. In contrast, Færch and Kasper (1983a), after placing CSs within a general model of speech production, focus on individual learners, who may or may not appeal to their interlocutors when they need help, and define CSs as "potentially conscious plans for solving what to an individual presents itself as a problem in reaching a particular communicative goal" (Færch and Kasper 1983a:36).

Both definitions have been influential, but Færch and Kasper's seems to have gained more popularity, as most subsequent research studies have employed their conceptualization. Several taxonomies have been proposed, with considerable overlap in the categories (Bialystok 1983; Blum-Kulka and Levenston 1983; Chen 1990; Corder 1983; Dörnyei and Scott 1995; Færch and Kasper 1983a, 1984; Haastrup and Phillipson 1983; Kumaravadivelu 1988; Labarca and Khanji 1986; Paribakht 1985; Tarone 1980, 1981; Tarone, Cohen, and Dumas 1976; Tarone and Yule 1987; Váradi 1973; Yarmohammadi and Seif 1992). There seems to be general consensus, however, at least about the two main types: reduction and compensatory strategies. The former refers to learners' attempts to reduce their intended meaning, for instance by topic avoidance or message abandonment, while the latter consists of learners' efforts to express their original intentions with their limited linguistic means (for reviews see Bialystok 1990, Cook 1993, and DeKeyser 1989). Table 1 summarizes a widely used taxonomy of CSs.

In the late 1980s this classification came under strong criticism from the researchers of the Nijmegen Group (Bongaerts and Poulisse 1989, Kellerman 1991, Poulisse 1987), who claimed that all these taxonomies were product- rather than process-based, and therefore they could take only the surface linguistic representations of CSs into account instead of focusing on the underlying cognitive processes learners used to arrive at them. They proposed a new, process-based taxonomy, which consisted of the following two main strategy types: *conceptual strategies*, which are employed to manipulate the intended concept, and *linguistic (or code) strategies*, which are used to manipulate the available linguistic resources.

Despite the seemingly big differences between the product- and the process-based approaches, obvious similarities can be noticed as well. Both conceptualize CSs as comprising two main categories: changing the intended meaning to be conveyed or making do with the linguistic means available to express meaning. This fundamental distinction can serve as the basis for further investigation into the nature of CSs.

1.2 *Foreigner Talk*

Foreigner Talk (FT) refers to the linguistic modifications native speakers (NSs) make to adjust their speech to their non-native interlocutor's (NNS) perceived level of proficiency. This "register of simplified speech" (Ferguson 1971:143) is characterized by linguistic adjustments in pronunciation, vocabulary, and grammar (for a summary of these features—adapted from Hatch 1983—see Gass and Selinker 1994).

These linguistic adjustments are essentially non-interactional, but Foreigner Talk Discourse (FTD) also incorporates conversational adjustments that may be utilized in the interactional phenomenon of meaning negotiation (for a review of FTD see Long 1981, 1983a, 1983b). Long (1981) observes the predominance of questions and present-tense oriented topics in FTD (these findings are also confirmed by Gaies 1982). In a later study, Long (1983b) distinguishes between modified input (simplified linguistic forms directed at the NNS) and modified interaction (changes in the functions of those forms in conversational discourse), and claims that conversational modifications can be found much more frequently in NS-NNS discourse than in its NS-NS counterpart. Focusing on the former, Long lists fifteen devices NSs use to modify the interactional structure of their conversations with NNSs. These are grouped into three subsets: (a) strategies of topic management, which are used to avoid conversational trouble; (b) tactics to repair communication problems; and (c) strategies and tactics to both avoid and repair trouble. Three of these devices are of crucial importance in further analysis of negotiated interaction: comprehension checks, which are used to check NNSs' comprehension; clarification requests, which are employed to find out what the interlocutor's preceding utterance(s) mean; and confirmation checks, which are made by NSs to see if their own understanding is correct.

Examiners also use FTD in language proficiency interviews (LPIs). Since the LPI is a "hybrid of interview and conversational interaction" (Ross and Berwick 1992:160), it shares some basic features of both modes of social interaction (van Lier 1989, Lazaraton 1992), but unlike conversation it is characterized by an

Table 1. *A Traditional Taxonomy of Communication Strategies*

Avoidance or Reduction Strategies

1	Message abandonment	Leaving a message unfinished because of language difficulties
2	Topic avoidance	Avoiding topic areas or concepts that pose language difficulties

Achievement or Compensatory Strategies

3	Circumlocution	Describing or exemplifying the target object or action (e.g., *the thing you open bottles with* for *corkscrew*)
4	Approximation	Using an alternative term that expresses the meaning of the target lexical item as closely as possible (e.g., *ship* for *sailboat*)
5	Use of all-purpose words	Extending a general, empty lexical item to contexts where specific words are lacking (e.g., the overuse of *thing, stuff, make, do,* as well as using words like *thingie, what-do-you-call-it*)
6	Word-coinage	Creating a nonexisting L_2 word based on a supposed rule (e.g., *vegetarianist* for *vegetarian*)
7	Use of nonlinguistic means	Mime, gesture, facial expression, or sound imitation
8	Literal translation	Translating literally a lexical item, an idiom, a compound word, or structure from L_1 to L_2
9	Foreignizing	Using a L_1 word by adjusting it to L_2 phonologically (i.e., with a L_2 pronunciation) and/or morphologically (e.g., adding to it a L_2 suffix)
10	Code switching	Using a L_1 word with L_1 pronunciation or a L_3 word with L_3 pronunciation in L_2.
11	Appeal for help	Turning to the conversation partner for help either directly (e.g., *What do you call . . . ?*) or indirectly (e.g., rising intonation, pause, eye contact, puzzled expression)

Stalling or Time-Gaining Strategies

12	Use of fillers/ hesitation devices	Using filling words or gambits to fill pauses and to gain time to think (e.g., *well, now let me see, as a matter of fact*)

Note. Adapted from "On the Teachability of Communication Strategies" by Zoltán Dörnyei, 1995, *TESOL Quarterly* 29, 55–85. Copyright 1995 by Teachers of English to Speakers of Other Languages, Inc. Excerpt from p. 58 used with permission.

asymmetrical allocation of control. This "asymmetrical contingency" (Jones and Gerard 1967, cited in van Lier 1989 and in Young and Milanovic 1992) means that only the interviewer has control over the interview, which is conducted according to a (largely predetermined) plan. Young and Milanovic (1992), investigating discourse variation in Cambridge First Certificate in English oral interviews, attribute discourse variation to the effect of four variables: the examiner, the participants' gender, the theme of the interview, and the task to be performed. They propose a working model of interview discourse, and call for further research into the effect of discourse variation on examiners' judgments.

Ross and Berwick (1992) take up part of this task by examining the discourse of accommodation in LPIs, and find that control exponents (which are used by the interviewer to control the interview process) and accommodation exponents (which "reflect the interviewer's attempts to facilitate the communication of information during the process of the interview" [Ross and Berwick 1992:164]) are both at play. Only accommodation exponents, however, can discriminate successfully among candidates' ratings. As a result, the researchers recommend the integration of accommodation in interview training procedures and among the rating criteria.

Central to the notion of FTD is the negotiation of meaning, which refers to interlocutors' attempts to clarify a lack of understanding in the course of conversation. Varonis and Gass (1985) set up a model for the concept consisting of two parts: a trigger (the speaker's utterance that poses a problem to the hearer) and the resolution (comprising the indication of the hearer's nonunderstanding, the speaker's attempt to solve the problem, and the hearer's optional response), with comprehension checks that can occur at any point in the process. As this model focuses on instances of nonunderstanding only, it can be viewed as a subgroup of their more general framework (Gass and Varonis 1991), which consists of two types of problematic communication, non-engagement and miscommunication, depending on the outcome of the communicative encounter (on the negotiation of meaning and outcome, see also Young 1984). Miscommunication is of special interest to us as it occurs frequently in NS-NNS oral interaction.

Aston (1986) questions the assumption that maximal meaning negotiation provides optimal conditions for SLA (cf. Ehrlich, Avery, and Yorio 1989). In place of Varonis and Gass's (1985) term "nonunderstanding routines," he suggests "troubleshooting machinery" to account for the facts that not all conversational trouble concerns comprehensibility, and there is no one-to-one correspondence between the presence of trouble and the use of troubleshooting procedures, which perform the two functions of locating and repairing conversational trouble. Aston claims that the frequency of these procedures may be linked to the perceived difficulty of the interaction. As he argues, "it is not simply or even primarily the frequency, but above all the social context of negotiation to influence acquisition"

(Aston 1986:140). These procedures are worthy of investigation as they provide interlocutors with the opportunity to maintain good rapport and to negotiate a mutually satisfactory outcome. Thus Aston, drawing on Varonis and Gass's (1985) approach, calls for further research that considers "these procedures not as isolated acts, but as contributions to routines which are constructed by both participants" (Aston 1986: 138).

This review of the literature underlines the importance of negotiated interaction as a central process in face-to-face interaction involving second-language learners. Consequently, if we want to gain deeper insights into negotiated communication between more and less proficient interlocutors, we need to examine the CSs that *both* participants use in case of communication difficulty.

2 Background to the Study

The research project reported on in this chapter was carried out at the State Foreign Languages Examination Board (SFLEB), the national testing agency of Hungary, which offers language proficiency testing in a variety of foreign languages to approximately 90,000 people a year, about half of whom take the test in English. The certificate of language proficiency issued by the SFLEB is a job requirement in many places in Hungary. In addition, it also means a salary supplement or bonus points in university entrance examinations, and it may exempt secondary school students from taking the final exams in the foreign language. Thus the results of the test are of crucial importance to the candidates, and it is essential to constantly improve the quality of FL testing at the SFLEB. One way of doing so is to learn more about the construct of language proficiency by investigating learners' test performances in the different types of examinations. The study reported on below is part of this larger project, and it focuses on the OPE, which involves more than 30,000 people annually.

3 Method

3.1 *Subjects*

The experiment was conducted at the SFLEB in the spring of 1992. The subjects were twelve adult Hungarian learners of English studying at the language school section of the SFLEB and preparing for the language proficiency interview at the intermediate level. Nine of the twelve subjects were working adults in their twenties, thirties, or forties, but the sample also included three high school students. There were five males and seven females among them, none of whom had spent a long period of time in an English-speaking country. They had been studying English at the SFLEB for three years in an intensive course consisting of twelve forty-minute classes a week. These subjects may be termed a "convenience sample;" they all volunteered to take part after the aims and procedures of the research were explained to them. Nevertheless, they are considered fairly typical of the whole population of candidates who take the EFL oral exam at the SFLEB.

Apart from the subjects, three female interviewers, who work for the SFLEB as full-time teachers and examiners, also participated in the experiment. All of them are non-native speakers of English with near-native competence. Two examiners have long years of experience in both fields, whereas the third interviewer (Examiner 3) was a relatively inexperienced examiner at the time the data were collected. Examiner 1 was the group's course instructor; she knew the candidates quite well, as she had taught them for three years. In contrast, the other two examiners (Examiners 2 and 3) had not met the subjects before. It was hypothesized that this variable (the subjects' familiarity with the examiner) might affect the quality of the candidates' oral discourse, since conversing with a familiar interlocutor or a completely unfamiliar interlocutor, especially in the stressful conditions of an oral test, can provide very different circumstances. It was also assumed that, for lack of shared experience and/or knowledge, the number of misunderstandings is likely to increase when complete strangers talk to each other for the first time in a foreign language. This, in turn, may lead to the use of various kinds of meaning negotiation strategies by both participants and, consequently, may result in differing types of oral discourse in the two contexts.

3.2 *Materials*

Two different sets of interview batteries were used at the two OPEs, each containing 15 pictures and 15 situation cards. The pictures selected for this experiment depict common scenes to describe (e.g., in a hospital, on holiday, or in a shop), just like the situation cards, which contain detailed written instructions in Hungarian for both interlocutors to act out. The topics cover a wide range (e.g., entertainment, work, health care, weather, and travel). Following the standard practice at the SFLEB, the candidates were asked to choose a picture and a situation card before the OPE began in order to ensure that several different topics were dealt with during the interview.

3.3 Procedure

The subjects took part in two oral tests: first a mock exam with their course instructor, and about a month later, a live exam with the two unknown examiners (one of whom was the interlocutor, while the other assessed the candidate's oral language performance; the examiners took turns in performing these duties). Both interviews lasted approximately 15 minutes and followed the standard procedures of the Hungarian OPE, which consists of three tasks: a general conversation, a picture description, and a role-play based on the Hungarian situation cards.

After the candidates' written permission was obtained to do so, all 24 oral exams were audio- and videotaped. They were transcribed partly by the author and partly by two research assistants, whose work was checked by the author.

3.4 Analyses

The main research question is whether there exist any significant interlocutor-related differences in oral test discourse in instances of problematic communication. The narrower focus of the study is on how the participants negotiate mutually understandable meaning in case of (potential) communication breakdown. To answer these questions I analyzed the collected data both quantitatively and qualitatively; for lack of space, this study reports mainly on the findings of the qualitative analysis.

After the data were collected and transcribed, the 24 transcripts were thoroughly examined to find all instances of communication problems (CPs) where the subjects used some kind of CS. A CP was defined as "a manifestation of a 'gap' in communicative competence" (Harper 1985:86), whereas for the identification of CSs Færch and Kasper's (1983a) definition served as the starting point. Because I did not have access to retrospective data on the candidates' CS use (see Poulisse, Bongaerts, and Kellerman 1987 on the reliability and usefulness of retrospection), only those utterances were identified as CSs that were accompanied by the co-occurrence of other performance features indicating strategic planning (such as self-repair, nervous laughs, rising intonation, and temporal variables, for instance, slower rate of articulation, pauses, drawls or repeats) (cf. Færch and Kasper 1983b, Raupach 1983, Willems 1987). In doubtful cases the utterances were checked against the videotape for concomitant signals of problematic communication (hesitation phenomena and paralinguistic features such as mime, gestures, or facial expressions). Altogether 363 CPs were found, in which the subjects used 460 CSs. The resulting CSs were carefully analyzed, and a partly new classification was proposed based on the results of the most influential taxonomies summarized in Table 1. In the new taxonomy the CSs were grouped into three categories and their frequency distribution was examined (Table 2). To compare the interviewers' meaning negotiation strategies a chi-square test of significance was performed.

The qualitative analysis was based on analytic induction, a method of both discovery and testing that aims at building a hypothesis from a transcribed set of data by frequent rereading and reexamination until some salient patterns or recurring themes emerge. Then these patterns or themes are tested against possible counterexamples to see if they *de facto* provide an adequate account of the analyzed phenomenon (Jackson 1986).

4 Results and Discussion

Table 2 shows the raw and relative frequencies of the observed CSs. From an interactional point of view, the observed CSs can be divided into three main groups.

4.1 *Help-Requesting Strategies*

In this testing context, where the two participants share the same mother tongue but speak in the FL, the two reduction strategies, as well as appeals for help and code switching, all function as the candidate's (direct or indirect) appeal for assistance that triggers some kind of help from the interlocutor.

4.2 *Meaning-Evoking/Approximating Strategies*

This category comprises the candidates' own efforts to convey their message. Most of the compensatory strategies belong to this group, as the candidates most often resort to them when they want to approximate their intended meaning (by using literal translation, approximation, word coinage, circumlocution, or restructuring) or to evoke the intended meaning in the listener's mind (by employing foreignizing, opposites, simplification, phonological similarity, or grammatical strategies).

4.3 *Survival Strategies*

This group contains the strategies that candidates use to continue the conversation when they are faced with communication difficulty. This category occurs infrequently in the data but is worth mentioning because it represents a different type of strategy, the main function of which is conversation maintenance.

The taxonomy presented in Table 2 draws considerably on previous classifications, but it also contains some elements that, to my knowledge, have not been reported in the research literature previously or have been under-researched so far. These include opposites, simplification, phonological similarity, and grammatical strategies, as well as the survival strategies of repeating, interpreting, and giving inappropriate responses to keep the conversation going. As these strategies are believed to be (relatively) new, I will define them and illustrate them with some examples from my data.

The strategy of opposites is defined as using a word opposite in meaning to the intended one. These are divided into two subcategories: ordinary opposites (e.g., *take* for *put*, *go* for *come*) and negative opposites, that is, the strategy of negating a word or expression in an attempt to evoke the intended meaning in the hearer's mind (cf. Blum-Kulka and Levenston 1983), as in Excerpt 1. (See the appendix for notation used in these transcripts.)

(1)

```
    I:  Can you tell me — something about her hairstyle?
    C:  Erm + erm — I think maybe + er this? ((pointing to
        the woman's bun in the picture))
    I:  Uhum.
→   C:  ++ E mm + not on bone ++ It isn't a bone, I know
        ((laughs)).
```

Simplification is the strategy of using an existing word that is only a part of the intended word or expression (e.g., *ice* for *ice cream*, *highway* for *highway code*—cf. Levenston and Blum 1977). Phonological similarity refers to the strategy of using an existing word that sounds similar to the intended one (cf. Dörnyei and Scott 1995, who also identify this type and refer to it as the "use of similar sounding words"). This strategy may be further divided into ordinary similarity (e.g., *prepare* for *repair*, *wool* for *wood*) and faulty retrieval, the strategy of using a nonexisting word that sounds approximately the same as the intended one (e.g., *rescriptions* for *prescriptions*, *short-leeved* for *short-sleeved*). Restructuring is the strategy that is used when learners realize they cannot express their intended meaning, so they stop in mid-sentence and develop an alternative way of conveying their message.

In addition to lexical strategies, I have also found several examples of grammatical strategies, in which the speaker uses a word or expression to approximate the intended grammatical meaning. These strategies are not the same as the grammatical types of formal reduction that Færch and Kasper (1983a) speak about. Færch and

Table 2. Taxonomy and Frequency Distribution of Communication Strategies

Strategy type	Number of instances	Percentage of all strategies
Help-requesting strategies		
Topic avoidance	31	7%
Message abandonment	40	9%
Appeal for help	24	5%
Code switching	29	6%
Meaning-evoking/approximating strategies		
Foreignizing	7	2%
Literal translation	71	15%
Opposites	26	6%
Approximation	35	8%
Word coinage	27	6%
Simplification	6	1%
Phonological similarity	27	6%
Circumlocution	62	13%
Restructuring	17	4%
Grammatical	42	9%
Survival strategies		
Repeating	2	0%
Interpreting	3	0%
Inappropriate response	11	2%
Total	460	99%

Note. Total is less than 100% due to rounding.

Kasper refer to the avoidance of a morphological or syntactic structure (such as the subjunctive or the passive voice), whereas in my data the subjects make an attempt (even if a faulty one) to express the grammatical structure they have in mind (see also Bialystok 1990, Littlewood 1984). Excerpt 2 illustrates this phenomenon.

Meaning Negotiation in the Hungarian Oral Proficiency Examination   251

(2)

→   C: . . . they − er said that + er − <u>the Japanese − er people − would like to − would have been like to er − to get worked them ((smiles)) − a lot.</u>

        I: Mmmm

→   C: <u>To make work er − er</u> . . .

             ((10 lines omitted))

→   C: . . . <u>they would like to er − to er − work − er very low − er salary − i- in</u> Japan, too.

        I: Wer- I I don't think anybody would like to work for a low salary.

        C: ((laughs)) Workers wouldn't like it.

In Excerpt 2 the candidate wants to use a causative structure and tries to express himself using three different grammatical strategies. As the last sentence shows, he is well aware of the difference between what he is trying to say and what he can actually say.

In addition to the two main CS groups, the Hungarian subjects used a third type that I call survival strategies. This category comprises three different coping strategies that can be used to stay in the conversation. The first one is repeating, that is, using the same word or expression again to keep the conversation going (cf. Chen 1990, Tarone and Yule 1987), as illustrated in Excerpt 3.

(3)

        C: It's great + er − but − er yesterday − I − wasn't − er so lucky − because − er − the − mm − rain fell, − and the wind − blew, <u>it was awful</u>, I I almost got froze − er when I arrived at my − er − office

→   I: Well, *it was really awful* yesterday.

→   C: And − er <u>it was really awful</u>, but − a few years − ever − ago − it was er -extra − extra-ordinary bad, <u>it was awful</u>, − it was − er even more cold − than this − er − it was very cold for the season [- and − <u>awful</u>.

        I: [Oh yes, it's terrible when you would think that − erm − it's summer already,

→   and it isn't − *it's really awful*.

        C: Yes, and − there was − aa − big catastrophe − on the − er north part − of the country. <u>It was awful</u>, I − I er − just − arrived − er − arrived − er in there, − and <u>it was awful</u>.

As can be seen from this example, it is not only the candidate who uses this strategy; the interviewer may also resort to it. The next type of survival strategy is interpreting, which is used when learners are in doubt about the other speaker's intended meaning, therefore feigning understanding, they try to interpret it and reply accordingly (cf. Dörnyei and Scott 1995, who also identify this CS type and call it "carrying on as if understood"), as illustrated in Excerpt 4.

(4)

```
        I:   Are you a commuter?
        C:   I'm a . . .?
             ((12 lines omitted))
        I:   Yes — how — how do you — well, — commute?
  →     C:   I I think it's — it's quite well ((laughs)) — but —
             but — my communication skills — er no — er — er
             isn't developing well ((laughs)) — I I think . . .
```

In this example the candidate first tried to clarify the meaning of the unknown word, *commuting*, but when the interviewer later returned to the same question, he decided to risk an interpretation of it, *communicating*, and answered according to that meaning. This strategy may result in misunderstanding, but at the same time it can also indicate where the candidate's communication (and not necessarily commuting) problem lies and thus may help the participants solve it.

The last type of survival strategy is that of giving an inappropriate response, which is when learners use a highly automatized, grammatically correct, but socioculturally or contextually inappropriate word or expression to keep the conversation going, as in Excerpt 5.

(5)

```
        I:   If you have any ideas, please + tell me.
  →     C:   What is it really?
        I:   + Erm well, look at +++ erm — look at the wallpaper.
```

In sum, the classification described above is based on the solution the candidates choose when they have a CP. In this case, three options are available to them: they can ask for help, or they may try to solve the CP themselves, either by approximating/evoking their intended meaning or by feigning understanding and employing a survival strategy to keep the conversation going. This interactional classification

Table 3. Numbers of Non-negotiated Communication Strategies in the Two Tests

Type of interviewer's follow-up	Number of Communication Strategies		
	Familiar interlocutor	Unfamiliar interlocutor	Total
Acknowledgment	35	28	63
Okay (interviewer continues)	26	23	49
No follow-up (candidate continues)	22	45	67
Total	83	96	179

will serve as the starting point for further analysis of the data from the point of view of meaning negotiation.

4.4 *Non-negotiated Strategies*

As my research question involves the comparison of how meaning gets negotiated across interlocutors, we need to establish which CSs result in negotiation. From this viewpoint the observed CSs can be divided into two main groups: non-negotiated and negotiated strategies, depending on whether they are involved in negotiated communication, which is "the process by which speakers attempt to resolve difficulties" (Gass and Varonis 1991:127). Before examining the types of negotiated communication present in the data let us look at instances of non-negotiated meaning. Of the 460 CSs the candidates used in the two tests, 39% (179 strategies) initiated no negotiation of meaning (Table 3).

As can be seen from the table, non-negotiated CSs occurred in similar distribution in the two testing conditions (with the familiar interlocutor vs. the unfamiliar one) and triggered three kinds of follow-up from the interviewers: acknowledgment (e.g., *Uhum, I see*), after which either the candidate or the interviewer could continue; *okay*, in which the interviewers accepted the candidate's CS and continued as if the previous utterance were okay; and no follow-up, when the candidate could continue without interruption. The majority of the non-negotiated CSs comprised some kind of literal translation (48 cases) or circumlocution (28 instances), and these two categories made up almost half the total number.

4.5 Descriptive Framework for the Analysis of Negotiated Communication

Let us now examine the instances of negotiated communication that make up 61% of the observed CSs: 281 strategies were negotiated by the interviewer and the interviewees, resulting in 201 negotiation exchanges, "in which there is some overt indication that understanding between participants has not been complete and there is a resultant attempt to clarify the nonunderstanding" (Gass and Varonis 1985:39).

Following Sinclair and Coulthard's (1975) seminal work on the structure of classroom discourse, in which they proposed a three-part exchange (initiation, response, and follow-up) as the basic unit of organization, Tsui (1994) expanded their framework to the analysis of non-classroom discourse, suggesting that the same organizational unit is at work in conversational interactions. Thus her analytical framework consists of the same three moves of initiation, response and follow-up, the head acts of which are divided into several subclasses. Initiating may comprise elicitation, requestive, directive, and informative; responding can be made up of positive/negative responses and temporization (that is, postponing the decision-making); and finally, follow-ups may consist of endorsements, concessions, acknowledgments, or turn-passing as an optional move. I adopted Tsui's framework and modified it to suit the analysis of negotiated communication under testing conditions. The framework I propose was also influenced by Varonis and Gass's (1985) model for negotiation of meaning.

I employed the qualitative research method of analytic induction, and the (re)analysis of my data resulted in the following descriptive framework of negotiated communication: initiation (I) – first response (R1) – first follow-up (F1) – second response (R2) – second follow-up (F2) [– third response (R3) – third follow-up (F3) – fourth response (R4) – fourth follow-up (F4) – fifth response (R5) – fifth follow-up (F5), etc.], in which the initiation and the follow-up moves are made by the interviewer, and the response moves belong to the candidate. The elements in angular brackets occur with much lower frequency, and the framework can be represented as follows.

$$(I) \rightarrow R1 \rightarrow F1 \rightarrow R2 \rightarrow F2 [\rightarrow R3 \rightarrow F3 \rightarrow R4 \rightarrow F4 \rightarrow R5 \rightarrow F5, \text{etc.}]$$

Thus from my data a symmetrical interaction pattern emerges in which each participant takes turns in making a contribution. This pattern seems to apply to instances of problematic communication when both participants must take a more active part and make a joint effort in order to solve the arising communication problem(s) effectively. Therefore my finding does not necessarily contradict the overall asymmetrical pattern of the interaction found by, for instance, Young and Milanovic (1992:421), who assume that "this kind of discourse is a unique product of the interview situation." Now let us examine the elements of the framework in more detail.

4.6 Discourse Moves and Acts

4.6.1 Initiation

Initiation refers to the interviewer's (optional) move to initiate a (new) conversation exchange with the interviewee. In oral test discourse this move consists only of elicitation, "whose discourse function is to elicit an obligatory verbal response or its nonverbal surrogate" (Tsui 1994:65), and it may also be omitted if the candidate is already in the middle of answering a previous question or describing the picture.

4.6.2 First Response

The first response consists of the candidates' attempt to respond, that is, to express their intended meaning (usually in reply to a previous initiation) when they encounter a communication problem and consequently they employ CSs. Most of the negotiated strategies (199 out of the 281 CSs) occur in this position, and sometimes the candidates use more than one CS to get out of their conversational trouble. In addition, this move may also comprise the interviewees' efforts to clarify, when they do not understand the interviewer's question, and ask her to repeat or modify it. This discourse act can also be performed by the interviewer, and it occurs in the follow-up move(s) with much higher frequency.

4.6.3 First Follow-up

The first follow-up consists of the interviewer's first attempt to negotiate mutually understandable meaning with the interviewee, and it may comprise the following discourse acts: Help, which represents the interlocutor's efforts to assist the candidates when they lack the proper linguistic means to express themselves adequately; Elicit, which refers to the interlocutor's attempt to obtain (further) language samples from the candidates; Clarify, which occurs when the interlocutor is in doubt about the speaker's intended meaning or finds its linguistic realization unacceptable (cf. candidates' clarify in R1); and Acknowledge, which signals that the candidate's message has been received and accepted.

4.6.4 *Second Response*

The second response is already optional, and it may consist of the following discourse acts. Acknowledge is when the candidates signal they have received and accepted the interviewer's previous attempt to help. We can see that acknowledgment may be performed by both the interviewer and the candidate, and is differentiated according to its position (that is, according to which discourse move it occurs in and who it is performed by). Respond is when the candidates try to improve on the quality of their earlier reply, and in doing so they may self-repair their previous (faulty) utterance or employ another CS (or more than one) in an attempt to further elaborate on the first one(s). The use of a second/third CS may, in turn, initiate other negotiation sequences within the exchange.

4.6.5 *Second Follow-up*

The second follow-up is also optional if R2 consisted of the candidate's acknowledgment(s). Even if R2 was a response containing another CS, F2 may still comprise any of the four subclasses mentioned under F1, which can also trigger further elements of response and follow-up.

4.7 *Negotiation Sequences*

Negotiation exchanges, containing the three main parts of initiation – response(s) and follow-up(s)—are made up of one or more negotiation sequences that belong to three subclasses: helping, eliciting, and clarifying sequences, depending on the type of meaning negotiation the interviewer chooses to employ (in the follow-up moves).

4.7.1 *The Helping Sequence*

This is the most frequent and thus most basic sequence occurring in the data. It consists of an (optional) initiation, a response including one or more CSs, a follow-up move containing the discourse act of Help, an (optional) second response move (in which the interviewer's help is usually acknowledged, although it may also be rejected or ignored), and an (also optional) second follow-up move (in which the interviewer acknowledges the candidate's response). This sequence is represented below and illustrated in Excerpt 6.

$$(I) \rightarrow R1 \rightarrow F1: Help \rightarrow (R2) \rightarrow (F2)$$

(6)

```
(R1)     C: This is a a er er big er er auto er way
(F1) →   I: Uhum, motorway
(R2)     C: Motorway, motorway
(F2)     I: Right.
```

This is a fairly typical sequence, in which the initiating move is not quoted as it consists of the instruction the interviewer gives the candidate in order to make him describe the chosen picture. The candidate produces a CS in R1, which gets corrected by the interviewer in F1. The correct answer is repeated (twice) in R2, and is acknowledged by the interviewer in F2.

4.7.2 The Eliciting Sequence

The second most frequent type of negotiation sequence in the data was the eliciting sequence, in which the interviewer chooses to elicit further FL information from the candidate with the aim of getting a better, more precise linguistic solution to the CP. This sequence may consist of an (optional) initiation, a response including one or more CSs, a follow-up move containing some kind of Elicit, and a second response (which may contain some CSs). The R2 usually triggers another sequence. The sequence is represented as:

$$(I) \rightarrow R1 \rightarrow F1: Elicit \rightarrow R2 [\rightarrow F2 \rightarrow R3 \rightarrow F3 \text{ etc.}]$$

(7)

```
(I)      I: And what topics did you touch upon if I may ask?
(R1)     C: Er +
(F2) →   I: What did you speak about?
(R2)     C: Er we — we were speaking about er — one of our er
            nice experience-s . . .
```

Excerpt 7 is an illustrative example of this sequence type. It consists of an initiating move (with an instance of Elicit: inform) that proves too difficult for the candidate, so she does not answer anything. Her reduction strategy (topic avoidance) in R1 serves as an indicator of nonunderstanding (in practice, it performs the function of a clarification request); thus the interviewer modifies her question in F2. This simplified question triggers a second response, which already contains the requested information.

4.7.3 The Clarifying Sequence

The least frequent sequence in the data occurred when the interviewer wanted to clarify what the candidate's previous utterance(s) had meant. This sequence consists of an (optional) initiation, a response including one or more CSs, a follow-up move with some kind of Clarify, a second response (in which the candidate may self-repair, use some more CSs or (dis)confirm the interviewer's confirmation check or *you mean?* clarification request), and an (optional) follow-up move (in which the interviewer acknowledges the second response). This sequence is represented below.

(I) → R1 → F1: Clarify → R2 → (F2)

(8)

```
(R1)    C:  Er — it's a problem that er — our company — is er
            — is building now.
(F1)→   I:  You mean it is developing, it's being developed?
(R2)    C:  Is is deve is the time — is — under def
            developing.
(F2)    I:  I see.
```

In Excerpt 8 there is no immediate initiating move present because the candidate is already in the middle of explaining what kind of problems his company has to face these days. So he employs a CS (circumlocution) in R1, which makes it difficult to understand what he means exactly. The interviewer wants to clarify his meaning by trying to interpret what he said and uses an instance of Clarify, *you mean?* in F1. The candidate, however, is not satisfied with the offered solution and tries to express himself by using another CS in R2, which is even less successful than the first one. Still, the interviewer acknowledges it without further negotiation in F2, perhaps because the intended meaning has already been clarified to a certain extent and it seems clear that the candidate cannot use more adequate linguistic means to convey his message.

Excerpt 8 also demonstrates the cyclical nature of CS use (cf. Poulisse 1987). In my data the candidates also resort to the use of two or even more CSs to overcome their communication difficulties. As Poulisse (1987:148) argues, "this often occurs when a speaker runs into a second lexical problem in the course of trying to solve the first one." It is worth noting, however, that the use of multiple CSs can occur simultaneously, that is, in the same discourse move as well.

Table 4. Numbers of Negotiation Sequence Types in the Two Tests

Type of sequence	Number of Communication Strategies		
	Familiar interlocutor	Unfamiliar interlocutor	Total
Helping sequence	131	69	200
Eliciting sequence	26	44	70
Clarifying sequence	11	25	36
Total	168	138	306

4.7.4 Frequency of Negotiation Sequences

Table 4 displays the numbers of the negotiation sequence types observed in the two testing conditions. A chi-square test of significance for two-way designs was performed on the data, which resulted in $\chi^2 = 26.59$, $df = 2$, $p < 05$. Therefore we can state that the two variables (familiarity of the candidates with the interlocutor and the sequence types the interlocutors used) are related for our sample. To estimate the strength of association, Cramer's V was calculated. It is 0.543; thus there seems to be a relatively strong relationship between the two variables.

Eyeball analysis of the data also shows that the unknown interlocutor employs fewer negotiation sequences than the known interviewers. In addition, helping sequences are used most often in both conditions, making up approximately two thirds of all the sequences. But their distribution differs greatly in the two tests: their number is almost doubled with the familiar interlocutor. Eliciting is the second most popular type, which is followed by clarifying sequences, but by contrast with helping sequences, both of them occur more frequently with the unfamiliar examiner. Thus, comparing the interlocutors' meaning negotiation strategies, we can say that the familiar examiner uses mainly "help-based" types, whereas the unfamiliar examiners rely on a "mixed type," with a more marked preference for elicitation and clarification.

This difference may be due to the differing nature of the two testing contexts. The interview conducted by the familiar interlocutor resembles a natural conversation to a greater extent, possibly because the participants have known each other longer and thus have established a closer, more personal relationship. Besides performing the primary function of FL assessment, this test also provides a greater opportunity for social interaction, which requires a bigger amount of personal involvement from both participants. As a result, the interviewer pays more attention not only to the linguistic realization but also to the content of her partners' FL utterances, and when

Table 5. Type and Number of Negotiation Exchanges in the Two Tests

Type of exchange	Number of exchanges		
	Familiar interlocutor	Unfamiliar interlocutor	Total
1-sequence	91	46	137
2-sequence	22	13	35
3-sequence	7	12	19
4-sequence or greater	3	7	10
Total	123	78	201

CPs arise, both interlocutors feel more obliged to solve them and to fully clarify potential misunderstandings.

By contrast, the interview done by the unknown examiners is a more impersonal and formal encounter between people who have not met before. Its primary purpose is to elicit a representative language sample from the candidates with the aim of evaluating their oral test performance; thus the social and interpersonal aspects do not play such an important role. Misunderstandings are more likely to occur between two strangers, and when they do, they are negotiated only to a certain extent, as it is not the content but the linguistic form of the candidates' utterances that really matters.

4.7.5 Combination and Frequency of Sequence Types

As we have seen in the previous section, negotiation sequence types may occur independently of each other, or some may be combined in order to negotiate meaning when the participants face serious communication difficulty and want to reach mutual understanding. Table 5 shows the breakdown of negotiation exchanges according to the different testing conditions.

As can be seen from the table, the observed sequences make up 201 negotiation exchanges altogether. Far more exchanges take place with the familiar interlocutor than with the unfamiliar one (123 versus 78). It should be noted that in both testing conditions one-sequence exchanges occur most frequently, and there is an inverse relationship between the frequency and the number of sequences that constitute the exchanges. One- and two-sequence exchanges dominate in the test with the familiar examiner, while the number of exchanges made up of three, four, or more sequences increases in the exam conducted by the unknown interlocutor. This difference must be closely related to the differing numbers of miscommunications in the two tests.

4.8 Instances of Miscommunication

Miscommunication occurs "when there is a mismatch between the speaker's intention and the hearer's interpretation" (Gass and Varonis 1991:124–125). It can be divided into two types: incomplete understanding and misunderstanding, depending on whether the problem is overtly recognized or not. The framework described above is based mainly on instances of incomplete understanding that get resolved through negotiated communication. In some cases, however, the negotiation exchanges lead to misunderstanding, which may or may not get resolved.

When a CP arises, either participant may initiate negotiation of meaning, but in the data mostly interviewers do so, which gives further support to the dominant role they play in the OPE (see the section on the clarifying sequence). The candidates initiate negotiation exchanges very rarely (in only ten cases), and when they do, they use either the different types of Clarify or some kind of self-repair or self-check (and self-confirm). In addition, the interviewer can interpret the candidates' topic avoidance as a request for clarification. It is worth noting, however, that topic avoidance may also be caused by the candidates' effort to come up with a solution; thus one strategy for interviewers is to allow sufficient time to let candidates think over the answer. Another strategy that can cause CPs is the interviewer's attempt to help, which sometimes results in the candidates' nonunderstanding (signaled by a comprehension check).

Misunderstandings did not occur frequently in the data: only fourteen cases were observed (with both the candidates and the interviewers producing seven instances each), and all of them occurred when the candidate was unfamiliar with the interviewer. In the data the candidates' misunderstandings were caused by the following factors:

- The candidate did not understand the interviewer's question (five times).
- The candidate did not have the necessary world knowledge to answer the question (one instance).
- The candidate did not know what kind of answer the interviewer expected (1 occasion).

All of the interviewers' misunderstandings belong to one category: deliberately misunderstanding the candidate's utterance in order to elicit the expected answer. Excerpt 9 illustrates this phenomenon.

(9)

```
(I)      I:   . . . And how do you have to start this washing
              machine?
(R1)     C:   Er — only — you — er — put — er — the bottom
(F1)→    I:   Put? + The bottom? My bottom into the washing
              machine? No, I don't want to do that ((laughs)).
              + What do I have to do? I have to . . . ?
              ((prompting the candidate to answer))
(R2)     C:   To +++ push.
(F2)     I:   Push [ — a what?
(R3)     C:        [push a — bottom — [ — buttom
(F3)     I:                           [bu . . . buttoN — a
              [buttoN — push the
(R4)     C:   [button ((laughs)) button — all right.
```

As the excerpt shows, the candidate's CS (phonological similarity between *bottom* and *button*) does evoke the intended meaning, but the interviewer first feigns misunderstanding (in F1), trying to elicit the right answer. She partly succeeds as the candidate recalls the first expected word (in R2) but fails to remember the second one and repeats the CS in R3. Finally, the interviewer tells him the missing word in F3. The candidate repeats it in R4 (but it overlaps with the interviewer's previous utterance). This negotiation ends successfully, but it must be noted that an interviewer's strategy of deliberate misunderstanding often confuses the candidates further instead of helping them clarify the CP, and thus it may not be the most effective elicitation strategy.

5 Summary and Conclusions

The findings of this study indicate noticeable differences in the ways meaning gets negotiated in the two testing conditions. The independent variable—familiarity of the candidate with the interlocutor—appears to have affected both the frequency and the type of negotiation exchanges the participants engaged in.

The main difference between the two testing conditions seems to lie in the frequency and type of sequence the interlocutors employ to negotiate meaning: while the familiar interlocutor uses far more negotiation sequences and seems to prefer the help-based type, the unfamiliar interlocutors would rather resort to a combination of all three sequences. The other interlocutor-related difference concerns the frequency of exchange types. Most negotiation exchanges contain one or two sequences in both testing contexts. This may be due to the relatively simple nature of the CPs to be solved, the time constraints of the examination, and perhaps also to the face-saving concerns of the participants. But the number of longer exchanges increases in the test conducted by the unfamiliar interviewers, which is believed to be related to two factors (which may also be causally related):

- the differing nature of negotiated communication in the two tests (i.e., the dominance of help-based vs. mixed exchanges), and
- the greater likelihood of misunderstandings between the two unknown conversation partners.

In sum, the use of the various negotiation sequences/exchanges resulted in differing types of oral discourse in the two testing conditions: the one with the known interlocutor seemed to resemble natural NS-NNS oral interaction to a greater extent, whereas the one with the unknown examiner often resulted in misunderstandings, and represented a more artificial, formal kind of talk.

On the basis of the results of this preliminary analysis, further research is recommended into the negotiated communication between interviewees and (known or unknown) interviewers to determine to what extent familiarity with the interlocutor affects meaning negotiation in oral test discourse, and to specify what kinds of exchanges and sequences are most conducive to the elicitation of representative FL samples from learners. It would also be important to examine which types of exchange most resemble conversation, and what combination of them provides the most effective assistance to candidates when they struggle to realize their communicative goals.

In addition, further research is needed to determine how generalizable the results are across differing testing conditions and to subjects with various language backgrounds. Thus the study could be replicated with larger samples and with participants who do not share the same mother tongue. The oral test discourse produced at other speaking tests should be examined to decide whether the findings of this study and the proposed descriptive framework can be applied to the analysis of other candidates' FL test performance as well.

Transcription Notation

I	Interviewer
C	Candidate
-	Short pause
+	Long pause
(( ))	Extra-textual remarks
[	Overlapping speech

underlined words   Candidate's CS
italicized words   Interviewer's meaning-negotiating strategy
→   Relevant speech phenomenon

Acknowledgments

I gratefully acknowledge the grants I received from the Hungarian Academy of Sciences and the Fulbright Commission, which made this research possible. I also wish to thank Fred Davidson, Zoltán Dörnyei, and the editors of this volume for their insightful comments on earlier versions of this chapter.

References

Aston, Guy. 1986. "Trouble-Shooting in Interaction with Learners: The More the Merrier?" *Applied Linguistics* 7.128–143.
Bialystok, Ellen. 1983. "Some Factors in the Selection and Implementation of Communication Strategies." In *Strategies in Interlanguage Communication*, ed. by Claus Færch and Gabriele Kasper, 100–118. London and New York: Longman.
Bialystok, Ellen. 1990. *Communication Strategies*. Oxford: Blackwell.
Blum-Kulka, Shoshana, and Eddie A. Levenston. 1983. "Universals of Lexical Simplification." In *Strategies in Interlanguage Communication*, ed. by Claus Færch and Gabriele Kasper, 119–139. London and New York: Longman.
Bongaerts, Theo, and Nanda Poulisse. 1989. "Communication Strategies in L_1 and L_2: Same or Different?" *Applied Linguistics* 10.253–268.
Canale, Michael. 1983. "From Communicative Competence to Communicative Language Pedagogy." In *Language and Communication*, ed. by Jack C. Richards and Richard W. Schmidt, 2–25. London and New York: Longman.
Canale, Michael, and Merrill Swain. 1980. "Theoretical Bases of Communicative Approaches to Second Language Teaching and Testing." *Applied Linguistics* 1.1–47.
Chen, Si-Qing. 1990. "A Study of Communication Strategies in Interlanguage Production by Chinese EFL Learners." *Language Learning* 40.155–187.
Cook, Vivian. 1993. *Linguistics and Second Language Acquisition*. New York: St. Martin's Press.
Corder, S. Pit. 1983. "Strategies of Communication." In *Strategies in Interlanguage Communication*, ed. by Claus Færch and Gabriele Kasper, 15–19. London and New York: Longman.
DeKeyser, Robert M. 1989. "Communicative Processes and Strategies." *Annual Review of Applied Linguistics* 9.108–121.
Dörnyei, Zoltán. 1995. "On the Teachability of Communication Strategies." *TESOL Quarterly* 29.55–85.

Dörnyei, Zoltán, and Mary Lee Scott. 1995. "An Overview of Communication Strategies: An Empirical Analysis with Retrospection." Paper presented at the annual conference of the American Association for Applied Linguistics, Long Beach, CA, March 25–28.

Ehrlich, Susan, Peter Avery, and Carlos A. Yorio. 1989. "Discourse Structure and the Negotiation of Comprehensible Input." *Studies in Second Language Acquisition* 11.397–414.

Færch, Claus, and Gabriele Kasper. 1983a. "Plans and Strategies in Foreign Language Communication." In *Strategies in Interlanguage Communication*, ed. by Claus Færch and Gabriele Kasper, 20–60. London and New York: Longman.

Færch, Claus, and Gabriele Kasper. 1983b. "On Identifying Communication Strategies in Interlanguage Production." In *Strategies in Interlanguage Communication*, ed. by Claus Færch and Gabriele Kasper, 210–238. London and New York: Longman.

Færch, Claus, and Gabriele Kasper. 1984. "Two Ways of Defining Communication Strategies." *Language Learning* 34.45–63.

Ferguson, Charles A. 1971. "Absence of Copula and the Notion of Simplicity: A Study of Normal Speech, Baby Talk, Foreigner Talk, and Pidgins." In *Pidginization and Creolization of Languages*, ed. by Dell Hymes, 141–150. Cambridge: Cambridge University Press.

Gaies, Stephen J. 1982. "Native Speaker-Nonnative Speaker Interaction Among Academic Peers." *Studies in Second Language Acquisition* 5.74–81.

Gass, Susan M., and Larry Selinker. 1994. *Second Language Acquisition: An Introductory Course*. Hillsdale, NJ: Erlbaum.

Gass, Susan M., and Evangeline Marlos Varonis. 1985. "Variation in Native Speaker Speech Modification to Non-Native Speakers." *Studies in Second Language Acquisition* 7.37–57.

Gass, Susan M., and Evangeline Marlos Varonis. 1991. "Miscommunication in Nonnative Speaker Discourse." In *"Miscommunication" and Problematic Talk*, ed. by Nikolas Coupland, Howard Giles, and John M. Wiemann, 121–145. Newbury Park, CA: Sage.

Haastrup, Kirsten, and Robert Phillipson. 1983. "Achievement Strategies in Learner/Native Speaker Interaction." In *Strategies in Interlanguage Communication*, ed. by Claus Færch and Gabriele Kasper, 140–158. London and New York.

Harper, H. 1985. "How to Do a Lot with Little: Learner Strategies of Communication in Verbal Interaction." *Revue de Phonétique Appliquée* vol. 73–75. Mons, Belgium: Université de l'État.

Hatch, Evelyn. 1983. *Psycholinguistics: A Second Language Perspective*. Rowley, MA: Newbury House.

Jackson, Sally. 1986. "Building a Case for Claims About Discourse Structure." In *Contemporary Issues in Language and Discourse Processes*, ed. by Donald G. Ellis and William A. Donohue, 129–147. Hillsdale, NJ: Lawrence Erlbaum Associates.

Jones, Edward E., and Harold B. Gerard. 1967. *Foundations of Social Psychology*. New York: Wiley.

Kellerman, Eric. 1991. "Compensatory Strategies in Second Language Research: A Critique, a Revision, and Some (Non-)Implications for the Classroom." In *Foreign/Second Language Pedagogy Research: A Commemorative Volume for Claus Faerch*, ed. by Robert Phillipson, Eric Kellerman, Larry Selinker, Michael Sharwood-Smith, and Merrill Swain, 142–161. Clevedon, Avon: Multilingual Matters.

Kumaravadivelu, B. 1988. "Communication Strategies and Psychological Processes Underlying Lexical Simplification." *IRAL* 25.309–319.

Labarca, Angela, and Rajai Khanji. 1986. "On Communication Strategies: Focus on Interaction." *Studies in Second Language Acquisition* 8.68–79.

Lazaraton, Anne. 1992. "The Structural Organization of a Language Interview: A Conversation Analytic Perspective." *System* 20.373–386.

Levenston, Eddie A., and Shoshana Blum. 1977. "Aspects of Lexical Simplification in the Speech and Writing of Advanced Adult Learners." In *The Notions of Simplification, Inter-languages and Pidgins and Their Relation to Second Language Pedagogy*, ed. by S. Pit Corder and Eddie Roulet (= Actes du 5ème colloque de linguistique appliquée de Neuchâtel), 51–71. Geneva: Droz.

Littlewood, William. 1984. *Foreign and Second Language Learning*. Cambridge: Cambridge University Press.

Long, Michael H. 1981. "Questions in Foreigner Talk Discourse." *Language Learning* 31.135–157.

Long, Michael H. 1983a. "Linguistic and Conversational Adjustments to Non-native Speakers." *Studies in Second Language Acquisition* 5.177–193.

Long, Michael H. 1983b. "Native Speaker/Non-native Speaker Conversation and the Negotiation of Comprehensible Input." *Applied Linguistics* 4.126–141.

Paribakht, Tahereh. 1985. "Strategic Competence and Language Proficiency." *Applied Linguistics* 6.132–146.

Patil, Prabhakar B. 1994. "Strategies of 'Teacher Talk'." *IRAL* 32.154–165.

Poulisse, Nanda. 1987. "Problems and Solutions in the Classification of Compensatory Strategies." *Second Language Research* 3.141–153.

Poulisse, Nanda, Theo Bongaerts, and Eric Kellerman. 1987. "The Use of Retrospective Verbal Reports in the Analysis of Compensatory Strategies." In *Introspection in Second Language Research*, ed. by Claus Færch and Gabriele Kasper, 213–229. Clevedon, Avon: Multilingual Matters.

Raupach, Manfred. 1983. "Analysis and Evaluation of Communication Strategies." In *Strategies in Interlanguage Communication*, ed. by Claus Færch and Gabriele Kasper, 199–209. London and New York: Longman.

Ross, Steven, and Richard Berwick. 1992. "The Discourse of Accommodation in Oral Proficiency Interviews." *Studies in Second Language Acquisition* 14.159–176.

Selinker, Larry. 1972. "Interlanguage." *IRAL* 10.209–231.

Sinclair, John M., and R. Malcolm Coulthard. 1975. *Towards an Analysis of Discourse: The English Used by Teachers and Pupils*. London: Oxford University Press.

Tarone, Elaine. 1980. "Communication Strategies, Foreigner Talk, and Repair in Interlanguage." *Language Learning* 30.417–431.
Tarone, Elaine. 1981. "Some Thoughts on the Notion of Communication Strategy." *TESOL Quarterly* 15.285–295.
Tarone, Elaine, Andrew D. Cohen, and Guy Dumas. 1976. "A Closer Look at Some Interlanguage Terminology: A Framework for Communication Strategies." *Working Papers on Bilingualism* 9.76–90.
Tarone, Elaine, and George Yule. 1987. "Communication Strategies in East-West Interactions." In *Discourse Across Cultures: Strategies in World Englishes*, ed. by Larry E. Smith, 49–65. New York: Prentice Hall.
Tsui, Amy B. M. 1994. *English Conversation*. Oxford: Oxford University Press.
van Lier, Leo. 1989. "Reeling, Writhing, Drawling, Stretching, and Fainting in Coils: Oral Proficiency Interviews as Conversation." *TESOL Quarterly* 23.489–508.
Váradi, Tamás. 1973. "Strategies of Target Learner Communication: Message Adjustment." Paper presented at the 6th conference of the Rumanian-English Linguistics Project, Timisoara, Rumania.
Varonis, Evangeline Marlos, and Susan Gass. 1985. "Non-Native/Non-Native Conversations: A Model for Negotiation of Meaning." *Applied Linguistics* 6.71–90.
Willems, Gerard M. 1987. "Communication Strategies and Their Significance in Foreign Language Teaching." *System* 15.351–364.
Yarmohammadi, Lotfollah, and Shahrzad Seif. 1992. "More on Communication Strategies: Classification, Resources, Frequency, and Underlying Processes." *IRAL* 30.223–232.
Young, Richard. 1984. "Negotiation of Outcome and Negotiation of Meaning in ESL Classroom Interaction." *TESOL Quarterly* 18.525–526.
Young, Richard, and Michael Milanovic. 1992. "Discourse Variation in Oral Proficiency Interviews." *Studies in Second Language Acquisition* 14.403–424.
Yule, George, and Elaine Tarone. 1991. "The Other Side of the Page: Integrating the Study of Communication Strategies and Negotiated Input in SLA." In *Foreign/Second Language Pedagogy Research: A Commemorative Volume for Claus Faerch*, ed. by Robert Phillipson, Eric Kellerman, Larry Selinker, Michael Sharwood-Smith, and Merrill Swain, 162–171. Clevedon, Avon: Multilingual Matters.

Part 4

Language Proficiency Interviews as Cross-Cultural Encounters

Maintaining American Face in the Korean Oral Exam: Reflections on the Power of Cross-Cultural Context

Catherine E. Davies
University of Alabama

1 Introduction

This chapter analyzes American students' strategies in an oral exam with a Korean bilingual examiner for displaying understanding and attempting to present self as simultaneously an appropriately proficient speaker of Korean, a serious language learner, and a competent interactant. The study suggests that the complex cross-cultural context of the face-to-face interaction creates competing role expectations for the participants. Under such conditions, both examiner and examinee may code switch into English as they frame the event, laminate frames, attempt to negotiate reframings, adopt different footings—all in the service of situated self-presentation. If the institutional goals of a language program (and the personal goals of the students) are not only communicative but also interactional competence in the target language, then such code switching works against them.

Whereas previous psychometrically oriented work on language proficiency interviews (LPIs) has tended to treat them as relatively unproblematic assessment instruments, this paper is a contribution to a critical trend (Bachman 1987; Carroll 1980; Douglas and Selinker 1984; Duran 1984; Lantolf and Frawley 1985, 1988; Raffaldini 1988; Shohamy 1988, 1991; Spolsky 1978; van Lier 1989) toward examining the sociolinguistic dimensions and discourse organization of LPIs as key to the central issue of validity. Other manifestations of this research trend can be seen in studies that examine the discourse of LPIs from the point of view of the nature of the discourse genre actually enacted (Johnson and Tyler 1998, Young and Milanovic 1992), discourse domains and their effect on performance (Douglas and Selinker 1993), topic-framing and accommodation by interviewers (Ross 1992, Ross and Berwick 1992), elaboration of responses by interviewees (He 1998, Young

1995), and problem management by the participants (Egbert 1998). Since almost by definition an LPI is a cross-cultural encounter, cultural differences must be considered as a potential source of significant effects. Cultural differences as a possible explanation for behavior of participants has been set forth by Berwick and Ross (1993) and Young (1995). A number of studies of other types of gatekeeping encounters, such as job interviews (Gumperz, Jupp, and Roberts 1979), academic counseling (Erickson and Shultz 1982), and academic advising sessions (Bardovi-Harlig and Hartford 1990, Fiksdal 1990, He 1995, Shea 1994) indicate that cultural differences among participants in shared social activity may have important interactional consequences that participants are unaware of.

This study uses the tools of interactional sociolinguistics to document the power of context to shape discourse, by showing how the complex cross-cultural context of the face-to-face interaction may create unforeseen problems. These problems arise from culturally shaped strategies of self-presentation by American undergraduate examinees and attempts at mutual face-maintenance during the co-construction of situated social identities with a Korean bilingual examiner. Under these conditions, culturally based interactional preferences lead to the co-construction of behavior that is potentially self-defeating for both the individual being assessed and the institution that requires the assessment. This study thus reinforces the importance of Shohamy's (1988) call to design oral language tests with systematic attention to context.

2 Data

The data analyzed here are eighteen oral exams of an average length of 15 minutes, some audiotaped and some videotaped, administered by the same bilingual Korean external examiner at semester's end in a self-instructional language program. In this language program, operating under the auspices of the National Association of Self-Instructional Language Programs (NASILP), the focus is on the development of oral skills in languages that are not offered at the university in typical instructional formats. The student signs a contract to work with a text and audiotapes for a minimum of five hours per week, and to attend three practice sessions per week in which a native-speaking tutor works with a small group of learners. At the end of the semester, the student's grade is largely determined by performance in an LPI administered by an external examiner, typically a linguist and language educator who travels to all participating universities to administer exams in a particular language. The examiner gives the students ratings for listening comprehension, verbal proficiency, grammatical accuracy, and general responsiveness. Such LPIs are not intended to be typical proficiency exams. They are instead a combination of an achievement and a proficiency test, evaluating "the student's *proficiency* in the *specific material covered*" (Sukle 1992:4, emphasis in original). The format of the interviews seems, in fact, to follow that of a typical LPI (Clark and Clifford 1988), as will be discussed below in the analysis.

3 Method

I collected data over the course of three semesters by means of video- and/or audiotaping, depending upon permission granted by the examinees.[1] I operated the video equipment from the back of the room and made notes unobtrusively during the exams. After each exam, I interviewed the examiner about certain aspects of the oral exam interaction. Native speakers of Korean helped with transcription and translation, and responded to my questions concerning interpretations of recorded interaction; I interviewed American students concerning interpretations of the English produced by the interviewees. Finally, I acted as participant observer by enrolling in Korean 101 and taking the exam myself during the third semester of data collection. Thus the perspectives of the examiner and examinees are represented through this methodology, as is my role as an American student of Korean.

4 Analytic Perspective

The basic theoretical perspective taken in this study is that of interactional sociolinguistics, which draws together research traditions in linguistics (particularly pragmatics and discourse analysis), anthropology (particularly the ethnography of speaking and cognitive anthropology), and sociology (particularly ethnomethodology and conversation analysis) in an attempt to understand the situated interpretation of communicative intent in face-to-face interaction. Taking Gumperz's (1982a, b) theory of conversational inference as a framework, the approach also draws on the cross-disciplinary work of Bateson (1972), Brown and Levinson (1987), Erickson (Erickson and Shultz 1981), Goffman (1974), and Ochs (1993) for understanding nonverbal aspects of communication, the framing of messages, and the relationships between such framing and individual presentations of self.

A theme in this theoretical orientation is the elaboration of our understanding of what is meant by context (Duranti and Goodwin 1992). The approach taken here is to conceptualize context as dynamic and emergent, both constraining interaction and created through it. An important framework for use as a starting point in identifying all possibly relevant dimensions of context is Hymes's (1974) SPEAKING framework. After laying out contextual dimensions of the oral exam within Hymes's framework and identifying instrumentalities and norms of interaction and interpretation as particularly important, I draw on other tools within interactional sociolinguistics in order to understand the process of the interview as an emergent cross-cultural encounter, in which attempts at mutual face-maintenance during the co-construction of situated social identities are both reflective and constitutive of the overall context of the exam.

5 The Oral Exam as Speech Event

I will first discuss the oral exam from the point of view of Hymes's (1974) SPEAKING parameters: scene/setting, participants, ends, act sequence, key, instrumentalities, norms, and genre.

5.1 *Scene/Setting*

The scene, which is culturally defined, is an institutionally organized oral exam that determines in large part the grade the student will receive for a semester's work in an American university-level self-instructional language program. The setting, which refers to the physical arrangements and location of the event, is a university classroom, where the examiner meets privately with an examinee for the fifteen-minute exam. The examiner sits at the teacher's desk in the front of the classroom, and the examinee sits in a student desk, the front of which abuts the side of the teacher's desk

5.2 *Participants*

The participants are the examiner and an examinee. The examiner is a native speaker of Korean, a linguist and a language educator, who has been engaged through NASILP to serve as external examiner. The examiner has been in touch with the university director of the program and the tutor in the language, so he knows what the students have studied and he has designed the exam on the basis of that knowledge. The examiner's institutional role is to elicit performance by the examinee relative to the material covered in the text in an atmosphere in which the examinee's anxiety level will be low enough that an accurate assessment can be achieved. Since the examiner comes from another university, he is not known to the students; they encounter him as a stranger in their 101 exam. In this data set, students in their second and third semesters (Korean 102 and 201, respectively) had previous experience with this particular examiner. The other participant, the examinee, is an American undergraduate student of Korean who knows that s/he is expected to display what s/he has learned during the semester in response to elicitation by the examiner. The first time around the student has a relatively unclear idea about the format of the exam but knows that it is based on the material covered in the text and that it is a face-to-face interview.

5.3 Ends

Hymes's *ends* refers to the purposes/outcomes of the speech event. From an institutional point of view, the purpose of the oral exam is to accurately assess the language proficiency, in relation to the textual material studied, of the examinee. From the examinee's point of view, the purpose is to get as good a grade as possible. The examiner operates with a set of rating criteria (listening comprehension, verbal proficiency, grammatical accuracy, and general responsiveness) provided by the institution. The students know the general framework but not the details of the rating scales that the examiner uses.

5.4 Act Sequence

The act sequence can be considered at two levels. The first is the overall structure of the oral exam as speech event. The format of the exam in the data under consideration here appears to follow that of a typical LPI, reflecting the examiner's familiarity with such exams. It begins, after greetings, with what could be seen as a warm-up phase in which the examiner asks questions based on the text material about the student's major, family, living situation, favorite foods, and so on. This phase is followed by a series of role-plays based on text material. The final phase of the exam is again a series of text-based questions asked by the examiner and at the end of the exam the examinee is requested to reciprocate by posing some questions to the examiner. The second level at which act sequence can be considered is at the level of utterances. A version of the three-part sequence identified as typical of classroom discourse (Mehan 1979, Sinclair and Coulthard 1975) can be seen in the first and final phases of the exam in that the examiner poses a question, the examinee answers, and then the examiner provides a minimal acknowledgment of some sort before moving on to the next question.

5.5 Key

Hymes's *key* refers to the spirit in which the event is carried on. It is conducted in a serious manner befitting an important institutional exam. More jocularity occurs than one might expect, however, because the first and third parts of the exam consist of questions associated with friendly small talk and because the examiner has a friendly demeanor and attempts consciously to put the students at ease. There are elements of a real conversation present in that the examiner does not know in advance the answers to the small talk questions that he is asking, and yet there inevitably remain aspects of what van Lier (1989) calls the "pseudo-social."

5.6 *Instrumentalities*

By instrumentalities, Hymes refers to channels, codes, and forms of speech. In this case the exam is conducted orally in Korean, but the examinees are aware that the examiner speaks English. The different sections of the exam are typically indicated in English by the examiner. The role-play instructions are also given in written English to the examinees, and sometimes the examiner clarifies the instructions in English. These and other instances of the use of English by the participants, especially the unexpected use of English by the examinees, were the aspects of the interaction that first attracted my attention as analyst.

5.6.1 *Summary of Use of English by Participants*

The examiner uses English (a) to ask for permission to record; (b) to indicate that the student is to participate in a role-play and direct the student to read the role-play instructions in English, and also to tell the student to ask him questions for the last phase of the exam; (c) "for clarification,"[2] using examples such as *McDonald's*, *football* to help the student understand; (d) "to translate something which student is not responsible for knowing because it is not in the material covered" (typically during the third phase of the exam when the examiner responds to student questions); and (e) "to deal with extreme awkwardness," when the examiner has exhausted other clarification strategies. Examinees use English (a) to refer to specific local items such as places, names of buildings, and majors; (b) to answer the examiner's questions; (c) to translate the examiner's questions; (d) to create hesitation markers and some self-talk; and (e) to metacommunicate about the interaction. Actual utterances in English as produced chronologically within three representative exams are reproduced in Excerpts 1–3 to give the reader a feeling for the nature of the discourse as well as for the range of variation between an expert bilingual student and a struggling monolingual novice.

(1a) English produced by "expert": Korean-American female, Korean 202. This student is a fluent bilingual. The examiner commented that she even used Korean backchannels appropriately.

business (her major), international marketing, tv, convenience store, Peace Corps, South America, Indiana

(1b) Examiner's English

I need to ask your permission to record, video, semester, business, building, role-play 1, role-play 2, role-play 3 (indicating initiation of those segments of the exam)

(2a) English produced by intermediate novice: American monolingual English-speaking female in Korean 101

well let's see, um, Who's in my family?, volleyball I'm on the volleyball team, Let's see . . . I am . . . (produces Korean), yeah, cereal . . . oatmeal, physical therapy, (Korean) I mean (Korean), hamster, tarantula, snake, rat, okay, okay, okay, ahm, Supply Store, ahm, um, fire station?, I'm not sure how to say "fire station," University Drive . . . can I say that?, I don't know how to say "to the left," Are we supposed to know that?, we haven't done "left" or "right" . . . sorry, can I say (Korean)?, You're asking me where the fire station is, Oh THIS one . . . I didn't read that part . . . I'm sorry, (when examiner volunteers that he has an Oldsmobile): That was my next question . . . I was gonna ask you what kind, vegetarian, (under breath) Oh I can't remember . . . dang!, I can't think of the one I wanted to ask so badly . . . it was such a good question.

(2b) Examiner's English

(gives Korean backchannel in response to student's initial self-talk in English), I'm a taxi driver . . . you're a passenger going to fire station, okay, read

the instructions here, in response to her question
"Are we supposed to know that?" "Yes," now the second
one (role-play), ask me questions, Oldsmobile, just
one more

(3a) English produced by struggling novice: American
monolingual English-speaking male in Korean 101

I misunderstood, I take it, oh . . . ah, ah, I'm sorry,
oh . . . ah, (makes voiceless alveolar tap
periodically in groups of four), doughnuts, I don't
know, you lost me on that one . . . I got about half of
it, ah . . . it's a good question, Wal-Mart, this is so
different . . . I'm sorry, am I from here, right?,
sorry, oh . . . oh I'm sorry, sorry about that, yeah, I
don't know my left or right, [as part of role-play 2 he
says "I'm sorry" in Korean], oh . . . well . . . I was
gonna say something else.

(3b) Examiner's English

that's your name (when student doesn't understand
question asking him what his name is), okay (in
response to apology), say it in English (when student
says he doesn't know his left or right [meaning how to
say those words in Korean]), okay the second one (re
role-play).

5.7 *Norms*

Norms of interaction and of interpretation draw attention to potentially relevant cultural differences. In principle what is being assessed is Korean communicative competence, within which the roles and relative statuses of participants dictate the forms both of grammar and interactional behavior. In terms of politeness, the examinee would have learned two basic kinds of grammatically encoded resources: verb forms associated with an appropriate speech style for the situation, and honorific affixes associated with forms of address (Sohn 1983). In Korean, it is important to use the honorific infix when addressing a person to whom respect is due but it is just as critical to omit it when using the same verb form to refer to self. The social significance of this form was indicated by my tutor's reaction in class when we made the mistake of using the honorific infix when referring to ourselves: he said "If you respect you, I shoot you!"

In terms of interactional behavior, my consultants confirm the analysis presented in Scollon and Scollon (1981) that in a typical interaction between Korean teacher and student, the teacher initiates interaction and controls topics, and the student responds to the teacher's initiations but within a silent display of attention as part of the enactment of deference. American students, on the other hand, know that they are expected to be voluble and active (responding at length to the teacher's requests to display knowledge, asking questions of the teacher, etc.), especially in a situation in which they know that their oral ability is being assessed. The fluent bilingual Korean-American students display such behavior. The fact that the exam is structured as if it were a conversation presents additional cultural imperatives for the American students in that they must strive to present themselves as competent interactants by never failing to respond and by not allowing appreciable gaps between turns (Sacks, Schegloff, and Jefferson 1974; Pomerantz 1984a, b). The consequences of this situation will be discussed below in relation to face-maintenance.

A related aspect of interactional competence, and the final one to be considered here, is the ability to produce strategic utterances oriented to the negotiation of meaning, such as indications of partial understanding and requests for repetition, as well as appropriate listenership behavior such as hesitation noises and backchannels. The placeholder and hesitation verbalizations in Korean have more of a velar nasal quality than do the typical American English ones, and there is a versatile backchannel (an alveolar nasal followed by a mid-front vowel) that can convey a range of meanings depending on intonation contour.

5.8 Genre

Finally, genre, as we have seen, is potentially problematic in that there are elements of an interview structure and yet the examiner attempts to create a conversation in order to make the examinee feel more at ease. This attempt consists of organizing the questions in a topically related series such as one would find in small talk of the sort that occurs between a teacher and student who are meeting in a social setting. Of course, as I have noted, there is also the kind of three-part turn structure that is associated with teacher-centered classroom discourse, since the examinee's opportunity to ask questions of the examiner is not integrated throughout the test but rather limited to a special section right at the end. Thus we find a kind of fictive conversation, a pseudo-conversational encounter.

6 The Oral Exam as an Emergent, Cross-Cultural Process

Having laid out the parameters of the oral exam as a speech event, we now turn to an examination of the situated signaling and interpretation of communicative intent—in particular a consideration of the use of both Korean and English within the speech event—as discussed above under instrumentalities, as a resource that participants deploy in presentation of self and attempts at mutual face-maintenance during the co-construction of situated social identities. Three sets of theoretical notions will be drawn upon in the analysis: (a) frames, laminations, and footings; (b) code switching as contextualization cue; and (c) face as a multidimensional phenomenon.

6.1 *Frames, Laminations, and Footings*

Compared with other less formal interactions, the oral exam as speech event lends itself rather neatly to an analysis in terms of frame (Bateson 1972, Goffman 1974, Tannen 1979). In fact, one might be tempted to assume that this speech event is relatively unproblematic, apart from possible complications arising out of the cross-cultural nature of the encounter: the participants enter the exam as a framed event, enact their roles as examiner and examinee through the sections of the test, and then pass out of the frame at the moment the exam ends.

If we look closely at the emergent discourse, however, we find that even in such a clearly defined event, broader frames as well as subframes are signaled within the frame of the exam. Such "laminations" (Goffman 1974) present a set of emergent possibilities that examinees then use to establish different footings within the frame of the exam. Goffman's (1981:128) definition of footing as "the alignment we take up to ourselves and the others present as expressed in the way we manage the production or reception of an utterance" implies a different stance toward the interaction on the part of the initiator, which may or may not then be taken up by the other participants. These footings form part of a culturally shaped strategy for presentation of self and attempts at mutual face-maintenance. We can also see them as part of an interpretive frame, which Ellis and Roberts (1987:24) distinguish from the broader sense of frame as schema, as establishing "speaker intentionality at any point in the interaction."[3]

6.2 *Code Switching as a Contextualization Cue*

The original impetus for the present study was the observation of unexpected code switching from Korean to English in an LPI. The theoretical notion of contextualization cue (Gumperz 1982a, 1992) is useful in understanding this phenomenon. It attempts to capture the idea that participants in a conversation are continuously assessing and interpreting all aspects of interaction and are sensitive to the co-occurrence of certain constellations (across prosodic, paralinguistic, phonological, semantic, syntactic, pragmatic, nonverbal dimensions of the discourse) as signaling a shift in "what is going on here." This interpretive frame evokes cultural background knowledge and social expectations necessary to interpret speech. A simple example is the mother calling her child who shifts from nickname to full name with louder volume and a different prosodic pattern. The native English speaker has learned, through the socialization process, to interpret that configuration of changes in lexicalization, amplitude, and prosody as a contextualization cue indicating that the mother is redefining the context as one in which her child must acknowledge her authority immediately or face the consequences. Sohn (1983:114), however, indicates that the opposite is true in Korean: "Koreans ... try to lower the addressee in terms of power through downgrading of address terms and speech styles." Such contextualization cues are conventionalized. Typically, participants in a conversation are not dealing with such obvious cues but rather with subtle constellations that are always interpreted in context and that the participants may be more or less aware of. The interpretation of contextualization cues across cultures is a significant problem that Gumperz and others have begun to address (Tannen 1985, Tyler and Davies 1990, Gumperz 1992).

In the case of code switching, we have a very obvious change—from one language to another—that could constitute an aspect of a contextualization cue (Gumperz 1992). An extensive literature has documented code switching in bilingual and multilingual contexts and considered a range of motivations and effects, beginning with Blom and Gumperz (1972) who demonstrated how a code switch served to redefine context. Blom and Gumperz documented cases in which the shift from one language variety to another conveyed social meaning in that it signaled a shift in definition of the situation, because each variety was associated with a different type of situation or relationship.

7 The Creation of Laminations in the Emergent Process

A significant aspect of an LPI is what the examinee knows or believes about the testing situation. In the LPIs studied here it would be possible, in principle, to sustain examinees' belief in the essentially monolingual Korean status of the examiner. He is a stranger to them, his name is Korean, and he appears to be Korean; they hear Korean leave taking ritual expressions as the classroom door opens and the previous student exits. The examiner calls the next name from the list, and then greets the student in Korean as the student approaches the door and enters the classroom. Any use of English by the examiner provides the examinee with the information that utterances in English will be understood by the examiner. Of course, any conversations in English with the examiner that the student might have had an opportunity to overhear would have the same effect. In interviews, American students indicated that knowing whether or not the examiner spoke English was very important.

The examiner's use of English early in the exam is a result of competing role expectations: He needs to get an accurate assessment of the examinee's ability to perform in Korean. But he also knows that he is unlikely to achieve his goal unless he creates an environment that is as comfortable as possible (Underhill 1987). The examiner, sensitive to the high level of face-threat to the examinee, signals by code switching that he speaks English. This, in addition to the ethical requirements of asking for permission to record, could be seen as a rapport-building strategy oriented to the positive face of the examinee (conveying, in effect, "I have this in common with you: We both speak English"). Further evidence of this motivation is provided by the examiner's comments about other cases in which he used English. In attempting, as he says, to provide "clarification" and "to deal with extreme awkwardness," he is indicating his sensitivity to degrees of face-threat for the examinee.

Switches into English by the examiner accomplish several things in terms of frame and laminations. In terms of the examinee's frame, they provide further information about instrumentalities, indicating, in effect, that this is *not* a situation in which nothing but Korean will be understood. Utterances in English will probably be understood, even if they are not responded to. Such information has significant effects in terms of the potential for focusing one's use of communicative resources. The code switches also create a lamination of the frame of the exam, the broader English-speaking world within which the exam is embedded. The code switches that seem most obviously to create the broader lamination are those concerning permission to record the exam and those that translate material that the examinee is not responsible for knowing because it is not in the material covered in the text. The creation of the lamination potentially conveys the message that the interaction is truly an artificial testing situation. It suggests that it is not a real conversation in which participants have to use Korean to communicate and learn things about each other.

The examiner's use of English to mark the different phases of the exam ("role-play one," "role-play two," "now ask me questions") reinforces the broader lamination at the same time that it creates subframes within the frame of the exam.

Within the subframes of the role-plays the examinee has to take on different social relationships to the examiner. Again, this manipulation of context reinforces the artificiality of the situation. The fact that the examiner was unaware that he had switched into English to mark the different phases of the exam suggests that he may also have been using the code switches unconsciously as convenient discourse markers in the bilingual situation. Evidence of this is his code switching with the most fluent Korean-American bilingual (see Excerpt 1b).

8 Attempts to Renegotiate Context

Ironically, then, the code switch by the examiner as a rapport-building move oriented to the examinee's positive face creates a set of emergent possibilities that examinees may seize upon to renegotiate context or to distance themselves from the exam. As the American examinees pointed out, they are only too willing to interpret the examiner's use of English as permission for them to use more English and thus to renegotiate the instrumentalities of the speech event. Such matching of the examiner's choice of language could even be seen as a responsive rapport-building move on the part of the examinee. The examiner typically responds indirectly by switching back to Korean and asserts his greater power in the interaction by continuing in that language. He never directly tells the examinee to speak Korean. In switching into English the examinees are also invoking the broader English-speaking context lamination, so that they can metaphorically step outside the frame of the exam and seek to establish a footing at a distance from their communicative difficulties.

9 Face

Turning now from the examiner's dilemma of competing role expectations, we shift to a consideration of the examinee's. As we do so, we will also extend the footing metaphor upward to "face." Even though the notion of "face," in the sense of social valuation of participants in relationships—something that could be saved or lost—is associated stereotypically with Asian cultures, Goffman (1967) introduced the term with reference to Western culture in his early work to refer to the presentation of self in social interaction. Brown and Levinson (1987) developed the notion in their universal theory of politeness, positing a tension for each social actor between the need to maintain both negative face (i.e., to be unimpeded in one's actions—a need addressed by negative politeness) and positive face (i.e., to be included, valued by significant others—a need addressed by positive politeness). Within Brown and

Levinson's theory, social interaction consists of a series of potentially face-threatening acts. The degree of threat is calculable according to culturally and contextually defined assessments of relative power, social distance between interactants, and rank of imposition of behavior. Participants in interactions then choose from among a set of possible strategies for the accomplishment of the act, with appropriate redress. Brown and Levinson (1987) suggest that Asian cultures generally favor negative politeness, in contrast to the relative favoring of positive politeness within American culture. Given that an LPI is a face-threatening event for the examinee regardless of culture, we have seen in the foregoing discussion of norms of interaction that the behavior of the examinee in a negative-politeness ethos would be different from that of the examinee in a positive-politeness ethos. We have also seen that the examiner's switch to English is revealed as serving multiple functions within the discourse.

Although Brown and Levinson's notions of positive and negative face are a source of insight, we need to return to Goffman's original focus on the presentation of self in order to understand the behavior of the American students. As examinees they are attempting to enact (and construct with the examiner) the culturally shaped but situatedly instantiated social identity of a successful examinee. This social identity, which can be thought of as their face, appears to have three significant dimensions. The next section will show how American examinees go about the presentation of self in this context, revealing their strategies for displaying understanding and attempting to present self as simultaneously an appropriately proficient speaker of Korean, a serious language learner, and a competent interactant.

9.1 *The Dimensions of Face of an American Examinee*

From the point of view of the American examinee, obviously the ideal course of action is to demonstrate appropriate proficiency in Korean. In the absence of this possibility, there are certain fall-back strategies that are oriented to different dimensions of one's face in the context. The following are examples of strategies that maintain three different dimensions of face for the examinee.

An appropriately proficient speaker of Korean:
- Answer, do role-play, ask questions appropriately in Korean. (This simultaneously meets other levels of face needs as well.)

- Try to treat the interaction as if it were an ordinary bilingual conversation. (E.g., answer the Korean question in English—implying: I understand even though I'm not responding in Korean.)

A serious language learner:
- Give an indication that you understand some of what's going on even though you are not sure about it. (E.g., translation of Korean question into English "Who's in my family?"—implying: I have tried.)
- Give some indication that you studied it but you've forgotten or are too anxious in the situation to call it up. (E.g., "This is so DIFferent [from the classroom context] . . . I'm sorry"—implying: I could perform if this were more like the classroom.)
- Give some indication that you're not supposed to know it because it wasn't in the text. (E.g., "Are we supposed to know that? We haven't done 'left' or 'right'"—implying: Otherwise I would know it.)

A competent interactant:
- Maintain interactional role by producing hesitation noises (in English) during your turn while stalling for time. (E.g., oh ah ahm.)
- Provide metacommentary on the interaction in English in your turn. (E.g., "I misunderstood, I take it," "I don't know . . . you lost me on that one . . . I got about half of it"—implying: I'm not a *total* idiot.)

The examples given for the serious language learner represent increasingly explicit accounts (Scott and Lyman 1968) that are interpretable as excuses but that seem intended to claim acknowledgment or recognition for effort as well as for some level of undisplayed proficiency. I am not yet sure to what extent the intended conveyed implications given above require culturally based inferences to interpret communicative intent; neither am I sure to what extent evaluations of the implications would differ cross-culturally—for example, a different tendency to give credit for effort (demonstrated or claimed) in the absence of achievement. But the production of these utterances does serve to fill the slot for the examinee in the conversation, which leads us to the next dimension of face.

The third dimension of face I call the competent interactant, invoking the dread specter of Goffman's "faulty interactant," the label that Americans wanted most to avoid. In the discussion of norms of interaction and interpretation of the speech event, responsiveness (Pomerantz 1984a, b) and a preference for "no gap and no overlap" between turns (Sacks, Schegloff, and Jefferson 1974) were indicated as characteristic of interaction among white middle-class Americans. Scollon and Scollon (1981) also cite a preference for volubility, which seems clearly related to a positive-politeness ethos. Silence is often interpreted within such an ethos as a lack of commonality, a lack of interest in the other person, a lack of willingness to disclose, or a reluctance to get close to the other person, whereas within a deference ethos it could be interpreted as indicating respect for the other's space, a reluctance to intrude or impose, or delicacy in not disclosing unwanted information to the other person (Tannen and Saville-Troike 1985). Thus the more the examiner moves away from the genre of interview within the oral exam and toward the genre of conversation, the more pressure the American examinee will potentially feel to keep talking, using whatever resources can be mustered even if they are in English. One American student pointed out that all of the utterances and noises produced so painfully by the struggling novice illustrate the incredible pressure to produce that American students feel.

10 Footings, Aspects of Face, and the Co-construction of Situated Sociocultural Identities

Thus we see that in the context of language proficiency assessment, whereas there is necessarily some attention to the assumed face needs of the examiner, the main focus of the student is on his/her own multifaceted presentation of self as examinee. We have also seen that a code switch typically serves as the most salient dimension of a contextualization cue that signals a shift in footing and is then interpretable (and maybe evaluated) by culturally based situated inferences. Excerpt 4 from an interview with an intermediate novice illustrates these processes and highlights the potential multifunctionality of utterances in discourse context.

```
(4) Student has heard examiner read role-play instructions
in English, and is now beginning a role-play in Korean.

Student:    I don't know how to say "to the left." Are we
            supposed to know that?
Examiner:   Yes.
Student:    We haven't done "left" or "right." Sorry.
```

In this excerpt, the examiner had already switched into English to give verbal instructions for the role-play and to indicate that the student should also read instructions in English, invoking the broader lamination of the English-speaking environment, at the same time as he signaled the initiation of the subframe of a role-play. After beginning the role-play in Korean the student realizes that she doesn't know some essential expressions, and she switches back to English to metacommunicate about the circumstances of the role-play just as the examiner had done, shifting her footing to the broader lamination. From my own experience of Korean 101, I know that the student does in fact know how to say something in Korean approximating *I don't know how to say "to the left" in Korean.* Thus this student is clearly choosing English as the language of metacommunication. She is presenting the face of the serious language learner—one who is sure enough of herself as having mastered the designated material that she can freely acknowledge something that she doesn't know. And of course she is also presenting herself as a competent interactant by filling the slot and keeping the conversation going.

The next segment of her utterance, *Are we supposed to know that?*, she would probably not know how to say in Korean. Her social deictic move through switch of pronouns from first person singular *I* to plural *we* was picked up on by American students as an attempt to shift responsibility away from herself, perhaps to the examiner for not being aware of what the class had covered. One consultant commented on "the American grade-conscious student," who might be "trying to get the examiner to conform to what she knows." The examinee seems to be defining the event as a contractual one, in which she has the right to challenge anything she perceives to be outside of the established boundaries of the contract between her and the examiner. In fact, as we have seen in the discussion of the examiner's uses of English, the examiner shares that view and translates when he knows that something is legitimately unknown to the examinee (usually in the final segment of the exam). In this case, however, the utterance is too direct a challenge to the examiner's power in the situation: evidence for this in the discourse is his immediate response in English, *Yes*. The challenge is confronted quickly, directly, without mitigation, and in the same code.[4]

The student then backs down with, *We haven't done "left" or "right." Sorry*, offering an account and something that looks like an apology. She maintains the plural pronoun, shifting responsibility to the class she was in. One consultant commented, "The point is: Don't count off on this. I'm not responsible." The utterance thus is intended to inform the examiner that the class hasn't had those words, and to convey the implication that her inability to perform is not a question of her lack of mastery of material or lack of studiousness. Her *sorry* has multiple potential interpretations that address face needs of both participants in the interaction and possibly even indirectly the face needs of the absent tutor. Assuming that this *sorry* is not an expression of sympathy but rather a form of apology, and also ruling out the possibility that it was said with attitude, it would be analyzed within

Brown and Levinson's (1987) framework as addressing the negative face of the hearer. The data here, however, affirm Holmes's (1990:192) findings for English that apologies are oriented to the speaker's face as well as to the hearer's: " . . . remedial interchanges involve a complex interweaving of the face needs of S and H." In this case, *sorry* is interpretable as a possible apology for any and/or all of the following: (1) for having overstepped the role of examinee and challenged the examiner, (2) for putting the examiner (who is supposed to know) in an awkward situation of having asked something that hadn't been covered (in which case it could simultaneously be an expression of sympathy), (3) indirectly for the teacher (who hadn't covered the material), and (4) for the student's own inability to respond (i.e., in relation to her own face).[5]

An expression that is apparently used in some cases where American English speakers use *sorry* is in fact learned by students early in Korean 101. Thus, just as in the case of *I don't know how to say "to the left,"* the examinee does know how to express the idea or perform the speech act in Korean. The question then becomes, why doesn't the examinee use her Korean resources? One answer to that question, which also applies to the other uses of English by the examinee in the oral exam, is that the oral exam as emergent cross-cultural context shapes the discourse in the ways that have been analyzed in this paper. Another answer to the question is obviously the context of language learning.

11 Developing and Assessing Interactional Competence

What we are concerned with here is interactional competence, Kramsch's (1986) extension of the notion of communicative competence (Hymes 1972, Canale and Swain 1980, Canale 1983, Savignon 1985) toward a richer view of the knowledge and skills involved in participating effectively in a sociocultural world. As Kasper (1989) has pointed out, interactional competence (in particular learning how to use compensatory strategies and how to signal listenership appropriately) is not likely to be learned in a typical teacher-centered classroom. This is the case partly because the classroom context rarely allows naturally occurring models of such discourse skills and also because such competence is typically not systematically taught.[6] A self-instructional language program, such as the one described here, has great potential for developing interactional competence in the following areas: in learning culturally appropriate strategies for signaling interactional difficulties and going about repairing them; in developing skill in the use of listenership signals (backchannelling as well as prosodic, paralinguistic, and nonverbal signals); and in learning appropriate sociolinguistic patterns. The use of selected representative videotaped oral exams as cross-cultural texts for analysis could serve throughout the course not only to reduce student anxiety about the exam but also and primarily as a means of analyzing and modeling interactional competence.[7]

Interactional competence means in principle that we want these American students to be able to carry on conversations and enact role-plays with the examiner as if they were Korean, supposedly indicating thereby that they could perform in the same way if they were to find themselves in a Korean-speaking context. Thus we want them to be able to interpret contextualization cues, to make appropriate culturally based inferences, as well as cultural evaluations of those inferences. We want the American students to be able to use and experience Korean as a means to communicate and interact, not as a parallel system into which they are constantly translating from English. They should gradually become comfortable with Korean as a means for presentation of self and the negotiation of situated social identities.

Such a view of interactional competence allows new ideas for assessment, such as appropriate use of honorifics as a gauge of proficiency. We have seen in this chapter how aspects of the American examinees' face as competent interactants and serious language students may work against self-presentation as proficient speakers of Korean by intruding various material in English. This contextual problem could in fact be turned to advantage for assessment purposes because the intrusion of English (especially in cases where the student has demonstrably learned the appropriate Korean) can be used as an index of the degree to which the student really has internalized practices such as apologizing as doable in the target language. In other words, even though the student knows how to say *I'm sorry*, it won't be used unless the student really has come to experience Korean as a means of communicating aspects of self and managing interaction.

12 Conclusion

This study has taken an interactional sociolinguistic perspective on maintaining American face in the Korean oral exam. It has analyzed the interactional consequences of strategies of self-presentation and attempts at mutual face-maintenance in the LPI, revealing the power of cross-cultural context. It has attempted to shed some light on the process of the LPI as an emergent cross-cultural encounter, in which aspects of face as part of the presentation of self in the co-construction of situated social identities—as examiner and examinee manage potentially competing role expectations—are both reflective and constitutive of the overall context of the exam as speech event.

The study contributes to the literature that documents the situated signaling and interpretation of contextualization cues. It also raises theoretical issues in relation to politeness, cross-cultural pragmatics, and communicative/interactional competence. In terms of theories of politeness, it poses questions both in relation to the contextual shaping of strategies for face-work (Fiksdal 1988) and the complexity and situated relevance of aspects of face in the enactment of cultural identity. For cross-cultural pragmatics it poses questions about how the context may shape the operational definition of a speech act, as well as about the multifunctionality of speech acts in discourse. For theories of communicative or interactional competence it invites us to consider how such competence might overlap with and differ from cross-cultural communicative/interactional competence (Blommaert and Verschueren 1991, Scollon and Scollon 1995).

Finally, the study has direct implications for oral language assessment as well as language teaching. As others have urged (Duran 1984, Olshtain and Blum-Kulka 1985, Raffaldini 1988, Shohamy 1990, Savignon 1985), research in communicative and interactional competence must provide the theoretical basis on which exams are designed, and attempts at application must be systematically critiqued (Schachter 1990). The design of LPIs must include an analysis of how culture informs the content of the exam (for example, including a role-play in a Korean exam in which the examinee must demonstrate bargaining skills) and also of how culture affects the structure and process of the exam. As we have seen in this study, the American cultural context of the exams and the cultural identities of the examinees had unforeseen consequences. A related area for analysis is what examinees know and/or believe about the circumstances of the exam, such as whether the examiner also speaks their native language. In terms of assessment, the study suggests that the theoretical framework of communicative/interactional competence may provide new ways of thinking about how and what to evaluate, such as code switching as an index of degree of socialization into the language. With regard to language instruction, the study suggests the potential for using oral exams as an integrated part of the teaching process (Shohamy 1990).

Notes

1. By way of compensation for their participation in the study, students were offered copies of the tapes of their own exams. Such an offer also represented an attempt to create a positive "washback" (Morrow 1986) within the program. The examiner as well as the tutor and director of the program were offered copies as appropriate, and a presentation was made at the annual conference of the National Association of Self-Instructional Language Programs that emphasized the opportunity to teach interactional competence in such programs.

2. The text in quotation marks represents the examiner's own words, as taken from interviews with him.

3. See Labov and Fanshel (1977) and Ribeiro (1994) for a similar analysis of psychotherapeutic interviews.

4. See Tyler (1995) for an interactional sociolinguistic analysis of a tutoring session in which an American undergraduate challenges a Korean tutor on slightly different grounds.

5. For an interactional sociolinguistic analysis of the problematic use of *sorry* by a Korean teaching assistant using English, see Tyler and Davies (1990).

6. The teaching of aspects of interactional competence has been addressed by, among others, Bardovi-Harlig, Hartford, Mahan-Taylor, Morgan, and Reynolds (1991), Davies and Tyler (1994), Davies, Tyler, and Koran (1989), Gumperz and Roberts (1980), Kramsch (1993), and Roberts, Davies, and Jupp (1992).

7. See Davies and Tyler (1994) for such use of video in the training of international teaching assistants.

References

Bachman, Lyle F. 1988. "Problems in Examining the Validity of the ACTFL Oral Proficiency Interview." *Studies in Second Language Acquisition* 10.149–164.

Bardovi-Harlig, Kathleen, and Beverly Hartford. 1990. "Congruence in Native and Nonnative Conversations: Status Balance in the Academic Advising Session." *Language Learning* 40.467–501.

Bardovi-Harlig, Kathleen, Beverly A. S. Hartford, Rebecca Mahan-Taylor, Mary J. Morgan, and Dudley W. Reynolds. 1991. "Developing Pragmatic Awareness: Closing the Conversation." *ELT Journal* 45.4–15.

Bateson, Gregory. 1972. *Steps to an Ecology of Mind*. New York: Ballantine.

Berwick, Richard, and Steven Ross. 1993. "Cross-Cultural Pragmatics in Oral Proficiency Interview Strategies." Paper presented at the 15th annual Language Testing Research Colloquium, Cambridge, England, August 2-4, and Arnhem, The Netherlands, August 5-7.

Blom, Jan-Petter, and John J. Gumperz. 1972. "Social Meaning in Linguistic Structures: Code-Switching in Norway." In *Directions in Sociolinguistics*, ed. by John J. Gumperz and Dell Hymes, 407–434. New York: Holt, Rinehart and Winston.

Blommaert, Jan, and Jef Verschueren, eds. 1991. *The Pragmatics of International and Intercultural Communication*. Amsterdam/Philadelphia: Benjamins.

Brown, Penelope, and Stephen C. Levinson. 1987. *Politeness: Some Universals of Language Usage*. Cambridge: Cambridge University Press.

Canale, Michael. 1983. "From Communicative Competence to Communicative Performance." In *Language and Communication*, ed. by Jack C. Richards and Richard Schmidt, 2–27. New York: Longman.
Canale, Michael, and Merrill Swain. 1980. "Theoretical Bases of Communicative Approaches to Second Language Teaching and Testing." *Applied Linguistics* 1.1–47.
Carroll, Brendan J. 1980. *Testing Communicative Performance: An Interim Study*. Oxford: Pergamon Press.
Clark, John J., and Ray Clifford. 1988. "The FSI/ILR/ACTFL Proficiency Scales and Testing Techniques: Development, current status, and needed research." *Studies in Second Language Acquisition* 10.129–147.
Davies, Catherine E., and Andrea Tyler. 1994. "Demystifying Cross-Cultural (Mis)communication: Improving Performance Through Balanced Feedback in a Situated Context." In *Discourse and Performance of International Teaching Assistants*, ed. by Carolyn G. Madden and Cynthia L. Myers, 201–220. Alexandria, VA: TESOL.
Davies, Catherine E., Andrea Tyler, and John J. Koran, Jr. 1989. "Face-to-Face With English Speakers: An Advanced Training Class for International Teaching Assistants." *English for Specific Purposes* 8.139–153.
Douglas, Dan, and Larry Selinker. 1984. "Principles for Language Tests Within the 'Discourse Domains' Theory of Interlanguage: Research, Test Construction, and Interpretation." *Language Testing* 2.205–226.
Douglas, Dan, and Larry Selinker. 1993. "Performance on a General Versus a Field-Specific Test of Speaking Proficiency by International Teaching Assistants." In *A New Decade of Language Testing Research*, ed. by Dan Douglas and Carol Chapelle, 235–256. Alexandria, VA: TESOL, Inc.
Duran, Richard P. 1984. "Some Implications of Communicative Competence Research for Integrative Proficiency Testing." In *Communicative Competence Approaches to Language Proficiency Assessment: Research and Application*, ed. by Charlene Rivera, 44–58. Clevedon, Avon: Multilingual Matters.
Duranti, Alessandro, and Charles Goodwin, eds. 1992. *Rethinking Context*. Cambridge: Cambridge University Press.
Egbert, Maria M. 1998. "Miscommunication in Language Proficiency Interviews of First-Year German Students: A Comparison with Natural Conversation." In *Talking and Testing: Discourse Approaches to the Assessment of Oral Proficiency*, ed. by Richard Young and Agnes W. He, 147–169. Amsterdam and Philadelphia: Benjamins.
Ellis, Rod, and Celia Roberts. 1987. "Two Approaches for Investigating Second Language Acquisition." In *Second Language Acquisition in Context*, ed. by Rod Ellis, 3–30. Englewood Cliffs, NJ: Prentice Hall.
Erickson, Frederick, and Jeffrey Shultz. 1981. "When Is a Context? Some Issues and Methods in the Analysis of Social Competence." In *Ethnography and Language in Educational Settings*, ed. by Judith L. Green and Cynthia Wallat, 147–160. Norwood, NJ: Ablex.

Erickson, Frederick, and Jeffrey Shultz. 1982. *The Counselor as Gatekeeper: Social Interaction in Interviews*. New York: Academic Press.

Fiksdal, Susan. 1988. "Verbal and Nonverbal Strategies of Rapport in Cross-Cultural Interviews." *Linguistics and Education* 1.3–17.

Fiksdal, Susan. 1990. *The Right Time and Pace: A Microanalysis of Cross-Cultural Gatekeeping Interviews*. Norwood, NJ: Ablex.

Goffman, Erving. 1967. *Interaction Ritual*. New York: Pantheon.

Goffman, Erving. 1974. *Frame Analysis*. New York: Harper and Row.

Goffman, Erving. 1981. *Forms of Talk*. Philadelphia: University of Pennsylvania Press.

Gumperz, John J. 1982a. *Discourse Strategies*. New York: Cambridge University Press.

Gumperz, John J., ed. 1982b. *Language and Social Identity*. New York: Cambridge University Press.

Gumperz, John J. 1992. "Contextualization Cues and Understanding." In *Rethinking Context*, ed. by Alessandro Duranti and Charles Goodwin, 229–252. New York: Cambridge University Press.

Gumperz, John J., Tom Jupp, and Celia Roberts. 1979. *Crosstalk: A Study of Crosscultural Communication* [film]. London: National Center for Industrial Language Training in association with the BBC.

Gumperz, John J., and Celia Roberts. 1980. *Developing Awareness Skills for Inter-ethnic Communication* (Occasional Paper No. 12). Singapore: SEAMEO Regional Language Centre.

He, Agnes W. 1995. "Co-constructing Institutional Identities: The Case of Student Counselees." *Research on Language and Social Interaction* 28.213–231.

He, Agnes W. 1998. "Answering Questions in LPIs: A Case Study." In *Talking and Testing: Discourse Approaches to the Assessment of Oral Proficiency*, ed. by Richard Young and Agnes W. He, 101–116. Amsterdam and Philadelphia: Benjamins.

Holmes, Janet. 1990. "Apologies in New Zealand English." *Language in Society* 19.155–199.

Hymes, Dell. 1972. "On Communicative Competence." In *Sociolinguistics: Selected Readings*, ed. by John B. Pride and Janet Holmes, 269–293. Baltimore, MD: Penguin.

Hymes, Dell. 1974. *Foundations in Sociolinguistics*. Philadelphia: University of Pennsylvania Press.

Johnson, Marysia, and Andrea Tyler. 1998. "Re-analyzing the OPI: How Much Does It Look like Natural Conversation?" In *Talking and Testing: Discourse Approaches to the Assessment of Oral Proficiency*, ed. by Richard Young and Agnes W. He, 27–51. Amsterdam and Philadelphia: Benjamins.

Kasper, Gabriele. 1989. "Interactive Procedures in Interlanguage Discourse." In *Contrastive Pragmatics*, ed. by Wieslaw Oleksy, 189–229. Amsterdam/Philadelphia: Benjamins.

Kramsch, Claire. 1986. "From Language Proficiency to Interactional Competence." *Modern Language Journal* 70.366–372.

Kramsch, Claire. 1993. *Context and Culture in Language Teaching.* New York: Oxford University Press.
Labov, William, and David Fanshel. 1977. *Therapeutic Discourse: Psychotherapy as Conversation.* New York: Academic Press.
Lantolf, James P., and William Frawley. 1985. "Oral Proficiency Testing: A Critical Analysis." *Modern Language Journal* 69.337–345.
Lantolf, James P., and William Frawley. 1988. "Proficiency: Understanding the Construct." *Studies in Second Language Acquisition* 10.181–195.
Mehan, Hugh. 1979. *Learning Lessons.* Cambridge, MA: Harvard University Press.
Morrow, Keith E. 1986. "The Evaluation of Tests of Communicative Performance." In *Innovations in Language Testing,* ed. by Matthew Portal, 1–13. Berkshire, England: NFER-Nelson.
Ochs, Elinor. 1993. "Constructing Social Identity: A Language Socialization Perspective." *Research on Language and Social Interaction* 26.287–306.
Olshtain, Elite, and Shoshana Blum-Kulka. 1985. "Crosscultural Pragmatics and the Testing of Communicative Competence." *Language Testing* 2.16–30.
Pomerantz, Anita. 1984a. "Agreeing and Disagreeing with Assessments." In *Structures of Social Action,* ed. by J. Maxwell Atkinson and John Heritage, 57–101. Cambridge: Cambridge University Press.
Pomerantz, Anita. 1984b. "Pursuing a Response." In *Structures of Social Action,* ed. by J. Maxwell Atkinson and John Heritage, 152–164. Cambridge: Cambridge University Press.
Raffaldini, Tina. 1988. "The Use of Situation Tests as Measures of Communicative Ability." *Studies in Second Language Acquisition* 10.197–216.
Ribeiro, Branca. 1994. *Coherence in Psychotic Discourse.* Oxford: Oxford University Press.
Roberts, Celia, Evelyn Davies, and Tom Jupp. 1992. *Language and Discrimination: a Study of Communication in Multi-Ethnic Workplaces.* New York: Longman.
Ross, Steven. 1992. "Accommodative Questioning in Oral Proficiency Interviews." *Language Testing* 9.173–86.
Ross, Steven, and Richard Berwick. 1992. "The Discourse of Accommodation in Oral Proficiency Interviews." *Studies in Second Language Acquisition* 14.159–176.
Sacks, Harvey, Emanuel A. Schegloff, and Gail Jefferson. 1974. "A Simplest Systematics for the Organization of Turn-Taking in Conversation." *Language* 50.696–735.
Savignon, Sandra J. 1985. "Evaluation of Communicative Competence: The ACTFL Proficiency Guidelines." *Modern Language Journal* 69.129–34.
Schachter, Jacquelyn. 1990. "Communicative Competence Revisited." In *The Development of Second Language Proficiency,* ed. by Birgit Harley, Patrick Allen, Jim Cummins, and Merrill Swain, 39–49. Cambridge: Cambridge University Press.
Scollon, Ron, and Suzanne Wong Scollon. 1981. *Narrative, Literacy and Face in Interethnic Communication.* Norwood, NJ: Ablex.

Scollon, Ron, and Suzanne Wong Scollon. 1995. *Intercultural Communication: A Discourse Approach.* Cambridge, MA: Blackwell.
Scott, Marvin B., and Stanford M. Lyman. 1968. "Accounts." *American Sociological Review* 33.46–62.
Shea, David. 1994. "Perspective and Production: Structuring Conversational Participation Across Cultural Borders." *Pragmatics* 4.357–389.
Shohamy, Elana. 1988. "A Proposed Framework for Testing the Oral Language of Second/Foreign Language Learners." *Studies in Second Language Acquisition* 10.165–179.
Shohamy, Elana. 1990. "Language Testing Priorities: A Different Perspective." *Foreign Language Annals* 23.385–394.
Shohamy, Elana. 1991. "Discourse Analysis in Language Testing." *Annual Review of Applied Linguistics* 11.115–131.
Sinclair, John, and Malcolm Coulthard. 1975. *Towards an Analysis of Discourse.* Oxford: Oxford University Press.
Sohn, Ho-Min. 1983. "Power and Solidarity in the Korean Language." *Korean Linguistics* 3.97–122.
Spolsky, Bernard. 1978. "Introduction: Linguists and Language Testers." In *Advances in Language Testing Series* vol. 2, *Approaches to Language Testing*, ed. by B. Spolsky, 1–10. Washington, DC: Center for Applied Linguistics.
Sukle, Robert. 1992. "Is There a Place for ACTFL Proficiency Testing in NASILP Programs?" *National Association of Self-Instructional Language Programs Journal* 1–8.
Tannen, Deborah. 1979. "What's in a Frame? Surface Evidence for Underlying Expectations." In *New Directions in Discourse Processing*, ed. by Roy O. Freedle, 137–81. Norwood, NJ: Ablex.
Tannen, Deborah. 1985. "Cross-Cultural Communication." In *Handbook of Discourse Analysis*, vol. 4: *Discourse Analysis in Society*, ed. by Teun van Dijk, 203–215. London: Academic Press.
Tannen, Deborah, and Muriel Saville-Troike, eds. 1985. *Perspectives on Silence.* Norwood, NJ: Ablex.
Tyler, Andrea. 1995. "The Co-construction of a Cross-Cultural Miscommunication: Conflicts in Perception, Negotiation and Enactment of Participant Role and Status." *Studies in Second Language Acquisition* 17.129–152.
Tyler, Andrea, and Catherine E. Davies. 1990. "Cross-Linguistic Communication Missteps." *Text* 10.385–411.
Underhill, Nic. 1987. *Testing Spoken Language: A Handbook of Oral Testing Techniques.* New York: Cambridge University Press.
van Lier, Leo. 1989. "Reeling, Writhing, Drawling, Stretching, and Fainting in Coils: Oral Proficiency Interviews as Conversation." *TESOL Quarterly* 23.489–508.
Young, Richard. 1995. "Conversational Styles in Language Proficiency Interviews." *Language Learning* 45.3–42.

Young, Richard, and Michael Milanovic. 1992. "Discourse Variation in Oral Proficiency Interviews." *Studies in Second Language Acquisition* 14.403–424.

Confirmation Sequences as Interactional Resources in Korean Language Proficiency Interviews

Kyu-hyun Kim
Kyung Hee University

Kyung-hee Suh
Hankuk University of Foreign Studies

1 Introduction

In this chapter we provide a detailed analysis of the interactional aspects of interviews conducted with learners of Korean as a second language. The main goal is to explicate the structure of talk in Korean language proficiency interviews (LPIs) and examine some of its interactional features, which may provide us with the means to better understand learners' interactional and sociolinguistic competence (Canale and Swain 1980, Kramsch 1986). First, we analyze confirmation sequences where the interviewer (IR) asks for confirmation regarding the answer that the non-native speaker (NNS) provided in the preceding turn in response to IR's question. We are especially concerned with analyzing ways in which features of confirmation sequences constitute a significant part of the asymmetrical structure of LPI talk (ten Have 1991) by examining how IR and NNS organize their turns and how they are oriented to them. The analysis centers on whether and how IR's confirmation request is responded to by NNS, which will be related to the issue of how participants' status and power relationships are constituted by their orientation to confirmation sequences.

Second, we will analyze other-initiated repair sequences (Schegloff, Jefferson, and Sacks 1977) and clarification sequences (Ochs 1988), where NNSs, following IR's question, ask for confirmation through a candidate understanding or repeat. An analysis of this type of confirmation sequences gives insight into some of the ways in which politeness strategies are practiced through particular sequential organizations. It is suggested that sociolinguistic competence in Korean is reflected not only by the ability to draw upon the rich honorific and politeness system of Korean language but also by the ability to exploit devices of repair as a politeness strategy for such interactional purposes as softening a "dispreferred" response (Pomerantz 1984, Sacks 1987).

2 Methodology and Data

This study is conducted within the framework of Conversation Analysis (CA). The major concern of this approach is to provide a systematic account of ordinary conversational interaction from the interactants' perspectives. CA researchers attempt to account for the course taken by particular episodes of interaction and to analyze the recurrent practices of talking in natural interaction by capturing the orientation of participants (Sacks, Schegloff, and Jefferson 1974). CA methodology is useful not only in analyzing spontaneous conversations but also in other genres of discourse such as interviews. The former provides a basis for analyzing the latter, a more institutionalized form of language use (Boden and Zimmerman 1991, Drew and Heritage 1992).

The data analyzed here were collected during language proficiency interviews conducted at the University of California at Irvine in the United States. The interviews, which were conducted by the first author, were administered as part of a placement test for courses to be offered in the 1995 spring quarter for high-intermediate undergraduate students who were then completing an intermediate-level Korean course during winter quarter (Korean 2B). The IR, a 34-year-old native Korean male instructor, had been teaching university-level Korean for more than seven years in the United States at the time of the interviews.

The subjects for this study were all Korean-Americans who were taking the course as part of their foreign language requirements. A total of 34 students were interviewed and videotaped, each for ten to fifteen minutes. For this study, data from nine interviews were analyzed. The interviews were conducted informally; the IR tried to make the talk as conversational and casual as possible. The interview format, designed by the IR, includes questions regarding NNSs' backgrounds, hobbies, school activities, relationships with parents, future plans, and the cross-cultural experiences they had as Korean-Americans. Brief background information on the nine NNSs is presented in Table 1.

The NNSs had each taken between one and four courses of Korean. In general, they were able to engage in casual conversation with native speakers of Korean.

Table 1. Backgrounds of Non-Native-Speaking Subjects in This Study

Name	Gender	Class	Proficiency level
TG	M	Sophomore	Low-intermediate
AJ	F	Sophomore	Low-intermediate
SU	F	Senior	Low-intermediate
LN	F	Junior	Low-intermediate
TP	M	Junior	High-intermediate
CY	M	Junior	High-intermediate
HK	M	Senior	Advanced
EK	F	Junior	Advanced
PN	F	Junior	Advanced

Those NNSs categorized as low-intermediate, however, could manage conversation in Korean only with some difficulty, often shifting to English. When speaking Korean, they were able to use only a limited range of vocabulary, they spoke with noticeable English accents, and they reported feeling uncomfortable and awkward.

The high-intermediate NNSs reported that they could carry on casual conversation in Korean without any difficulty. But they often had some difficulty understanding certain vocabulary, particularly hybrid Sino-Korean words. Despite their limited lexical ability, they were perceived as fluent in Korean, with native-like accent and intonation, and were capable of long conversations in Korean with some switches to English for particular lexical items.

Advanced NNSs, by comparison with high-intermediate NNSs, had a wider range of vocabulary use (both Sino-Korean and pure Korean). They had acquired native-like accents and could pass as native speakers of Korean. But their reading and writing skills were very much limited, they had difficulty in reading authentic Korean texts, and they made numerous spelling and grammar mistakes in writing. Compared with peers taking an advanced Korean language course (Korean 3B) at the same time, they lagged far behind not only in their writing ability but also in the ability to speak formally—for example, when making a formal presentation.[1]

3 Background

As background to the following analysis, we can note several points that are relevant to Korean LPIs. First, a general feature of LPIs is that IR asks questions and elicits information from NNS with the aim of evaluating NNS's competence in the target language. LPIs are distinguishable from other types of interviews by their relative lack of concern with the content of NNS's response as compared with the linguistic form of the response.

Second, the Korean language is characterized by a system of highly elaborate politeness markers and honorifics that structurally index hierarchical relationships between the participants. Because sociolinguistic competence in acknowledging status differences is considered the most important interactional skill for a Korean speaker, the asymmetrical structure of Korean LPIs constituted by the unequal status of IR and NNS is one of the most important features of LPI interaction (Bardovi-Harlig and Hartford 1991).

Third, the asymmetrical structure of Korean LPIs is indexed not only by linguistic means but also by the different interactional patterns displayed by IR and NNS. That is, the difference in status is manifested not only directly through the use of linguistic forms but also indirectly through particular interactional modes involving expressions of collaborative stance.

In the following sections we will discuss various interactional and conversational features of confirmation sequences observed in LPI talk that play a significant role in shaping and characterizing the interaction between IR and NNS as that of an LPI. We will attempt to show that NNSs' interactional and sociolinguistic proficiency in Korean can be explicated, to some extent, by their ability to relate to IR's confirmation request, which is situated in the third turn, following IR's question and NNS's answer. IR's confirmation request and NNS's collaborative response are taken to be some of the constitutive features of Korean LPIs, to which the participants orient themselves. We also examine confirmation requests that NNS makes as a repair initiator in response to IR's question and point out that the ability to use them for interactional purposes constitutes a socially valued politeness strategy reflecting a high level of proficiency in conversational Korean.

4 IR's Confirmation Request as Third-Turn Assessment

4.1 *Question-Answer Sequences in the LPIs*

The examination of the data shows that the interview discourse displays a particular type of turn-taking pattern different from spontaneous conversations. For example, interviews in general are basically constituted by question-answer sequences, with IR asking most of the questions. In Korean LPIs, the question-answer sequence often contains a confirmation sequence, where IR, following NNS's answer, makes a confirmation request and NNS gives confirmation.[2]

The confirmation sequence often serves to link the prior question-answer sequence to a follow-up question (Schiffrin 1994). This format is illustrated in Excerpt 1, which was produced by the high-intermediate NNS, *TP*. Here the single arrow (→) marks the turn that contains the confirmation request initiating the confirmation sequence, and the double arrow (⇒) marks the turn where a follow-up is provided.³

```
(1) From the interview with TP, a high-intermediate speaker

1    IR:   hh taykay  ka-myen eti-  eti  -eyse (.) uh
              usually go-COND where where-LOC

2          stay-hay -yo, //eti  -eyse iss -eyo,
           stay-do  -POL   where-LOC stay-POL
           hh If you go (to Korea), where do you usually stay?
                                                [
3    NNS:                ah     eti-- halmeni-lang
                         filler where- grandmother-COM
           kachi     sal -myen
           together  live-COND

4          pangpaydong-ey -yo.
           Pangpaydong-LOC-POL
           If I stay with my grandmother, I stay in Pangpay-
           Dong.

5→   IR:   ah kulay    -yo?
           CST like:that-POL
           Oh, really? (=Is that so?)

6    NNS:  ney.
           Yes.

7 ⇒  IR:   eng::: kulem iss -ul  -tey   iss  -kwu, cal
           RM     then  stay-ATTR-place exist-CONN well
           haycwu
           do:for:you-

8          -si  -keyss-ney,
           HONOR-MOD  -FR
           I see. Then I presume that you had a place to stay,
           and that she must have treated you very well,

9          (.)
```

```
10 NNS:    yey. yey.
           Yes. Yes.
```

Here we can observe a pattern of question (lines 1 and 2) – answer (lines 3 and 4) – confirmation request (line 5) – answer (line 6) – follow-up assessment (lines 7 and 8) – answer (line 10). In response to NNS's answer in lines 3 and 4, IR, in line 5, initially produces a change-of-state token *ah* (Heritage 1984a), translatable into "oh" in English, by which he registers the informativeness of the content of NNS's answer. The change-of-state token is followed by a confirmation request in the form of newsmark (*kulayo*? "Is that so?") (Jefferson 1981). This confirmation request is then responded to by NNS in line 6. Following NNS's confirmation, IR produces what may be called a "realization marker" (*eng:::* "I see") in line 7, which often functions as a turn-holding device.[4] The realization marker frames IR's follow-up assessment.

This format is recurrently observed throughout the data, where IR's confirmation request acts as a pivot in organizing the talk. This recurrently observed pattern can be represented as follows.

a	1st	IR:	Question
b	2nd	NNS:	Answer
c	3rd	IR:	Confirmation request
d	4th	NNS:	Confirmation
e	5th	IR:	Follow-up assessment/question

Following IR's question *a*, NNS produces answer *b*, which is treated as newsworthy by IR, who makes a confirmation request *c*. IR's confirmation request *c* is then answered by NNS's confirmation in fourth turn, *d*, which leads to IR's follow-up assessment or question. The third and fourth-turn utterances, *c* and *d*, leading to the fifth-turn assessment/question, are taken to form a "confirmation sequence," which constitutes the major object of inquiry in this section.[5] The confirmation sequence is followed by IR's follow-up *e*, which may be framed by an acknowledgment token such as a realization marker (e.g., *eng:::* "I see" in Excerpt 1) or a receipt marker (e.g., *yey* "yes"—see Excerpt 3).[6]

The confirmation request as defined in this context is thus produced in third turn by IR who targets NNS's answer in the immediately preceding turn and asks for NNS's confirmation. It usually takes the form of a question such as a newsmark (e.g., *really?*), as in Excerpt 1, but as the following discussion will show it may take the form of a questioning repeat, whereby IR repeats part or all of NNS's preceding answer (see Excerpt 2). Also, IR may produce a realization statement as a confirmation request, showing that NNS's answer is newsworthy (see Excerpt 3).[7]

As we will demonstrate in the following discussion, IR's confirmation request constitutes a collaborative move on the part of IR to elicit participation and involvement from NNS. The sequential place where IR's confirmation request is situated is an important one in terms of assessing prior talk and developing subsequent talk. This sequential place is a locus where IR assesses the prior talk and projects subsequent talk. It thus warrants scrutiny as one of the places where participants' interactional competence may be gauged, especially with regard to the response made by NNSs with different proficiency levels.

4.2 NNS's Confirmation as a Collaborative Response

What is important with respect to IR's confirmation request is that it is accountably and normatively to be responded to in the following turn. An absence of confirmation in response to a confirmation request is often perceived as interactionally noticeable, with smooth interaction between IR and NNS hinging significantly upon whether IR's confirmation request is properly responded to by NNS. This point suggests that, as we will demonstrate in the following sections, a confirmation sequence constitutes a structural place in LPI talk where IR and NNS mutually negotiate and consolidate their relationship in a way that has significant implications for topic transition and the organization of LPI discourse.

The examination of how confirmation sequences are generated in LPIs shows that whether and how appropriately NNSs respond to IR's confirmation requests can be related to their interactional or sociolinguistic competence (or more broadly, to communicative competence). High-intermediate and advanced NNSs, for instance, were much more interactive than low-intermediate NNSs in responding collaboratively to IR's confirmation requests. We can see in Excerpt 1 that a high-intermediate NNS, *TP*, quickly affirms IR's newsmark. Also, in Excerpt 2, IR's confirmation request in the form of a partial repeat is quickly confirmed by a high-intermediate NNS, *CY*, in line 5. In the excerpts that follow, including Excerpt 2, the arrows (→) at lines 1, 3, 4, 5, and 6 represent first, second, third, fourth, and fifth turns in a question-answer sequence, as displayed in the schematic representation presented above. The arrow at line 4 marks the third turn where IR's confirmation request is situated, and the arrow at line 5 marks the fourth turn where NNS's confirmation is due.

(2) From the interview with CY, a high-intermediate speaker

```
1→a  IR:  taykay   hankwukmal:-un ettay-yo  ku     cip -eyse
          usually  Korean     -TOP how -POL that   home-LOC

2         pwumonim-tul-hako hankwukmal//-ul  ssu-eyo?
          parent  -PL -COM  Korean     -OBJ use-POL
          Do you usually use Korean when speaking to
          your parents at home?
                                      [
3→bNNS:                         ney hankwukmal
                                Yes Korean
          -man   sse-   yo(hh)
          -only  use    -POL
          Yes. I use only Korean (hh).

4→c  IR:  hankwukmal-man  sse-yo?=
          Korean     -only use-POL
          You use only Korean?

5→dNNS:   =ney=
          Yes.

6→e  IR:  =ung:: .h kulikwu tongsayng-hako-to  -yo?
          RM        and     brother  -COM -also-POL
          I see. .h and the same with your brother
          (=And do you also use Korean when speaking to your
          brother?)
```

Here NNS's collaborative stance is displayed by the fact that his confirmation in line 5 latches on to IR's confirmation request. The student's confirmation, then, is again latched on to by IR's follow-up in line 6.

Excerpts 1 and 2 show that IR's confirmation requests in interrogative forms (newsmark and questioning repeat, respectively) invite a confirming response from NNS. The sequence of confirmation request and confirmation, though often brief, serves to provide mutually ratified common ground for the participants to proceed to the next stage of dialogue. Note that IR's confirmation request sometimes takes a non-interrogative form—a "realization statement" (see note 7)—as illustrated in Excerpt 3, which was produced by an advanced NNS, *HK*.

(3) From the interview with *HK*, an advanced speaker

```
1→a  IR:   chinchek-pwun -tul-un   ta  hankwuk-ey
           relative-HONOR-PL -TOP  all Korea   -LOC

2          kyesi         -nketkat-ney-yo,
           exist:(HONOR)-seem    -FR -POL
           I guess your relatives are all in Korea.

3→bNNS:    . . . wuli apeci--  ameni    ccok-un  ta  yeki-ey
           . . . our  father   mother side-TOP  all here-LOC
           sal  -kwu -yo
           live-CONN-POL
           My father- the relatives on my mother's side
           are living here.

4→c  IR:   ah    kule       -nun -kwu//n -a,
           CST like:that-ATTR-UNASSIM-IE
           Oh, I see (=I've now realized that that is the
           case),
                                 [
5→dNNS:                          ney.
                                 Yes.

6→e  IR:   yey: (2.0) kulem ku   ttay malko -nun kyesok
           yes        then  that time except-TOP continuously

7          hankwuk-- hankwuk-ey  an  ka-po  -ass-kwu -yo,
           Korea     Korea   -LOC NEG go-see-PST-CONN-POL
           I see. (2.0) Then except for that period,
           you've never been in Korea?
```

Following NNS's answer in line 3, IR produces a realization statement, which contains the post-verbal particle *kwun*. By using this particle, which is termed "unassimilative," the speaker proposes the informativeness of the preceding response by treating it as information that has not yet been assimilated by the speaker (Lee 1991). While the realization statement does not take the form of an interrogative, and hence does not require an answer, there is a sense in which it serves as a confirmation request; it still virtually demands NNS's confirmation as part of the ongoing co-assessment. Indeed, in Excerpt 3, the NNS promptly confirms the confirmation request collaboratively, and the collaborativeness of NNS's response to IR's confirmation request is displayed by the overlap in line 5.[8]

The collaborative stance displayed through a response to IR's confirmation request is often expressed in a highly active and elaborate manner by advanced NNSs. Excerpt 4 is a case in point. In lines 70 and 71, IR asks *PN*, an advanced NNS, what she thinks of Korea, and beginning on line 74, she answers that she has heard only negative things about Korea from her friends. In response, in lines 81 and 82, IR produces a collaboratively formulated confirmation request, to which the NNS, in lines 83 and 84, collaboratively responds in partial overlap with IR in the manner of co-assessing the prior point.

(4) From the interview with *PN*, an advanced speaker

```
70→a   IR:  hankwuk-ila -n     nala    -eytayhayse ettehkey
            Korea   -QUOT-ATTR country-about       how

71          sayngkak-hay-yo? . . .
            thought -do -POL
            What do you think of Korea?

              .
              .
              .

74→b   NNS: kulssey       -yo, . . .
            let:me:see    -POL
            Well, . . .

              .
              .
              .

81→c   IR:  .h (kunikka) pwucengcekin negative-ha -n-key
            so           negative     negative -do-ATTR-thing:SUB

82          mence tuli-ci//-yo, (ku  -ci  -yo?)
            first hear-COMM-POL  that-COMM-POL
            So you hear negative things first, right?
                          [                     ]
83→d   NNS:              ney:::::::         ta-yo. //
                         yes                all-POL
            mwucoken.
            no:matter:what
            Right. Everything (I hear about Korea is
            negative). No matter what.
                                                  [
84→e   IR:                                       ney.
                                                 Yes.
```

In line 83, we can see that NNS responds to IR's confirmation request by producing a stretched affirmation (*ney:::::::* "yes") in overlap with the utterance-final elements in IR's utterance. Here NNS further heightens her collaboration with IR's point by adding two intensifiers (Labov 1984), *ta-yo* "everything" and *mwucoken* "no matter what," and IR collaboratively acknowledges NNS's confirmation in overlap in line 84.

As a whole, Excerpts 1, 2, 3, and 4 show that high-intermediate and advanced NNSs quickly confirm IR's confirmation request, thereby displaying proficient assessment skills, sometimes acting as co-tellers doing co-assessment. In contrast, low-intermediate students were often not skillful in dealing with IR's third turn. For instance, we find in Excerpt 5 that *AJ*, a low-intermediate NNS, does not respond to IR's confirmation request.

```
(5)  From the interview with AJ, a low-intermediate speaker

1→a IR:   eti   eti   noll-e    ka-ss -eyo?
          where where play-PURP go-PST-POL
          Where did you go (during the vacation)?

2         (.)

3→bNNS:   uh las vegas ka-ss -eyo. hh
          Las Vegas go-PST-POL
          I went to Las Vegas. hh

4→c IR:   las vegas ka-ss -eyo?
          Las Vegas go-PST-POL
          Did you go to Las Vegas?
5→d       (.)

6→e IR:   las vegas manhi coh -aci    -ess-takwu
          Las Vegas much  good-become-PST-QUOT
          ha-nuntey
          do-CIRCUM

7         manhi coh -aci    -ess-eyo?
          much  good-become-PST-POL
          I've heard that Las Vegas has become better.
          Has it become better?

8    NNS: ney.
          yes
```

```
           Yes.
```

In response to IR's question about whether NNS has visited anyplace during the vacation, NNS, in line 3, answers that she has visited Las Vegas. In line 4, IR produces a confirmation request in the form of questioning repeat. As his repeat is not responded to, IR goes on to produce a follow-up without NNS's confirmation. We can observe the same pattern in Excerpt 6, which was produced by another low-intermediate student, *LN*.

```
(6)   From the interview with LN, a low-intermediate speaker

1→a IR:   hankwuk-eyse elma     dongan iss -ess-eyo ku
          Korea    -LOC  how:long during stay-PST-POL that
          ttay,
          time
          At that time how long had you been in Korea?

2         (1.0)

3→bNNS:   kunyang han tal,
          just    one month
          Just one month,

4         (.)

5→c IR:   han tal   iss -ess-eyo?
          one month stay-PST-POL
          Had you stayed for one month?

6→d       (.)

7→e IR:   eti (.) nol -le   ka-n   tey  iss  -eyo?
          where   play-PURP go-ATTR place exist-POL
          Can you tell me about any places you visited?

8   NNS:  uh      ithaywon (.)  shopping
          filler  Itaewon       shopping
          uh, Itaewon, for shopping.
```

In line 1, IR asks a question, which is answered by NNS in line 3. IR's ensuing confirmation request in line 5, however, is left answered. Notice that NNS's answer in line 3 (*kunyang han tal,* "Just one month") is produced with slightly rising intonation expressing uncertainty, as marked by the comma. Here NNS is probably asking IR to check whether her utterance was grammatically or appropriately formulated. Her lack of response in the subsequent context may be attributable to NNS's stance, which is mainly oriented to informational and grammatical rather than interactional aspects of her response. The formulation of an answer as a statement with a rising question intonation marking uncertainty is frequently observed in the case of low-proficiency-level students (see line 3 in Excerpt 9).

While this lack of confirmation on the part of NNSs may look trivial, one begins to sense that the interaction is unilateral. Excerpts 5 and 6 clearly show this one-sidedness: the confirmation request is formulated as a question, which requires an answer as a second action in the following turn. The lack of confirmation in these excerpts constitutes a context where an answer (i.e., confirmation) is "officially" absent (Heritage 1984b), and IR is placed in a situation where he should go ahead and produce a follow-up without the prior question-answer cycle being completed.

While the lack of confirmation in response to a question may be noticeable due to its turn status as a second pair part, the absence of NNS's answer in response to IR's confirmation request in a non-question format (i.e., a realization statement) also tends to be viewed as noticeable, though to a lesser degree than in a question, as shown in Excerpt 7.

(7) From the interview with *AJ*, a low-intermediate speaker

```
1→a  IR:   ah cwulo    emeni   malssum       -ul ttalu -nun
           usually mother telling:HONOR-OBJ follow-ATTR
           phyen-I  -eyo?
           side -COP-POL
           ah do you usually follow what your mother tells you
           to do?

           (2.0)

2→bNNS:    eccelttay-yo h
           sometimes-POL
           Sometimes. h

3→c  IR:   eccelttay-nun ttalunun-kwun   -a,
           sometimes-TOP follow   -UNASSIM-IE
           (I see, so) sometimes you obey her,

4→d        (4.0)
5→e  IR:   uh::   way-   uh way kyengceyhak-ul ha-key
```

```
              filler why         why economics  -OBJ do-CONN
              toy-   ss  -eyo
              become-PST-POL
              Uh:: why- uh why did you choose economics (as your
              major)?
```

Following IR's confirmation request in the form of a realization statement in line 3, an awkward four-second gap ensues, where some kind of response is obviously due. This state of interaction, causing an untoward sense of unilateralness, leads IR to bring up a topic in a "bounded" manner, rather than in a "shaded" manner (Jefferson 1984), presumably requiring more cognitive effort on the part of IR as a topic-initiator. Notice in line 5 that IR's follow-up (about NNS's major) is rather disjunctive from the preceding topic (about the relationship with mother). It is also prefaced by disfluencies in talk, characterized by fillers and a cutoff, which can be taken as suggesting that IR is troubled and burdened by the need to develop the talk unilaterally.[9]

Excerpts 5, 6, and 7 contrast sharply with the preceding excerpts produced by high-intermediate and advanced NNSs, where we noted a smoothly coordinated turn exchange in a pattern of confirmation request by IR, quick confirmation by NNS, acknowledgment, and follow-up by IR. On the basis of the preceding discussions of Excerpts 5, 6, and 7 we may point out that, without any confirmation from NNS, more interactional burden falls on IR, who finds himself in a situation where he must initiate a new follow-up question without a mutual sense of having completed the preceding cycle of talk. This state of affairs may not only result in disfluencies and/or a disjunctive follow-up in IR's turn, but may sometimes lead IR to overtly cover up the absence, as shown in Excerpt 8.

(8) From the interview with AJ, a low-intermediate speaker

```
1→a IR:   caymi iss  -eyo?
          fun   exist-POL
          Do you like (your major)? (Is your major fun?)

2→bNNS:   acik    molla    -yo.
          not-yet not:know-POL
          I don't know yet.

3→c IR:   acik molu     -kyess-eyo?
          yet  not:know-MOD  -POL
          You don't know yet?
4→d       (.)
```

```
5→e IR:    ney, colep     -ha-kwu -nun  acik acik (.) mwe
           yes graduation-do-CONN-ATTR  yet  yet      what

6          kwucheycekin kyewhek-un epkeyss -ciman . . .
           specific     plan     -TOP    not:exist-but
           I see, I presume that you don't have a specific
           plan yet about what to do after graduation, but . .
```

The micro pause in line 4 points to a place where this NNS might have responded. Noticing that nothing is forthcoming, IR goes on to produce a follow-up in line 5. Here, faced with a gap in line 4 where NNS's answer is due, IR generates an acknowledgment token (*ney*) in line 5, even though there is nothing to acknowledge. In this context, the use of the acknowledgment token is opaque in terms of whether IR assumes the presence of NNS's prior response, which does not exist, or reiteratively assesses NNS's answer in line 2. In either case we can point out that the use of the "dummy" acknowledgment token framing a follow-up functions to cover up and delete the immediately preceding problematic sequence, where an expected confirmation is absent.

In some cases the problem is apparent from the lack of verbal response. That is, it was observed that some low-intermediate NNSs often responded to IR's confirmation request by simply nodding. This is illustrated in Excerpts 9 and 10, produced by two low-intermediate NNSs, *TG* and *SU*.

(9) From the interview with *TG*, a low-intermediate speaker

```
1→a  IR:    uh: .h cikum-un  ku- (.) aphatu   -eyse ttalo
            filler now -TOP  that   apartment-LOC  separately

2           honca sal -ko iss-eyo?
            alone live-PROG  -POL
            uh: are you living alone in an apartment now
            (separate from your family)?

3→b NNS:    uh:     ani    -yo  ku-  roommate tul-i  iss//-
            filler  no:COP-POL  that roommate two-SUB exist-eyo,
                                                      POL
            uh: no. I've two roommates,
                                                    [
4→c  IR:                                            ah
                                                    CST
```

```
               roommate twul-i    iss  -eyo?
               roommate two -SUB  exist-POL
               Oh, do you have two roommates?

5→dNNS:        ((nodding))

6     IR:      ney.
               yes
               I see.
```

(10) From the interview with *SU*, a low-intermediate speaker

```
1→a   IR:      elma      dongan iss -ess-nuntey?
               how:long  for    stay-PST-CIRCUM
               How long did you stay (in Korea)?

2→bNNS:        i    cwuil.
               two  week
               Two weeks.

3→c   IR:      i    cwuil,
               two  week
               Two weeks,

4→dNNS:        ((nodding))

5→e   IR:      sewul-ey  iss -ess-eyo?
               Seoul-LOC stay-PST-POL
               Did you stay in Seoul?
```

    In these cases the nodding was conducted not in the manner of an enthusiastic collaboration but by a slight tilting of the head two or three times. The presence of the nonverbal confirmation certainly serves as a response to IR's confirmation request. The act of confirming in the form of nodding, however, not accompanied by any verbal response, is perceived as rude, especially in the context of interacting with higher status persons. In this respect we still find in such cases as Excerpts 9 and 10 that an appropriate form of confirmation is obviously missing.

    As IR's confirmation request is situated in the third turn in a question-answer sequence where he assesses the prior talk and projects a follow-up, a collaborative response by NNS to IR's confirmation request contributes to establishing mutually affirmed common ground, on the basis of which the IR can initiate subsequent talk. Confirmation sequences, in this sense, are places where we can observe interactional differences deriving from differing levels of NNS proficiency (Young 1995:13). The lack of displayed skills of less proficient NNSs in dealing with IR's confirmation request undermines the basis for collaboratively building the talk, and often results in a state where IR has the burden of unilaterally terminating and initiating a topic. It often causes the interaction to be one-sided, with a barrage of questions one after another from IR. The expected collaborative confirmation from NNS toward IR's confirmation request, then, serves as a go-ahead with respect to IR's next move.

In the context of the hierarchically organized Korean discourse system, the lack of confirmation from NNS may also violate the interactional norm that Bardovi-Harlig and Hartford (1991:42) call the "maxim of congruence," which dictates that participants make their contribution congruent with their status. Through a confirmation request, IR claims his/her right to evaluate prior talk and initiates subsequent talk, and expects NNS to respond in kind. The lack of confirmation on the part of NNS not only results in more burden on IR in having to initiate topics unilaterally, but also threatens IR's face by not performing a speech act congruent with NNS's status, i.e., not collaboratively ratifying IR's right to confirm the prior talk and initiate a topic.

This pattern of interaction between IR and NNS results from the fact that the act of giving information constitutes a delicate act of negotiating status as well as rapport between the interlocutors. As Tannen (1993:244) observes,

> To the extent that giving information, direction, or help is of use to another, it reinforces bonds between people. But to the extent that it is asymmetrical, it creates hierarchy: Insofar as giving information frames one as the expert, superior in knowledge, and the other as uninformed, inferior in knowledge, it is a move in the negotiation of status.

Tannen makes this observation in the context of discussing gender differences in conversational styles. But this point seems to be relevant to any type of interaction involving status differences, which are manifested by the patterns of information-giving (Coates 1993). In the excerpts analyzed, we can note that NNSs, as they provide information in response to IR's question, take the role of information givers, which puts them in a superior position toward IR. Given the many situations where those who give information are higher in status, this state of affairs may not be in line with the status relationship between the higher status IR and the lower status NNS. IR's confirmation request, in this sense, is an attempt on the part of IR to reverse this role relationship in which he is placed in a lower position as the information receiver: IR, through his confirmation request, claims that he is not in the lower status position any more. Viewed in this light, NNS's response to IR's confirmation request takes on a special meaning that has great implications for interactional management in LPIs. It will constitute NNS's affirmation of IR's move to place himself back in the superior (or more precisely, a non-inferior) position.

In the Korean sociocultural context of the interaction, unequal distribution of power and control manifested through confirmation sequences between the higher status IR and the lower status NNS constitutes "a psychologically convergent orientation" of the participants (Coupland, Coupland, and Giles 1991:32). That is, from the Korean perspective, the higher status person's status-imposing move, which may be treated as not highly accommodating to the lower status interlocutor from the egalitarian perspective (Giles, Coupland, and Coupland 1991), is taken by the latter as something to affirm with due respect. This attitude, of course, is rooted in the Korean sociocultural norm highlighting hierarchical relationships.

These observations strongly suggest that NNS's close orientation toward IR's confirmation request in Korean LPIs constitutes a crucial aspect of sociolinguistic competence by indexing that NNS treats IR as a socially higher status person whose assessment he or she respects and values. Confirmation sequences in Korean LPIs thus display interactional patterns in which we observe a subtle interplay of topic-initiating and status-negotiating moves by IR and NNS, made in the direction of limiting NNS's opportunity to initiate topic development. These sequential characteristics point to a cultural "rich point" (Agar 1994), which, as "signals of frame differences" between language cultures (what Agar calls "languacultures"), are those clues to culture that appear blatantly in speech, indexing behaviors that the natives command effortlessly but seem bizarre to outsiders (Young and Halleck 1998).

In the next section, we discuss the interactional import of confirmation sequences as a constitutive feature of Korean LPI talk, showing that the status-indexing nature of confirmation sequences are expressly oriented to both by IR and NNS.

4.3 *Confirmation Sequences as Constitutive Features of Asymmetry*

The preceding discussion suggests that confirmation sequences are a potential site of co-assessment and mutual ratification of different status. Through confirmation requests, IR does not simply ask for confirmation regarding the informational status of a given answer but negotiates and exerts his/her status as someone who takes the initiative in assessing prior talk and developing topics. NNS's appropriate response to IR's confirmation request serves to acknowledge and ratify the higher status of IR, and it is in this sense that different proficiency levels in interactional competence can be correlated, at least partly, with the ability to engage in collaborative joint activities with IR's confirmation request.

When advanced NNSs respond to the IR's confirmation request collaboratively, they are showing expressly that they are oriented to the request. It is through such a display of focused orientation to IR's confirmation request that NNSs acknowledge and ratify their relationships with IR. This point is further supported by Excerpt 11, where an advanced-level student, *PN*, displays her orientation to IR's confirmation request by terminating her ongoing answer and by quickly responding to it in the fourth turn in line 8, marked by arrow *d*.

```
(11)   From the interview with PN, an advanced speaker

1→a IR:  ettehkey,    etten       tension iss   -ess-eyo?
         how          what:kind   tension exist-PST-POL
         So, what kind of tension have you had (with your
         parents)?

2→bNNS:  kunyang (.) nay-ka  kocip            -i    sey -kw//u,
         just        I      -SUB stubbornness-SUB strong-CONN
         It's just that I was stubborn, and,
                                               [
3    IR:                                     ung.
                                              yes
                                              I see.

4→bNNS:  mot         toy        -kwu(h)  k//ulay(h)-ss -unikka(h)
         not:able    become-CONN         like:that -PST -CAUSE
         because I was not a good girl,
                                       [
5    IR:                              hhhhhhhhhhhhhh
                                      hhhhhhhhhhhhhh

6→bNNS:  kuntey khu -myense cikum-un  acwu coh -ayo=
         but    grow-SIMUL  now  -TOP very good-POL
         But as I grew up, now it's very good.

7→c IR:  =kulay     -yo?=
          like:that-POL
          Really?

8→dNNS:  =emma    appa -ka   //ney.
         mother  father-SUB   yes
         My mom and dad (are very good), yes.
```

```
9→e   IR:                  [
                           eng::: okay .h um tayhwa -ha-
                       RM         okay   um-conversation-do-
10                  lttay-nun hankwukmal-lo    hay-yo, . . .
                    when -TOP Korean      -INSTR do -POL
                    I see. Okay .h uhm do you use Korean in
                    conversations,
```

In response to IR's question as to whether she has had any tension with her parents, NNS produces an extensive answer through lines 2, 4, and 6. IR then produces a confirmation request in line 7, and NNS responds in line 8 by initially continuing her answer, where the subject portion is tagged onto her prior utterance. Notice that she immediately affirms IR's confirmation request after quickly completing her answer (*emma appa-ka ney*, "My mom and dad [are very good], yes"). NNS makes her post-completion utterance very brief (*emma appa-ka*, "My mom and dad") and immediately responds to the confirmation request without any pause (*ney*, "yes"). That is, the utterance, *emma appa-ka*, which is tagged onto the prior utterance and grammatically completes it, is said very fast and produced as one intonation unit along with the following brief response *ney*, "yes," without any gap between them. This practice shows that NNS swiftly shifts her orientation from her own utterance toward IR's confirmation request (also see Excerpts 2, 3, and 4).

The preceding discussion shows that NNS displays a collaborative stance toward IR's confirmation request and that IR smoothly embarks on initiating a follow-up on the basis of NNS's ratification. It is worth noting in this regard that IR, for his part, also displays his orientation to the interactional import of his confirmation request. Excerpt 12 illustrates a dialogue showing how IR responds to a high-intermediate NNS who has not explicitly responded to his confirmation request.

```
(12)   From the interview with CY, a high-intermediate
       speaker

8→a    IR:  uh      cwulo etten ke    manhi po    -ayo?
            filler mainly which thing a:lot watch-POL
            Uh, which program do you usually watch?

9→b    NNS: uh      yocum    -un ku  nukkim -i   caymi-
            filler these:days-TOP that feeling-SUB fun-
            iss  -eyo.
            exist-POL
10          nukk//im.
```

```
                    feeling
                    Uh these days, "Feelings" is fun. "Feelings."
                    [
11→c1  IR:          nukkim, //ah,
                    feeling CST
                    "Feelings," oh.
                                [
12→d?NNS:                       kulikwu ku (      )
                                and    that
13                  pam  -ey  M  -po   -ayo(   //    )
                    night-LOC "M"  watch  -POL
                    And (      ) I watch "M" on (        ).
                            [
14→c2  IR:                  M.  yey yey yey yey I see
                            "M" yes yes yes yes I see
                            "M." Yes, yes, yes, yes. I see.

15→e   IR:  tut    -nun  ke    -nun taykang mwuncey-nun
            listen -ATTR thing -TOP roughly problem-TOP
            peyllwu . . .
            not:much
            What do you think of your listening skills. I
            presume you don't have any problem . . .
```

In line 8, IR asks NNS about his favorite Korean TV program, and NNS answers by providing the name of his favorite program in line 9. Following this question-answer sequence, IR, in line 11, produces a confirmation request by repeating the name of NNS's favorite TV program, followed by a change-of-state token *ah*. In response, NNS, instead of attending to IR's confirmation request, goes on to talk about another TV program he watches (*"M"*) in lines 12 and 13. We have marked this place with arrow (d?) to show that the utterance does not respond to IR's confirmation request. Notice in line 14 that IR, after repeating the name of the program collaboratively, produces an agreement token (*yes*) as many as four times. Here we can see that IR's production of a series of affirming responses functions as a *pro forma* agreement, which does not express genuine agreement but simply works toward terminating the sequence. In line 15, then, IR produces a follow-up question.

From this sequence of talk, we can see that IR, after noticing that NNS has not attended to his confirmation request and has just proceeded to list a second TV drama, discourages NNS from further continuing his talk. That is, IR's confirmation request made in the form of a partial repeat (line 11) has not been taken up by NNS, who goes on to extend his turn. Given this move by NNS, which does not affirm IR's confirmation request, IR initiates another confirmation request (line 14) through another repeat, and it is in this sequential context that IR produces a *pro forma* agreement, which works toward terminating the sequence.

There is a sense in which the NNS in Excerpt 12 does not affirm IR's confirmation request partly because he is employing a peer-to-peer conversational style. In other places of the interview talk, for example, this particular NNS, *CY*, was observed to interact with IR in a highly casual manner by bringing up a topic and completing IR's question. It is important to note, in this respect, that in Korean conversation one should apply a different rule of interaction when interacting with higher status persons (for example, higher in terms of age, social status, kinship, etc.) than when interacting with peers. As Scollon and Scollon (1995) observe, in many East Asian societies one generally applies the hierarchical politeness system for the former, and the solidarity politeness system for the latter; as most long-term observers can attest, in the former, one is not supposed to take the initiative in generating conversation. If we regard the LPI talk as a type of discourse where there is a clear difference in status between the interviewer-teacher and the interviewee-student, we can see that NNS's application of conversational strategies that may be proper for peer-to-peer interaction is socially inappropriate here.

The preceding discussion suggests that IR and NNS mutually build talk in such a way that confirmation sequences index their different, reciprocating orientations. The asymmetrical structure of LPI talk is thus partly constituted by participants' practice of displaying different types of orientations. The predominant role that IR plays in initiating topics and developing them is shown to be something that is interactionally achieved through the sequence of talk that is closely attuned, mutually ratified, and collaboratively enacted by IR and NNS.

4.4 *Orientation to Asymmetry as Sociolinguistic Competence*

IR has the role of a higher status person in the context of Korean discourse, where the primary attention is given to indexing of a hierarchically organized relationship between participants. As the preceding discussion suggests, IR and NNS are both oriented to the status-indexing import of confirmation request as third-turn assessment, where IR and NNS mutually collaborate to sustain different expectations and different roles. It is partly through this type of mutual work that the asymmetrical structure of the LPI is constituted, and the higher status of IR and the lower status of NNS are constituted and reconfirmed as an interactional achievement.

A crucial part of learning Korean involves appropriate interaction with higher or lower status persons by using appropriate forms—marking politeness and honorific relations in a variety of social situations—but sociolinguistic competence in Korean involves more than being able to use appropriate politeness and honorific forms. Sociolinguistic competence hinges largely on the learner's ability to work collaboratively with the interlocutor through details of talk geared toward expressing and indexing an appropriate social relationship.

5 NNS's Confirmation Request: Repair as Politeness Strategy

As we saw in the preceding discussion, a participant's orientation to the interactional import of confirmation sequences constitutes and reflects one aspect of sociolinguistic competence in the context of Korean discourse that demands careful attention to managing different statuses between participants. It is against this linguistic and sociocultural background that both IR's confirmation request and NNS's collaborative response can be significantly related to the maxim of congruence or polite strategies: through the confirmation sequence, NNSs show that they recognize and ratify IR's right to distribute turns and initiate topics in relation to the prior answer.

While we have examined how participants in Korean LPIs are oriented to confirmation sequences, we can also observe that NNS's interactional competence can be measured in terms of how NNSs themselves are able to use confirmation requests as an interactional resource. Instances of NNSs' confirmation requests are produced in such forms as repeats or collaborative completions. In contrast with the observation that IR's confirmation request, following NNS's answer, invites NNS's confirmation to set the stage for IR's follow-up, NNS's confirmation request, following IR's question, functions to invite IR's confirmation, thus checking that NNS understood IR's question correctly before answering it. In this respect, NNS's confirmation request is situated in an "other-initiated repair sequence" (Schegloff 1979) or a "clarification sequence" (Ochs 1988), in which the speaker, after noticing a problem in prior talk, prompts the hearer to repair the trouble.

Frequently, advanced NNSs' use of a confirmation request takes on a highly interactional character providing a collaboratively negotiated point at which NNSs can initiate some action in a polite manner. In contrast, low-intermediate NNSs' use of confirmation requests, usually taking the form of questioning repeats, is mostly limited to checking information they did not understand, as shown in Excerpt 13.

(13) From the interview with *LN*, a low-intermediate speaker

```
1       IR:   cohaha-nun    cakka  iss    -eyo?
              like   -ATTR  writer exist-POL
              Do you have any favorite writer?

2→i     NNS:  cakka?
              writer
              cakka (writer)?

3→ii    IR:   ney. writer
              yes  writer
              Yes. Writer

4             (0.8)

5       NNS:  eng (.) cikum eps         -eyo.
              filler  now   not:exist-POL
              Uh, I don't have any for now.
```

Noticing that IR used a word that she did not know, NNS makes a confirmation request in line 2 by repeating the word. The confirmation request functions as an other-repair initiator, which prompts IR to repair the problem in line 3, where he provides the meaning of the word in English. Here NNS's confirmation request is mainly concerned with checking the meaning of the trouble source term.

In contrast with low-intermediate NNSs, advanced NNSs often made a confirmation request for interactional purposes as well as for the purpose of checking information. Excerpt 14 illustrates this. In this case NNS, following IR's question, makes a confirmation request through a repeat in line 5 (marked by arrow *i*). After IR's response in line 6 (marked by arrow *ii*), NNS provides an answer to the question.[10]

(14) From the interview with *HK*, an advanced speaker

```
1       IR:   mwe  ettehkey mwe   i    -pen  yelum  panghak-
              what how      what  this-time  summer vacation-
              ttay
              when

2             mwe  ku    pakkey talun    ha-n   il
              what that  outside different do-ATTR event
              iss  -eyo, (.)
```

```
                  exist-POL

3                 mwusun mwe    eti (.) thukpyelhi   kiek   -ey
                  what   what   where   especially   memory-LOC
                  nam    -nun   il,
                  remain-ATTR   event
                  So, tell me, during summer vacation, is there any
                  other thing that you did? For example any special
                  event that you remember?

4                 (0.7)

5→i    NNS:       yelum   panghak  -ttay  //-yo?
                  summer  vacation-time   -POL
                  During summer vacation?
                                                [
6→ii   IR:                                      ney
                                                yes
                                                Yes.

7                 (2.0)

8      NNS:       um,     mwe   caymi-nun eps        -eyo
                  filler  what  fun       -TOP not:exist-POL

9                 kunyang tep-kwu h//hhhuh
                  just    hot-CONN
                  Um, it is not fun. It's just hot.
                                          [
10     IR:                                ku:  tew-ess-ci   -yo
                                          that hot-PST-COMM-POL
                                          It was really hot, right?

11     NNS:       ney.
                  yes
                  Yes
```

In lines 1, 2, and 3, IR asks whether NNS has done anything else during summer. The question is followed by a pause in line 4, and in line 5 NNS produces a confirmation request by repeating part of IR's question, which is responded to swiftly by IR in overlap. Following another pause in line 7, NNS answers negatively by saying that there was nothing fun in Korea and the weather was just hot. As a whole, we find that the confirmation sequence or other-initiated repair sequence (lines 5 and 6) is "inserted" between IR's question and NNS's answer (lines 8 and 9) (Schegloff 1972).

Notice here that NNS's confirmation request targets an item (summer vacation) that is retrievable from IR's preceding question, which suggests that it was produced for interactional purposes rather than for genuine information-checking purposes. It is important to note in this respect that the NNS's confirmation request occurs before he provides a negative answer, a type of dispreferred response such as refusing an invitation or an offer (Sacks 1987, Pomerantz 1984). Given that NNS is responding to IR in a dispreferred manner, we find a sense in which the insertion sequence, which is initiated by NNS's confirmation request, is interactionally motivated to soften his dispreferred response. This practice allows NNS to avoid potential display of nonalignment with IR.

NNS's attempt to align and collaborate with IR is also shown here by the fact that NNS laughs in line 9. His laugh tokens in line 9 further contribute to relieving the mutual interactional burden of providing and receiving a dispreferred response by inviting IR's collaboration, which is indeed displayed in line 10 in overlap. IR's collaborative response in line 10 then changes the course of talk from NNS's summer experiences to hot weather. A similar pattern is observed in Excerpt 15, which was produced by *EK*, another advanced NNS.

(15)   From the interview with *EK*, an advanced speaker

```
1        IR:  pwumonim-hako-nun ettehkey kwankye      -ka
              parents   -COM -TOP how      relationship-SUB

2             ettay-ess-yo, . . . mwusun tension katun
              how   -PST-POL     what   tension like

              ke    ep          -ess-eyo?=
              thing not:exist-PST-POL
              How was your relationship with your parents? . .
              . Haven't you had any tension (with them)?

3→i      NNS: =wuli pwumonim-hako ce       -hako-yo?
              our  parents   -COM I:HONOR-COM -POL
              Between my parents and me?

4→ii     IR:  ney.
              yes
              Yes.
```

```
5      NNS:  ani    -yo,
             no:COP-POL
             No.

6      IR:   ung, .hh tongsayng      -un  iss  -eyo?
             I:see    younger:brother-TOP exist-POL
             I see, .hh Do you have a younger brother?
```

In response to IR's question as to whether NNS has had any tension with her parents, NNS, in line 3, produces a confirmation request through a partial repeat, i.e., by producing a questioning repeat whose material is found in IR's preceding question. As in Excerpt 14, NNS repeats information that is easily retrievable from IR's question in the form of a confirmation request and, after receiving IR's confirmation, produces a negative answer.

We find a similar pattern in Excerpt 16, where an advanced-level NNS, *PN*, produces a confirmation request as other repair initiator by offering her candidate understanding of IR's question (line 29).

```
(16) From the interview with PN, an advanced speaker

21    IR:   .hh taykay ettay-yo ku   Korean-American-tul-hako
             usually how    -POL that Korean-American-PL-COM

22           yayki-hay-po -mye -nun, (.) pwumonim chinkwu-tul
             talk -do -see-COND-TOP      parents  friends-PL

23           pwumonim-in//a ilehkey   hankwuk-cal al-ci
             parents  -or  like:this Korean well know-CONN
                                          [
24    NNS:              ney.
                        Yes

25           mot ha-nun elun -tul-hako yayki-ha-l-ttay
             can:not do-ATTR elder-PL -COM  talk -do-ATTR-time

26           cham pwulphyenha -ko kule-    -nunte//y, attay-yo
             very uncomfortable-CONN like:that-CIRCUM how-POL
                                              [
27    NNS:                              ney::.
                                        Right.

28           ku- kulen    kyenghem  iss -ess-eyo?
             that like:that experience exist-PST-POL
```

```
                .hh Usually, how is it? You know, when I talk to
                Korean-Americans, they say that they feel awkward
                when interacting with friends of their parents, or
                with elders that they don't know well. Do you have
                such an experience? (=Has such a thing happened to
                you?)

29→NNS:    na-hanthey-yo?
           I -to      -POL
           To me?

30→ IR:    ney.
           Yes.

31         (1.2)

32  NNS:   ani-yo, (.) pwulphyenhan-ke    -nun eps        -eyo
           NEG-POL     awkward    -thing-TOP not:exist-POL
           No, there is nothing I find uncomfortable with.

33  IR:    eps       -ess-eyo?=
           not:exist-PST-POL
           Nothing?

34  NNS:   =ney.=
           yes
           Right.

35  IR:    =um.
           I:see
           I see.
```

In response to the question about whether she has had a hard time interacting with Korean elders, NNS, in line 29, produces a confirmation request in the form of a collaborative completion (*na-hanthey-yo?*, "To me?"), which is, as in Excerpts 14 and 15, highly interactional rather than informational in nature—it is clear from the context that the IR's question is targeting this particular NNS, not anyone else.[11] After receiving IR's confirmation, NNS, following a pause, answers in the negative to IR's question, saying that she has not had such an experience.[12]

As a whole, we can see in Excerpts 14, 15, and 16 that advanced NNSs are exploiting the other-initiated repair strategy for some interactional purposes other than double-checking the information at hand. In response to IR's question, they make a confirmation request (and initiate repair) as a way of inviting IR's collaboration before going on to produce a dispreferred response. This strategy serves to soften the dispreferred response, which is inherently destructive of social solidarity and hence potentially face-threatening (Heritage 1984b). Advanced NNSs' uses of confirmation requests, in this sense, can be understood as a politeness strategy of negotiating ground to mitigate the degree of dispreferredness of the projected action and to avoid showing disrespect.

If we now focus on NNS's production of a dispreferred response, we find that this face-considering practice of using a confirmation request as a frame for the following dispreferred response is in contrast with the practice of low-intermediate NNSs, who tend to produce a dispreferred response directly without any attempt to mitigate the degree of assertion. Excerpt 17 is a case in point. In the preceding segment of talk, NNS said that she had come to the U.S. when she was three years old.

(17)   From the interview with *LN*, a low-intermediate speaker

```
1   IR:  kulem yeki-se hakkyo-ey ccwuk           naka  -ko
         then  here-LOC school-LOC continuously attend-CONN

2        kulehkey mwusun (1.0) mwncey-nun       pyello -ess
         like:that any      problem-TOP not:much not:exist-PST

3        -kyess-ney-yo? mwe (.) kunikka hankwuk-eyse
         -MOD -FR -POL  what    I:mean  Korea  -from

4        nut  -nutkey o   -mye -nun (.) hankwuk salam-i
         late late    come-COND-TOP    Korean person-COP

5        -kittaymwuney ene mwuncey-to sayngki-kwu
         -because    language problem-also come:out-CONN

6        kule       -lthey-ntey. kulen    -ke  -n
         like:that-MOD-CIRCUM   like:that-thing-TOP cenhye
         not:at:all

7        eps-ess    -eyo?
         not-exist-POL
```
         Then you have attended school here (in the U.S.)
         throughout all those years, and I presume you
         haven't had many problems, right? (.) I mean, if
         one comes to the U.S. from Korea later in his/her
         life, he/she is likely to have language problems

```
                   and the like. Haven't you have any problem like
                   that?

 8→NNS:    ani-yo.
           NEG-POL
           No.

 9   IR:   .h pwumonim-hako kwankye -nun ettay-ss -eyo?
           parents -COM    relation-TOP how   -PST-POL

10         pwumonim-un  amwulayto        hankwukcek-i-ko
           parents -TOP no:matter:what   Korean       -COP-CONN

11         kule-canh- kulenikka, .h mwusun tension-katun-ke
           -nun
           like:that-ASSER I:mean any tension-like -thing-
           TOP

12         eps        -ess-eyo?
           not:exist-PST-POL
           .h What about your relationship with your parents?
           Given that your parents are more Korean, you know-,
           I mean, have you had any tension with them?

13→NNS:    ani-yo,   eps      -eyo.
           NEG-POL   not:exist-POL
           No. I don't have (any tension with them).

14   IR:   hankwuk-- uh    pwumonim malssum cal tut-nun
           Korea     filler parents  words   well listen-ATTR

15         phyen-I -eyo?
           side  -COP-POL
           Korea- uh do you usually listen to your parents
           (when they tell you to do something)?
```

We can first observe that IR's queries are very long, while NNS's responses are fairly short. As noted above, this form of turn-taking suggests that a great burden is placed on IR to unilaterally develop topics, which often occurs when NNS's proficiency is not high. From line 1 to line 3, IR makes a confirmation request regarding NNS's school life: "Then you have attended school here (in the U.S.) throughout all those years, and I presume you haven't had many problems, right?" Noticing that no answer is forthcoming, IR, up to line 7, produces an extended turn where the question is more specifically formulated. Notice that NNS not only has passed the transition relevance place (Sacks, Schegloff, and Jefferson 1974) after the first question in line 3, but also has not responded to IR in any form throughout his lengthy turn, and in line 8 she produces only a minimal dispreferred response.

More or less the same format continues in the subsequent talk, where IR's question, ranging from line 9 to line 12, is not collaboratively responded to. The NNS again passes a transition relevance place in line 9 following IR's question, and it is only after the question is further elaborated that she produces a minimal dispreferred response in line 13.

From the pattern of interaction shown in Excerpt 17, we find a sense in which NNS responds to IR on a simply factual basis, and does not make any attempt to make face-saving comments in interactionally preparing a ground for mitigating the dispreferredness of her response. Such a lack of a collaborative attempt on the part of NNS, as we mentioned above, works against building a mutually ratified interaction. Compared with Excerpts 14, 15, and 16, we can observe striking differences in interactional skills in designing and formulating dispreferred responses, which relate to different proficiency levels in using details of talk for politeness strategies.

An unmitigated dispreferred response to IR's question has highly negative implications for not only interactional management but also topic management. If we treat the sequence initiated by IR's question as a topic-proffering sequence, NNS's production of dispreferred response constitutes an act of declining IR's topic proffer. In this sense, NNS's ability to use confirmation requests for the purpose of softening dispreferred responses constitutes an important aspect of the interactional and sociolinguistic competence to respect IR's topic proffer and to remedy the projected lack of uptake. It reflects sensitivity both to face work and to topic management.

6 Conclusions

The findings reported in this chapter suggest that differences in proficiency can be related to features of talk, such as how NNSs respond to IR's confirmation request or how NNSs interactionally use the practice of confirmation request as repair. As we observed above, NNSs' use of features of talk as interactional resources involves using them as politeness and topic management strategies. Confirmation sequences thus furnish rich interactional resources that a NNS uses to act on a mutually sustained collaborative ground—he/she ratifies IR's higher status, mitigates threats to face, and responds favorably to a topic proffer.

While this study explicates the structure of LPI talk as oriented to and constituted by IR and NNS, it is limited because there exists to date little research into the structures of Korean conversational discourse. The lack of baseline research analyzing Korean conversation means that there is nothing to which features of LPI talk can be compared. Given this absence of baseline data, the goal of the present study is to raise some basic questions through detailed analysis of how LPI talk is organized, and to bring up research topics that are relevant both to the study of LPI talk and to an analysis of Korean conversation in general. The fact that only one interviewer's interaction with NNS is examined is another limitation.

The participants' mutual orientation toward IR's confirmation request as status-relevant or status-impinging reflects one of the chief attributes of the Korean language, which indexes hierarchically organized social norms associated with topic development when a lower status person interacts with the higher status person (Scollon and Scollon 1995). Though further research is certainly needed to verify this point, informal observation suggests that such interactional features associated with confirmation sequences are observed not only in other types of interviews but also in spontaneous conversations between status unequals, with the higher status participant having the right to initiate and terminate a topic. Given the importance of hierarchically structured sociocultural organization in Korean discourse, it is certainly worth pursuing further how such hierarchical relationships are constituted and sustained by mutually reinforcing orientations in spontaneous Korean conversations as well as in other types of talk.

In this respect, we should look at how NNSs, or lower status persons in general, manage to use various features of talk such as confirmation requests as politeness strategies, focusing more on the interactional side than on the informational side. In fact, some of the general problems observed in relation to NNSs with lower proficiency is that they do not (or cannot) attend to small details of talk that, from an informationally oriented perspective, may look very minor but whose social consequences belie their seeming triviality. In many cases, what NNSs need to acquire is the ability to display a collaborative stance toward the IR. Such competence is especially important in most of the contexts involving Korean discourse systems, social norms, and ideologies, which are intertwined with Korean language indexing hierarchically organized politeness and honorific systems. While producing or inviting a minimal response collaboratively may look unimportant from an informationally oriented perspective, it should be noted that such activities often serve the highly significant interactional purposes of negotiating status, expressing politeness, and managing face work.

We have attempted to identify some of the basic features of the recurrent structure of Korean LPI talk from a conversation analytic perspective, with the focus on the interactional and sequential implications of IR's and NNS's confirmation requests. The ability to relate to these features of LPI may well serve as a ground for devising measures of interactional and sociolinguistic competence. We hope that these initial insights into Korean LPIs will stimulate future research. Further studies and commentary will provide more specific information for the study of language testing as well as for the study of general practice in conversations and other types of talk-in-interaction occurring in institutional settings.

Acknowledgments

We wish to thank Richard Young and Agnes He for their insightful comments and suggestions. They significantly strengthened the major thesis of this chapter by bringing up critical issues relevant to LPIs and conversation analysis hitherto overlooked. Any remaining problems and errors, however, are all ours.

Notes

1. In general, a discrepancy was noted between the speaking and writing skills of all NNSs. The much higher proficiency level in spoken Korean is due to the fact that, as Korean-Americans, they had been verbally interacting with Korean-speaking parents, siblings, and others.

2. Schiffrin (1994:170) calls confirmation requests "information-checking questions."

3. The data were generally transcribed according to the transcription conventions of Conversation Analysis (Sacks, Schegloff, and Jefferson 1974; Atkinson and Heritage 1984). Interruption is marked by "//" placed in the interrupted utterance, as well as by "[," placed between turns. Cut-offs are marked by double dashes "--" to distinguish them from the morpheme boundary marker, while in English glosses they are marked by a single dash "-". Inhalations are marked by ".h". Questioning intonation is marked by a question marker (?), and continuing intonation is marked by a comma (,). In the English glosses, two or more English words linked by a colon (:) indicate that the linked words are realized as a single morpheme in Korean. The following abbreviations are used in the glosses: ATTR—Attributive, CAUS—Causative, CIRCUM—Circumstantial, COM—Comitative, COMM—Committal, COND—Conditioner, CONN—Connective, COP—Copula, CST—Change-of-State Token, FR—Factual Realization, HONOR—Honorific, IE—Informal Ending, INSTR—Instrumental, LOC—Locative, NEG—Negative Particle, OBJ—Object, PL—Plural, POL—Polite Suffix, PST—Past Tense, QUOT—Quotative, RM—Realization Marker, SIMUL—Simultaneous, SUB—Subject, TOP—Topic, UNASSIM—Unassimilated.

4. Note that the realization marker in line 7 (*eng:::*) is distinct from the change-of-state marker in line 5 (*ah*). The former, with its stretched sound and rising-falling intonation, may register informativeness of some utterance further back in prior talk (i.e., it may not register informativeness of the

immediately preceding utterance), while the latter is usually responsive to the immediately preceding utterance. While an analysis of these differences is beyond the scope of this chapter, it can be noted that the use of the realization marker *eng:::*, in contrast with that of the change-of-state token *ah*, often projects that the speaker is about to take the floor.

5. The sequence of confirmation request and confirmation may recursively occur when a further attempt is made by IR to dwell on assessing NNS's preceding answer after NNS's response to his confirmation request.

6. According to Jefferson (1981), news announcement sequences in English conversation may run as follows: (1) news announcement, (2) "oh really?", (3) reconfirmation, and (4) assessment. In this sequence "oh really?" and reconfirmation correspond to confirmation request and confirmation respectively as defined in this chapter. It is noteworthy that Jefferson observes that this type of sequence is "generally terminal or topic-curtailing" (quoted in Heritage 1984), which is congruent with the characteristics of confirmation sequences in Korean LPIs examined below.

7. Here a term like "confirmation prompt" rather than "confirmation request" may be more appropriate because a realization statement does not constitute a request (in the sense that newsmarks and questioning repeats do). In any case, a realization statement, compared with newsmarks or questioning repeats, may not require an answer as a second action because it does not constitute the first action (Sacks, Schegloff, and Jefferson 1974). We still find, however, a strong sense that, despite its non-question form, a realization statement functioning as a confirmation request invites NNS's confirmation just like a newsmark or a questioning repeat (see Excerpt 7). For this reason, and for the sake of convenience, we will use the term "confirmation request" to refer to realization statements as well as newsmarks and questioning repeats.

8. In the sequential context following IR's realization statement, lack of NNS response would have been highly noticeable (see Excerpt 7).

9. When no confirmation is forthcoming from NNS, IR is not likely to prod NNS to produce confirmation by repeating or rephrasing his prior confirmation request. This is because what is officially absent is not an answer with some informational value but an answer that is expected to collaboratively affirm IR's confirmation request.

10. Notice that this question-answer sequence is followed by IR's collaborative confirmation request in line 10, to which NNS responds in line 11.

11. As Kim (1993:11) observes, this type of collaborative completion is frequently constructed by Korean speakers in spontaneous conversations. This is normally attributed to the structure of Korean, where referents are often not explicitly marked. Kim suggests that Korean speakers tend to use this typological feature as an interactional resource by collaboratively filling in the empty slot in the interlocutor's utterance with a noun phrase. This practice is motivated not so much by the need to provide some information as by the interactional need to be collaborative and cooperative with the interlocutor by showing interest in his/her utterance and preparing mutually constructed common ground for subsequent interaction.

12. It is worth noting that sometimes politeness strategies conflict with one another at various levels of organization. For instance, in Excerpt 16, NNS, in her confirmation request in line 29, uses a non-honorific form *na*, "I" (*na-hanthey-yo?*, "To me?") instead of the more appropriate honorific form *ce*. This is seriously face-threatening to IR. While this may be attributed to the NNS's use of solidarity-based peer-to-peer interactional strategies (see also Excerpt 12), her highly proficient interactional competence seems to make up for this shortcoming at the linguistic level.

References

Agar, Michael. 1994. *Language Shock: Understanding the Culture of Conversation*. New York: Morrow.
Atkinson, J. Maxwell, and John Heritage, eds. 1984. *Structures of Social Action: Studies in Conversation Analysis*. Cambridge: Cambridge University Press.
Bardovi-Harlig, Kathleen, and Beverly S. Hartford. 1991. "Saying 'No' in English: Native and Nonnative Rejections." *Pragmatics and Language Learning* 2.41–57.
Boden, Deirdre, and Donald H. Zimmerman, eds. 1991. *Talk and Social Structure*. Berkeley and Los Angeles: University of California Press.
Canale, Michael, and Merrill Swain. 1980. "Theoretical Bases of Communicative Approaches to Second Language Teaching and Testing." *Applied Linguistics* 1.1–47.
Coates, Jennifer. 1993. *Women, Men, and Language*. New York: Longman.
Coupland, Nikolas, Justine Coupland, and Howard Giles. 1991. *Language, Society, and the Elderly*. Cambridge, MA: Blackwell.
Drew, Paul, and John Heritage, eds. 1992. *Talk at Work: Interaction in Institutional Settings*. Cambridge: Cambridge University Press.
Heritage, John. 1984a. "A Change-of-State Token and Aspects of its Sequential Placement." In *Structures of Social Action*, ed. by J. Maxwell Atkinson and John Heritage, 245–299. Cambridge: Cambridge University Press.
Heritage, John. 1984b. *Garfinkel and Ethnomethodology*. Cambridge, MA: Blackwell.
Jefferson, Gail. 1981. "The Abominable 'Ne?': A Working Paper Exploring the Phenomenon of Post-Response Pursuit of Response." Unpublished ms, University of Manchester, Department of Sociology.
Jefferson, Gail. 1984. "On Stepwise Transition from Talk About a Trouble to Inappropriate Next-Positioned Matters." In *Structures of Social Action*, ed. by J. Maxwell Atkinson and John Heritage, 191–222. Cambridge: Cambridge University Press.
Kim, Kyu-hyun. 1993. "Other-Initiated Repairs in Korean Conversation as Interactional Resources." In *Japanese/Korean Linguistics*, vol. 3., ed. by Soonja Choi, 3–18. Palo Alto, CA: Center for the Study of Language and Information, Stanford University.
Kramsch, Claire. 1986. "From Language Proficiency to Interactional Competence." *The Modern Language Journal* 70.366–72.
Labov, William. 1984. "Intensity." In *Meaning, Form, and Use in Context: Linguistic Applications* (= *Georgetown University Round Table on Languages and Linguistics*

1984), ed. by Deborah Schiffrin, 43–70. Washington DC: Georgetown University Press.

Lee, Hyo-Sang. 1991. "Tense, Aspect, and Modality: A Discourse-Pragmatic Analysis of Verbal Affixes in Korean from a Typological Perspective." Unpublished Ph.D. dissertation, University of California, Los Angeles.

Ochs, Elinor. 1988. *Culture and Language Development*. Cambridge: Cambridge University Press.

Pomerantz, Anita. 1984. "Agreeing and Disagreeing with Assessments: Some Features of Preferred/Dispreferred Turn Shapes." In *Structures of Social Action: Studies in Conversation Analysis*, ed. by J. Maxwell Atkinson and John Heritage, 57–101. Cambridge: Cambridge University Press.

Sacks, Harvey. 1987. "On the Preference for Agreement and Contiguity in Sequences in Conversation." In *Talk and Social Organization*, ed. by Graham Button and John R. E. Lee, 54–69. Clevedon, Avon: Multilingual Matters.

Sacks, Harvey, Emanuel A. Schegloff, and Gail Jefferson. 1974. "A Simplest Systematics for the Organization of Turn-Taking in Conversation." *Language* 50.696–735.

Schegloff, Emanuel A. 1972. "Notes on Conversational Practice: Formulating Place." In *Language and Social Context*, ed. by Pierpaolo Giglioli, 95–135. New York: Penguin.

Schegloff, Emanuel A. 1979. "The Relevance of Repair to Syntax-for-Conversation." In *Syntax and Semantics 12: Discourse and Syntax*, ed. by Talmy Givón, 261–286. New York: Academic Press.

Schegloff, Emanuel A., Gail Jefferson, and Harvey Sacks. 1977. "The Preference for Self-Correction in the Organization of Repair in Conversation." *Language* 53.361–82.

Schiffrin, Deborah. 1994. *Approaches to Discourse*. Cambridge, MA: Blackwell.

Scollon, Ron, and Suzanne Wong Scollon. 1995. *Intercultural Communication*. Cambridge, MA: Blackwell.

Tannen, Deborah. 1993. "Asymmetries: Women and Men Talking at Cross-Purposes." In *Linguistics for Teachers*, ed. by Linda M. Cleary and Michael D. Linn, 235–251. New York: McGraw-Hill.

ten Have, Paul. 1991. "Talk and Institution: A Reconsideration of the 'Asymmetry' of Doctor-Patient Interaction." In *Talk and Social Structure*, ed. by Deirdre Boden and Donald H. Zimmerman, 138–63. Cambridge: Polity Press.

Young, Richard. 1995. "Conversational Styles in Language Proficiency Interviews." *Language Learning* 45.3–42.

Young, Richard, and Gene B. Halleck. 1998. "'Let Them Eat Cake!' or How to Avoid Losing Your Head in Cross-Cultural Conversations." In *Talking and Testing: Discourse Approaches to the Assessment of Oral Proficiency*, ed. by Richard Young and Agnes W. He, 355–382. Amsterdam and Philadelphia: Benjamins.

Divergent Frame Interpretations in Language Proficiency Interview Interaction

Steven Ross
School of Policy Studies
Kwansei Gakuin
Sanda, Japan

1 Interviews

As one of the most direct and increasingly used methods of second language assessment, language proficiency interviews deserve close and critical examination. In the last decade a number of applied linguists have considered the content of language proficiency interviews from a number of perspectives with a view to comparing the content of the interview with discourse characteristic of interaction in the world outside the assessment context. The critical scrutiny that language proficiency interviewing has received is motivated by the fact that its popularity has surpassed the available research base that might constrain uncritical use of interviewing methods. An orthodoxy has arisen, apparently without detailed consideration of the phenomena within the interview, and has instigated considerable critical reexamination of the content and construct validity of many language proficiency interview formats (Bachman and Savignon 1988, Young 1995).

Because the interview is widely recognized as the most feasible direct method of assessment, its status as the preferred method of authentic language testing (Stevenson 1985) has increased dramatically in the last twenty years. The fact that candidates must directly reveal their skill in participating in conversation-like interaction provides the basis for the face validity of the interview.

Among possible alternatives such as simulation, tape-mediated interviews, and role-plays, the face-to-face interview is widely taken to be the most realistic sampling of a second language speaker's pragmatic competence (Bachman 1990) if not communicative competence itself. The overwhelming preference for the interview method of communicative language testing has led to a widely held position that what is sampled in the context of the oral interview is in fact the most valid basis for inferring candidates' second language proficiency (Bachman 1988, van Lier 1989). The source of interview face validity may come from the emphasis placed on the candidate's speech without much reference to the authenticity or sampling adequacy of the questions posed in the interview genre of interaction. When proficiency is defined according to ordinally scaled criteria defining real world competence that must be extrapolated from the content and context of direct interview questions rather than from the world external to the interview, there is an immediate potential discrepancy between the content validity of questions used in the interview and the meanings ascribed to answers to those questions (Bachman and Savignon 1986, Lantolf and Frawley 1985). In the orthodox view of interview processes (Educational Testing Service 1982, Lowe 1982), candidate answers are interpreted as direct evidence of proficiency, but are apparently less understood as conditionally relevant to interviewer questions. The emphasis on defining proficiency as the well-formedness of morphosyntax and facility of speech act realization, as opposed to understanding the construct of proficiency as one depending on the interaction of two speakers engaged in continuous mutual negotiation of meaning, has led to objections to the view that second language proficiency is directly assessable through language proficiency interviews (Bachman and Savignon 1988, Lantolf and Frawley 1988, Ross and Berwick 1992, van Lier 1989).

As with many innovations in second language pedagogy, the procedures and criteria for defining proficiency according to the oral interview protocol were initially accepted without extensive examination of the underlying presuppositions regarding the procedures by which the protocols would be met. This tendency for unreflective acceptance coincided with the newfound orientation to communicative competence and the concept of teaching for proficiency (Omaggio 1983, James 1985). Eventually a reassessment of the implications and methodology of language proficiency testing began to emerge in the research literature. In particular the rating scale used in the Foreign Service Institute oral proficiency interview (Clark and Clifford 1988), which provided ordinally scaled descriptions of proficient speakers and was later adapted in the American Council on the Teaching of Foreign Languages (ACTFL) Guidelines (Byrnes and Canale 1987), has been the object of much discussion and critical review (Bachman and Savignon 1988, Lantolf and Frawley 1988). Much of this critical reexamination stems from perceived mismatches between the face validity of interviews and the construct of context-independent second language proficiency.

Lantolf and Frawley (1985, 1988) note that the definitions of proficiency are not linked to any observation of natural communication but are instead lists of characteristics presumed to be in the repertoire of a proficient speaker. The problem, they argue, is that there is no such ideal non-native speaker against whose competence any given level of proficiency can be calibrated, and that "very little is known about how speakers, native or otherwise, relate linguistic structure to language function in the everyday world" (Lantolf and Frawley 1988:183). A similar critical analysis of the definitions of proficiency relating to oral interview outcomes has been articulated by Bachman and Savignon (1986) and Bachman (1988), who assert that the interview method influences the candidate's demonstration of language behavior, which may not have a referent in non-test settings. Since the goal of the interview is to obtain a specimen of second language speech through a standardized procedure, the interview presumes rules of behavior and interaction (Briggs 1986, Dillon 1990, Schegloff 1984) that may not reflect the types of interaction second language speakers are likely to encounter outside the interview situation (van Lier 1988). Standardization of the interview and the rating criteria process may increase the reliability of the procedure at the expense of the generalizability of the ratings—a problem that potentially threatens the content validity of the procedure and the predictive validity of the level awarded to the candidate. The effect of standardization of interview protocols may portend serious consequences in other forms of diagnostic interviews as well, and may in fact influence the interaction and discourse in ways that are detrimental to the candidate (Marlaire and Maynard 1990).

The foregoing critiques of the Foreign Service Institute type of oral proficiency interview have tended to focus on the criteria by which definitions of proficiency were formulated. Interview discourse remains opaque and, until very recently, unexamined. Ross and Berwick (1992) and Young (1995) have considered how differing orientations to the enterprise of interviewing often result in conflicting frames of reference for interpreting questions and responses.

How discourse in the interview is framed and reframed and how participants orient themselves to the interview as a speech event are the foci of the present chapter. The rationale for this analysis may not seem obvious. What is said by the candidate is contingent upon, and consequent to, the candidate's accurate framing of interview questions (MacLachlan and Reid 1994, Tannen 1979). As a candidate's speech occurs within the interview, what is perceived by the interviewer as indicative of proficiency is to a large degree how well the candidate is attuned to contextualization cues (Gumperz 1992a). This requirement brings up a basic condition on interpreting how well-suited the candidate's answers to interview questions are: the candidate's pragmatic competence.

Knowing which strategies successfully achieve communicative goals in everyday interaction is the basis of pragmatic competence (Bachman 1990). A candidate's pragmatic competence to no small degree depends on his or her understanding of the form and purpose of questions embedded in the context of the interview. Pragmatic competence here requires a selection of interpretation and responding strategies appropriate for the context of the interview interaction, which itself projects to situations external to the immediate context. Crucial for a demonstration of pragmatic competence is the candidate's recognition that questions are motivated by the goals of the interview, and may not necessarily require an exact correspondence to events outside the immediate context of interaction.

As Levinson (1992) points out, an interview question as a form of institutional discourse orients the participants to follow a procedure (the interview question-and-answer sequence) that may simulate a discourse domain characteristic of non-institutional interaction. An example of such a procedure in the oral interview is the asking and answer of known-information questions, as shown in Excerpt 1.

(1)
```
→   I:  and once I get to Tokyo I have to call my friend (.)
        ahh so could you tell me how to use a coin telephone?
    C:  coin telephone?
    I:  ummm
    C:  (1.0) well fff where are the fffffriends hhehehh?
    I:  ahh my friend lives in Saitama so from
    C:                            [saiTAMA
    I:  Tokyo Station I'll probably have to call Saitama.
    C:  I sssee so you should (.) you (.) should look for the
        telephone colored with yellow or green
    I:  uh hum
```

Here the interviewer (I) presumably already knows how to use a public telephone. The procedure the candidate (C) must be oriented to is that such questions in the context of the interview are not literally information questions. The information of interest in this context is whether or not the candidate can answer appropriately—and not to inform the asker specifically to the factual details of public telephone operation. As we will examine later in this paper, a candidate's success in the interview procedure as a form of institutional discourse depends on an inferential framework different from noninstitutional talk (Drew and Heritage 1992). Within the interview framework are individual questions that invoke potentially conflicting frames of reference. Here the frame in Goffman's (1974) sense impacts on how interview questions are understood by candidates as questions to be answered literally, or as questions intended to be an invitation to talk in the second language about a relevant topic.

In order to participate in the structured interaction of an interview, both participants must orient themselves to a set of rules that may differ from those governing conversational interaction. For the candidate, these often require a demonstration of pragmatic competence atypical of non-interview interaction. The candidate must understand the context of the question, and weigh the implications of possible answering strategies. Answers need to be encoded in a form that betokens second language speaking skill first and foremost—even if such answers may not necessarily be accurate in factual detail.

Central to successful performance in the interview is the candidate's accurate determination of the interview frame. Accurate framing crucially depends on an awareness of the purpose of the interaction (i.e., language assessment) and secondarily depends on the comprehension of questions in light of that purpose. The framing hierarchy is represented schematically in Figure 1. The outer (darkened) frame signifies the interview as the context of interaction and as a speech event. The inner frame represents the reference of questions posed within the boundaries of the interview frame. Candidate answers (A) within the inner frame are relevant to questions understood as part of the interview. These serve to fulfill the candidate's obligation to respond, and are interpreted as answers directly relevant to the first pair part question. The inner frame presents potential pragmatic difficulty for many second language interview candidates. If questions are not accurately comprehended, or are not ratified by candidates, accounts (A') that explain *why* an answer will not be forthcoming are still likely to be accepted as surrogate answers because they remain within the interview frame boundary. This phenomenon suggests that a criterion for marking candidates' adherence to a cooperative principle is a response relevant to the context of the interaction, even if it does not strictly correspond to the question-and-answer sequence. This point is corroborated by the common interviewer practice of not reformulating questions to which a non sequitur (A'') was provided. Here again cooperation is marked by a response, even if the response is not specifically an answer to the intended question.

Although rarer than accounts, non sequiturs are frequently accepted as responses (Ross 1992). Their acceptance is evidenced by non-formulation of the original question and progression to other interview topics. The analysis offered here is that

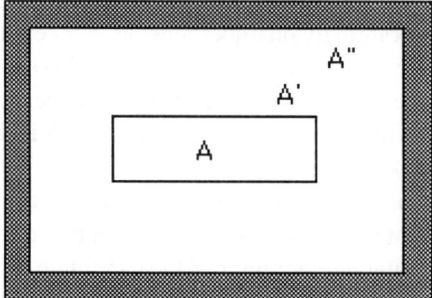

Figure 1. Interview Context and Question Frames

even non-answers are meaningful because they can be interpreted in the interview context frame. Answers, accounts, and responses are seen here as variants of second pair parts indicating a hierarchical preference structure (Levinson 1983). As long as responses are *within* the interview frame they are interpretable for the purposes of the interaction and consonant with the goals of the interviewer.

Under the rules of interview interaction, the interviewer retains the sole right to ask questions and to nominate topics for which such questions will be relevant. The candidate must correctly comprehend the propositional content of such questions and interpret them within the context of the interview interaction. The extent to which candidates can employ appropriate framing interpretations to no small degree constrains their ability to participate in interview interaction successfully and project an image of communicative competence. When candidates misinterpret the content of interviewer questions outside the interview frame, there is usually an overt signal indicating a perception of deficiency in the interaction, which instigates a compensatory reinterpretation of the frame on behalf of the candidate. Repetition or recasting of the intended question is a typical interviewer compensatory move in such instances. When candidates comprehend interviewer questions but consistently opt for an answering strategy that does not provide a sufficient basis for continued interaction about the topic within the intended frame, a perception of noncooperation may ensue. Such a perception may translate into the formation of negative attributes about the candidate's second language proficiency.

2 Minimalism in Interviews with Japanese

In interview interaction, the outer boundary of the frame for interaction is the participants' orientation to the interview itself. Both candidate and interviewer

Divergent Frame Interpretations

ideally understand that the questions and answers in the interview are motivated by the purposes of the assessment process, and only secondarily for the information value candidates' answers have. The specific questions posed by the interviewer are within the bounds of the interview frame. The candidates must initially be attuned to the propositional content within the topical frame of each question. It is at this point in cross-cultural interactions that interpretations of the frame content may vary and lead to interactional difficulties and miscommunication. Some questions, that is, may invoke differential framing of schemata in candidates—incomplete understanding (Gass and Varonis 1991)—which may lead to an apparent self-defensive and noncooperative stance in the interview. Such stances by Japanese candidates involve the withholding of superficially trivial factual information from non-intimate interlocutors (Barnlund 1975), or resorting to silence as a form of metacommunication (Lebra 1987). When interviewers, who may be oriented to a different set of cultural norms, pose questions requiring self-disclosure, the Japanese candidate may often opt for a minimalist approach. The minimalist approach to interview participation creates plentiful instances in which the candidate is perceived as apparently capable of answering questions across a wide spectrum of topics, but chooses to underelaborate answers to questions in a variable manner. Underelaboration of answers to interview questions typically provokes accommodative restructuring of the interaction by the interviewer. Such accommodation is correlated with proficiency rating outcomes (Ross and Berwick 1992). An examination of the contexts of underelaboration is thus essential for separating differing frame orientations from pragmatic breakdowns and cross-cultural miscommunication.

The first category of underelaboration to be examined is related to the phenomenon of minimalism in interview answers. This phenomenon may reveal an interactional strategy on the part of many Japanese candidates in which they transfer the pragmatics of interview interaction from their own culture (House 1993). Candidates' perceptions of the interview frame may lead them to answer interviewer questions concisely without appearing superfluous or verbose—two traits that are not particularly valued in the Japanese speech community (Lebra 1987). In the minimalist style, Grice's maxim of quantity (making a response as informative as needed for the purpose of the exchange), is breached—leading to uninformative answers that typically lead to repeated questioning on the same topic. As seen in Excerpt 2, the interviewer poses a question about the candidate's extensive travel overseas. Although the question is articulated with the syntax of an interrogative that could be answered with a yes or no response, the interviewer's question invites the candidate to talk *informatively* on the topic of travel to South America, not to verify that he has been there—a fact that the interviewer has already established through his asking of the question. In opting for the minimalist style, the candidate forces the interviewer to reiterate the essential question (→) and pry out an answer.

(2)
```
    I:  I see here you've ahh (.) you've been overseas~ quite
        a f::ew countries:: (.) ahh (.) you've been to South
        America?
    C:  yes (1.0)
→   I:  on sightseeing?
    C:  (.) yes
→   I:  when was that?
    C:  (2.0)
    I:  when did you go to South America (.) how many years
        ago.
```

The purpose of questions in the context of the language proficiency interview is rarely to establish the truth of particular facts about a candidate's life experiences. Rather, interview questions are invitations for the candidate to talk about the topics introduced through the questioning process. The task of decoding interviewer questions as *invitations* to speak to a topic constitutes such a challenging test of second language pragmatic competence that many Japanese candidates at the advanced level of proficiency apparently have considerable difficulty with it. This phenomenon potentially confounds the interpretation of second language proficiency, since candidates need the pragmatic wherewithal to determine that interview questions are for the purposes of the interview—and may not constitute questions necessarily requiring factual information about the candidate.

Literal interpretation of interview questions may be the default strategy for candidates. In Excerpt 3, the interviewer reveals in the second question turn (→) that the original question as posed was not merely to confirm the fact that there is a closing time for the company dormitory but was rather an invitation for the candidate to speak on the topic of life in the company dormitory and the manner in which employees manage to accommodate their schedules to this imposition. The evidence that the interviewer *expected* an answer other than the affirmative answer provided is the pause after the candidate's answer, followed by an explicit reformulation of the intended question.

(3)

```
    I: there's a time limit at ah dormitories right?
    C: yes
→   I: (1.0) uhhhm whats:::the time limit.
    C: uhhn:: it's eleven o'clock umm-but we can (.) we can
       go back (.)
    I: uhhm
    C: we can go back to the dormitory by (.) twelve in the
       midnight
```

Excerpt 3 provides an instance in which the anticipated answer to the question was explicitly seeded in the second question. As in the first excerpt, the candidate was not attuned to the interview interaction as a context in which opportunities for extensive show of speaking skills was to be demonstrated. Rather, the candidate's erroneous interpretation is that the question was motivated by a genuine need for information—which was arguably *not* the intention of the interviewer.

The two excerpts examined thus far suggest that interviewers are obliged to reorient their interlocutors to the question frames they pose when answers are underelaborate. That there are responses to the questions is apparently interpreted to signify that candidates are capable of answering. The answers as they are articulated, however, are not taken by interviewers as sufficient interview responses. To the extent that the responses underrepresent what the candidate can potentially say about the current topic of talk, interviewers rarely abandon the topic in the face of underelaboration. Here interviewer strategies vary. Some interviewers plod on with staccato question-and-answer sequences in scaffolded interactional sequences. Others spend long prefatory turns in framing or reframing the topic of talk so as to increase the likelihood of topical uptake in the candidate responses.

Excerpt 4 presents another example of answering in the minimalist mode. At the arrow bar (→), the candidate responds literally to the topic initiated by the interviewer, but does not hear it as an invitation to take the floor and comment on her many trips overseas. The interviewer hereafter resorts to a scaffolding strategy in order to coax out commentary on the different places the candidate has visited. In this excerpt, it appears that the interviewer has acquiesced to the answering strategy of the candidate. The interviewer opts for rapid replacement of underelaborated topics by reaching further into the list of referents within the original topic until there is one on which the candidate will take the floor. By the end of the question-and-answer sequencing in this excerpt, the interviewer has reduced the length of the wait time from the two seconds after the second elaboration, which includes a metacomment possibly revealing the interviewer's perception of underelaboration in this interlocutor's previous responses, to overlapping speech in the last answer-question pairing.

(4)

```
      C: that's the fun part
      I: [ummmh
      C: of going (.) abroad
      I: [so you've been to Turkey, Greece, Italy, France,
         Spain, and the United Kingdom and- and Finland
  →   C: yes hehh (1.0)
      I: what did you ah think of Finland.
      C: ah hh it is it was very cccoold hehheheh
      I: hheheheh what time of year were you there.
      C: it was at March
      I: ah °so it could be real cold°
  →   C: yeah (2.0)
      I: that's your only impression of Finland it's cold.
  →   C: yeah hhehh coold
      I: so Turkey was hot.
  →   C: well
      I: [what about Greece.
```

A different approach to managing the question frame orientation of the candidate may include longer interviewer prefatory turns. The strategy of orienting the candidate to observing the boundaries of frame through extensive prefatory turns usually comes at a cost in terms of interviewer speaking time and effort. When long preliminaries to interview questions are met with consistent minimalist answers from candidates, the impression of a candidate's unwillingness or inability to communicate may likely develop in the mind of the interviewer or assessor. In the case of unwillingness to communicate (avoidance), the assessment of proficiency is potentially confounded. Rating scale criteria (e.g., Educational Testing Service 1982) are predicated on evidence provided by the speech of the candidate. If candidates show variable evidence of speaking skill, interpretation of the available speech is perhaps the most difficult aspect of the rating process because such evidence is inconsistent. Nonparticipation in the interview through apparent inability to respond apropos the interview questions is usually taken as unambiguous evidence of a lack of communicative ability in the second language. A potential assessment dilemma is in determining whether the shortcoming in candidate performance is due to unwillingness to respond or a fundamental inability to formulate adequate answers. We can surmise that reformulations and repetitions of questions first met with minimalist answers reveal that interviewers expected substantive answers.

Excerpt 5 provides an example of a candidate responding with an underelaborate response to a saliently introduced new topic of talk. A pause in the answer turn could be taken as a sign of noncomprehension in many question answer turns. Here, however, the candidate's response projects an understanding of the complex propositional content underlying the question. The interpretation of the question is at variance with the interviewer's motive for asking it. The explicit asking for a rationale for the agreement can be taken as a sign that the interviewer's intention was not to solicit agreement but to exercise a different speech act. The candidate's literal interpretation of the question may in this instance reveal a shortcoming in his pragmatic competence, or it might simply reveal his adherence to an interactional strategy in which answers are kept minimal until the floor is formally structured for extended answer turns.

(5)

```
    I:  (10.0) It has been said that ah because Japan is a
        rich country (.) it should start helping financially
        ah underdeveloped countries in Asia (.) do ah do you
        agree with this?
→   C:  (1.5) Yes, I am agree
    I:  why-why do you agree-what reasons do you have.
```

The phenomenon of underelaboration in candidate answer turns is ambiguous in the context of the language assessment interview. Candidates may underelaborate for different reasons. The interpretation given in the analyses of the four excerpts assumes that underelaboration is the result of negative pragmatic transfer from Japanese (Maeshiba, Yoshinaga, Kasper, and Ross 1995; Takahashi and Beebe 1987). The context of the interview is understood by candidates as one that bestows the speaking rights to the interviewer, while the candidates' role is to provide exact responses to questions—no more, no less. This interpretation is consonant with Young's (1995) observation that Europeans and Asians are members of different speech communities and are oriented to different contextualization cues in a language proficiency interview. Unfamiliarity with the interview as a speech event may also confuse some candidates as to what is expected from a cooperative interlocutor. An alternative to these interpretations is that many candidates do not in fact possess sufficient proficiency in the second language to understand that interview questions are not to be interpreted as information questions. Literal answers to such questions are indicative of a systemic shortcoming in second language communicative ability.

3 Self-Disclosure

A source of miscommunication in cross-cultural interaction is the boundary of question and topic frames and misperceptions of interlocutors' orientation to them (Gumperz 1992b). When interviewers pose a seemingly innocuous question pertaining to the inside of the Japanese candidate's personal space—the domains of the home, work, religious, or romantic life, for instance—underelaboration in answers may be doubly ambiguous (Hinds 1983; Loveday 1982; Triandis, Bontempo, Villareal, Asai, and Lucca 1988). Underelaborate answers may mark the boundaries of what are considered by the candidate as private matters. In the context of the proficiency interview, when interviewers do not perceive the frame boundaries in the same way as candidates, and trespass into personal space with probing questions, underelaborate answers may be interpreted as signs of an inability to answer as opposed to a culture-specific strategy to indicate an unwillingness to answer.

Excerpt 6 below provides an example of the difference in the interview participants' orientation to a topic. The interviewer may well have invaded the candidate's familiar space by querying reactions of the candidate's family after he had been selected by his current employer. Here differing understandings of face are possibly at work. The candidate's response underelaborates an answer about his family's reaction to his recent employment at the company. By revealing his attitude, he potentially reveals their expectations about his position in society as manifested in his membership in a particular Japanese company. Their happiness could indicate their attitude toward the company—as a desirable career choice for their sons, or not, and as a indication of the family's status in Japanese vertical society. The candidate's reply "maybe" is understood by the interviewer as a non-answer to the question. The fact that it was punctuated by pauses and articulated with laughter, possibly a sign of embarrassment, further corroborates the interpretation that the question frame was face-threatening for the candidate.

(6)

```
I: so- so tell me a little about your family
C: family (.) ahum I have a (.) ah (.5) father and br-eh
   mother and grandmother (.) I have no brother
```

```
    I:  °I see° (.) and how do your parents feel about you
        joining (this company) are they happy?
→   C:  (.5) mayhhbehhh: (2.0)
·   I:  what did they say: when you told them: you: were:
        going to work at (this company)
```

The culturally dependent concept of personal space varies as much in orientation to talk as it does in proxemics. When candidates are confronted with topics that in their own society mark them according to culture-based expectations about normal behavior and desirability, their opaque, underelaborate answers to questions become interpretable. In Excerpt 7, the topic is marriage. For both males and females in Japan, the pressure to conform to expectations in traditional society is particularly pervasive. In this excerpt the question, punctuated by a three-second pause after the candidate's previous answer, is likely heard as revealing the male interviewer's expectation that the candidate (a male in his mid-thirties) should be planning to get married. As in the previous excerpt, the laughter and subvocalization in the answer turn suggest that the candidate's response is encoded as a dispreferred second pair part—as if a positive response to the question would somehow be more correct than that offered.

(7)
```
    I:  and ah (.) are you married?
    C:  no I am single.
    I:  (3.0) do you plan to get married?
→   C:  °hhha-nohh°
    I:  (1.0) I see you're not a- ↑you have no plans right now
    C:  yeah
```

Here the interviewer's hearing of the candidate's reply evidently is attuned to the sensitivity to the topic of marriage. The short pause suggests an expectation that further talk from the candidate would be forthcoming. The interviewer may interpret this instance of underelaboration as an inability to speak, since he proceeds to provide the candidate with a surrogate answer to his own question. Surrogate or loaned answers in the context of language proficiency interviews usually betoken an interpretation by the interviewer that candidates are *incapable* of supplying answers that would close a question-answer sequence (Berwick and Ross 1993). From the perspective offered in this paper, however, the underelaboration remains ambiguous.

It can be argued that part of second language competence involves transcending cultural expectations transferred from the native language. But recent research in the acquisition of second language pragmatics suggests that even advanced-level second language users to some degree interpret and operate within the frame orientations characteristic of their first language pragmatic system (Takahashi and Beebe 1987, Gass and Varonis 1991, Kasper 1992). The implications of recent work in interlanguage pragmatics (Kasper and Blum-Kulka 1993) suggest that second language morphosyntactic knowledge may develop to a considerable degree in advance of pragmatic knowledge. Knowing how to say things in a second language often predates knowing when (or when not) to say them. Knowing how to interpret the frames for many indirect speech acts is an aspect of language that may be acquired only well into adulthood (Levinson 1983).

This brings us to a different challenge in understanding underelaborations in interview discourse. When questions are potentially face-threatening, as we have seen in the example above, candidates signal discomfort in a culturally specific manner. Without such within-frame interpretive clues, however, understanding underelaborations is more complex. In Excerpt 8, for example, the candidate apparently understands the literal content of the interviewer's question but does not detect the nuance that his frequent transfers from one assignment to another in the company is an oddity inviting an explanation. The candidate in the first answer turn acknowledges emphatically that it is indeed strange to have been transferred, prompting the interviewer to reformulate the question into an answerable one.

(8)
```
    I: Isn't that ah (.) isn't that strange to have been(.)
       transferred so many places in such a short time.
 →  C: yes
    I: Is there any special reason why you were moved.
 →  C: [°yes°] [sp- very special
    I: what's the reason.
```

The candidate's understanding of the first uttering of the question was not apparently at fault, since his overlapping speech with the rephrased question confirms the interviewer's interpretation that his frequent transfers were both strange and special. The result of his two underelaborated responses is the interviewer's asking the same question three times to get one answer that would have been relevant, appropriate, and expected after only the first asking.

Excerpt 8 illustrates a conflict inherent in the interview as a form of interrogation in which the candidate is, within the definition of the interview frame itself, unable to dismiss topics broached by the more powerful interviewer/examiner. By acknowledging an understanding of the topic, the candidate may involuntarily ratify it and thus license further unwanted and potentially face-threatening talk. Here the interviewer presumably wanted an explanation of the frequent rotations. The underelaborations were not taken as signals for the interviewer to close down the topic; they failed to provide an explanation of the candidate's special status; and they failed to provide evidence that the candidate could interpret the theme of the question framed in the passive voice. Such a sequence could be interpreted as detrimental to the candidate's creating a positive impression of advanced proficiency, since the interviewer expended three turns to ask essentially the same question. The candidate either did not have the wherewithal to comprehend that a *reason* for the frequent transfers would be the basis of a viable answer, or resorted to a strategy that was not acknowledged by the interviewer as a token of an unwillingness to answer.

A final example should suffice to provide evidence of the interaction of underelaborations in the conflict of differing frame orientations. In Excerpt 9, a probing question about a political topic is posed by the interviewer. The interviewer is querying the candidate about his interpretation of a (then) recent political scandal in which a large company (Recruit) had secretly sold preferred stocks to senior officials of the Liberal Democratic Party. The first asking is met with a half-second micropause, which is interpreted by the interviewer as evidence that the lexical content of the question was beyond the candidate's ability to comprehend it. In restating the question, the interviewer paraphrases the content of the question. The candidate's response to this political topic is baldly under-specific. The subvocalization again suggests that the candidate anticipates that a mere affirmative is an insufficient response for the intended purpose of the question. The interviewer provides, in reaction to the affirmative response, a long pause of three seconds to signal that the floor is still open and that a more elaborate account is expected. With a slower rate of articulation, the interviewer thereafter restructures the question further to facilitate an answer from the candidate.

(9)
```
I:  do you think (.) that the scandal has hurt the
    credibility of LDP.
C:  (.5)
```

```
I:  ah do you think tha- (1.0) that the recruit case has
    has damaged the - the image of the ah LDP.
→ C: °yes°
I:  (3.0) do you think (.) that perhaps (.) maybe it'll be
    difficult in the future for the LDP to maintain its
    control of the government.
C:  (2.0) the other party the other government is not so
    strong in Japan as LDP
```

Of particular interest here was the interviewer's apparent expectation that the candidate *could* answer such a complex question in a second language. Indeed, the interviewer's persistence leads to the candidate providing a suitably elaborate response, supplying what the interviewer was after in the first place—a rich sample of second language speaking ability. If such complex probes are contingent on interviewers' anticipation of elaborate responses, the underelaborate answers occurring in the manner and position they do can be taken to indicate differences in frame orientation. Such differences may lead to potential misreadings of candidate proficiency when interviewers are less persistent and interpret underelaborations as indicative of inability to formulate answers apropos the questions.

A potential threat to this interpretation concerns the interviewer's anticipation that extended responses will be forthcoming, especially to probing questions. If the language proficiency interview were scripted—with interviewers asking the same questions to all candidates—the argument that questions project extended answers could be seriously challenged. The FSI-type language proficiency interview is *not* scripted, which means that interviewers craft their questions to candidates based on the impression of proficiency formulated at that time in the interview. The asking of probing questions projects responses that will confirm the candidate's upper limits of second language speaking proficiency.

4 Conclusions

Seemingly misplaced underelaborations in answer turns may portend troubles other than the candidate's apparent inability to articulate a suitable response because of a fault in second language comprehension or production skill. A possible source of an underelaborate answer may be pragmatic transfer from the candidate's sociocultural background. In the excerpts examined above, all candidates were Japanese speakers. Both the minimalist strategy in responding to questions crafted to give the candidate an open speaking turn and the underelaborate responses attributable to face-threat for the candidate may well be linked to an aspect of second language proficiency that goes beyond the literal interpretation of the form and propositional content of interview questions.

The positioning of underelaborate responses in answer turns may indicate interviewer insensitivity to cultural differences between the candidates' sociocultural backgrounds and those of the interviewers. The goal of these language proficiency interviews is ostensibly to assess candidates' communicative competence in English as it might be invoked in interaction with native speakers of English. The construct of communicative competence for second language speakers may not be defensibly premised on an assumption of native-speaker-like linguistic usage, nor on the presumption of equivalent speech community norms. This leads to an inferential dilemma. The transfer of pragmatic rules into second language performances used as assessments of competence creates a potential misconstrual of the evidence of candidate ability. Candidates may be able, but unwilling, to demonstrate second language ability because of conflicts of face and self-disclosure. Or the interview process may reveal that candidates mistakenly respond out of frame by interpreting interview questions as *real* questions.

Recent conceptualizations of second language proficiency have found a place for the notion of pragmatic competence as an aspect of a second language user's ability to interpret and create meaning within a given context (Canale and Swain 1980, Bachman 1990). The importance of pragmatic competence as a component of the content validity of an assessment of interactional skills is taken as self-evident. The main constraint for the assessment of pragmatic competence, however, has been in how it can be assessed within the confines of the contrived interactions so typically used in language assessment procedures. Part of the problem in operationalizing the construct of pragmatic competence has been the manner in which adequate procedures could be devised to capture pragmatic performances in a reliable and content valid manner.

In the present data, the picture of pragmatic competence we can infer is exclusively within the context of the interview interaction. Although candidates may well comprehend the surface propositional content of questions, they may not have sufficient pragmatic competence to decode questions as implicating meanings different from the propositions such questions might possess in the candidates' own first language and culture. The communicative task here may be for the candidate to realize that the norms for talk about certain topics differ from Japanese norms, and that minimalist strategies or underelaborate responses may not adequately serve to inform the interviewer that questions of a private nature won't beget answers.

Another aspect of candidates' second language competence may be their ability to discern interviewers' motivation for asking questions that apparently require a degree of self-disclosure in the answers. That is, pragmatic competence, if it is demonstrated in the context of the interview, should lead the candidates to the anticipation that such questions are asked for the purposes of generating talk suitable for the aims of assessment—and not for genuine self-revelation. Successfully interpreting questions within the interview frame may constitute a major criterion for pragmatic competence as it is manifested in oral interview interaction.

The excerpts in this chapter have demonstrated ways in which questions crafted to be optimally answerable by candidates often go mysteriously underelaborated. It has been argued that underelaborations are a form of miscommunication stemming from differing orientations to the frame of the interview question. For the interviewer, the game of question and answer is a facsimile of real world interaction in which questions are not literally motivated by the transactional goals that their propositional contents indicate. Interview questions are not always posed, that is, to get the information the questions apparently request. Rather, the information is in *how* the answers are formulated and articulated. It is argued that an aspect of pragmatic competence on the part of second language speakers may be how well they are attuned to the interview frame and how well they understand that the game of answering may have to transcend the constraints of transfer of sociocultural pragmatic norms. Such a requirement constitutes a very tall order for the majority of second language interview candidates. It means, in effect, that in the process of being interviewed, candidates must invoke metapragmatic knowledge in order to realize when the questions they hear are not literally questions necessarily inviting authentic self-disclosure and potential loss of face, but are rather a sophisticated form of language display. The fact that underelaborate answers are frequent even in high-level interviews would suggest that pragmatic transfer survives despite the acquisition of other complex second language skills.

Acknowledgments

I would like to thank Richard Young, Agnes Weiyun He, and Gabi Kasper for comments on an early draft of this chapter.

References

Bachman, Lyle F. 1988. "Problems in Examining the Validity of the ACTFL Oral Proficiency Interview." *Studies in Second Language Acquisition* 10.149–164.

Bachman, Lyle F. 1990. *Fundamental Considerations in Language Testing*. Oxford: Oxford University Press.

Bachman, Lyle F., and Sandra J.Savignon. 1986. "The Evaluation of Communicative Language Proficiency: A Critique of the ACTFL Oral Interview." *Modern Language Journal* 70.380–390.

Barnlund, Dean C. 1975. *Public and Private Self in Japan and the U.S.* Tokyo: Simul Press.

Berwick, Richard, and Steven Ross. 1993. "Cross-Cultural Pragmatics in Oral Proficiency Interview Strategies." Paper presented at the 15th Language Testing Research Colloquium, Queens College, Cambridge, England.

Briggs, Charles L. 1986. *Learning How to Ask: A Sociolinguistic Appraisal of the Role of the Interview in Social Science Research.* Cambridge: Cambridge University Press.

Byrnes, Heidi, and Michael Canale. 1987. *Defining and Developing Proficiency: Guidelines, Implementations, and Concepts.* Lincolnwood, IL: National Textbook.

Canale, Michael, and Merrill Swain. 1980. "The Theoretical Bases of Communicative Approaches to Second Language Teaching and Testing." *Applied Linguistics* 1.1–47.

Clark, John L. D., and Ray T. Clifford. 1988. "The FSI/ACTFL Proficiency Scales and Testing Techniques: Development, Current Status, and Needed Research." *Studies in Second Language Acquisition* 10.129–147.

Dillon, J. T. 1990. *The Practice of Questioning.* London: Routledge.

Drew, Paul, and John Heritage. 1992. "Analyzing Talk at Work: An Introduction." In *Talk at Work: Interaction in Institutional Settings*, ed. by Paul Drew and John Heritage, 3–65. Cambridge: Cambridge University Press.

Educational Testing Service. 1982. *Oral Proficiency Testing Manual.* Princeton, NJ: Author.

Gass, Susan M., and Evangeline M. Varonis. 1991. "Miscommunication in Nonnative Speaker Discourse." In *Miscommunication and Problematic Talk*, ed. by Nikolas Coupland, Howard Giles, and John M. Wiemann, 121–145. Newbury Park, CA: Sage.

Goffman, Erving. 1974. *Frame Analysis: An Essay on the Organization of Experience.* Cambridge, MA: Harvard University Press.

Gumperz, John J. 1992a. "Contextualization Cues and Understanding." In *Rethinking Context*, ed. by Alessandro Duranti and Charles Goodwin, 229–252. Cambridge: Cambridge University Press.

Gumperz, John J. 1992b. "Interviewing in Intercultural Situations." In *Talk at Work: Interaction in Institutional Settings*, ed. by Paul Drew and John Heritage, 302–327. Cambridge: Cambridge University Press.

Hinds, John. 1983. "Intrusion in Japanese Conversation." *Papers in Linguistics* 16.1–33.

House, Juliane. 1993. "Toward a Model for the Analysis of Inappropriate Responses in Native/Nonnative Interactions." In *Interlanguage Pragmatics*, ed. by Gabriele Kasper and Shoshana Blum-Kulka, 161–183. New York: Oxford University Press.

James, Charles J., ed. 1985. *Foreign Language Proficiency in the Classroom and Beyond.* Lincolnwood, IL: National Textbook.

Kasper, Gabriele. 1992. "Pragmatic Transfer." *Second Language Research* 8.203–231.

Kasper, Gabriele, and Shoshana Blum-Kulka. 1993. "Interlanguage Pragmatics: An Introduction." In *Interlanguage Pragmatics*, ed. by Gabriele Kasper and Shoshana Blum-Kulka, 3–17. New York: Oxford University Press.

Lantolf, James P., and William Frawley. 1985. "Oral Proficiency Testing: A Critical Analysis." *Modern Language Journal* 69.337–345.

Lantolf, James P., and William Frawley. 1988. Proficiency: Understanding the Construct. *Studies in Second Language Acquisition* 10.181–195.

Lebra, Takie Sugiyama. 1987. "The Cultural Significance of Silence in Japanese Communication." *Multilingua* 6.343–357.

Levinson, Stephen. 1983. *Pragmatics*. Cambridge: Cambridge University Press.

Levinson, Stephen. 1992. "Activity Types and Language." In *Talk at Work: Interaction in Institutional Settings*, ed. by Paul Drew and John Heritage, 66–100. Cambridge: Cambridge University Press.

Loveday, Leo J. 1981. "Communicative Interference: A Framework for Contrastively Analysing L_2 Communicative Competence Exemplified with Linguistic Behavior of Japanese Performing in English." *International Review of Applied Linguistics* 20.1–16.

Lowe, Pardee, Jr. 1982. *ILR Handbook on Oral Interview Testing*. Washington, DC: Defense Language Institute.

MacLachlan, Gale L., and Ian Reid. 1994. *Framing and Interpretation*. Carlton, Victoria: Melbourne University Press.

Maeshiba, Naoko, Naoko Yoshinaga, Gabriele Kasper, and Steven Ross. 1996. "Transfer and Proficiency in Interlanguage Apologizing." In *Speech Acts Across Cultures: Challenges to Communication in a Second Language*, ed. by Susan M. Gass and Joyce Neu, 155–187. Berlin: Mouton de Gruyter.

Marlaire, Courtney L., and Douglas W. Maynard. 1990. "Standardized Testing as an Interactional Phenomenon." *Sociology of Education* 63.83–101.

Omaggio, Alice. 1983. *Proficiency-Oriented Language Testing*. Washington, DC: Center for Applied Linguistics.

Ross, Steven. 1992. "Accommodative Questions in Oral Proficiency Interview Discourse." *Language Testing* 9.173–186.

Ross, Steven, and Richard Berwick. 1992. "The Discourse of Accommodation in Oral Proficiency Interviews." *Studies in Second Language Acquisition* 14.159–176.

Schegloff, Emanuel A. 1984. "On Some Questions and Ambiguities in Conversation." In *Structures of Social Action*, ed. by J. M. Atkinson and J. Heritage, 28–54. Cambridge: Cambridge University Press.

Stevenson, Douglas K. 1985. "Authenticity, Validity, and a Tea Party." *Language Testing* 2.41–47.

Takahashi, Tomoko, and Leslie Beebe. 1987. "The Development of Pragmatic Competence by Japanese Learners of English." *JALT Journal* 8.131–155.

Tannen, Deborah. 1979. "What's in a Frame? Surface Evidence for Underlying Expectations." In *New Directions in Discourse Processes*, ed. by Roy O. Freedle, 137–181. Norwood NJ: Ablex.

Triandis, Harry C., Robert Bontempo, Marcelo J. Villareal, Masaaki Asai, and Nydia Lucca. 1988. "Individualism and Collectivism: Cross-Cultural Perspectives on Self-Ingroup Relationships." *Journal of Personality and Social Psychology* 54.323–338.

van Lier, Leo. 1989. "Reeling, Writhing, Drawling, Stretching, and Fainting in Coils: Oral Proficiency Interviews as Conversation." *TESOL Quarterly* 23.489–508.

Young, Richard. 1995. "Conversational Styles in Language Proficiency Interviews." *Language Learning* 45.3–42.

"Let Them Eat Cake!" or How to Avoid Losing Your Head in Cross-Cultural Conversations

Richard Young
University of Wisconsin-Madison

Gene B. Halleck
Oklahoma State University

1 Introduction

In this chapter we will discuss some dispreferred patterns of speaking that we and several other researchers are beginning to find in the discourse of language proficiency interviews (LPIs). We will attribute these patterns to three causes: transfer of conversational style from speakers' first language, personality differences among learners, and differences of second language proficiency.[1] Because neither participant in an LPI is generally aware of the cultural or personal reasons for the way learners speak, we argue that the interviewer forms an impression of the learner that leads to a poor evaluation of the learner's ability to speak the second language. Such an impression can have damaging consequences for the learner in the context of the assessment.

The fact that the patterns of speaking may have damaging social consequences is familiar to sociolinguists. To illustrate this point, we begin with a historical anecdote. The story of Marie-Antoinette and the French Revolution is a familiar one; we retell it here because it bears centrally on the theme of culture and conversational style. In the version of events retold in the *Encyclopaedia Britannica* ("Marie-Antoinette" 1994), the story goes like this:

Marie-Antoinette was born Maria Antonia Josepha Joanna von Österreich-Lothringen in Vienna in 1755 and she grew up speaking the German of the Viennese aristocracy. She was married at the age of 15 to the dauphin Louis, grandson of France's King Louis XV. The timid, uninspiring Louis proved to be an inattentive husband; by the time he ascended the throne of France in 1774, Marie-Antoinette had proved to be stronger and more decisive than her husband. She successfully prodded him to resist the attempts of the revolutionary National Assembly to abolish feudalism and restrict the royal prerogative. As a result, she became the main target of the popular agitators, who attributed to her a celebrated and callous remark. On being told that the people had no bread, she is believed to have said "Qu'ils mangent de la brioche!" (Let them eat cake!). After the revolutionaries took control in 1789, Louis XVI and his Queen Consort were arrested. In order to shore up their position, Marie-Antoinette urged her brother, the Holy Roman emperor Leopold II, to conduct a counterrevolutionary crusade against France but Leopold avoided acceding to her demands. After France declared war on Austria in April 1792, Marie-Antoinette's continuing intrigues with the Austrians further enraged the French. Popular hatred of the Queen provided impetus to the insurrection that overthrew the monarchy on August 10, 1792. Marie-Antoinette spent the remainder of her life in Parisian prisons. Louis XVI was executed on orders from the National Convention in January 1793, and in August the Queen was put in solitary confinement in the Conciergerie. She was brought before the Revolutionary tribunal on October 14, 1793, and guillotined two days later.

Clearly, it is an oversimplification to claim a direct relationship between Marie-Antoinette's reputed remark, "Let them eat cake!" and her end at the hands of the revolutionaries. Nevertheless we would like to claim that the outrage that the French people felt at her remark reveals a great deal about how certain elements of conversational style can be greatly misunderstood when transferred from one language and cultural context to another.

Michael Agar, in his book *Language Shock* (1994), reveals that Marie-Antoinette's remark could be heard as what the Viennese call "Schmäh" or "Schmähreden." "Schmäh" is a difficult word to translate because it seems to encapsulate a very Viennese way of looking at life, a basic cultural premise, a general attitude toward life. In Agar's words (1994:102),

> *Schmäh* as a worldview rests on irony, on the fact that things are not as they appear, on the difference between dream and reality, to use another Austrian cliché. And reality is cruel, full of harmful events and ill-intentioned others.... [*Schmäh*, then,] is a way to convert this reality into humor, a release of hardship—real or imagined—through laughter.

Recall that Marie-Antionette/Maria Antonia had been brought up in Vienna and it is likely that she had absorbed the Viennese attitude to life that *Schmäh* expresses. It is not difficult, however, to see how her remark "Qu'ils mangent de la brioche" might lose quite a lot in translation into French from her inbred Viennese value system.

Such phenomena as *Schmäh* are what Agar calls *rich points*. Rich points are those interactional phenomena experienced by us as users of a second language that seem to contrast greatly with our native practices. Rich points are not just linguistic differences, however; they are deep clues to the culture and values that appear saliently in speech that the natives command effortlessly but that may appear strange, weird, and even despicable to outsiders. Rich points may be addressed in second language instruction but more often than not they are ignored. Perhaps if Marie-Antoinette had been taught that the French masses would be less than appreciative of her native Viennese sense of irony, she might have managed to keep her head.

2 Rich Points in Cross-Cultural Interviews

Rich points are noticeable in all cross-cultural conversations and in particular in LPIs. To bring this point home, Kim and Suh (1998) describe the discourse of LPIs conducted at the University of California at Irvine involving American learners of Korean and Korean interviewers. In these interviews, Kim and Suh observe a recurrent question-answer sequence over five turns as follows (IR is the native-speaking Korean interviewer, NNS is the American speaker of Korean as a second language).

```
(1) From Kim and Suh (1998)

1st Turn (IR)              Question

2nd Turn (NNS)             Answer

3rd Turn (IR)              Confirmation request (news-
                           mark, repeat, realization
                           statement, etc.)

4th Turn (NNS)             Confirmation

5th Turn (IR)              Follow-up
```

The rich point in this sequence is the interviewer's request for confirmation in the third turn and the learner's reply in fourth turn. Note that by confirmation request, Kim and Suh do not mean here one of the conversational modifications that Pica and others have described as characteristic of conversations in which meaning is being negotiated (e.g., Pica 1987). In Kim and Suh's data, there is no misunderstanding of the propositional content of the NNS's utterance in the second turn, and although the confirmation request takes the form of an interrogative, it is not designed to test IR's understanding of the NNS's utterance. A translated example from Kim and Suh's Korean data exemplifies this sequence.

```
(2) From Kim and Suh (1998)

1    IR:  Hh if you go (to Korea) where usually do you stay?
2    NNS: Uh if I stay with my grandma, I stay in Pangpay-
3         Dong
4→  IR:  Oh is that so?
5→  NNS: Yes.
6    IR:  Oh I see. Then I presume that you had a place to
7         stay, and she must have treated you very well
8    NNS: Yes. Yes.
```

As we can see, the interviewer's confirmation request is situated in the third turn in line 5 and is a response to the NNS's prior response in the second turn (lines 3–4). This seemingly innocuous exchange is, according to Kim and Suh, a crucial part of the discourse in which both participants in the conversation co-construct and confirm a social hierarchy. It is a place where "IR claims his/her right to evaluate prior talk and initiates subsequent talk" (p. 313). The Korean interviewer expects the learner to respond by confirming the interviewer's right to evaluate and to wait for him or her to initiate a topic. The learner's close orientation toward and confirmation of the interviewer's third turn "constitutes a crucial aspect of sociolinguistic competence by indexing that NNS treats IR as a socially higher status person whose assessment he or she respects and values" (p. 314). This particular sequence is, in other words, a rich point—a hot line, if you will, between conversational practice and cultural values. Indeed, Kim and Suh mention this as one way in which Korean interviewers assess the proficiency of a conversational partner. Less proficient students respond to the interviewer's confirmation request in one of two ways, both of which the interviewer perceives as threats to his/her positive face. One way in which these less proficient students respond is by silence, as in line 4 in Excerpt 3.

(3) From Kim and Suh (1998)

```
1    IR:  How old were you when you came from Korea?
2    NNS: Four years old.
3→   IR:  When you were four years old?
4→  NNS: (.)
5    IR:  Do you have any memories of Korea?
```

According to Kim and Suh, the lack of collaboration by less proficient NNSs often causes the interaction to seem one-sided, characterized by a barrage of questions one after another from the IR (p. 313). The other strategy that less proficient NNSs use is to continue the topic they began in the second turn, ignoring the interviewer's confirmation request. Excerpt 4 shows the impatient way that an interviewer responds to such a challenge to his higher status position.

(4) From Kim and Suh (1998)

```
1    IR:  Uh which TV programs do you usually watch?
2    NNS: Uh these days, Feelings is fun. Feelings.
3         [
4→   IR:  Feelings, oh.
5              [
6→  NNS:           And (        ) I watch M on (      )
7                                                    [
8    IR:  M. Yes, yes, yes, yes. I see.
9         What do you think of your listening skills. I
10        presume you don't have any problem . . .
```

In this sequence of talk, the interviewer notices that the learner has not attended to his confirmation request in line 4. The learner has instead proceeded to give the name of another TV drama in line 6, whereupon the interviewer discourages the learner from continuing this sequence by shifting topic in lines 9-10.

When participants in Korean LPIs successfully co-construct a confirmation sequence, the social hierarchy of interviewer and student is recognized, ratified, and re-created. Participants recognize and accept their place in the hierarchy. In contrast, when the confirmation sequence goes awry, the higher status participant—the interviewer—perceives the lower status participant—the learner—as challenging the hierarchy, and a negative evaluation of proficiency in Korean results. Although we presume it is perfectly possible in Korean for the learner to deliberately challenge the status of the interviewer—snubs and other forms of verbal hostility are a communicative resource available to speakers of Korean as they are in any other language—we assume that the low proficiency learners in Kim and Suh's study are not aware of the effects of their verbal actions, any more than Marie-Antoinette was aware of the likely reaction of the French masses to her infamous *Schmäh*.

2.1 Topic Elaboration as a Rich Point in English Conversational Style

In cross-cultural conversations in English, a rich point that Young (Young 1995, Young and Milanovic 1992) has noted is related to topical development. In studies of LPIs conducted within the First Certificate in English (FCE) examination administered by the University of Cambridge Local Examinations Syndicate, Young (1995) observed two significant discourse differences between interviews involving high proficiency learners of English and those involving learners with only intermediate proficiency. The first difference occurs in responses to display questions asked by the interviewer. During the FCE interview the learner and interviewer have access to a set of what are called interaction materials. These materials consist both of photographs and short texts (one or two sentences in length) related by a similar broad theme, such as "places where people live" or "clothes and fashion." In part of the interview, the interviewer asks the NNS to relate a text to one of the photographs in the interaction pack. There is only one correct match of text and picture, which is known to the interviewer in advance of asking the question; the task is thus very similar to the display question-and-answer sequence familiar from studies of classroom interaction (see, e.g., Mehan 1979). In a study of topical organization in FCE interviews, Young (1995) found that high proficiency learners talked almost twice as much as intermediate learners in response to the interviewer's display question (median amount of NNS talk from high proficiency learners 27 t-units, from intermediate learners 15 t-units; $Z = -2.43$; $p < .05$).

The following two excerpts from interviews with learners at different proficiency levels illustrate this point. In Excerpt 5, Vincent, an intermediate learner, responds to the interviewer's questions with "just the facts" until at the end of the task, the interviewer is constrained to provide an expansion of Vincent's answer.

```
(5) From Young (1995)

1  IR:   Now. (.5) I want to move onto the (.1) next part of
2        the exam. (.5) I want you to look at: this little
3        paragraph here number one, all right? (.1) Just
4        read it to yourself (.1) and try and then think
5        where you might: read something like that, where
6        would you see it.
7  NNS:  (42.) I think it may be a: advertisement (.2) of
8        holiday.
```

```
 9 IR:   Right,
10 NNS:  About (.2) um (2.) maybe on a beach?
11 IR:   Mhm?
12       (3.)
13 IR:   What's what do you think is the (.2) the intention
14       of the (.2) the writer of this, what is what's the
15       writer trying to- to say.
16 NNS:  (3.) The writer is trying to: (1.) recommend,
17 IR:   Yeah?
18 NNS:  a pla:ce [ (2.) ] to people.
19 IR:            [Mhm? ] Or (.5) the w- it's gives me the
20       feeling of giving advice. (.2) °of some kind°. (2.)
21       Yeah?
22 NNS:  Yes.
23 IR:   About traveling by car. Some of the problems (.2)
24       that can happen.
25 NNS:  Mm (2.) ↑yeah.
26 IR:   Okay (.5) now let's move on.
```

The exchange begins with a display question from IR in lines 1–6. After a 42-second pause during which Vincent reads the paragraph that IR has indicated, Vincent responds with a short answer in lines 7 and 8. IR indicates with rising intonation in line 9 that Vincent still has the floor, and Vincent adds an extra prepositional phrase to his answer in line 10. Although IR's rising intonation and three-second pause in lines 11 and 12 indicate that he expects Vincent to elaborate further on his answer, Vincent does not take the hint, and IR has to prompt him with an explicit question in lines 12–15. Vincent answers IR's second question, again briefly, in lines 16 and 18, and IR's tokens of active listenership in lines 17 and 19 again encourage Vincent to elaborate. Despite a two-second pause in line 18, Vincent does not elaborate further and IR himself completes the answer that he sought from Vincent in lines 19–24.

By contrast, in Excerpt 6, Marco, an advanced learner, goes beyond the brief responses to questions that Vincent displayed and elaborates and expands on his answers.

(6) From Young (1995)

```
1 IR:Okay so if we could move on to the s:econd section
2     which is these short (.5) pieces of writing, (.5)
3     uhm (1.) if you could >have a look at the first one,<
4     (.5) uh read it for a moment and then (.5) tell me
5     if you think it has any connection with the pictures=
6 NNS:Mm.
```

```
7   IR:   =and also where you think it might possibly come
8         from.
9   NNS:  Yes (1.) should I: read it loudly?
10  IR:   No no don't bother, no just to yourself.
11  NNS:  (22.) Yeah the connection is with (1.) is with this
12        (1.) picture.
13  IR:   The same one (    ).
14  NNS:  Mhm,
15  IR:   Yeah.
16  NNS:  And uh (.2) you see here it says (.2) not to leave
17        children (.5) in the car (1.) with a hot weather,
18        must suffocating. So I can say that uh (1.5) this
19        motorist know (1.) uh this kind of thing and that's
20        why (.2) maybe he asked to his wife to (.2) feed the
21        child outside [maybe=]
22  IR:                 [Yes. ]
23  NNS:  =you know some [fresh air.]
24  IR:                  [Exactly. ] Yeah.
25  NNS:  And uh well the hot weather can be connected with
26        this picture as well this is summertime so,
27  IR:   The last one. Yes.
28  NNS:  Yes.
29  IR:   Yeah.
```

Excerpt 6 begins in a similar way to Excerpt 5, with a display question from IR, followed by 22 seconds of silence as Marco reads. Marco's answer to the question comes in lines 12–13, and IR confirms this as the expected answer in lines 14 and 16. Up to this point the exchange has been very similar to the three-part Initiation-Response-Evaluation sequence noted by Sinclair and Coulthard (1975) and many others as the most common sequence in teacher-led speech events. Marco goes on, however, to elaborate on his answer in lines 17–22, and after overlapping evaluation by IR the two participants collaboratively construct a closing of the topic.

So the tendency for intermediate learners to simply answer display questions while high proficiency learners elaborate is one difference between the two proficiency levels. The second difference that Young observed also involves length and elaboration of topics. This occurred in the part of the FCE interview where learners were given the opportunity to freely express their own opinions and comment about a list of activities related to the theme of the interaction pack. Here topics initiated by high proficiency learners lasted almost three times as long (in t-units) as those initiated by the intermediate learners. (Median persistence of topics initiated by high proficiency learners 24 t-units, by intermediate learners 8.5 t-units; $Z = 2.21; p < .05$.)

Thus in two important phases of the interview, a topical analysis reveals that high proficiency learners expand and elaborate on topics in LPIs more than intermediate learners. The only other difference was in the mean rate of speaking of the two groups, with high proficiency learners speaking faster (in t-units per minute) than intermediate learners, a difference that can be accounted for by longer unfilled pauses in the speech of the intermediate learners. (Mean rate of speaking for high proficiency learners 10.71 t-units/minute, for intermediate learners 8.09 t-units/minute; $t = -2.949$; $p < .005$.) The difference in rate of speaking can most convincingly be accounted for by differences in cognitive processing between the two groups: as Dreyfus and Dreyfus (1986) and Mislevy (1993) have suggested, experts command fast, automatized procedures whereas for novices the same procedures are slow and attention-consuming. The high proficiency learners seem to have automatized their speech production in a second language to a degree that the intermediate learners have not, and thus they speak faster.

Initially it seemed that the differences in topic elaboration between the two groups were also due to differences in cognitive processing. But there was a cultural factor that confounded the effect of proficiency: the majority of the high proficiency learners came from Western European backgrounds, while the majority of the intermediate group came from East Asia, principally Japan, Thailand, and Hong Kong. Recent results from other researchers (e.g., van Betteraij, Kellerman, and Schils 1996) suggest that while proficiency-related differences in cognitive processing may play a part, there are also cultural factors at work and that, in fact, degree of elaboration of a topic is a rich point of English conversational style that ESL learners, especially those from East Asian countries, must come to terms with.

The quantity of a rational conversational participant's contribution to a conversation is defined within Grice's comprehensive pragmatic theory. According to Grice (1989), rational conversationalists tacitly accept the Cooperative Principle, which states "Make your conversational contribution such as is required, at the stage [of the talk exchange] at which it occurs," together with its four sub-cases, the Maxims of Quality, Quantity, Relation, and Manner. For the purposes of this discussion, the relevant Maxim is that of Quantity (Grice 1989:26), which states:

1. Make your contribution as informative as is required (for the current purposes of the exchange).
2. Do not make your contribution more informative than is required.

We wish to make the case that, for a variety of reasons that we will detail later, some speakers of English as a second language interpret the degree of informativeness required in LPIs very differently from their native-speaking interviewers. As a consequence, their interviewers either perceive them to be uncooperative conversationalists or simply evaluate their oral proficiency at a lower level than might otherwise be the case.

In the particular case of Japanese learners of English, Ross (1998) has revealed two reasons why these learners appear to American interviewers to be uncooperative in LPIs. Ross terms *minimalism* a strategy that Japanese ESL learners use in LPIs. It derives from transfer of the pragmatics of interview interaction from their own culture (House 1993). According to Barnlund (1975), Japanese interviewees withhold superficially trivial factual information and respond concisely and briefly to interviewer questions. They do so, according to Lebra (1987), because they do not wish to appear superfluous or verbose, two traits that are not particularly valued in Japanese society. Ross illustrates Japanese minimalist response strategy with Excerpt 7 from a Foreign Service Institute oral proficiency interview administered in Japan.

(7) From Ross (1998)

```
1  IR:  I see here you've ahh (.) you've been overseas~ quite
2       a f::ew countries:: (.) ahh (.) you've been to South
3       America?
4 NNS:  Yes (1.0)
5  IR:  On sightseeing?
6 NNS:  (.) Yes
7  IR:  When was that?
8 NNS:  (2.0)
9  IR:  When did you to South America (.) How many years ago.
```

The lengthy process punctuated by long pauses in lines 4, 6, and 8 by which the NS interviewer gradually draws from the Japanese candidate the information about his South American vacation is familiar to many teachers of Japanese ESL students, who have compared it to pulling teeth. As a strategy, this cooperative oral surgery is very similar to the interaction we saw with Vincent in Excerpt 5. As Ross (1998:340) comments, however,

> the purpose of questions in the context of the LPI is rarely to establish the truth of particular facts about a candidate's life experiences. Rather, interview questions are invitations for the candidate to talk about the topics introduced throughout the questioning process. The task of decoding interviewer questions as *invitations* to speak to a topic constitutes such a challenging test of second language pragmatic

competence that many Japanese candidates at the advanced level of proficiency have considerable difficulty with it.

An alternative reason why Japanese learners may appear uncooperative in LPI conversations lies in the different Japanese and American perceptions of the boundaries of personal space. As Ross points out, "When interviewers pose a seemingly innocuous question pertaining to the inside of the Japanese candidate's personal space—the domains of the home, work, religious, or romantic life, for instance—underelaborate answers may be doubly ambiguous (Hinds 1983; Loveday 1982; Triandis, Bontempo, Villareal, Asai, and Luca 1988)" (p. 344). Excerpt 8 from Ross shows a male Japanese learner's response to a male American interviewer's direct question, "Are you married?"

```
(8)   From Ross (1998)

1    IR:    And ah (.) are you married?
2    NNS:   No I am single.
3    IR:    (3.0) do you plan to get married?
4→ NNS:    °hhha- nohh
5    IR:    (1.0) I see you're not a- ↑you have no plans right
6           now
7    NNS:   Yeah
```

After the learner's factual reply to the interviewer's question, the three-second pause in line 3 indicates that the interviewer expects the learner to elaborate on his reply. The fact that he does not do so is interpreted by Ross (1998:345) as follows.

> For both males and females in Japan, the pressure to conform to expectations in traditional society is particularly pervasive. In this excerpt, the question, punctuated by a three-second pause after the candidate's previous answer, is likely heard as revealing the male interviewer's expectation that the candidate (a male in his midthirties) should be planning to get married.

The laughter and subvocalization in the answer at line 4 suggest that the candidate recognizes his response as a dispreferred second pair part—as if a positive response to the question would somehow be more appropriate than the one he offered.

In both of these instances of short responses to an interviewer's questions, the learners appear to American English conversationalists to flout the Maxim of Quantity. Clearly, in both examples, the interviewer invites a more informative response than the learner provides. If we assume that the Cooperative Principle and its attendant maxims are universal, we must conclude that by superficially flouting the Maxim of Quantity, the Japanese learner generates a conversational implicature; that is, a non-logical and context-dependent inference that comprises the meaning conveyed (Horn 1992:261). If we are to understand exactly what that implicature is, we need a situated understanding of Japanese culture and conversation such as Ross provides us. Without such an understanding, we are left with a sense of dissatisfaction with the learner's response that may easily result in a negative evaluation of his ability as a conversationalist in English.

We have suggested so far that both American and British interviewers prefer talkative over taciturn interlocutors and, when they encounter taciturn learners, they may underevaluate such interlocutors' proficiency in English. The reason they do so is that different speech communities value different aspects of conversational style. Talkativeness—the gift of the gab—is particularly valued by native speakers of English. Hymes (1974) reports that this is far from being a universal value, however, and cites the ancient Spartans, the Aritama of Colombia, and the Paliyans of south India as societies in which talkativeness is not valued. Equally, as Reisman (1989) points out, although in many contexts of American speech, rapid, fluent responses in dialogue and the avoidance of silence are considered desirable conversational style, in other societies—Denmark is one example—silences indicate "the well-being of those present, at least a kind of affirmation that people speak only when moved to do so, that their feelings are genuine, etc." (p. 112). Talk and the social construction of silence are valued differently in different situations by different people. Indeed as Basso (1970), Samarin (1965), and Hymes (1974) have noted, the distribution of required and preferred silence perhaps most immediately reveals in outline form a community's structure of speaking.

3 Culture and Conversational Style: Comparing Mexicans and Japanese

Returning once more to *Schmäh* as a rich point in Viennese language and culture, Agar (1994:100) offers the following comments.

> The *rich points* in a languaculture you encounter are relative to the one you brought with you. The juxtaposition of English and German highlights rich points that a juxtaposition of English and Hopi wouldn't. And a native speaker of Austrian German might be struck by different rich points than I would be if he or she set out to study how people talk in a Viennese neighborhood.

Table 1. Backgrounds of NNS Informants

Pseudonym of NNS	Sex	L₁	Site of interview	ACTFL rating	Duration of initial Q&A phase (minutes:seconds)
Fuki	F	Japanese	U.S.	Superior	11:22
Ana	F	Spanish	Mexico	Superior	8:22
Takahiro	M	Japanese	U.S.	Advanced	17:29
Fernando	M	Spanish	Mexico	Advanced	14:36
Minoru	M	Japanese	U.S.	Intermediate-Mid	21:41
Angeles	F	Spanish	Mexico	Intermediate-Mid	9:05

Thus it is with talkativeness. We have seen how an understanding of an American interviewer's expectations and cultural frame is related directly to the degree of elaboration expected of a learner's response in an LPI. For a Japanese learner of English, then, elaboration of responses is a rich point in understanding how in the United States language is used to express cultural attitudes. But this may not be the case for learners from other cultural backgrounds. What we will describe in the remainder of this chapter is a comparison between the performances of two groups of learners in LPIs: a group of Japanese learners and a group of native speakers of Spanish from Mexico. The aim of the comparison is to investigate to what extent talkativeness in LPIs is a rich point of English conversational style for Japanese learners of English.

These two groups of learners were chosen to represent two quite different cultural styles of interaction. The learners were also chosen to represent different levels of proficiency in English as a second language. Background data on the learners and the interviews are summarized in Table 1.

These interviews were part of a larger testing program carried out by the second author of this chapter and followed the format of the Oral Proficiency Interview (OPI) of the American Council on the Teaching of Foreign Languages (ACTFL). The interviewer was an ACTFL-certified tester. The interviews with Mexican informants were conducted on a private university campus in Mexico; those with Japanese informants were conducted on a state university campus in the northeastern part of the U.S. All six informants were either university students or researchers.

For the purposes of comparison, two interviews—one with a Japanese and one with a Mexican—were chosen for analysis at each proficiency level. The proficiency of the learners was assessed by the interviewer to be at one of three levels: *Intermediate-Mid, Advanced,* and *Superior.* These levels of speaking proficiency are defined by ACTFL (1989) as follows:

Intermediate-Mid: Able to handle successfully a variety of uncomplicated, basic and communicative tasks and social situations. Can talk simply about self and family members. *Can ask and answer questions and participate in simple conversations on topics beyond the most immediate needs* [italics added]; e.g., personal history and leisure time activities. Utterance length increases slightly [from Intermediate-Low level], but *speech may continue to be characterized by frequent long pauses, since the smooth incorporation of even basic conversational strategies is often hindered as the speaker struggles to create appropriate language forms* [italics added]. Pronunciation may continue to be strongly influenced by first language and fluency may still be strained. Although misunderstandings still arise, the Intermediate-Mid speaker can generally be understood by sympathetic interlocutors.

Advanced: Able to satisfy the requirements of everyday situations and routine school and work requirements. *Can handle with confidence but not with facility complicated tasks and social situations, such as elaborating, complaining, and apologizing* [italics added]. Can narrate and describe with some details, linking sentences together smoothly. Can communicate facts and talk casually about topics of current public and personal interest, using general vocabulary. Shortcomings can be smoothed over by communicative strategies, such as pause fillers, stalling devices, and different rates of speech. Circumlocution which arises from vocabulary or syntactic limitations very often is quite successful, though some groping for words may still be evident. The Advanced-level speaker can be understood without difficulty by native interlocutors.

Superior: Able to speak the language with sufficient accuracy to *participate effectively in most formal and informal conversations* [italics added] on practical, social, professional, and abstract topics. Can discuss special fields of competence and interest with ease. *Can support opinions and hypothesize* [italics added], but may not be able to tailor language to audience or discuss in depth highly abstract or unfamiliar topics. Usually the Superior-level speaker is only partially familiar with regional or other dialectical variants. The Superior-level speaker commands a wide variety of interactive strategies and shows a good awareness of discourse strategies. The latter involves the ability to distinguish main ideas from supporting information through syntactic, lexical and suprasegmental features (pitch, stress, intonation). Sporadic errors may occur, particularly in low frequency structures and some complex high-frequency structures more common to formal writing, but no patterns of error are evident. Errors do not disturb the native speaker or interfere with communication.

The italicized portions of the ACTFL descriptors make clear one indication of increasing proficiency: while the Intermediate-Mid learner can answer questions, the Advanced learner can elaborate and the Superior learner can support opinions and hypothesize. According to these descriptors, differing degrees of topical elaboration—of talkativeness, if you will—are indicative of differing degrees of proficiency in English as a second language. Our belief was that the same conversational phenomenon also distinguished Mexican from Japanese conversationalists; and we were concerned to find out whether *culture* or *proficiency* was the main determinant of topic elaboration among the six subjects.

3.1 *Organization of the Interview and Timing*

All interviews contained the same eight phases arranged in the same sequence. The phases are listed below together with a brief description of each.

Warm-up. The interviewer turned on the tape recorder immediately before a brief opening exchange consisting of an exchange of greetings.

Initial Question-and-Answer Phase. The opening was immediately followed by an extended question-and-answer phase lasting between 8 and 21 minutes. The IR began this phase with some general questions about the NNS's hometown and background, and often asked the NNS to compare aspects of his/her home culture with life in the United States. Topics shaded into one another in a mostly coherent way. The IR marked the end of this phase and the beginning of the next by some explicit instruction such as "All right, let's do something different."

Set up Role-Play. IR then gave instructions to the NNS regarding the parts that NNS and IR would take in a role-play. Setting up the role-play generally took less than a minute.

Role-Play. The role-play itself generally lasted up to three minutes. Role-plays at the Intermediate level often involved typical survival situations such as ordering food in a restaurant, buying something in a department store, or getting information at a ticket booth. At the Advanced level the role-play involved a complication that required the interviewee either to complain about a problem (calling the landlord about a broken window) or to talk her way out of a difficult situation (an accident while driving a friend's car).

Second Question-and-Answer Phase. The role-play phase was followed by a second question-and-answer phase, which begins with IR making the transition from the imagined situation to personal history by asking a question such as "Has anything like that ever happened to you?" Some NNSs had difficulty recognizing this transition, in which case the IR made her rhetorical intent explicit: "Now I'm just asking you a regular question." The second Q&A phase was much shorter than the first, lasting between one and two and a half minutes. The topic was usually limited to the subject matter of the role-play.

Role Reversal. After the second Q&A phase in Intermediate-level interviews, the IR asked the NNS to exchange roles with her, using an instruction like "Okay I've been asking you all the questions in this interview and it's your turn now to ask me some questions." The role reversal phase was quite short and the questions that the NNS asked of the IR were often questions on her personal background such as "Where are you from?" or "Do you have any children?" The role reversal phase lasted between one and two minutes.

Third Question-and-Answer Phase. The transition to the third Q&A phase, in which IR and NNS took back their normal roles, could be marked explicitly by a phrase such as "I have a question for you if you can't think of one for me," or the transition back to the participants' normal roles in the interview could simply be implied by a question from the IR. The third and final Q&A phase was shorter than the first interview phase because the entire interview was supposed to last no more than 30 minutes.

Closing. The transition to the closing phase of the interview was marked by the IR expressing her good wishes or thanks to the NNS. The closing was brief, although in all cases longer than the opening.

The most substantial phase of the interview is what we have termed the initial question-and-answer phase, lasting from the conclusion of the warm-up phase until the time when IR begins to set up the role-play. Because it represents a significant proportion of the complete interview and because it followed a similar format in all six interviews, this was the part of the interview that was chosen for analysis.

3.2 *Topical Structure Analysis*

An analysis of the discourse was carried out that focused on the ways in which topics were introduced, developed, and changed by IR and learner. The identification and analysis of topics was carried out using the methods described in Crow (1983) and Young (1995).[2] In this study, a comparison was made of topic persistence,[3] rate of speaking,[4] and frequency of topic shift[5] in these interviews across two different cultures and across three different levels of proficiency in spoken English. The reason for doing so was to problematize the descriptions of topical elaboration that are given in the ACTFL descriptors. As mentioned above, we believed that the same conversational phenomena characterizing proficiency in the ACTFL descriptors also distinguished Mexican from Japanese conversationalists.

Table 2. Topical Structure Analysis of Six ACTFL Oral Proficiency Interviews

ACTFL Proficiency			Median persistence of topics measured in t-units across			Rate of speaking (t-units/minute)	Topics shift every
	NNS	L₁	IR turns	NNS turns	All turns		
Superior							
	Fuki	J.	3.5	6.0	10.5	9	57 secs
	Ana	Sp.	2.0	9.0	13.0	14	39 secs
Advanced							
	Takahiro	J.	3.0	6.5	9.5	9	48 secs
	Fernando	Sp.	3.0	6.0	10.0	8	58 secs
Intermediate-Mid							
	Minoru	J.	5.5	8.5	15.0	8	72 secs
	Angeles	Sp.	4.0	8.0	12.5	12	55 secs

The approach taken was first to conduct a quantitative analysis of topical organization in the six interviews along the lines of work that Young has previously done, and for which by now there exists a solid body of results and an established methodology for analyzing topical organization. The small number of LPIs analyzed here, however, makes generalization difficult; the use of inferential statistics is not warranted, and general statements about the crosscutting effects of culture and proficiency in LPIs are difficult to make on the basis of a quantitative analysis alone. After examining the quantitative results, the transcripts were examined to see how the tendencies revealed by the quantitative analysis appeared in the moment-by-moment shifts of conversation. By combining both quantitative and qualitative analyses, we hope to have described in rich detail the six interviews that were studied and to suggest hypotheses that may be tested in further larger-scale studies of LPI conversations. This study should therefore be read as a focused description of these six interviews, a description that is enriched by using both quantitative and qualitative analyses.

Figures 1 through 4 illustrate the results of the quantitative analysis reported in Table 2. Figures 1 and 2 show the median persistence of topics across turns at talk by the IR and by the NNS. The three sets of bars represent the three proficiency levels, with the lowest proficiency level (Intermediate-Mid) at the bottom and the highest (Superior) at the top. The darker bars in each figure represent the Japanese and the lighter bars represent the Mexican speakers of Spanish.

Figure 1 shows that, in general, the American interviewer had to contribute more t-units per topic with a lower proficiency learner. In interviewing the Superior and Intermediate-Mid learners, it was true—as hypothesized—that she contributed more

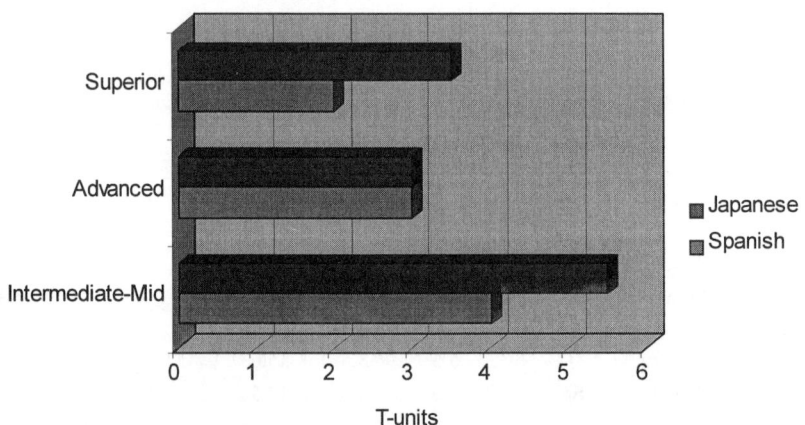

Figure 1. *Median Persistence of Topics Across IR Turns (in T-units) as a Function of L_1 and ACTFL Proficiency Level*

t-units per topic with the Japanese learners than with the Mexicans. But with the middle of the three levels of proficiency—the Advanced-level learners—the interviewer contributed as many t-units per topic with Fernando, her Mexican

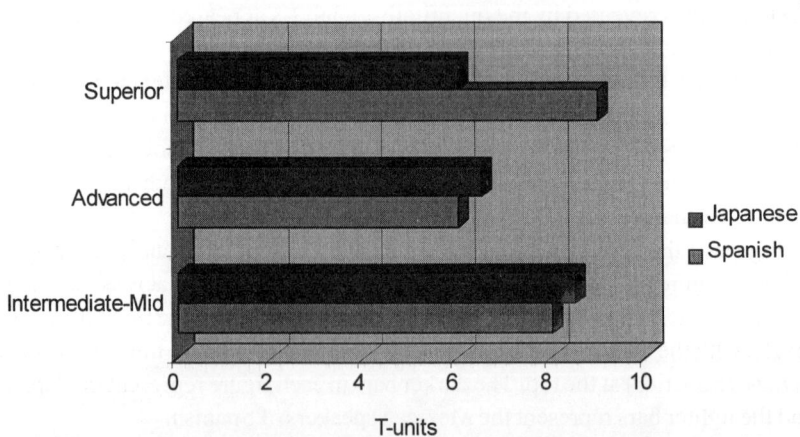

Figure 2. *Median Persistence of Topics Across NNS Turns (in T-units) as a Function of L_1 and ACTFL Proficiency Level*

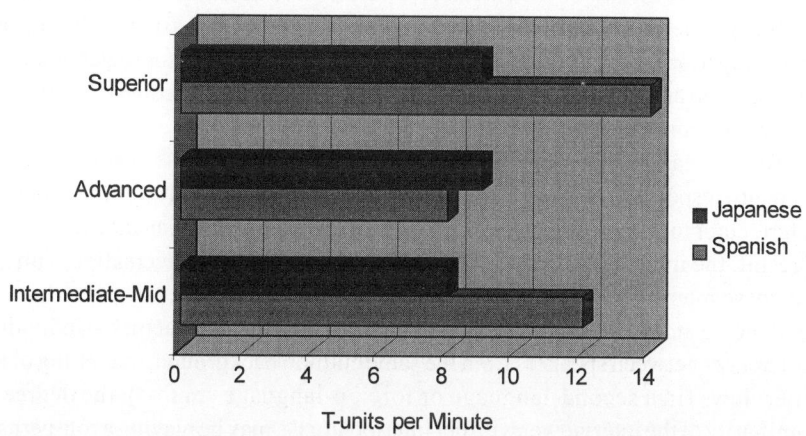

Figure 3.   Rate of Speaking (in T-units per Minute) as a Function of L_1 and ACTFL Proficiency Level

interlocutor, as she did with Takahiro, her Japanese interlocutor.

Figure 2 shows how many turns at talk the NNSs contributed to each topic. In this case, there seems to be no clear relationship between proficiency and the contribu-

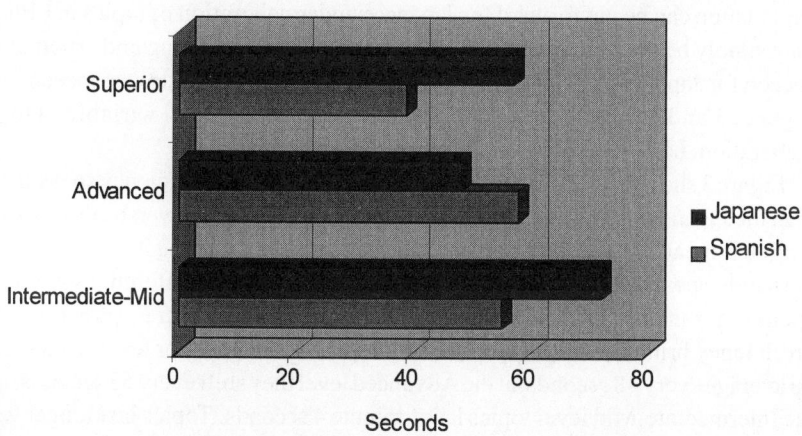

Figure 4.   Frequency of Topic Shift (in Seconds) as a Function of L_1 and ACTFL Proficiency Level

tions of the NNSs: the two Intermediate-Mid learners contributed most, followed by the Superior learners, and the Advanced learners contributed least. In addition, only at the Superior level was there a marked difference between the topic elaboration of the Mexican and Japanese speakers, with Ana contributing a median of 9 t-units to each topic, compared with a median of 6 t-units from Fuki.

To summarize this phase of the investigation, then, these results reveal a tendency, especially marked at the Superior level of proficiency, for the Japanese interlocutor to contribute fewer t-units per topic than the Mexican interlocutor. As a result, the interviewer must work harder to keep up the conversation with her Japanese interlocutor than with the Mexican. It is noteworthy, however, that this tendency is not to be found in all interviews. Clearly other factors—individual differences between speakers from the same cultural background, the setting of the interviews (in a second-language or foreign-language context), the degree of familiarity of the interviewer with her interlocutors—may be playing a role perhaps as important as the differences between the Japanese and Mexican conversational styles.

One possible explanation for the underelaboration by Japanese in conversations with Americans lies *not* in transfer of Japanese conversational style but rather in the comparative difficulty that Japanese have in speaking English, a difficulty caused either by the typological dissimilarities between Japanese and English or by the relatively small amount of practice that Japanese have in speaking English during the course of their education in Japan. If this is the case, then an alternative explanation can be put forward for Japanese underelaboration of topics in LPIs: it may simply be that English places extra demands in formulating and articulating speech for Japanese than it does for Mexicans, resulting in a slower speech rate. Figures 3 and 4 show how rate of speaking affects a crucial variable in topic elaboration: how often one topic shifts or shades into the next.

Figure 3 shows that the Mexican speakers at all levels of proficiency speak faster than the Japanese speakers. Ana speaks at 14 t-units per minute versus Fuki's 9 and Angeles speaks at 12 t-units per minute to Minoru's 8.[6] At the Advanced level, Fernando speaks very slightly faster than Takahiro. These differences in rate of speaking translate into more rapid topic shifts. As shown in Figure 4, higher proficiency brings more frequent shifts of topic. At the Superior level, topics shift on average every 48 seconds; at the Advanced level they shift every 53 seconds; and the Intermediate-Mid level topics last 1 minute 4 seconds. Topics last longer with Japanese speakers than with Mexicans at the two extremes of proficiency, with the situation somewhat reversed in the case of the Advanced speakers, Fernando and Takahiro.

4 Conclusions

What can we conclude from this admittedly small-scale study of topical organization in LPIs between cultures and across proficiency levels? The first set of results speaks to the differences between the conversational styles of Japanese and Mexican candidates. In our sample of OPIs in English, the following tendencies have been observed.

1. Mexican candidates require less work from the interviewer than Japanese in terms of the number of t-units she contributes to each topic in the conversation.

2. Mexican candidates speak faster than Japanese, as measured by the number of t-units uttered per minute.

And, perhaps as a consequence of this greater speed,

3. Mexican candidates shift topics more frequently than Japanese.

The conclusions that we can draw when we compare topical organization across the three proficiency levels are remarkably similar.

1. High proficiency NNSs require less work of the interviewer than lower proficiency NNSs, as measured by the number of t-units that she contributes to each topic in the conversation.

2. High proficiency NNSs speak more rapidly than lower proficiency speakers.

And, perhaps as a consequence of this faster speed,

3. Higher proficiency speakers tend to shift topics more frequently than lower proficiency speakers.

From these results we can infer that two factors influence topical organization in LPIs: transfer of L_1 conversational style and proficiency level. Most important, the effects of these two factors appear to be indistinguishable. On the basis of topical organization alone, therefore, we cannot say whether the assessment of a given candidate reflects his or her oral proficiency or whether it is conveyed by transfer of his or her native conversational style. In the particular case that we have presented here, it appears that Mexican candidates have the advantage over Japanese.

We have argued in this paper that certain features of L_1 conversational style, combined with difficulty of processing English, transfer into these learners' interlanguage discourse, and that these features may be the cause of negative judgments about their speaking proficiency in English, at least at the Intermediate level. In the case of the Japanese and Mexicans in this study it does indeed appear that the Japanese conversationalist at the Intermediate level is, like Marie-Antoinette, losing his head in an LPI and is being assessed at a lower level of proficiency precisely because his interlanguage conversational style contains features of topical structure that are judged negatively by Americans.

Even at the Superior level of proficiency, we notice that the Japanese interviewee's responses appear underelaborate by American standards. Excerpts 9 and 10 illustrate how, notwithstanding her ability to speak in paragraph-length discourse, demonstrated in more than a dozen turns throughout the interview, there are several turns in which Fuki's answers resemble the unelaborated type of response that Ross characterizes as "minimalist."

(9)

```
    IR:   Mhm (.) so you will live in Tokyo?
  Fuki:   Yes.
    IR:   Mhm where is your family now?
  Fuki:   Uh in ( ) Prefecture.
    IR:   How far is that?
  Fuki:   Uh it's about six hundred or seven hundred
          kilometers away so it's very far.
    IR:   Far away.
  Fuki:   Very far.
```

(10)

```
  Fuki:   . . . opportunities to enjoy entertainment like you
          know going to see concerts or plays,
    IR:   In Tokyo?
  Fuki:   In Tokyo.
    IR:   Mm?
  Fuki:   Uhm.
```

It is difficult to tell, from the excerpts illustrated above, that Fuki is a Superior-level speaker, since these isolated segments of her interview resemble the conversational style of Minoru, the Intermediate Japanese speaker. In the interview segments illustrated in Excerpts 11 and 12 below, Minoru's responses seem, from an American point of view, to violate Grice's Maxim of Quantity:

(11)
```
    IR: It's a big city.
Minoru: Yes, I think so.
    IR: Living in Osaka must be very different from living
        in Tate College.
Minoru: Yes.
```

(12)
```
    IR: How long have you been here?
Minoru: For one month
    IR: Oh okay why did you come to State U?
Minoru: For my research
    IR: Research?
Minoru: Yes.
```

Minoru's restrained style contrasts with the uninhibited ease with which the Mexican Intermediate interviewee, Angeles, elaborates. In a typical response to a question about her hometown, illustrated in Excerpt 13, Angeles volunteers information without any prompting.

(13)
```
     IR: I don't know anything about Chihuahua could you
         tell me something about Chihuahua=
Angeles: Okay this is the ehm a state has a state
     IR: Mhm
Angeles: More big of the republica republica Mexican and ehm
         you can go to the Sierra Tarahumara I dunno how to
         say sierra in ingles in English
     IR: Mm
Angeles: But you can go there you can uh ( ) Barranca del
         Cobre also uhm uh can I say that how d'you say eh
         animal uh person's uhm works with the animals
         ganadería?
```

Whereas the Intermediate-level Japanese speaker's responses, excerpted in 11 and 12, are reserved and unelaborated, the Intermediate-level Mexican speaker's answers are much more informative. Although Angeles has trouble forming grammatically accurate answers in English and sometimes gropes for the right word, her style seems more cooperative than Minoru's and her responses provide a lot more information.

These conclusions are only general tendencies, however, and there are exceptions to them. In particular, the topical organization found in the interview with the Advanced-level Japanese speaker, Takahiro, does not fit the general pattern we have outlined. Figure 1 shows no difference between Takahiro and the Mexican Advanced-level speaker, Fernando, in terms of interviewer work by topic. Figure 3 shows no significant difference between the two in terms of rate of speaking, and Figure 4 shows that Takahiro's interview goes against the general Japanese trend toward more rapid topic shifting than Mexican candidates. It is important to recognize the behavior of this outlier lest we overestimate the effect of cultural differences on second language speech style.

Two further words of caution need to be entered at this point before we rush to remedy the perceived inequities in oral assessment procedures and before we rush to attribute all aspects of learners' conversational style to transfer from L_1 conversational practices. First, assessment of oral proficiency is not based on topical organization alone. The ACTFL descriptors do make mention of learners' abilities to hold the floor and discuss a range of different topics. But the descriptors make clear that learners are assessed on a range of features of their conversation, including pronunciation, fluency, and grammatical and lexical accuracy. Further research is needed before we know the effect of the interviewers' perceptions of topical organization on assessment as a whole. Finally, we have tried to show a tendency for a conversational style to transfer. It may also be the case, however, that those Japanese interviewees rated Advanced and Superior have learned ways of compensating for the conversational style typical of their L_1. We do not know from this analysis whether the Intermediate-level Japanese speaker would have been judged at a higher level if he, too, had compensated for the conversational style of his L_1, or whether other factors also caused him to be rated Intermediate.

In this chapter we have argued that transfer of L_1 conversational style into English explains in large measure the differences in topical organization in the LPIs of Mexicans and Japanese. Because of the value that American and British NSs place on topical elaboration, the transfer of a Japanese speech style where topics are underelaborated may result in negative assessments of Japanese learners' proficiency in English. This study of ACTFL OPIs has provided some evidence of transfer of speech style. The study has also shown, however, that stylistic transfer does not explain all the facts of conversational variation across cultures. There are stylistic differences between individuals from the same culture, and there may also be personality differences that result in differing degrees of adjustment to the preferred speech styles of English. Thus although cultural differences explain much, we should beware of too readily interpreting all conversational mismatches in intercultural settings as resulting from cultural differences.

Notes

1. In this chapter we use "conversational style" in the sense used by Tannen (1984, pp. 1–2) to refer to those interactional resources such as turn-taking, intonation, topical choice, and organization that are used by speakers to communicate something more than the propositional content of their utterances. Speakers use these resources to communicate images of themselves, their affective reaction to what is being said, and their understanding of the particular speech event that is under way.

2. The initial interview phase was divided into discrete topics at points in the transcript which indicated a topic change. A change of topic is defined by Maynard (1980:280) as "an utterance which employs referents unrelated to prior talk in order to implicate a new set of mentionables." A mixture of functional and structural criteria were used to identify a topic change, and often these criteria co-occurred. They were:
- Explicit boundary markers such as "So," "Okay," etc.
- Imperatives in the speech of the IR such as "Tell me . . "
- Long unfilled pauses
- Introduction of new information
- Rounding off by repetition or paraphrase in closing of a salient lexical item that was used to initiate the topic
- Framing moves such as "Okay I wanna ask you a question . . ."
- High pitch on a new lexical item as an indication of a topic opening
- Low pitch on the same item that opened a topic (or a paraphrase of it) as an indication of closing.
- Explicit abandonment of a topic

3. The persistence of a topic was measured by counting the number of t-units across both IR and NNS turns from one topic shift to the next. Since turn-taking was fairly orderly in these interviews with very little overlapping speech, the identification of turns was not problematic. Continuers or backchannels, which were often uttered by the IR while the NNS was speaking, were not counted in measuring topic persistence; neither were tokens of laughter.

4. Rate of speaking was measured in t-units per minute. A t-unit is one clause plus any subordinate clauses and was used as the basic unit of analysis for several reasons. First, since a t-unit is based on a clause, it is an easier unit to identify in speech than a sentence. Second, more than any other unit such as turns or words, t-units have identifiable referential meaning and can thus be used as a basis for studies of topical continuity. Third, t-units were chosen in order to provide comparability of results from this study with results from previous studies that had used this unit (e.g., Schneider and Connor 1990, Young 1995, Young and Milanovic 1992). The rate of speaking of the NNS in a given

interview was calculated by totaling the t-units uttered by the NNS during the initial interview phase of the LPI and then dividing by the duration in minutes of this phase. Such a measure is not a perfect measure of rate of speaking of the NNS because it includes the IR's talk as well as the NNS's. The IR was the same person in all these interviews, however, and she followed a similar pattern of questioning in all. It is thus reasonable to take the IR's contribution to the rate of speaking measured in this way to be constant. Since we are concerned in this study with comparisons of the rate of speaking of different NNSs, the constant IR contribution to each interview disappears in comparisons across different NNSs.

5. The frequency of topic shift in a given interview was measured by dividing the duration of the first interview phase of the LPI by the number of topic shifts within that phase. For example, the first phase of Ana's LPI lasted 8:22 and there were a total of 13 topic shifts during that time (including the initial topic initiation but not the transition to the next phase), averaging a shift of topic approximately every 39 seconds.

6. It should be noted, however, that since Fuki's t-units are significantly longer than Ana's, the difference in "speed" noted here may not, in fact, be significant.

References

ACTFL Proficiency Guidelines. 1989. Hastings-on-Hudson. NY: American Council on the Teaching of Foreign Languages.
Agar, Michael. 1994. *Language Shock: Understanding the Culture of Conversation*. New York: Morrow.
Barnlund, Dean C. 1975. *Public and Private Self in Japan and the U.S.* Tokyo: Simul Press.
Basso, Keith. 1970. "To Give Up on Words: Silence in the Western Apache Culture." *Southwestern Journal of Anthropology* 26.213–230.
Crow, Bryan K. 1983. "Topic Shifts in Couples' Conversations." In *Conversational Coherence: Form, Structure, and Strategy*, ed. by Robert T. Craig and Karen Tracy, 136–156. Beverly Hills, CA: Sage.
Dreyfus, Hubert L., and Stuart E. Dreyfus. 1986. *Mind over Machine: The Power of Human Intuition and Expertise in the Era of the Computer*. New York: The Free Press.
Grice, H. Paul. 1989. "Logic and Conversation." In *Studies in the Way of Words*, 3–143. Cambridge, MA: Harvard University Press.
Hinds, John. 1983. "Intrusion in Japanese Conversation." *Papers in Linguistics* 16.1–33.
Horn, Laurence R. 1992. "Pragmatics, Implicature, and Presupposition." In *International Encyclopedia of Linguistics*, vol. 3, ed. by William Bright, 260–266. New York: Oxford University Press.
House, Juliane. 1993. "Toward a Model for the Analysis of Inappropriate Responses in Native/Nonnative Interactions." In *Interlanguage Pragmatics*, ed. by Gabriele Kasper and Shoshana Blum-Kulka, 161–183. New York: Oxford University Press.
Hymes, Dell. 1974. *Foundations in Sociolinguistics: An Ethnographic Approach*. Philadelphia: University of Pennsylvania Press.

Kim, Kyu-hyun, and Kyung-hee Suh. 1998. "Confirmation Sequences as Interactional Resources in Korean Language Proficiency Interviews." In *Talking and Testing: Discourse Approaches to the Assessment of Oral Proficiency*, ed. by Richard Young and Agnes W. He, 297–332. Amsterdam and Philadelphia: Benjamins.

Lebra, Takie Sugiyama. 1987. "The Cultural Significance of Silence in Japanese Communication." *Multilingua* 6.343–357.

Loveday, Leo J. 1981. "Communicative Interference: A Framework for Contrastively Analysing L_2 Communicative Competence Exemplified with Linguistic Behavior of Japanese Performing in English." *International Review of Applied Linguistics* 20. 1–16.

"Marie-Antoinette." (1994). In *The New Encylopaedia Britannica* (vol. 8, p. 844). Chicago: Encyclopaedia Britannica.

Maynard, Douglas W. 1980. "Placement of Topic Changes in Conversation." *Semiotica* 30.263–290.

Mehan, Hugh. 1979. "What Time Is It Denise? Asking Known Information Questions in Classroom Discourse." *Theory into Practice* 18.285–294.

Mislevy, Robert J. 1993. "Foundations of a New Test Theory." In *Test Theory for a New Generation of Tests*, ed. by Norman Frederiksen, Robert J. Mislevy, and Isaac I. Bejar, 19–39. Hillsdale, NJ: Erlbaum.

Pica, Teresa. 1987. "Second-Language Acquisition, Social Interaction, and the Classroom." *Applied Linguistics* 8.3–21.

Reisman, Karl. 1989. "Contrapuntal Conversations in an Antiguan Village." In *Explorations in the Ethnography of Speaking* (2nd ed.), ed. by Richard Bauman and Joel Sherzer, 110–124. New York: Cambridge University Press.

Ross, Steven. 1998. "Divergent Frame Interpretations in Language Proficiency Interview Interaction." In *Talking and Testing: Discourse Approaches to the Assessment of Oral Proficiency*, ed. by Richard Young and Agnes W. He, 333–353. Amsterdam and Philadelphia: Benjamins.

Samarin, William. 1965. "The Language of Silence." *Practical Anthropology* 12.115–119.

Sato, Charlene J. 1982. "Ethnic Styles in Classroom Discourse." In *On TESOL '81*, ed. by Mary Hines and William Rutherford, 11–24. Washington, DC: TESOL.

Schneider, Melanie, and Ulla Connor. 1990. "Analyzing Topical Structure: Not All Topics Are Equal." *Studies in Second Language Acquisition* 12.411–427.

Sinclair, John, and Malcolm Coulthard. 1975. *Towards an Analysis of Discourse*. New York: Oxford University Press.

Tannen, Deborah. 1984. *Conversational Style: Analyzing Talk Among Friends*. Norwood, NJ: Ablex.

Triandis, Harry C., Robert Bontempo, Marcelo J. Villareal, Masaaki Asai, and Nydia Lucca. 1988. "Individualism and Collectivism: Cross-Cultural Perspectives on Self-Ingroup Relationships." *Journal of Personality and Social Psychology* 54.323–338.

van Betteraij, Margo, Eric Kellerman, and Erik Schils. 1996. "Self-Disclosure and Safe Topics of Conversation: A Cross-Cultural Appraisal." In *EUROSLA 6: A Selection of*

Papers, ed. by Eric Kellerman, Bert Weltens, and Theo Bongaerts, 35–46. Amsterdam: Vrije Universiteit Uitgeverij.

Young, Richard. 1995. "Conversational Styles in Language Proficiency Interviews." *Language Learning* 45.3–42.

Young, Richard, and Michael Milanovic. 1992. "Discourse Variation in Oral Proficiency Interviews." *Studies in Second Language Acquisition* 14.403–424.

Index of Names

A

Agar, Michael, 11, 20, 314, 331, 356, 357, 366, 380
Ajirotutu, Cheryl Seabrook, 119, 121, 122, 142, 145
Akinnaso, F. Niya, 119, 121, 122, 142, 145
Alderson, J. Charles, 237
Alexander, Jeffrey C., 169
Allen, Patrick, 294
American Association for Applied Linguistics (AAAL), 23, 114
American Association of Teachers of German, 168
American Council on the Teaching of Foreign Languages (ACTFL), 10, 20, 27, 28, 69, 98, 117, 123, 145, 334, 367
Ammerlaan, Ton, 215, 236
Andersen, Elaine S., 235, 236
Anderson, Anne L., 54, 62, 66
Anderson-Hsieh, Janet, 103, 114
Asai, Masaaki, 344, 353, 365, 381
Aston, Guy, 244, 245, 264
Atkinson, J. Maxwell, 14, 20, 21, 50, 55, 65, 82, 98, 105, 114, 148, 150, 167, 294, 301, 331, 332, 352
Austin, John L., 4, 12, 16, 20
Avery, Peter, 244, 265

B

Bachman, Lyle F., 1–4, 20, 30, 49, 50, 53, 65, 103, 114, 117, 145, 147, 165, 167, 271, 291, 333–336, 349–351
Bailey, Kathleen M., 103, 114
Bakhtin, Mikhail M., 13, 20
Bardovi-Harlig, Kathleen, 7, 22, 272, 288, 291, 300, 313, 331
Barnes, Gregory A., 103, 115
Barnlund, Dean C., 57, 66, 339, 351, 364, 380

Basso, Keith, 366, 380
Bateson, Gregory, 273, 280, 291
Baugh, John, 168, 169
Bauman, Richard, 381
Beebe, Leslie, 213, 235, 343, 346, 352
Bejar, Isaac I., 381
Bennett, Adrian, 147, 167
Bennington, Martha, 103, 114
Bentlage, Andy, 215, 235
Berwick, Richard, 101, 102, 115, 117, 144, 146, 154, 168, 182, 183, 202, 203, 226, 227, 237, 242, 244, 266, 271, 272, 291, 294, 334, 335, 339, 345, 351, 352
Bialystok, Ellen, 206, 208, 209, 211, 228, 229, 235, 239, 241, 250, 264
Biemer, Paul P., 23
Blakemore, Diane, 124, 145
Blom, Jan-Petter, 281, 291
Blommaert, Jan, 290, 291
Blum-Kulka, Shoshana, 16, 20, 241, 249, 264, 266, 290, 294, 346, 352, 380
Boden, Deirdre, 298, 331, 332
Bongaerts, Theo, 207, 213, 215, 219, 235–237, 241, 247, 264, 266, 382
Bontempo, Robert, 344, 353, 365, 381
Boxer, Diana, 35, 46, 49
Bragger, Jeannette, 118, 145
Briggs, Charles L., 12, 21, 335, 351
Bright, William, 380
Brown, Gillian, 32, 40, 49, 62, 66
Brown, H. Douglas, 238
Brown, Penelope, 13, 21, 47, 49, 273, 283, 284, 288, 291
Buck, Kathryn, 66, 89, 98
Burkhalter, Amy J., 103, 115
Button, Graham, 14, 21, 101, 114, 169, 332
Byrd, Patricia, 103, 114
Byrnes, Heidi, 53, 66, 89, 98, 334, 351

C

Canale, Michael, 4, 5, 21, 53, 56, 66, 205, 235, 240, 264, 288, 292, 297, 331, 334, 349, 351
Carroll, Brendan J., 271, 292
Casey, Neil, 14, 21
Cazden, Courtney B., 183, 202
Chaiklin, Seth, 5, 21
Chapelle, Carol, 292
Chen, Si-Qing, 241, 251, 264
Choi, Soonja, 331
Christie, Frances, 178, 202
Clark, John L. D., 28, 48, 49, 69, 98, 117, 145, 181, 202, 218, 235, 273, 292, 334, 351
Clayman, Steve E., 14, 21
Cleary, Linda M., 332
Clifford, Ray T., 28, 49, 117, 145, 181, 202, 273, 292, 334, 351
Coates, Jennifer, 313, 331
Cohen, Andrew D., 53, 66, 241, 267
Cohen, Louis, 53, 66
Cole, Peter, 236
Connor, Ulla, 370, 381
Constantinides, Janet, 103, 114
Cook, Vivian, 241, 264
Cook-Gumperz, Jenny, 119, 145
Coombs, Jerrold, 180, 186, 190–192, 194, 199, 204
Corder, S. Pit, 208, 235, 241, 264, 266
Coulthard, Malcolm, 13, 24, 146, 254, 266, 275, 295, 362, 381
Coupland, Justine, 314, 331
Coupland, Nikolas, 265, 314, 331, 351
Crago, Martha, 57, 66
Craig, Robert T., 21, 380
Crow, Bryan K., 6, 21, 370, 380
Crymes, Ruth C., 238
Cummins, Jim, 181, 202, 294

D

Das, Bikram, 67
Davies, Alan, 4, 19, 21

Davies, Catherine E., 103, 114, 271, 281, 288, 289, 292, 295
Davies, Evelyn, 288, 294
Dechert, Hans W., 236, 237
Defense Language Institute (DLI), 28
DeKeyser, Robert M., 241, 264
Derrida, Jacques, 13, 21
Devlin, Brian, 178, 202
Dillon, J. T., 335, 351
Donahue, Frank, 149, 150, 155, 166, 168
Donitsa-Schmidt, Smadar, 70, 71, 98
Donohue, William A., 265
Dörnyei, Zoltán, 241, 243, 249, 252, 264, 265
Douglas, Dan, 13, 21, 271, 292
Drew, Paul, 11, 14, 20–22, 101, 110, 114, 147, 148, 159, 168, 298, 331, 337, 351, 352
Dreyfus, Hubert L., 363, 380
Dreyfus, Stuart E., 363, 380
Dumas, Guy, 241, 267
Duran, Richard P., 271, 290, 292
Duranti, Alessandro, 49, 273, 292, 293, 351

E

Educational Testing Service (ETS), 27, 28, 49, 181, 203, 206, 217, 235, 334, 342
Egbert, Maria M., 15, 16, 18, 106, 114, 147, 149–151, 153, 159, 168, 272, 292
Ehrlich, Susan, 244, 265
Ellis, Donald G., 265
Ellis, Rod, 213, 235, 236, 280, 292
Erickson, Frederick, 9, 14, 21, 272, 273, 292

F

Færch, Claus, 205–209, 211, 213, 215, 219, 229, 235, 236, 238, 241, 247, 249, 264–267
Fanshel, David, 9, 14, 22, 280, 294
Feagin, Crawford, 169
Ferguson, Charles A., 242, 265
Fiksdal, Susan, 55, 66, 119, 145, 147, 168, 272, 290, 293
Finger, Alexis, 103, 115
Firth, J. R., 4, 21

Fishman, Pamela, 43, 49
Foreign Service Institute (FSI), 18, 28, 206, 217, 334, 335, 364
Ford, Cecilia E., 14, 21, 105, 114
Frawley, William, 30, 49, 50, 117, 145, 181, 203, 271, 294, 334, 335, 352
Frederiksen, Norman, 381
Freebody, Peter, 178, 202
Freedle, Roy O., 295, 352

G
Gadamer, Hans-Georg, 13, 21
Gaies, Stephen J., 242, 265
Garfinkel, Harold, 13, 21
Gass, Susan M., 66, 107, 114, 145, 236, 238, 242, 244, 245, 253, 254, 261, 265, 267, 346, 351, 352
Gerard, Harold B., 30, 32, 49, 183, 203, 243, 265
Giesen, Bernhard, 169
Giglioli, Pierpaolo, 332
Giles, Howard, 265, 314, 331, 351
Givón, Talmy, 66, 168, 332
Goffman, Erving, 13, 21, 33, 41, 49, 55, 66, 118, 145, 273, 280, 283, 284, 293, 337, 351
Goodwin, Charles, 28, 33, 41, 47, 49, 273, 292, 293, 351
Goodwin, Marjorie H., 28, 33, 41, 47, 49
Gordon, Claire, 69, 98
Greatbatch, David, 14, 21
Green, Judith L., 292
Grice, H. Paul, 13, 16, 17, 21, 214, 236, 339, 363, 377, 380
Groves, Robert M., 23
Gumperz, John J., 12, 13, 15, 21, 27, 28, 32, 47, 49, 119, 145, 272, 273, 281, 288, 291, 293, 336, 344, 351
Guy, Gregory R., 169

H
Haastrup, Kirsten, 215, 236, 241, 265
Hall, Joan K., 5, 22
Halleck, Gene B., 16–19, 117, 314, 332, 355

Halliday, Michael A. K., 178, 179, 188, 199, 203
Harley, Birgit, 294
Harper, H., 247, 265
Hartford, Beverly S., 7, 22, 272, 288, 291, 300, 313, 331
Hasan, Ruqaiya, 178, 203
Hatch, Evelyn, 28, 33, 40, 47, 49, 224, 236, 242, 265
Hawkins, Barbara, 62, 66
He, Agnes W., 6, 14–18, 22, 101, 102, 108, 112, 114, 115, 271, 272, 292, 293, 329, 332, 350, 381
Heath, Christian, 14, 22
Henley, Nancy, 49
Heritage, John, 11, 14, 21, 22, 50, 55, 65, 82, 98, 101, 105, 114, 147, 148, 150, 167, 168, 294, 298, 301, 302, 309, 325, 331, 332, 337, 351, 352
Hildyard, Angela, 50
Hinds, John, 231, 236, 351, 365, 380
Hines, Mary, 381
Hoekje, Barbara, 103, 115
Holmes, Janet, 22, 236, 288, 293
Hood, Susan, 179, 203
Horn, Laurence R., 366, 380
House, Juliane, 16, 20, 339, 351, 364, 380
Hovy, Eduard, 185, 203
Howard, Irwin, 236
Hunt, Kellogg W., 223, 236
Hutchins, Edwin, 3, 22
Hymes, Dell, 4, 13, 15, 22, 118, 119, 145, 205, 236, 265, 273–276, 288, 291, 293, 366, 380

I
Inter-Agency Language Roundtable (ILR), 34
Irvine, Judith T., 154, 168

J
Jackson, Sally, 248, 265
Jacoby, Sally, 5, 22
James, C. L., 334, 351

Jefferson, Gail, 13, 14, 23, 28, 31, 41, 50, 101, 105, 106, 115, 118, 146, 148–151, 153, 155, 168, 169, 279, 285, 294, 297, 298, 301–303, 310, 327, 331, 332
Johnson, Marysia, 16–18, 27, 271, 293
Jones, Edward E., 30, 32, 49, 183, 203, 243, 265
Jones, Randall L., 235
Jupp, Tom, 272, 288, 293, 294

K

Kasper, Gabriele, 16, 20, 205–209, 211, 213, 215, 219, 229, 235, 236, 238, 241, 247, 249, 250, 264–266, 288, 293, 343, 346, 350–352, 380
Katona, Lucy, 17, 239
Kellerman, Eric, 208, 213, 215, 219, 226, 229, 235, 236, 241, 247, 266, 267, 363, 381
Kenyon, Dorry, 69, 92, 98
Khanji, Rajai, 215, 237, 241, 266
Kim, Kyu-hyun, 16, 19, 297, 324, 331, 357–359, 381
Koehler, Kenneth, 103, 114
Koike, Dale April, 16, 18, 69
Koran, John J., Jr., 103, 114, 288, 292
Krahnke, Karl J., 237
Kramarae, Cheris, 49
Kramsch, Claire, 5, 22, 50, 117, 145, 288, 293, 297, 331
Krashen, Stephen D., 235, 236
Kroll, Barry M., 56, 66
Kumaravadivelu, B., 213, 236, 241, 266

L

Labarca, Angela, 215, 237, 241, 266
Labov, William, 9, 14, 22, 76, 98, 280, 294, 307, 331
Lado, Robert, 4, 22
Lantolf, James P., 30, 49, 50, 117, 145, 181, 203, 271, 294, 334, 335, 352
Lave, Jean, 3, 5, 21, 22
Lazaraton, Anne L., 8, 22, 48, 50, 101, 102, 115, 147, 168, 224, 236, 242, 266

Lebra, Takie Sugiyama, 339, 352, 364, 381
Lee, Hyo-Sang, 305, 332
Lee, John R. E., 169, 332
Levenston, Eddie A., 241, 249, 264, 266
Levinson, Stephen C., 11, 13, 14, 17, 21, 22, 32, 47, 49, 50, 112, 115, 273, 283, 284, 288, 291, 336, 338, 346, 352
Lewin, Miriam, 176, 203
Lightbown, Patsy M., 226, 237
Linn, Michael D., 332
Linnell, Kimberly, 103, 115
Littlewood, William, 250, 266
Long, Michael H., 107, 115, 266
Loveday, Leo J., 213, 231, 237, 344, 352, 365, 381
Low, Graham, 214, 237
Lowe, Pardee, Jr., 28–30, 50, 206, 218, 237, 352
Lucca, Nydia, 344, 353, 365, 381
Luke, Allan, 178, 202
Lyberg, Lars E., 23
Lyman, Stanford M., 285, 295

M

MacLachlan, G., 335, 352
Madden, Carolyn G., 66, 103, 115, 145, 173, 203, 238, 292
Maeshiba, Naoko, 343, 352
Magnan, Sally S., 218, 226, 237
Mahan-Taylor, Rebecca, 291
Malinowski, Bronislaw, 4, 16, 22
Manion, Lawrence, 53, 66
Marie-Antoinette, 355–357, 360, 376, 381
Marlaire, Courtney L., 14, 23, 102, 115, 335, 352
Martin, James R., 178, 179, 202, 203
Mathiowetz, Nancy A., 23
Maynard, Douglas W., 14, 23, 102, 115, 335, 352, 370, 381
Maynard, Senko K., 220, 233, 237
McCarthy, Michael, 28, 33, 37, 40, 43, 46, 47, 50
McHoul, Alexander, 13, 23
McLaughlin, Barry, 207, 219, 229, 237
McLeon, Beverly, 207, 219, 237

McNamara, Tim F., 3, 23
Mehan, Hugh, 275, 294, 360, 381
Meritt, Marilyn, 28, 33, 50
Meux, Milton, 180, 186, 190–192, 194, 199, 204
Meyers, Colleen M., 103, 115
Milanovic, Michael, 6, 24, 30, 51, 54, 67, 122, 146, 153, 169, 182, 183, 202, 204, 218, 224, 230, 238, 243, 244, 267, 271, 296, 360, 370, 382
Mishler, Elliot G., 9, 23
Mislevy, Robert J., 363, 381
Moder, Carol Lynn, 16–18, 117
Mohan, Bernard, 17, 19, 173, 174, 180, 184, 191, 201, 203
Monkhouse, Francis J., 175, 203
Morgan, Jerry L., 236
Morgan, Mary J., 291
Morrison, Donald M., 214, 237
Morrow, Keith E., 273, 294
Münch, Richard, 169
Myers, Cynthia L., 103, 115, 173, 203, 292

N

National Association of Self-Instructional Language Programs (NASILP), 272, 274
National Centre for English Language Teaching and Research of Australia, 179, 203, 204
Nehls, Dietrich, 237
Neu, Joyce, 352
New South Wales Adult Migrant English Service, 179, 203, 204
Nijmegen Group, 241
Nunan, David, 53, 66
Nuthall, Graham, 180, 186, 190–192, 194, 199, 204

O

Ochs, Elinor, 5, 12, 21–23, 32, 50, 56, 66, 114, 273, 294, 297, 319, 332
Ogden, Charles K., 22
Oleksy, Wieslaw, 293
Oller, John, 66

Olshtain, Elite, 290, 294
Olson, David R., 50
Omaggio, Alice, 145, 334, 352
Orestrom, Bengt, 118, 146

P

Palmer, Adrian S., 1–3, 20
Paribakht, Tahereh, 205, 208, 209, 215, 237, 241, 266
Patil, Prabhakar B., 266
Phillips, Susan U., 57, 66
Phillipson, Robert, 215, 236, 241, 265–267
Pialorsi, Frank, 103, 114
Pica, Teresa P., 103, 107, 115, 358, 381
Pomerantz, Anita, 43, 50, 279, 285, 294, 298, 322, 332
Portal, Matthew, 294
Poulisse, Nanda, 205–208, 211, 213, 215, 216, 219, 228–230, 236, 237, 241, 247, 258, 264, 266
Precians, Robert, 180, 186, 190–192, 194, 199, 204
Preston, Dennis, 145, 238
Pride, John B., 22, 236

R

Raffaldini, Tina, 117, 146, 271, 290, 294
Ramsey, S. Robert, 57, 66
Ranney, Susan, 6, 23
Raupach, Manfred, 220, 236, 237, 247, 266
Reid, I., 335, 352
Reisman, Karl, 366, 381
Reynolds, Dudley W., 291
Ribeiro, Branca, 280, 294
Richards, Ivor A., 22
Richards, Jack C., 213, 237, 264, 292
Riggenbach, Heidi R., 8, 23, 53, 58, 64, 67, 101, 115
Ringbom, Håkan, 230, 237
Rivera, Charlene, 168, 292
Roberts, Celia, 272, 280, 288, 292–294
Rogoff, Barbara, 3, 23
Rommetveit, Ragnar, 8, 23
Ross, Steven, 16, 17, 19, 101, 102, 109, 115, 117, 142, 144, 146, 154, 168, 182,

183, 202, 203, 226, 227, 237, 242, 244, 266, 271, 272, 291, 294, 333–335, 337, 339, 343, 345, 351, 352, 364–366, 376, 381
Rossman, Tammi, 207, 237
Roulet, Eddie, 266
Rounds, Patricia L., 103, 115
Rutherford, William, 381

S

Sacks, Harvey, 7, 13, 14, 23, 28, 31, 32, 41, 50, 101, 105, 106, 115, 118, 146, 148–151, 153, 155, 168, 169, 279, 285, 294, 297, 298, 301, 303, 322, 327, 332
Samarin, William, 366, 381
Sato, Charlene J., 381
Savignon, Sandra J., 30, 49, 50, 117, 145, 165, 167, 288, 290, 294, 333–335, 351
Saville, Nick, 202
Saville-Troike, Muriel, 55, 67, 286, 295
Scarcella, Robin C., 213, 220, 235, 236, 238
Schachter, Jacquelyn, 290, 294
Schaeffer, Nora C., 8, 23
Schegloff, Emanuel A., 13, 14, 21, 23, 28, 31, 32, 41, 42, 50, 101, 105, 106, 114, 115, 118, 146, 148–151, 153, 155, 168, 169, 279, 285, 294, 297, 298, 301, 303, 319, 322, 327, 332, 335, 352
Schieffelin, Bambi B., 50
Schiffrin, Deborah, 32, 48, 50, 118–122, 124, 125, 128, 134, 136, 137, 141, 142, 146, 169, 300, 301, 332
Schils, Erik, 363, 381
Schmidt, Richard W., 64, 67, 237, 264, 292
Schneider, Melanie, 370, 381
Schoepfle, G. Mark, 182, 186, 199, 201, 204
Schutz, Alfred, 13, 23
Schwartz, Joan, 214, 238
Scollon, Ron, 279, 286, 290, 294, 318, 328, 332
Scollon, Suzanne Wong, 279, 290, 294, 318, 328, 332

Scott, Marvin B., 285, 295
Scott, Mary Lee, 241, 249, 252, 265
Searle, John R., 12, 16, 17, 23
Seif, Shahrzad, 241, 267
Selinker, Larry, 13, 21, 145, 205, 236, 238, 239, 242, 265–267, 271, 292
Sharwood-Smith, Michael, 235, 236, 266, 267
Shea, David, 272, 295
Sherzer, Joel, 168, 381
Shillcock, Richard, 62, 66
Shohamy, Elana, 69–71, 73, 90, 92, 93, 98, 271, 272, 290, 295
Shultz, Jeffrey, 9, 14, 21, 272, 273, 292
Sinclair, John M., 13, 24, 254, 266, 275, 295, 362, 381
Slaughter, Helen, 147, 167
Smelser, Neil J., 169
Smith, B. Othanel, 180, 186, 190–192, 194, 199, 204
Smith, Jan, 103, 115
Smith, Larry E., 267
Sohn, Ho-Min, 278, 295
Sperber, Dan, 143, 146
Spolsky, Bernard, 18, 24, 235, 271, 295
Spradley, James P., 53, 67
Stansfield, Charles W., 69, 72, 92, 98, 237
State Foreign Languages Examination Board of Hungary, 245
Steele, Ross, 203
Stenstrom, Anna-Brita, 118, 146
Stevenson, Douglas K, 352
Sudman, Seymour, 23
Suh, Kyung-hee, 16, 19, 297, 357–359, 381
Sukle, Robert, 273, 295
Sukwiwat, Mayuri, 213, 237
Swain, Merrill, 4, 5, 21, 56, 66, 205, 235, 236, 240, 264, 266, 267, 288, 292, 294, 297, 331, 349, 351

T

Takahashi, Tomoko, 213, 220, 235, 238, 343, 346, 352

Index of Names

Tannen, Deborah, 28, 32, 33, 35, 48, 50, 56, 58, 67, 280, 281, 286, 295, 313, 332, 335, 352, 355, 381
Tao, Hongyin, 57, 67, 105, 116
Tarone, Elaine, 205, 206, 208, 209, 213–215, 238, 240, 241, 251, 267
ten Have, Paul, 297, 332
Thompson, Irene, 66, 89, 98
Thompson, Sandra, 14, 21, 57, 67, 105, 114, 116
Thorne, Barrie, 49
Threadgold, Terry, 178, 202, 203
Torrence, Nancy, 50
Tracy, Karen, 21, 380
Triandis, Harry C., 344, 353, 365, 381
Tsui, Amy B. M., 124, 146, 254, 255, 267
Tyler, Andrea, 16–18, 27, 103, 114, 116, 173, 204, 271, 281, 287–289, 292, 293, 295

U

Uliss-Weltz, Robin, 213, 235
Underhill, Nic, 53, 67, 282, 295
University of Cambridge Local Examinations Syndicate (UCLES), 5, 360

V

Valdman, Albert, 24, 181, 204
van Betteraij, Margo, 363, 381
van Dijk, Teun A., 168, 295
van Lier, Leo, 8, 24, 27, 30, 32, 48, 50, 54, 67, 101, 116, 117, 146, 147, 169, 182, 204, 218, 233, 238, 242, 243, 267, 271, 276, 295, 334, 335, 353
Vann, Roberta J., 66
Váradi, Tamás, 239, 241, 267
Varonis, Evangeline Marlos, 107, 114, 244, 245, 253, 254, 261, 265, 267, 339, 346, 351
Verschueren, Jef, 290, 291
Villareal, Marcelo J., 344, 353, 365, 381
Voloshinov, Valentin N., 13, 24

W

Wagner, Johannes, 215, 238
Waizer, Ronit, 70, 71, 98
Wallat, Cynthia, 292
Walton, Christine, 178, 202
Watzinger, Johanna, 155, 168
Weber, Elizabeth G., 124, 146
Weir, Cyril J., 64, 67
Weltens, Bert, 382
Werner, Oswald, 182, 186, 199, 201, 204
Wertsch, James V., 23
Wiemann, John M., 265, 351
Wilkinson, Louise Cherry, 50
Willems, Gerard M., 247, 267
Williams, Jessica, 103, 116, 173, 204
Wilson, Deidre, 143, 146
Wolfgang, Aaron W., 66
Wolfson, Nessa, 6, 24, 27, 50

Y

Yarmohammadi, Lotfollah, 241, 267
Yorio, Carlos A., 238, 244, 265
Yoshida-Morise, Yumiko, 16, 17, 19, 205, 223, 233, 238
Yoshinaga, Naoko, 343, 352
Young, Richard, 1, 4, 6, 16, 17, 19, 24, 30, 32, 48, 51, 54, 67, 93, 98, 101, 112–116, 122, 142, 144, 146, 147, 153, 166, 169, 182, 183, 204, 218, 224, 230, 233, 238, 243, 244, 255, 267, 271, 272, 292, 293, 295, 313, 314, 329, 332, 335, 343, 350, 353, 355, 360–362, 370, 371, 381, 382
Yule, George, 32, 40, 49, 62, 66, 215, 238, 240, 241, 251, 267

Z

Zimmerman, Donald H., 298, 331, 332
Zukowski/Faust, Jean, 114

Index of Topics

A

Accommodation, 117, 144, 244, 271, 339
Achievement test, 216, 273
Action knowledge, 174
Activity type, 11, 112, 174
Adjacency pair, 13, 14, 31, 32, 34, 42, 43, 101, 102
Advanced (level of speaking proficiency), 6, 54, 70–74, 81, 89, 123, 150, 299, 303, 304, 307, 310, 315, 319, 320, 322–324, 340, 346, 347, 365–369, 372, 374, 378
Affective schema, 3, 16
Asymmetrical contingency, 30
Asymmetry, 119, 120, 129, 154, 182, 218, 230, 297, 300, 313, 318
Austria, 356, 366
Authenticity, 1, 2, 8, 9, 11, 55, 65, 334
Avoidance strategy, 112

B

Backchannel, 35, 38, 53–55, 57, 60, 62, 64, 105, 123, 215, 220, 277, 279, 288, 370
Background knowledge, 19, 143, 148, 174, 218, 281
Boundary, 57, 154, 287, 337, 338, 344, 370
    signaling, 6, 7

C

Cambridge Assessment of Spoken English (CASE), 4
Clarification. *See also* Negotiation of meaning, 34, 57, 61, 64, 0, 107, 120, 121, 125–127, 131, 132, 134–138, 141–143, 242, 257–259, 261, 276, 282

Clarifying sequence, 256, 258, 259, 261, 297, 319
Classroom interaction. *See also* Discourse, 6, 180, 183
Co-construction, 5, 7, 11, 32–34, 144, 173, 174, 178, 182, 183, 191, 200–202, 272, 274, 280, 286, 289, 358, 359
Code switching, 243, 248, 250, 280
Cognitive processing, 3, 17, 226, 310, 363
Coherence, 32, 60, 62, 64, 182
Communication
    breakdown, 56, 57, 60, 164, 194, 195, 239, 240, 247, 260, 339
    problem, 14, 55, 57, 61, 65, 103, 104, 165, 173, 186, 206, 208, 247, 252, 254, 255, 261
Communication strategies, 12, 19, 30, 205, 208, 215, 239, 240
    achievement, 208, 209, 216, 234, 243
    avoidance, 57, 60, 208, 209, 214, 220, 221, 234, 241, 243, 250, 257, 261
    conceptual, 241
    lexical simplification, 239
    linguistic or code, 241
    message abandonment, 208, 209, 220, 234, 241, 250
    reduction, 208, 211, 213, 220, 224–227, 234, 241, 243, 248, 257
    taxonomy of, 208, 234
Competence
    communicative, 4, 7, 12, 56, 205
    discourse, 4, 53, 56, 62
    interactional, 2, 3–8, 19, 22, 145, 271, 279, 288–290, 293, 303, 314, 319, 331
    linguistic, 4, 10, 11, 14, 55
    pragmatic, 4
    strategic, 3, 4, 7, 56, 57, 62, 205, 216, 240

Confirmation request, 76, 91, 242, 258, 297, 300–305, 307–314, 316–321, 323–329, 358, 359
Confirmation sequence, 19, 359
Construct validity, see Validity, 1
Contextualization cue, 280, 281, 286, 289, 290
Contingency, 183, 185, 201
  asymmetrical, 30, 218, 243
  mutual, 30, 32
Conversation
  everyday, 2, 3, 6, 7, 9–12, 14, 18, 27, 28, 30–33, 40
  features of, 27, 28, 31–34, 40, 42, 48
  informal, 78
  natural, 1, 8–10, 27, 30–32, 34, 37, 43, 47
Conversation Analysis (CA), 13, 14, 50, 147, 148, 150, 166, 273, 298
Conversational implicature, 337, 366
Conversational involvement, 28, 32, 34, 48, 143, 259, 303
Conversational modification, 242, 358
Conversational style. *See also* Japanese; Journalistic interview style; Mexican, 112, 120, 133, 135, 137, 143, 278, 281, 313, 318, 355, 356, 360, 363, 366, 367, 374–378
Cooperative principle, 17, 214, 337, 363, 365
Cross-cultural, 192, 298, 339, 344, 355, 360
  communication, 12, 13, 290
  context, 271, 272, 288, 289
  encounter, 9, 12, 19, 269, 272, 274, 280, 289, 290
  interview, 12, 19, 20, 280, 289, 357
Culture, 4, 12, 16, 104, 112, 281, 283, 284, 290, 314, 339, 344, 345, 349, 355, 357, 364, 366, 369, 371, 375, 378

D

Dialogue, 3, 80, 177, 180, 202, 304, 316, 366
Discourse, 9, 32, 33, 38, 40, 44, 69, 80
  classroom, 6, 13, 92, 254, 275, 279
  institutional, 9–11, 118, 119, 121, 336
  interview, 9, 14, 15
  non-classroom, 32, 33, 54
  semantics, 9, 10
Discrete-point testing, 55
Display question, 360–362
Dutch, 216, 230

E

Elaboration. *See also* Underelaboration, 7, 15, 71, 76, 81, 83, 87, 89, 103, 108, 109, 112, 140–142, 154, 271, 273, 341, 360, 362, 363, 367, 369, 374, 378
Elicitation, 109, 174, 177, 181, 182, 185, 198, 200, 254, 255, 259, 262, 263, 275
  mode, 70, 71
  technique, 12, 27, 29, 34, 70, 71
English, 3, 5, 6, 18, 19, 34, 46, 57, 58, 63, 64, 70, 73, 74, 76–78, 82, 84, 92, 93, 104, 105, 112, 118, 122, 123, 128, 141, 142, 149, 152, 155, 157, 159, 162, 179, 206, 211, 215–220, 239, 245, 246, 271, 273, 276–289, 299, 301, 302, 304, 320, 349, 360, 363, 365–367, 369, 374–376, 378
Ethnography of speaking, 9, 12, 13, 15, 182, 273
Ethnomethodology, 13, 14, 273

F

Face, 10, 12, 19, 28, 31, 33, 37, 46, 47, 69–71, 102, 104, 117, 132, 245, 263, 271–275, 279–290, 313, 324, 325, 327, 328, 333–335, 344, 346, 349, 350, 358
Field, 173, 174, 178–180, 195, 198–200, 368
First Certificate in English (FCE), 102, 108, 244, 360
Follow-up, 41, 46, 60, 108, 109, 135, 184, 188, 190, 194, 195, 198, 201, 253–258, 301, 302, 304, 308–312, 316, 317, 319, 357
  acknowledgment, 253, 254, 256
  concession, 254
  endorsement, 254
Footing, 271, 280, 283, 286, 287

Foreigner talk, 239, 242
Frame, 9, 11, 17–19, 118, 119, 135–144, 174, 271, 280–283, 302, 313, 314, 325, 333, 337–339, 342, 344, 346–350, 367
France, 356
French Revolution, 355

G

Genre, 11, 15, 45, 54, 63–65, 71, 177–180, 199, 201, 271, 274, 279, 286, 298, 334
   analysis, 178–180
Georgetown Linguistics Society Conference, 114
German, 3, 18, 147–155, 158, 161–166, 355, 366

H

Hopi, 366
Hungary, 19, 239, 245–247, 251, 264
Identity, 5, 7, 108, 284, 290

I

Illocutionary act. *See also* Speech act, 17
Implication sequence, 179, 180
Initiating, 218, 254
Initiation-response-evaluation, 362
Institutional discourse. *See also* Discourse, 9
Interactional competence. *See also* Competence, 2, 3–8, 19, 22, 145, 271, 279, 288–290, 293, 303, 314, 319, 331
Interactional sociolinguistics, 13
Interactive practice, 6, 7, 12, 30, 36, 37, 40, 46
Interactiveness, 1–3, 33, 34, 93
Intermediate-mid (level of speaking proficiency), 74, 75, 150, 225–227, 366–368, 371, 374
International Education Achievement Test of Proficiency, 216
International teaching assistant (ITA), 19, 64, 103, 123, 173, 185, 289
Intersubjectivity, 8

Interview, 9–12, 18, 19, 27, 29, 30, 37, 40, 42–44, 46, 53–56, 58, 63, 69, 71, 73, 200
Irony, 356, 357

J

Japanese, 135
   conversational style, 19, 57, 59, 206, 212, 217, 220–222, 230, 231, 338–340, 343, 344, 348, 349, 364–367, 369–372, 374–378
Journalistic interview style, 40

K

Knowledge structure, 173, 174, 177, 180–185, 191, 198–202
Korean, 3, 19, 34, 39, 40, 271–290, 297–302, 304, 313, 314, 316–319, 323–326, 328, 329, 357–359

L

Lamination, 280–283, 286, 287
Language proficiency interview (LPI), 3, 10, 18, 27, 48, 53, 99, 101, 112, 117, 122, 142, 144, 147, 153, 164, 166, 171, 173, 242, 269, 271, 297, 355
Lexicogrammar, 20, 103, 173, 174, 179, 180, 182, 185, 187, 193, 198, 199, 201

M

Maxim
   of congruence, 313, 319
   of manner, 17, 363
   of quality, 17, 363
   of quantity, 339, 363, 365, 377
   of relevance or relation, 17, 40, 363
Meaning, 8, 13, 15, 16, 54, 76, 80
   natural, 17
   speaker, 17
Mexican conversational style, 366, 367, 369–372, 374–378
Michigan Test of English Language Proficiency, 216
Minimalism, 338–343, 348, 349, 364

Miscommunication, 14, 18, 147, 244, 260, 261, 339, 344, 350
Mode, 70, 102, 175, 178–180, 195, 241, 242, 300, 341
Monologue, 71, 72, 92, 93, 177, 180

N
Narrative, 76, 78–80, 90, 175
Navajo, 58
Negotiation exchange, 9, 118, 254, 256, 260–262
Negotiation of meaning, 17, 19, 57, 60–63, 107, 239, 244, 253, 254, 261, 279, 334
   clarification request, 242, 257, 258
   comprehension check, 242, 244, 261
   confirmation check, 242, 258
Non-classroom discourse. *See also* Discourse, 254
Non-native speaker (NNS), 10, 12
Nonunderstanding routine, 111, 113, 244, 254, 261

O
Oral Proficiency Examination (OPE), 239, 240
Oral Proficiency Interview (OPI), 9, 10, 18, 19, 27, 28, 69, 117, 149, 173, 181, 206, 217, 367

P
Persian, 215
Personality differences, 176, 215, 355, 379
Phases of an interview, 28, 29, 33, 118, 149, 151, 152, 154, 160, 275, 276, 282, 283, 363, 366, 369, 370
Politeness, 278, 283, 284, 286, 290, 298, 300, 318, 319, 324, 325, 327, 328
Portfolio assessment, 53–55, 64, 65
Pragmatic competence. *See also* Competence, 4, 333, 336, 337, 364
Pragmatics, 9, 10, 13, 16, 105, 273, 290, 339, 346, 364
Proficiency. *See also* Advanced, Intermediate-Mid, Superior (levels of speaking proficiency), 9, 11, 14, 15, 18, 27–30, 48, 53, 57, 58, 65, 69, 71, 75, 81, 90, 93, 102, 103, 108, 118, 123, 142, 147, 164, 165, 181

Q
Question-answer, 14, 15, 32, 37, 42, 43, 54, 73, 90, 101, 102, 173, 300, 301, 303, 309, 312, 317, 320, 345, 357, 360, 369, 370

R
Rating
   procedure, 30, 65, 69, 181, 182, 191, 199, 202, 272, 275, 335, 342, 378
   scale, 2, 4, 10, 28, 55, 63, 64, 69, 150, 165, 181, 217, 218, 227, 228, 244, 275, 334, 342
Register, 178, 179, 242
Reliability, 1, 2, 55, 58, 65, 218, 221, 222, 228, 229, 247, 335
Repair, 14, 18, 53–55, 57, 60, 62, 63, 65, 102, 105–108, 110, 112, 148, 150–159, 161–166, 208, 214, 219, 222, 224–227, 234, 288, 297, 298, 300, 319–321, 323, 324, 327
   organization, 14, 148, 149, 154
   tactics, 60, 242
   trajectory, 14
Response, 34, 35, 38, 43, 45, 46, 78, 92, 184, 185
   positive/negative, 254
Rhetorical script, 6, 55, 71, 74, 92
Rich point, 314, 357, 358, 360, 363, 366, 367
Role-play, 3, 29, 36, 41, 43, 44, 69, 73, 275–278, 282, 284, 286, 287, 289, 290, 333, 369, 370

S
Schmäh, 356, 357, 360, 366
Second language acquisition (SLA), 205, 346, 350
Self-disclosure, 339, 344, 349, 350
Self-presentation, 271, 272, 289
Semidirect test, 18, 69–71

Simulated Oral Proficiency Interview (SOPI), 69
Social hierarchy, 19, 313, 358, 359
Sociolinguistic competence. *See also* Competence, 56, 118, 297, 298, 300, 303, 314, 318, 319, 327, 329, 358
Spanish, 3, 18, 69–74, 76, 77, 84, 93, 94, 366, 367, 371
Speaking ability, 1–4, 9, 10, 19, 27–29, 31, 55, 64, 348
SPEAKING acronym, 15, 273, 274
Speech
    act, 6, 12, 13, 16, 19, 71, 72, 76–80, 90, 92, 124, 184, 185, 200, 201, 288, 290, 313, 334, 343, 346
    activity, 10, 15, 16, 103, 112
    community, 12, 15, 16, 339, 349
    event, 8–10, 12, 15, 16, 18, 30, 31, 48, 64, 117–119, 137, 144, 274, 275, 280, 283, 285, 289, 355, 362
    rate, 16, 71, 105, 123, 223, 247, 347, 363, 368, 370, 374, 378
Status, 70, 278, 281, 297, 300, 309, 312–314, 318, 319, 327, 328, 333, 344, 347, 358, 359
Strategies. *See also* Communication strategies, 56, 57
    for managing turns, 6
    metacognitive, 3
Structuralist theory of second language knowledge, 4
Superior (level of speaking proficiency), 78, 142, 150, 181, 366–368, 371, 374, 376, 378
Systemic functional linguistics, 173, 174, 178, 199

T

T-unit, 223, 360, 362, 363, 370–372, 374, 375
Talk-in-interaction, 10, 13, 16, 144, 147, 148, 329
Temporization, 254
Tenor, 178, 179
Texas Oral Proficiency Test (TOPT), 72–74

Topic, 10, 32
    coherence, 32, 45
    elaboration, 79
    initiation or nomination, 14, 28, 32, 34, 43
    management, 10, 40, 44
    negotiation, 32, 34, 40, 44, 47
    organization, 14
    shift, 6, 45
Topical structure analysis, 370–374
Transfer, 34, 41, 148, 157, 162, 165, 166, 207, 209, 220, 229, 339, 343, 346–350, 355, 356, 364, 375, 376, 378
Transition relevance place (TRP), 14, 327
Turn (of talk)
    claiming, 53, 57, 62
    distribution of, 31, 34, 75, 77, 78
    maintaining, 53, 54, 57, 62
    order of, 31, 34, 36
    signals of, 60, 74–76
    size of, 31, 40, 57, 72
    taking, 6, 28, 31, 34, 47, 53, 54, 57, 58, 74, 154
    yielding, 6, 57, 60, 62, 63
Turn-constructional unit (TCU), 14, 103, 105–108, 112, 164

U

Underelaboration, 183, 339, 341, 343–348, 350, 374

V

Validity, 1, 2, 12, 30, 48, 55, 56, 65, 69, 70, 144, 182, 201, 271, 333–335, 349
    construct, 1, 2
Viennese, 355–357, 366

In the series STUDIES IN BILINGUALISM (SiBil) ISSN 0298-1533 the following titles have been published thus far or are scheduled for publication:

1. FASE, Willem, Koen JASPAERT and Sjaak KROON (eds): *Maintenance and Loss of Minority Languages.* 1992.
2. BOT, Kees de, Ralph B. GINSBERG and Claire KRAMSCH (eds): *Foreign Language Research in Cross-Cultural Perspective.* 1991.
3. DÖPKE, Susanne: *One Parent - One Language. An interactional approach.* 1992.
4. PAULSTON, Christina Bratt: *Linguistic Minorities in Multilingual Settings. Implications for language policies.* 1994.
5. KLEIN, Wolfgang and Clive PERDUE: *Utterance Structure. Developing grammars again.*
6. SCHREUDER, Robert and Bert WELTENS (eds): *The Bilingual Lexicon.* 1993.
7. DIETRICH, Rainer, Wolfgang KLEIN and Colette NOYAU: *The Acquisition of Temporality in a Second Language.* 1995.
8. DAVIS, Kathryn Anne: *Language Planning in Multilingual Contexts. Policies, communities, and schools in Luxembourg.* Amsterdam/Philadelphia, 1994.
9. FREED, Barbara F. (ed.) *Second Language Acquisition in a Study Abroad Context.* 1995.
10. BAYLEY, Robert and Dennis R. PRESTON (eds): *Second Language Acquisition and Linguistic Variation.* 1996.
11. BECKER, Angelika and Mary CARROLL: *The Acquisition of Spatial Relations in a Second Language.* 1997.
12. HALMARI, Helena: *Government and Codeswitching. Explaining American Finnish.* 1997.
13. HOLLOWAY, Charles E.: *Dialect Death. The case of Brule Spanish.* 1997.
14. YOUNG, Richard and Agnes WEIYUN HE (eds): *Talking and Testing. Discourse approaches to the assessment of oral proficiency.* 1998.
15. PIENEMANN, Manfred: *Language Processing and Second Language Development. Processability theory.* 1998.